THE
COMMON MUSE

An Anthology of
Popular British Ballad Poetry
15th-20th Century

EDITED BY
VIVIAN DE SOLA PINTO AND
ALLAN EDWIN RODWAY
WITH AN INTRODUCTION
AND NOTES

PENGUIN BOOKS

IN ASSOCIATION WITH CHATTO AND WINDUS

Penguin Books Ltd, Harmondsworth, Middlesex, England
Penguin Books Pty Ltd, Ringwood, Victoria, Australia

—

First published by Chatto & Windus Ltd, 1957
Published in Penguin Books 1965

—

Made and printed in Great Britain
by Cox & Wyman Ltd,
London, Fakenham and Reading
Set in Monotype Bembo

PENGUIN POETS

D89

THE COMMON MUSE

'*I'm not particular; a brave story, or a quaint story, or a funny story, in good rough verse, that's all I ask for. But where to find one? Here's the doctor for umpire. I say, Doctor, don't you agree with me, now?*'

'*Not quite,*' *said the Doctor, looking up from his cold beef.* '*I dare say you wouldn't think them worth much; but there are plenty of ballads sung about which you never hear.*'

'*What! real modern ballads, written by some of the masses, in this century, for instance? Where did you ever hear one, Doctor? What are they like, now?*'

THOMAS HUGHES,
The Scouring of the White Horse,
Cambridge, 1859, p. 168

CONTENTS

NOTE ON THE TEXTS AND
ACKNOWLEDGEMENTS

THE texts of the ballads in this collection reproduce the spelling and punctuation of the original broadsides, manuscripts and old editions, with the following exceptions:

  (i) Obvious misprints have been corrected.

 (ii) Punctuation has occasionally been altered, but only when it seemed likely to interfere with the sense for the modern reader.

(iii) The modern s has been substituted for the old long ſ and the modern usage followed in the use of the letters u, v, i and j.

All editorial emendations are indicated by triangular brackets: ⟨⟩

The editors wish to thank Mr G. R. Hibbard for reading the introduction in typescript and making valuable suggestions which they have been glad to adopt; Dr David Daiches for the loan of his copy of the otherwise unobtainable *Merry Muses of Caledonia*; Mr M. Tarlton, to whose excellent memory they owe much of the contents of the Appendix to this work; the Duke of Portland for kindly allowing them to use his MSS. in Nottingham University Library; and Mr Stephen Sedley for invaluable assistance with the Discography.

They also acknowledge the kind permission given by the following publishers for the reprinting of copyright texts: Mr M. J. Graham, of the *Notts Free Press,* for kindly providing us with photographs of two early nineteenth-century broadsides; the Nonesuch Library Ltd for a poem from their edition of *Blake's Poetry and Prose*; Country Life Ltd for permission to reprint *The Bishop's See* and *My Master and I* from *Victorian Street Ballads,* edited by W. Henderson; the Cambridge University Press for permission to reproduce four poems from *The Pepysian Garland* and

NOTE ON THE TEXTS AND ACKNOWLEDGEMENTS

three from *Old English Ballads*, both edited by Hyder E. Rollins; the Clarendon Press, Oxford, for permission to reproduce texts from *The Poems of Jonathan Swift*, edited by H. Williams, and from *The Shirburn Ballads*, edited by A. Clark; Eric Partridge Ltd for ballads from *The Poems of Henry Carey*, edited by F. T. Wood; Lawrence and Wishart Ltd for the text of five poems from *Come All Ye Bold Miners*, edited by A. L. Lloyd; Bolton's Publishers, Preston, for *Blackpool Breezes* from *Billy's Weekly Liar*; the Navy Records Society for two poems from *Naval Songs and Ballads*, edited by the late Sir Charles Firth; Harvard University Press for a poem from *The Pack of Autolycus*, edited by Hyder E. Rollins; Mr Harry Pollitt for permission to print H—y P—tt in the Appendix to this work.

Finally, the editors wish to express their indebtedness to the following libraries for their courteous assistance: Bodleian, British Museum, Manchester Public Libraries (Reference Library), and Nottingham University Library.

PREFACE

THE object of this book is to make available to the general public a selection from a vast range of British popular poetry[1] which has hitherto been inaccessible to the 'common reader' and has been known only to a limited number of specialists. The editors believe that such a selection will not only fill a gap in the equipment of the student of English literature but will also introduce a number of readers to a new and exciting part of the English poetic heritage which has hitherto been grossly neglected and unfairly despised. The temper of the mid twentieth century is better adapted than that of the Victorian period to appreciate this vigorous popular realistic poetry, and the editors will consider that they have been richly rewarded for their labours if young poets of the present age obtain from these street Ballads a stimulus comparable with that which Coleridge and Scott received from the rediscovered oral ballads of the late Middle Ages. It is claimed, not that the verses printed in this book are 'great poetry' but that they are vital and genuine popular art to be valued as we value the English village churches of the Middle Ages, much of the anonymous carving in the Gothic cathedrals, the works of the English caricaturists of the eighteenth century and of the 'Sunday painters' of nineteenth-century France. Wordsworth, in his famous tribute in Book V of *The Prelude* (ll. 197–219) to the books to which he was indebted, couples the 'low and wren-like warblings' of these ballad poets with the music of Homer and Shakespeare and the 'loftiest notes' of English poetry. It is time that scholarship should, in its own way, follow Wordsworth's lead in 'asserting the rights' and 'attesting the honours' of these humble and

1. The term 'British' is used with reference to poems written and published in England, Scotland and Ireland. The editors have not attempted any selection from the popular poetry of the U.S.A. or other English-speaking countries.

neglected writers as the creators of an authentic and important part of the achievement of English poetry.

This collection, like all anthologies, necessarily represents a personal choice. Certain well-known ballads, however, have been deliberately omitted, despite their merits, as they are easily available elsewhere. The whole question of ballad music is considered to be outside the scope of this collection, but most of the street-ballad tunes are readily available in such works as those of W. Chappell, *Pills to Purge Melancholy*, and others listed in the Bibliography and Work in Progress. Indeed many of the ballads in this collection can now be heard, sung to period tunes, on some of the records in the Discography (Pt 1).

INTRODUCTION

I

THOUGH many of our greatest poets knew, used and imitated street songs and ballads, in modern times it is mainly the political and social historians and antiquaries who have so far paid serious attention to them. Literary critics and historians mention them, if at all, only to dismiss them as 'doggerel' or 'journalism in verse'. What was good enough for Shakespeare, apparently, is no longer good enough for us.

After the invention of printing, the ballad in the south of England fell into the hands of journalists like Thomas Deloney, who made it the vehicle of sensational news-items, printed on one side of the paper and hawked as broadsides in fairs and markets, a practice which has survived to this day.

So write Sir Herbert Grierson and Mr J. C. Smith in their *Critical History of English Poetry* – and of the street ballad they write nothing more. Whether as history or criticism, this is obviously inadequate for a genre which matches in life-span, quantity and often in quality many of the approved kinds of 'hallmarked' literature. Yet that one sentence is comparatively generous. Not all academic histories of literature allow so much. Indeed, eminent and scholarly writers[1] on the ballad itself seem to be unaware of the fact that, besides the traditional ballad of the Middle Ages and literary imitations by modern poets, there exists a third type no less vital and interesting than the first and

---

1. An exception is Professor Hyder E. Rollins, to whose editorial labours all students of the English Street Ballad owe a debt of gratitude. His article on 'The Black Letter Broadside Ballad' (*P.M.L.A.A.*, XXXIV, 2, 1919) is notable both for its scholarly treatment of the historical aspect of the subject and its well-balanced criticism.

far more so than the second, if we leave out of consideration Coleridge's single dazzling success in *The Ancient Mariner*. 'What is a ballad?' asks W. P. Ker, and his answer is that 'a ballad is *The Milldams of Binnorie* and *Sir Patrick Spens* and *Lord Randal* and *Childe Maurice*.' Professor Gregory Smith, in his article in the latest edition of *The Encyclopaedia Britannica*, says merely that 'it is the kind of verse preserved in Sir Walter Scott's *Minstrelsy of the Scottish Border*, and Professor Child's *English and Scottish Ballads*.' Similarly, Robert Graves, in his valuable little book on *The English Ballad*, asserts that 'the beginning of the end of the ballad proper is when no more are being composed; and it is a fact that the ballad proper gradually ceased to be composed after Tudor times.' This is the accepted view, but it is a 'fact' of which Marvell, Rochester, Congreve, Gay, Swift, Pope, Cowper and other major writers were unaware. During the seventeenth and eighteenth centuries 'the ballad' was a living form to be used when poetic diction, the Miltonic manner or the heroic couplet seemed inappropriate. They did not differentiate between 'traditional' and 'street' ballads. Nor did they feel that the old were necessarily superior to the new. In fact, such an excellent poet and critic as William Cowper considered that the golden age of the English ballad was not the Middle Ages but the early eighteenth century. Writing to William Unwin, on 4 August 1783, he says:

The ballad is a species of poetry, I believe, peculiar to this country, equally adapted to the drollest and most tragical subjects. Simplicity and ease are its proper characteristics. Our forefathers excelled in it; but we moderns have lost the art. It is observed, that we have few good English odes. But to make amends, we have many excellent ballads, not inferior in true poetic merit to the best odes that the Greek or Latin languages have to boast of. It is a sort of composition I was ever fond of. . . . I inherit a taste for it from my father, who succeeded well in it himself, and who lived at a time when the best pieces in that way were produced. What can be prettier than Gay's ballad, or rather Swift's, Arbuthnot's, Pope's and Gay's in the 'What do ye call it' – ''Twas when the seas were roaring'?[1]

Here is appreciation of quality and some historical sense, without any attempt to distinguish 'literary' from 'popular', 'traditional' from 'street' ballads.

Such elementary distinctions – and consequent lack of further discrimination – we owe to critics of the nineteenth century who were influenced by Romantic medievalism.

It is not difficult to see how this state of affairs came about. The medieval ballad could be considered picturesque, and it could plausibly be seen as a product of the 'folk'. The street ballad was vulgarly unromantic, it had little of that wistful idealism which the Victorians called 'poetry', and it was a product of the 'lower classes'. Moreover, it was contemporary.

Here, perhaps, is the crux of the matter. For the critic turning from Scott's *Minstrelsy* or Percy's *Reliques* to the street literature of his own day, it was self-evident that there *was* a difference, whatever might be the difficulties of defining it. It was not so evident that the difference might well have been exaggerated by the sudden change in focus: that lack of historical perspective which overlooked the fact that the street ballad of Victoria's reign bore much the same qualitative relationship to that of Elizabeth I's as the poetry of Tennyson bore to the poetry of Shakespeare. Unselfconsciously and effectively, Shakespeare could draw upon a common cultural store, where Tennyson and the Pre-Raphaelites were driven to the past – with the result that they appeared self-conscious and artificial. Even the editor of *Curiosities of Street Literature* (1871) has to write unflatteringly of his chosen material:

1. *Letters of William Cowper chosen and edited by J. G. Frazer* (Macmillan, 1912), I, 244 (Part I, 73).

It is humiliating in the midst of all the schools and teaching of the present day to find such rubbish continually poured forth, and eagerly read. Still, there are some redeeming features in this weary waste. *Taken as a whole*, the moral tone of the ballads, if not lofty, is certainly not bad; and the number of single stanzas that could not be quoted in these pages on account of their gross or indecent language is very small; while that of entire ballads, to be excluded on the same general ground, is smaller. [p. 118]

It seems necessary to admit, moreover, that what he considers a redeeming feature is but dubiously so. It is apparent, particularly in the amatory ballads, that the movement away from bawdry is accompanied by a movement towards sentimentalism or, more usually, the horrific. Wholesome Rabelaisian comedy is giving way to an unhealthy sensationalism.

Gruesome street ballads, of course, were printed in all periods, and were particularly popular in the Elizabethan age. But they were not so popular as in the nineteenth century, nor so insistently connected with sex. It is as if the repressions of a bleak age are here finding their nightmare expression. 'There's nothing beats a stunning good murder, after all' (EXPERIENCE OF A RUNNING PATTERER)[1] reads the epigraph to the *Curiosities*. No overstatement, if the following contemporary sales statistics (from the *Curiosities*, p. 159) are accurate:

1. The quotation is from Mayhew (v. Bibliog.). His chapter on the vendors of street literature is vividly informative about the Running Patterer, who ran through the streets shouting what purported to be the contents of his broadsides. Usually he was one of a 'mob' or 'school', from whose combined clamour only a few leading words were audible, 'Horrible', 'Dreadful', 'Murder', 'One Penny', 'Seduction', 'Pool of Blood' and the like. As Mayhew puts it, 'They usually deal in murders, seductions, crim-cons, explosions, alarming accidents, deaths of public characters, duels and love-letters. But popular or notorious murders are the "great goes".' (Cp. the gag-and-patter of a Standing Patterer: Part I, 89.)

1849	Rush's murder	.	.	.	2,500,000 copies
1849	the Mannings	.	.	.	2,500,000 copies
1840	Courvoisier	.	.	.	1,666,000 copies
1840	Greenacre	.	.	.	1,650,000 copies
1828	Corder ('Maria Marten')		.		1,166,000 copies

The quality of these ballads was not and could not have been high, since they had to be written with great speed (allegedly by 'the wretched victim' on the night before his execution) so that the Running Patterer could strike while the iron was hot. A shilling was the customary writer's fee. The sort of ballad excluded from the *Curiosities* is usually less degenerate, if less ostensibly 'moral';[1] it retains something of the vitality of its forerunners in the preceding century.

In short, it is true to say that the distinction of kind which seemed obvious in the nineteenth century would have been far more difficult to make before then. Nevertheless, this does not mean that it was wholly illusory.

2

No distinctions in this field can, however, be absolute. The traditional ballads of the Middle Ages probably owe much of their merit to individual creative minstrels, while their survival seems often to have been due not to 'folk memory' but to repeated broadsheet publication. The street ballads, in their turn, owe something to 'folk memory' and communal rephrasing, since they were often transmitted orally; witness the variant versions sometimes surviving in manuscript copies. Moreover, a broadsheet is often the only evidence available, and it cannot be relied upon to give any indication of date or manner of composition, though

1. Cp., for example, *Verses on Daniel Good*, Part II, 152, with *The Jolly Driver*, Part II, 173 (itself much inferior to the earlier *Gee Ho, Dobin*, Part II, 154).

sometimes it may do so. The language and some of the detail may be contemporary (since publishers liked to keep up to date), the woodcut much older (for economy's sake) and the story sometimes of immemorial antiquity.[1]

If the ballad is to be classified at all, it must be classified on aesthetic grounds; the best possible grounds, after all, for the literary critic. But logic then forces him to admit to the canon works obviously written by gifted individuals very far removed from the 'folk'. Thus M. J. C. Hodgart in his excellent book, *The Ballads* (1950), writes of the *Twa Corbies*:

No one but a purist could object to this reshaping by Scott, since the result is a ballad by any standard and it is good poetry. [p. 44]

Similarly, we have been obliged to class as 'street ballads' poems by well-known authors, even though they may not in every instance have been published (so far as we know) in broadside form.[2] Judging by the same aesthetic standards,

---

1. Most of these points are compactly illustrated by the ballad *As I Lay Musing* (Part II, 178). This version is taken from a MS., previously unpublished, of the Restoration period. As *The Fryer well fitted* it appears in broadside form in several collections. A variant version, *The Fryer and the Maid,* appears in D'Urfey's *Pills to Purge Melancholy*. But a reference by Skelton in *Colin Cloute* (ll. 879 ff.) seems to take it back to the early sixteenth century. Perhaps this is what caused Child to classify it as 'traditional'. Scottish versions also exist (Buchan's MSS., II, 351; Kinloch MSS., VI, 97, and V, 60). The story appears to be of Oriental origin.

2. Henry Carey's *Sally in our Alley* was at first included as an example of this category, only to be found afterwards in a collection of nineteenth-century street ballads in the Bodleian. Cowper's *John Gilpin*, obviously a street ballad, was originally published in a newspaper but was swiftly reprinted in chapbook form and followed by a broadside sequel (Firth, b. 22, 77. Bodl.) The poems by Dorset, Sedley and Byron (Part I, 72, 86, 48 respectively) definitely belong to the street-ballad genre though none of them has yet been found in broadside form.

we shall be compelled to exclude certain works which were published in this form.[1] The printers of broadsides were both piratical and heterogeneous in habit.

No very clear line can, indeed, be drawn between street ballads and 'hallmarked' literature. A ceaseless interchange took place between them from the sixteenth till the end of the nineteenth century. Just as many 'traditional' ballads have their origin in earlier literary romances and inspire later literary poems,[2] so many street ballads are shortened versions of famous plays or lengthened versions of playhouse songs,[3] and some literary poems are based on earlier street ballads.[4] Among the broadsides, too, many literary works are to be found. Thus both Marlowe's *Come live with me* and Ralegh's reply to it were printed anonymously on a single broadsheet (Rox. I, 205), and are an interesting borderline case. Taken together, they form a unit of a type common enough among street ballads. Taken separately, only Ralegh's perhaps has the true street-ballad flavour. Marlowe's is a little too airily brilliant and lacks the touch of realism that keeps the street ballad down to earth.

Can the street ballad, then, be distinguished and defined

1. E.g. Wordsworth's *We Are Seven,* which was circulating in English villages as a penny broadsheet in the early nineteenth century. See *John Clare,* J. W. and A. Tibble (1932), p. 35.

2. E.g. *Hind Horn* from the Horn cycle of romances, *Thomas Rymer* from the romance *Thomas of Erceldoune.* The influence of the traditional ballads (usually through Percy's *Reliques*) is to be found in the work of most of the Romantic poets, though Wordsworth seems to have been affected more by the street ballads.

3. It is difficult to say precisely when any particular 'ballad', of either variety, can be classed as a 'song'. All the ballads were sung, and the contents of a 'ballad' and a 'song' were often very similar. It is therefore a matter of taste at what point the amount of narrative in the poem justifies the use of the term 'ballad'.

4. A remarkable instance is Campbell's *Ye Mariners of England,* which is clearly based on Martin Parker's seventeenth-century street ballad, *Saylors for my Money* (Part I, 70).

at all? It seems possible to do so, provided that a high degree of precision is not demanded, for at their most typical these ballads are quite easily recognizable. They differ from the traditional ballads, for instance, in belonging to a less primitive world. Only at the edges do the two forms shade off into each other. The traditional ballad, in the main, was the product of the pre-literate rural community living in an atmosphere of beliefs and rituals of immemorial antiquity. The street ballad, as its name implies, was the product of a literate or semi-literate urban population, the new proletariat of the great city. The form slowly becomes dominant as the poetry of the poor man when the manufacture of paper, and the printing-press, has made possible the cheap production of the broadsheet,[1] or single sheet of paper with ballad and usually a woodcut printed on one side. This new type of ballad (as it was in the sixteenth century) *tended* to be comic, realistic and unheroic as the earlier type *tended* to be tragic, romantic and heroic. Both types are intended for simple people and are therefore written in a simple and direct diction, though the traditional ballad, like the primitive epic, tends to be composed in a standardized poetic diction which is rarely found in the street ballad.[2] The street ballad is certainly less independent of time and place than the traditional ballad; it is attracted to a more social (or anti-social) mode, and its meaning is more on the surface. It is not thereby *necessarily* superficial, any more than Chaucer is when he reflects humorously on the life of his times in *The Canterbury Tales*; simply, it is less akin to myth and primitive ritual and it rarely taps the deeper springs of the psyche. The arbitrary narrative 'shots'

1. It probably existed, however, before the introduction of printing. See below, pp. 32, 33, Introduction.

2. See F. B. Gummere, *The Popular Ballad* (1907), pp. 304-7, for the stock phrases used in traditional ballads: 'Heroes and Heroines are always yellow-haired. . . . Even the athletic heroes like Robin Hood are as white as milk . . . alliterative phrases like "purple and pall", "in the royal red" are conventional', etc.

of the traditional ballad,[1] and its vivid dreamlike images, would be out of place and are little used. The street ballad is usually more leisurely and circumstantial in the narrative; it is less wedded to one dramatic incident, though, like the traditional ballad and unlike learned narrative poetry, it prefers juxtaposition to explanation and relies more on action to express character than on analysis. It is rooted in common speech and its basic rhythmical unit is the musical phrase rather than the metrical foot.

The difference between 'street' and contemporary 'hall-marked' poetry is equally real and equally elusive: again, a matter of tendencies rather than clear-cut distinctions. The obvious distinction by *form* soon breaks down. Not all street poetry is narrative,[2] and some ballads are not written in normal ballad metres. In Scotland, moreover, rigorous repression tended to diminish printed and increase oral transmission, so that the distinction between folk song or folk ballad on the one hand and street song or street ballad on the other became blurred. Of those 'Scots' pieces which have survived in apparently pure form as printed broadsides, many are certainly English fakes. Again, it is characteristic of the street-ballad poet that he should parody the poetry of the *élite* and therefore often use the form he parodies.

The audience these poets write for is as varied as the form they write in, and any attempted distinction on the basis of *class* breaks down equally quickly. Even in Shakespeare's day the upper classes obviously knew popular ballads well. Snatches of them abound in his plays, sometimes in key passages, and these quotations often seem irrelevant and obscure till the context is known. Desdemona is reminded of a street ballad at a crucial moment (see Part II, 96). Edgar in the fourth scene of the third act of *King Lear* says obscurely, 'Pillycock sat on Pillycock hill', and there is a

1. A very good account of the technique of these ballads is to be found in Chapter II of *The Ballads*, by M. J. C. Hodgart.

2. See above, p. 19, note 3, on 'Song'.

method in his madness. If it is understood that the phrase comes from a lecherous ballad in which Pillycock hill is the *Mons Veneris*, this obviously enriches the theme of lechery and animalism so prominent in the play and it prepares the way for Edgar's important speech on this theme which follows a few lines later. Falstaff, Sir Toby Belch, Mercutio, Hamlet and even Queen Cleopatra are acquainted with this kind of poetry. Falstaff indeed aspires to figure in a street ballad, possibly of his own composition, when he tells Prince John (2 *Henry IV*, IV, iii) that if his exploit in capturing Colville of the Dale is not duly 'book'd' he will 'have it in a particular ballad with mine own picture on the top of it, Colville kissing my foot'. Highborn Ophelia in her madness shows herself acquainted with a surprising range of street poetry. Street ballads, moreover, were well known to literary and upper-class poets throughout the seventeenth, eighteenth and early nineteenth centuries and were often composed by them (see below, pp. 39–46).

We are thus left, finally, as for the distinction from the traditional ballad, with an aesthetic criterion. In the last analysis the distinguishing and defining factor seems to be *tone*. If there is one typical quality of street ballads it is that they tend to be 'lowfaluting': the opposite of whatever can be called 'highfaluting'. Thus the street ballads, though sometimes ingeniously fantastic rather than realistic, are nevertheless typically unsentimental, uncourtly and irreverent when they deal with the subject of love. It is no accident that Ralegh's sceptical reply should be wedded with Marlowe's *Come live with me* to form a single broadside poem. Nor is it surprising to find a parody of Marlowe's poem beginning with the lines

> Come live with me and be my Whore,
> And we will beg from door to door.[1]

1. See Part II, 108. C. Day Lewis's well-known modern adaptation of this poem is in the true tradition of the street-ballad parody

The street-ballad poet commonly came from a class that knew the simple life not from romantic idealizations but from personal experience. This, however, gives him an honest rather than a disdainful approach. The note of contempt, where it is sounded, marks the appearance of the sophisticated writer who has 'gone slumming'. G. A. Stevens's *A Pastoral* (Part II, 118) clearly belongs to this class:

> To a Hottentot offals have charms,
>   With garbage their bosoms they deck;
> She sluttishly open'd her arms,
>   He filthily fell on her neck.

The writer's sense of superiority and his self-conscious realism put this poem in an entirely different class from such a pastoral as *Andrew and Maudlin* (Part II, 117) in which the 'earth feet, loam feet, lifted in country mirth' are shown not in Eliotesque perspective but as a 'close-up' by a poet who writes from within a circle which is for ever closed both to the sentimental romantic and to the sophisticated intellectual:

> Here they did fling, and there they did hoist,
>   Here a hot Breath, and there went a Savour;
> Here they did glance, and there they did gloist,
>   Here they did Simper and there they did Slaver;
> Here was a Hand, and there was a Placket,
> Whilst, hey! their Sleeves went Flicket-a-flacket.

Even when a street ballad is written in what might be called the 'golden' pastoral mode, it is never so exquisite as to have no bearing upon life, and the vision offered is always an idealization which is fairly close to actuality. *Phillida Flouts Me* (Part II, 99), is well known and justly praised for its lyrical simplicity, but its beauty is shot through with gleams of common sense and it is full of concrete details of Elizabethan rustic life such as the 'clout' 'wrought with good coventry' and the succulent 'pie lids and pastry-crusts, pears, plums, and cherries' with which the swain tempts his nymph. It is matched by the far less widely known but equally delightful poem, *The Happy Husbandman*, which follows it in the present collection (Part II, 100). Though it has all the trappings – and the charm – of literary pastoral in the way of thistledown beds and quilts of roses, its love is solid and sensual, while the desire for a rural retreat seems to spring from a genuine psychological need rather than a mere graceful fantasy. Above all, it is saved by the strength of language that is characteristic of the street ballad.

Often indeed these ballad poets achieved without effort that ideal of a poetry using 'the real language of men' that Wordsworth aimed at and only occasionally succeeded in compassing. It can be terse, as in the summing up of the dangers of the London Miss:

> She masters your breeches, and takes your riches.

(Witness, too, the capture of the 'three daring poachers':

> At night we were trepann'd by the keepers hid in sand.
>
> Part I, 77.)

It can be effortlessly evocative, in the same pastoral, of all that is contrary to the London Miss, the country girl's yielding freshness:

> She's soft as the Air, as Morning fair

– a line that leads the Happy Husbandman naturally to evening:

> And then my little Love does lie
> All the Night long, and dye.

The shortening of the second line of this couplet is no metrical fault but a consummate stroke of art comparable with the similar shortening of the last line of each stanza in Blake's *Never seek to tell thy love*. The alliteration of the first line accelerates the reading as well as binding into the idea of love a suggestion of protective tenderness, and the pause after 'long'[1] slows down the rhythm and gives the needed emphasis to the last phrase. Worth noting, too, are the variations of tone and pace achieved by slight metrical variation in the ballad *A Pleasant New Ballad of Two Lovers* (Part II, 129).[2]

There is, indeed, more complexity of one sort or another in the street ballad than is apparent at first sight. Thus, for instance, the grandeur and dignity in the rhythm of Thomas Deloney's fine ballad, *The Winning of Cales* (Part I, 8) is combined with a slight touch of burlesque suggesting the pomposity of the strutting Spaniard:

> Long the proud Spaniard
>   advanced to conquer us,
> Threatning our Country
>   with fire and sword,
> Often preparing
>   their Navy most sumptuous,
> With all the provision
>   that *Spain* could afford.

1. Ballad punctuation, following the general practice before the eighteenth century, is almost always rhetorical rather than grammatical (where it is not simply erratic). Similarly, metrical irregularity, at least before the nineteenth century, is usually due not to incompetence but to the needs of tune, or sense, or to a desire to avoid an uncolloquial idiom. E.g. cf. *The Wooing Maid* (Part II, 194), who says that since 'one wedding produceth another':

> Before one shall scape me, Ile goe without bidding;
> O that I could find out some fortunate wedding!

The irregularity of the second line is *used*. The reader is forced to stress the 'I' to make the line scan. In doing so he adds a sense of character and speech rhythm, and an implication to the comedy.

2. Referred to in *Romeo and Juliet* as 'My heart is full of woe.'

In *The Town-Rakes*[1] (Part II, 140), to take an example of a rather different kind, the swagger only half conceals a disgusted awareness of the rake's superficiality, an awareness successfully sustained down to the chilling jollity of the final couplet:

> Then leaps in the Dark, and his Exit he makes,
> What Death can compare with the jolly Town-Rakes.

The ironical effect of the following stanza from that fine poem *The Map of Mock-Begger Hall* (Part I, 38) is enhanced enormously by the clatter of the double rhymes and the irregular movement of the penultimate line suggesting a gallop along the road to ruin:

> Young Landlords when to age they come,
> Their rents they will be racking,
> The tenant must give a golden sum,
> Or else he is turn'd packing,
> Great fines and double rent beside.
> Or else they'l not content be,
> It is to maintain their monstrous pride,
> *While mock begger hall stands empty.*

Again there are the Websterian overtones of *The Witch* (Part II, 136), a satire of great splendour of language:

> Shee that could reeke within the sheets of lust,
> And there bee searcht, yet passe without mistrust;
> Shee that could surfle upp the waies of sinne,
> And make streight Posternes where wide gates had bin:
> *Canidia* now drawes on.

Or there is the strange mixture of the macabre and the mock-heroic in *Captain Death* (Part I, 74):

1. This ballad, like *The Epicure* (Part II, 141) and others, serves as a reminder that the divisions in this collection are necessarily arbitrary. Such ballads deal with both amatory and social matters and could with equal justice be placed in Part I or Part II. They may serve as reminders that our anthological divisions did not exist in the mind of the ballad writer.

Grenades, fire, and bullets were soon heard and felt,
A fight that the heart of Bellona would melt,
The rigging all torn, the decks filled with blood,
And scores of dead bodies were thrown in the flood; –
The flood, from the time of old Noah and Seth,
Ne'er bore the fellow of brave Captain Death.

But at length the dread bullet came wingèd with fate,
Our brave Captain dropt, and soon after his mate;
Each officer fell, and a carnage was seen,
That soon dyed the waves to crimson from green,
Then Neptune arose and pulled off his wreath,
Instructing a Triton to crown Captain Death.

The mythological figures here are no mere frigid ornaments
but living elements in the popular imagination, treated half
humorously like the Biblical characters in the medieval
drama.

However, when all is said, 'complexity' – though more
common than might be supposed – is not the most useful
concept for the appreciation of street balladry, nor is 'inten-
sity'. These critical tools yield more valuable results when
applied respectively to Metaphysical and Romantic poetry.
The limitation of the street ballad is precisely that it is never
metaphysical and rarely romantic. It is the product of the
Muse of the common man, who is prompted rather to
take her to bed, as it were, then to analyse her or to set her
on a pedestal and adore her. Her greatest faults are those of
slovenly incompetence,[1] coarseness, scandalmongering and
garrulity: less ridiculous faults perhaps than some of
Melpomene's intenser inanities. On the other hand, it has

---

1. It should be emphasized, however, that these ballads were
usually written to go with a tune or tunes already in existence, and
apparently slovenly or pedestrian rhythms become transformed in
song. The words are of primary importance to the ballad singer –
hence his readiness to let one tune serve for several ballads – but
the music often adds another dimension of meaning, and almost
invariably accounts for apparent metrical differences.

to be admitted that the Common Muse at her best falls a good deal short of the Olympian sublime. Her characteristic virtues are those of the middle way: directness, simplicity, and honest earthly realism.

The street ballad, even in its degenerate nineteenth-century form, drew on that racy homely English which is the backbone of our language and with which the literary language loses touch at its peril. Tennyson's *Ballad of the Revenge* is doubtless a greater poem than the street ballad celebrating the Battle of Navarino (Part I, 30), but the idiom of the anonymous ballad poet is really stronger and healthier English than the carefully contrived literary language of the Laureate:

> You've heard of the Turks and the Greeks,
> For all Europe's been told their bad habits,
> How they cut down each other like leeks,
> And the Turks slaughter children like rabbits.
> But John Bull could bear it no more,
> Said he, you death dealers, I'll stop you,
> And if you don't both soon give o'er,
> I swear by St George, that I'll whop you.

This is certainly less noble, but perhaps has more genuine life in it than Tennyson's famous lines:

> Then spake Sir Richard Grenville: 'I know you are no coward;
> You fly them for a moment to fight with them again.
> But I've ninety men and more that are lying sick ashore.
> I should count myself a coward if I left them, my Lord Howard,
> To these Inquisition dogs and the devildoms of Spain.'

That we are today in danger of losing touch with this norm of the 'language really used by men' seems indicated, not only by esoteric qualities of much modern poetry but also by the fact that we are prone to find the ballad idiom too Rabelaisian in its gusto and coarseness, even though we admit its Chaucerian merits of apt and easy directness, artfully used colloquialism and everyday imagery. The language of *The Lass of Lynn's New Joy*, a street ballad of middling quality, is typical of the central strength of the genre. When the deceived bridegroom on his wedding night 'found she'd a Rising Belly'

> ... he began to Roar,
> Your Fancy it has been Itching;
> By th'Meat in your Pot, I find, you Whore,
> you've had a Cook in your Kitchin.
>
> (Part II, 221.)

This is, doubtless, brutal, but apt and aesthetically adequate to the character and situation. It attempts neither to raise nor to lower the subject to any other plane than its own: that appropriate to *l'homme moyen sensuel* at his most articulate. At the same time the language is sufficiently metaphorical and rhythmical to lift it from the world of mere *reportage* to the world of creative art, if that term is not too genteelly restricted.

A similarly effortless use of homely imagery is to be found throughout. Witness, for example, the ballad in which the wicked Judge Jeffreys is shown recounting his villanies to his wife (Part I, 24):

> What Justice I did, my dear Wife, you can tell;
> Right or wrong I spar'd none, like the Divel in Hell;
> But, Guilty or not, I sent all to *Bridewell*.
>
> . . .
>
> Unless it were those that greased my Fist,
> To them, I gave Licence to cheat whom they list,
> (For 'twas only those that my *Mittimus* miss'd)

Without straining for effect or holding up the narrative, the 'Divel in Hell' and the greasing of the Fist give a sense of vivid actuality to the situation.

It is obvious too from the 'vocational ballads' (Part I, Section 3; II, Section 3) that these writers had nothing to learn about the Freudian aspect of imagery. They use it, however, not obscurely or neo-romantically but consciously and wittily.

The ballad-monger was mobile and difficult to regulate; the ballad poet (often the same person) was usually anonymous. Hence, he was not overawed by Authority – legal, clerical or critical – or by Posterity. Though the limitations of his outlook bound him to his own time and place, and his earthiness prevented him from soaring, he was in all other ways free:

> Whether these lines do please, or give offence,
> Or shall be damn'd as neither Wit nor Sence;
> The Poet is for that in no suspence,
> For 'tis all one a hundred years hence.'[1]

Such an attitude is typical and it gave rise to the typical virtues of the tradition: good-natured humour, shrewd criticism of society, sturdy realism and powerful rhythm, well exemplified in the following lines from one of the many ballads in praise of the Good Old Times:

> Some years ago the farmer's sons were learnt to plough and sow,
> And when the summer-time did come, likewise to reap and mow;
> But now they dress like Squire's sons, their pride it knows no bounds,
> They mount upon a fine blood horse to follow up the hounds.
>
> The farmer's daughters formerly were learnt to card and spin,
> And, by their own industry, good husbands they did win;
> But now the card and spinning-wheel are forced to take their chance,
> While they're hopped off to a boarding-school to learn to sing and dance.

1. Lines prefixed to a later, expanded, broadside version of *The Epicure* (Part II, 141): *The Careless Gallant*, Bagford III, 53.

In a decent black silk bonnet to church they used to go,
Black shoes, and handsome cotton gown, stockings as
    white as snow,
But now silk gowns and coloured shoes they must be
    bought for them,
Besides they are frizzed and furbelowed just like a
    freizland hen.

          (*The Times have Altered*, Part I, 51)

Lyricism and pathos are certainly to be found (witness
their union with religious feeling in the fine Catholic ballad
Hierusalem, my happie home (Part I, 92) and with lover's
loyalty and wry humour in stanzas 7–9 of *The New Balow*
(Part II, 218)); but these qualities, after the mid seventeenth century at any rate, the ballad poet seems to aspire
after rather than inherit as a birthright. Pathetic ballads,
particularly after 1700, tend to become sentimental[1] and
to use stock poetic diction, whereas in the more robust
the poet uses his own vernacular, so that his rhythms have
life though they may lack a slick competence. It seems to
have been this living literature of the common people,
quite as much as the classics, which has been a main source
of vitality in our poetic tradition. For four hundred years
the street ballad and popular song formed a rich vernacular soil in which more aspiring poetry rooted itself
and thrived.

3

The great majority of those street ballads still extant have
survived as printed broadsides, and they seem to have first
appeared in that form early in the sixteenth century. The
'Broadsheet' or 'Broadside' was a single sheet or half sheet
of paper with matter printed on one side of it. These

---

1. This is particularly true of the nineteenth-century ballads. See,
for example, *Blue Ey'd Mary* or *The Lovely Village Fair* (Part II,
122, 126).

broadsheets were used very soon after the introduction of printing into England for proclamations and official notices. The type used was what is now called 'English' and is very similar to the 'Gothic' type which has continued to be used in Germany up to present times; hence these ballads were often known as 'Black-letter Ballads'. Long after the adoption of roman type for the printing of books, the 'English' fount continued to be used for ballads as well as for the documents issued by various crown offices. The ballads were often, though not always, illustrated by rough pictures in woodcut.

The earliest known example of a printed sheet ballad is John Skelton's *A Ballade of the Scottyshe Kynge* (Part I, 1), printed by Richard Fawkes immediately after the battle of Flodden in 1513, a unique copy of which survives in the British Museum.[1] The street ballad, however, undoubtedly existed – though not yet as the dominant form – before the sixteenth century and quite probably before the introduction of printing. The poem called *London Lickpenny* (Part I, 37),[2] formerly attributed to John Lydgate, survives only in two seventeenth-century manuscript copies, but it certainly dates from the second half of the fifteenth century. This powerful realistic work bears all the marks of the true street ballad in its loose swinging rhythm, its racy colloquial style, and its combination of good humour with hard-hitting criticism of social and economic conditions. Above all it conveys in almost every line the atmosphere of the crowded street and the jostling London crowds. It may indeed be described as the prototype of the English street ballad, and it embodies themes that were to reappear again and again in poems of this kind during the next three hundred years. It is hardly likely that it was the sole work of this kind produced in fifteenth-century London. More probably it is the only

1. See *A Ballade of the Scottyshe Kynge written by John Skelton*, edited by John Ashton, London, 1882.

2. See edition by P. Holthausen, *Anglia*, XLIII, 1919.

surviving example of an English street-balladry of the Middle Ages that existed before the introduction of printing.[1]

The street ballad was certainly flourishing in the reign of Henry VIII, though, apart from Skelton's ballad already mentioned, few extant broadside ballads can be certainly assigned to the first half of the sixteenth century. However, there is plenty of evidence to show that they existed in this period. William Gray was employed to write them as propaganda for high officials, though in 1540 he got into trouble for a ballad flyting with a certain Thomas Smyth, as a result of which both poets were committed to the Fleet.[2] In 1543 Parliament passed an Act for the Advancement of True Religion which specifically mentions 'printed ballads, rhymes and songs' as a means used 'to subvert the very true and perfect exposition, doctrine and declaration of the Scriptures'. A little later in the same year eight London booksellers were brought before the Privy Council for violating this statute. After a fortnight five of them were released on condition that they should furnish lists of 'books and ballads' sold by them. Soon afterwards twenty-five other booksellers were similarly bound.[3]

This statute was repealed under Edward VI, but the Privy Council continued to keep a watchful eye on the publication of ballads. Ballads were used extensively in this reign for propaganda in connexion with the great religious controversy of the day, and the anti-Catholic ballad of *Luther, the Pope, a Cardinal and a Husbandman* and the anti-Protestant *Little John Nobody* are typical products of the mid sixteenth century. Mary's accession to the throne was

1. See Hyder E. Rollins, *P.M.L.A.A.*, xxxiv, 1919, xv, p. 258. According to Professor Rollins, attempts were made to circulate manuscript broadsheet ballads 'early in the fifteenth century'.

2. See *Calendar of State Papers, Foreign and Domestic, Henry VIII*, Vol. xvi, pp. 212, 213.

3. E. G. Duff, *Century of the English Book Trade*, pp. xxiv ff.

greeted by William Forrest in his ballad *A New Ballade of the Marigolde* (Part I, 3), but her Government was aware that ballads could be used for other purposes besides panegyric, and soon after her coronation she issued a proclamation against the printing of 'books, ballads, rhymes and interludes'. All the same, many propagandist ballads appeared during her reign, and some contained virulent attacks on the queen's policy. In March 1554 Bishop Bonner was ordered to suppress 'ballads and other pernicious and hurtful devices'. Loyal Catholics like John Heywood were allowed to issue propaganda ballads, but printers of anti-Catholic ballads were severely punished. Elizabeth's accession to the throne was hailed by William Birche in *A songe betwene the Quenes majestie and Englande* (Part I, 4).

Henceforward Catholic balladry became outlawed and clandestine, while the Protestants, provided that they supported the Government, could print their ballads with impunity. The popular broadside ballad became as characteristic a production of the Elizabethan age as the court lyric and the drama. No less than a hundred ballads were licensed at Stationers' Hall for publication in 1569–70 alone, and about three-quarters of them dealt with the Northern Rebellion. It was in this period that the types of street ballad which flourished till the middle of the nineteenth century became established. They can be roughly classified according to their functions and subject matter. First, there are ballads which are the popular journalism of the day. Every important or exciting event, from the defeat of the Spanish Armada down to the latest robbery, rape or murder, was recorded in ballad form, and the ballad-monger who composed, sang, and sold his wares in street and market combined the functions of the journalist who writes and the newsagent who distributes the cheap sensational newspaper of our own day. Secondly, there are ballads which represent popular fiction. They tell stories of English domestic life and more highly coloured tales of the Italian *novelle*, and even anticipate the historical novel. Thirdly, there are many ballads written to satisfy the popular demand for moralizing and religious literature. Such ballads are rivals and auxiliaries of the pulpit; some of them deal with Bible stories and many others are meditations on the vanity of human life and the terrible and inevitable judgements of heaven on sinfulness and irreligion. Finally, there are ballads which are really merry tales or popular lyrics dealing with the perennial subjects of love, courtship and marriage. In the Elizabethan period some of the latter achieve an unforced melody not inferior to some of the best work of the courtly poets.[1]

Like the popular films of the twentieth century, they were often condemned by moralists. In Henry Chettle's pamphlet *Kind Hartes Dream* (1592) the old-fashioned minstrel Anthony Nownow describes the newfangled ballad-mongers as 'an idle upstart generation', and Philip Stubbes in his *Anatomie of Abuses* (1583) attacked them (along with contemporary drama) for immorality. Both in England and Scotland attempts were made to fit moralizing and religious words to the ballad tunes. In Scotland two men were hanged in August 1579 for writing satiric ballads; in October of the same year the Scottish Estates passed an act to suppress 'bards and sangsters'. In the Elizabethan period the ballad poets seem to have been distrusted by men of letters and courtiers as much as by the moralists. The professional authors from Thomas Nashe to Ben Jonson affected to regard them with the same sort of contempt[2] that Victorian men of letters felt for the

1. See above, p. 24, and Part II, 99 and 104.
2. Cf. the character of Nightingale, the ballad singer in Ben Jonson's *Bartholomew Fair* and the lines in *An Ode. To himselfe* by the same author:

> What though the greedie Frie
>   Be taken with false Baytes
> Of worded Balladrie
> And think it Poesie?

'penny-a-line' journalist of the nineteenth century, though Jonson's Cock Lorrel's song is a fine example of the street ballad written by the man of letters. As for the courtiers, Hotspur is no doubt voicing their opinion accurately enough when he says

> I'd rather be a kitten and cry mew
> Than one of those same metre ballad-mongers.

This courtly attitude may be due more to feeling about the vendors' character and social position than the quality of their wares – and, in any case, it applied equally to 'traditional' and 'street' ballads. Autolycus in *The Winter's Tale* is probably a fair specimen of the amusing light-fingered rogues who hawked their broadsides in the taverns, markets, and farmhouses of Elizabethan England. The dialogue between the ballad-monger and the country-folk in Act IV, Scene iv, of that play gives a vivid picture of the way in which Elizabethan popular ballads circulated, and it can be noted that Autolycus is quite willing to sing the ballads which he is peddling with his customers:

Clown. What hast here? Ballads?

Mopsa. Pray now, buy some: I love a ballad in print o' life, for then we are sure they are true.

Aut. Here's one to a very doleful tune, how a usurer's wife was brought to bed of twenty money-bags at a burthen and how she longed to eat adders' heads and toads carbonadoed.

Mop. Is it true think you?

Aut. Very true and but a month old.

Dorcas. Bless me from marrying a usurer!

Aut. Here's the midwife's name to't, one Mistress Taleporter, and five or six honest wives that were present. Why should I carry lies abroad?

Mop. Pray now, buy it.

Clo. Come on, lay it by.: and let's first see moe ballads; we'll buy the other things anon.

Aut. Here's another ballad of a fish,[1] that appeared upon the

1. Cf. Part I, 81.

36

coast on Wednesday the fourscore of April, forty thousand
fathom above water, and sung this ballad against the hard
hearts of maids: it was thought she was a woman and was
turned into a cold fish for she would not exchange flesh
with one that loved her: the ballad is very pitiful and as true.

Dor. Is it true too, think you?

Aut. Five justices' hands at it, and witnesses more than my
pack will hold.

Clo. Lay it by too; another.

Aut. This is a merry ballad, but a very pretty one.

Mop. Let's have some merry ones.

Aut. Why, this is a passing merry one and goes to the tune of
'Two maids wooing a man': there's scarce a maid west-
ward but she sings it; 'tis in request, I can tell you.

Mop. We can both sing it: if thou wilt bear a part, thou shalt
hear; 'tis in three parts.

Dor. We had the tune on't a month ago.

Aut. I can bear my part; you must know it is my occupation.
Have at it with you.

The king of the ballad-mongers in Shakespeare's London
was William Elderton, who was probably an actor and
whose character is doubtless fairly represented by Gabriel
Harvey's description of him as 'Elderton of the ale-crammed
nose'. He was the author of numerous ballads of the same
type as those which Autolycus hawked in Shakespeare's
Bohemia. Elderton's rival and successor was Thomas
Deloney, whose prose stories have received high praise
from modern critics. Deloney, however, was known to his
contemporaries chiefly as a popular ballad poet, 'the
balleting silkweaver of Norwich' as Nashe calls him. His
ballads are remarkable for their vigorous rhythm and
metrical virtuosity (see Part I, 7 and 8).

A development of the street ballad which was very
popular in the late sixteenth century was the jig or ballad in
dialogue; a short drama in ballad metre set to dance music,
which may be regarded as the ancestor of the eighteenth-
century ballad opera. Jigs were commonly performed in the

Elizabethan theatres (cf. Hamlet's remark about Polonius, 'He's for a jig or a tale of bawdry, or he sleeps'). The most interesting extant example is Francis Attowel's jig based on the ballad *As I went to Walsingham,* which has a plot resembling that of *Measure for Measure.*

The seventeenth century was perhaps the golden age of the English street ballad. The ballad poets did not yet have to contend with the rivalry of the newspaper, and the popular taste for poetry had not yet been destroyed by the effects of industrialism. Innumerable broadsheets containing satiric, religious, political, sentimental, amatory and comic verses were hawked and sung in the London streets and taverns. Chappell states[1] that he has traced more than 250 ballad publishers in London alone in the seventeenth century.

Social criticism was the theme of some of the best of the ballads of the late seventeenth century, such as the twin ballads of *The Old and the New Courtier* (Part I, 41) written in the reign of James I to satirize the manners of the new plutocracy. The fine ballad called *The Map of Mock-Begger Hall* (Part II, 38) is another vigorous and amusing indictment of the greed and snobbery of the new type of landlord as contrasted with the kindly patriarchal type of a society which was dying in the age of the Stuarts. The ballad of the Street Cries of London, of which there are many variations, gives a vivid impression of the richly coloured pageant of the old London streets with their warm, pulsating communal life:

> Ripe Chery ripe,
>   the Coster-monger cries,
> Pipins fine, or Peares,
>   another after hies,
> With basket on his head,
>   his living to advance,
> And in his purse a paire of Dice,
>   for to play at Mumchance.

1. Introduction to *The Roxburghe Ballads* (Ballad Society, Vol. II, Part 1, 1872).

> Hot Pippin pies,
>   to sell unto my friends:
> Or puding pies in pans,
>   well stuft with Candles ends,
> Will you buy any Milke?
>   I heare a wench that cries,
> With a paile of fresh Cheese and creame,
>   another after hies.

Martin Parker (d. 1656), a name which is not found in the histories of literature, succeeded Deloney and Elderton as a chief ballad poet of London. He is a writer of considerable power and versatility. He is capable of the lyrical sweetness of *The Milkemaids Life*, quoted by Izaak Walton in *The Compleat Angler* (1653):

> Base idleness they do scorne:
> They rise very early in the morn,
> And walk into the field,
> Where pretty birds doe yield
>   brave musick on every thorn
> The linet and the thrush
> Doe sing on every bush;
>   and the dulcid nightingale
> Her note doth straine
> In a jocund vaine
> To entertaine
> That worthy traine
> Which carry the milking pale.

An ardent royalist, he was the author of the cavalier poem with the famous refrain 'When the king enjoys his own again' (afterwards appropriated by the Jacobites), and he could write stirring ballads of action like his excellent *Saylors for my Money* (Part I, 70), which undoubtedly provided Thomas Campbell with the groundwork and even some phrases for *Ye Mariners of England*.

The Civil Wars and the subsequent political conflicts in the reigns of Charles II, James II and William III produced great crops of political and satiric ballads. Some of the best of the Cavalier ballads were reprinted in the collection called *The Rump* (1662) and some of the best of the Whig ballads in the *Poems on Affairs of State* (1689–97). Many amatory and humorous ballads also appeared in the *Drolleries*, which were originally collections of ballads and songs from the Drolls or theatrical entertainments which took the place of the banned plays under the rule of the Puritans. Later they came to incorporate unpuritanical or antipuritan poems of all kinds written by Cavaliers to console themselves in their eclipse or to celebrate their emancipation after the Restoration. It is noticeable that the same ballad publishers often printed for both political parties, thus ensuring the survival of the political or ideological ballad, a form which had vigorous life until well into the nineteenth century. Traditional ballads of the Middle Ages such as *The Twa Sisters* (1656) and *The Elfin Knight* (*c.*1670) were also occasionally reprinted as broadsides. The tradition of Elderton and Parker was carried on in the latter part of the century by Thomas D'Urfey (1653–1723). He not only wrote popular ballads but sang them himself to Charles II and Queen Anne, and he made a great collection of ballads and popular songs by himself and other writers called *Wit and Mirth or Pills to Purge Melancholy* (1719–20). The ballads in this collection are often coarse and scurrilous, but they have life, metrical dexterity, and in many cases real lyrical beauty. Henry Carey was the great balladmonger of the age of Hogarth, Swift and Fielding. His well-known *Sally in our Alley* (Part II, 146) is the classic example of the early eighteenth-century street ballad, the poetic counterpart of Hogarth's popular engravings; he wrote other ballads which are quite as good, such as the delicious *Sally Sweetbread*, the ballad of the citizen's wife who resolves to 'steal to the fair' and enjoy herself when the 'good man's from home' (Part II, 205). Carey, it may be noted, was the pioneer of the eighteenth-century ballad opera, which can be regarded as the remote descendant of the Elizabethan jig.

In the Elizabethan period there had been a sharp distinction between the ballad-monger and the courtly and educated poets. In the seventeenth century, however, scholars and courtiers began to take an interest in popular poetry. Collections of broadsides were made by the great scholar John Selden, by Samuel Pepys, the diarist, and by the courtier-poet Charles Sackville, Earl of Dorset. In the reign of Charles I literary poets seem to have started to write in the manner of the ballad-mongers, adopting their metres, idiom and style. John Aubrey in his *Brief Lives* tells how Richard Corbet, D.D., afterwards Bishop of Oxford, found a ballad singer in the market-place at Abingdon complaining that he could not sell his broadsides. Taking pity on the poor man, the 'jolly doctor' took off his gown, put on the ballad singer's leather jerkin and sang the ballads himself. As he had 'a rare full voice he vended a great many and had a great audience'. This incident symbolizes the new alliance of the scholarly poets and the ballad-mongers. Bishop Corbet not only sang street ballads; he wrote them too. One of the best of his own poems is a typical street ballad, the admirable poem on the fairies, with its exuberant ballad-monger's title: *A Proper New Ballad entitled the Fairies Farewell or God a Mercy Will; to be sung or whistled to the tune of Meadow Brow by the Learned; by the Unlearned to the tune of Fortune*. Corbet's contemporary, the courtier-poet Sir John Suckling, adopted the street-ballad form for his most famous poem, the delightful *A Ballade upon a Wedding* (Part II, 199), and the tradition was handed on from the courtiers of Charles I to the Restoration Wits who often write in the manner of the street ballad. Dorset's gay and witty *Song written at Sea in the First Dutch War* (Part I, 72) is a most successful use of the form by a courtier poet. The poem was originally sold as a broadside under the title of *The Noble Seaman's lament* and is written to an old street-ballad tune. Sedley also wrote a typical journalistic ballad on a contemporary murder trial[1] with a slight tang of irony, and a number of Rochester's satires were published as broadsides; many of them are in the true street-ballad manner, as, for example, the bitter satire on Charles II called *The History of Insipids,* with its dancing, mocking rhythm:

> Chast, pious, prudent, *Charls* the Second,
>   The Miracle of thy Restauration,
> May like to that of *Quails* be reckon'd
>   Rain'd on the Israelitick Nation;
> The wisht for Blessing from Heav'n sent,
> Became their Curse and Punishment.
>
>   .   .   .
>
> Never was such a Faiths Defender,
>   He like a politick Prince, and pious,
> Gives liberty to Conscience tender,
>   And doth to no Religion tye us.
> *Jews, Christians, Turks, Papists,* he'll please us,
> With *Moses, Mahomet,* or *Jesus.*[2]

But the man of letters who made the most successful use of the street ballad in the Restoration period was Andrew Marvell. Most modern readers think of Marvell as the subtle lyrical poet of *The Garden, Bermudas* and *To His Coy Mistress.* The political satires which he wrote in the latter part of his life are not so well known. These propaganda poems were powerful instruments in the political struggle between the 'country party' and the court. Marvell used the rollicking metres and the strong homespun style of the street ballad with great effect in several of his political poems, such as the satiric dialogue between the horses of the statue of Charles I at Charing Cross and Charles II at Woolchurch. The dialogue is a series of sledgehammer attacks on

1. See Part I, 86.
2. Part I, 14.

the Stuart kings, culminating in the crashing blow of the conclusion:

> But canst thou Divine when things shall be mended?
> When the Reign of the Line of the Stuarts is ended.
> Then, England, rejoyce, thy Redemption draws nigh;[1]
> Thy oppression together with kingship shall die
> A Commonwealth, a Commonwealth we proclaim to
>   the nation
> The Gods have repented the King's Restoration.

Cowper was right in pointing to the reign of Queen Anne as a great age of balladry. Most of the famous Queen Anne Wits wrote street ballads. Congreve wrote several, the best of which is, perhaps, the song of Ben the Sailor in *Love for Love* (Part II, 166). Pope, in spite of his devotion to the couplet, wrote at least two poems in the street-ballad manner, *A Farewell to London* and the gay little poem following in the footsteps of the Earl of Dorset:

> To one fair lady out of Court
>   And two fair ladies in
> Who think the Turk and Pope no sport
>   And wit and love no sin,
> Come these soft lines with nothing stiff in
> To Bellenden, Lepell and Griffin.

Prior, Swift and Gay were all masters of the street ballad. Prior wrote several spirited and vigorous poems in this style, the best of them being, perhaps, his mocking English ballad in answer to Boileau's pompous French ode on the taking of Namur, and that masterpiece of shadowed humorous realism *The Ballad of Down Hall*, describing his visit to the house given to him by Robert Harley, Earl of Oxford:

1. Marvell's *Poems and Letters*, ed. Margoliouth, I, 195. Cf. Chatterton's *The Prophecy* (1770), a political street ballad with the refrain, 'Look up, ye Britons! cease to sigh / For your redemption draweth nigh.'

Come here my sweet Landlady, pray how do you do?
Where is *Sisley* so cleanly, and *Prudence* and *Sue*?
And where is the widow that dwelt here below?
And the Hostler that sung about Eight Years ago?

And where is your Sister so mild and so dear?
Whose Voice to her Maids like a Trumpet was clear,
By my Troth, she replies, you grow Younger, I think,
And pray, Sir, what Wine does the Gentleman drink?

Why now let me Die, Sir, or live upon Trust,
If I know to which Question to answer you first.
Why Things since I saw you, most strangely have vary'd,
And the Hostler is hang'd, and the Widow is Marry'd.

In Swift's Dublin, as in Andrew Marvell's London, the
street ballad was a powerful weapon of propaganda and the
great Dean used it vigorously in his campaigns against Irish
social and economic injustice.

Gay wrote many ballads, the best of which are, perhaps,
Black-eyed Susan and *Molly Mog* (Part II, 142). The ballad
in the farce called *The What d'ye Call It* (Part I, 73), in
which Pope, Gay, Arbuthnot and Swift collaborated is a
masterpiece of virtuosity, which well deserves Cowper's
praise.[1] Cowper himself adopted the street-ballad form
for his most successful and popular poem, the sparkling
and delightful *Ballad of John Gilpin*, a poem which has
nothing to do with the revival of medieval balladry
sponsored by Cowper's contemporary Bishop Percy.[2] It is
the work of an artist in the tradition that goes back through
Carey and D'Urfey to Parker, Elderton and Deloney.
Burns was influenced probably almost as much by the
tradition of the street ballad as by that of Scottish folk song.
That Hogarthian masterpiece, *The Jolly Beggars,* is a

1. See above, p. 15.
2. Though Percy included some excellent sheet ballads in his
famous *Reliques of Ancient English Poetry* (1765).

sequence of poems in the street-ballad measures and style, and its vigorous anti-heroic realism and hearty sensuality clearly relate it to the work of the popular ballad poets of the seventeenth and eighteenth centuries.

Blake is another poet of the late eighteenth century who is profoundly influenced by the popular poetry of the street ballad. One of his early poems (Part I, 46) in the *Island in the Moon* might well have been written by the author of the *Old and the New Courtier* in the reign of James I. Indeed a number of the *Songs of Innocence and Experience* and some of the miscellaneous poems might be described as street ballads spiritualized and transfigured, and it is highly probable that Blake's beautifully engraved illustrations to these poems are inspired by the example of the crude popular art of the woodcut illustrations to the street ballads. Wordsworth was unquestionably influenced very considerably by the street ballad; if *The Ancient Mariner* is the descendant of the medieval traditional ballads, Wordsworth's characteristic contributions to *Lyrical Ballads* like *Harry Gill* and *The Idiot Boy* are attempts to use the manner of the eighteenth-century street ballad for studies in psychology beyond the reach of the ballad-mongers. That great and much-maligned poem *Peter Bell* bears much the same relationship to the moralizing street ballad that *The Ancient Mariner* bears to such traditional ballads as *Sir Patrick Spens*. It has the slow lumbering movement of the edifying ballad, its garrulity, and also its power of conveying emotion in simple colloquial language; here, of course, all these characteristics are transmuted by the genius of a great poet. Byron, like his predecessors, the aristocratic poets of the Restoration, delighted in popular poetry, and his letters are full of snatches of verse in the street-ballad manner. *So We'll Go No More A-Roving*, one of his best lyrics, seems obviously derived from the refrain of *The Jolly Beggar* (Part II, 95). When he defended the Luddites, or Nottinghamshire weavers, whose miseries had driven them to rise and smash the new machine-looms, he used the street-ballad form with an irony and gusto worthy of Marvell and Swift (Part I, 48). Shelley is not a poet whom most readers will associate with the street-ballad tradition. Nevertheless, it may be remarked that some of his most admired and effective metrical forms are certainly derived from street ballads. The stanza of *Arethusa* and *The Cloud* is an old street-ballad stanza used by Marvell and Swift and found in dozens of broadsides; the quatrain of four-accent anapaestic lines rhyming in couplets, which is used so admirably in *The Sensitive Plant,* is a popular street-ballad type used by Marvell in his *Dialogue between Two Horses,* Prior in his *Ballad of Down Hall* and by numerous ballad-mongers. When Shelley wanted to write in a popular manner, as in *The Masque of Anarchy* or *Song to the Men of England,* he used the street-ballad form and idiom, and acquired a directness and power which is rare enough in his other writings.

The street ballad belongs to the heroic or patriarchal age of capitalism, when every apprentice could aspire, like that popular ballad hero Dick Whittington, to be Lord Mayor of London, and when there was still little social distinction between wage-earner, shopkeeper, merchant and craftsman. It came to maturity in the seventeenth and early eighteenth centuries, before the advent of machinery on a large scale, and began to wilt in the age of industrial capitalism and mass employment, when the proletariat was losing its genuine culture of the street, the tavern and the fair, and coming to depend on the music-hall for its songs. Nevertheless, the street ballad continued to flourish until well into the nineteenth century. In the eighteenth century the 'black letter' fount had gone out of fashion and the broadsides were now printed in roman type or 'white letter'; they were still commonly illustrated by the traditional woodcut pictures. The ballads, as well as short popular prose stories, were also printed in cheap little paper-covered pamphlets called chapbooks and in smaller brochures called 'garlands'. The street ballad certainly retained its popularity in the early nineteenth century. Enormous numbers of them were printed and sold by James Catnach, an enterprising Scottish printer who came to London in 1813 and set up a press in Seven Dials. John Pitts, also of Seven Dials, was another specialist in this line; and others were to be found in Liverpool, Manchester, Birmingham, Nottingham, Newcastle and elsewhere. These early nineteenth-century ballads, though often crude and sensational, are extremely interesting expressions of the mentality of the uneducated classes in the early days of industrialism, and a few of them, like the famous Lincolnshire Poacher's Song (see note to Part I, 76, p. 617) have genuine poetic quality.

In the early Victorian period, however, the ballad-singer became a pitiable figure living rather on tips from better-class people who remembered him from palmier days than on the prcoeeds of his sales. He would recall the times when he sold 'four or five quires a day' instead of 'two or three dozen' ballads. Douglas Jerrold, in an article called *The Ballad Singer*, published in 1842, wrote that 'the public ear has now become dainty, fastidious, hypercritical; hence the Ballad-singer languishes and dies. Only now and then his pipings are heard. . . . With the fall of Napoleon declined the English ballad-singer.' He was almost certainly helped to extinction by the establishment of a regular police force. After 1829 the ballad-monger could be more easily discouraged by prosecutions for mendicity and obstruction. Moreover, he was exposed to new kinds of competition. The music-hall now became a regular feature of English urban life and produced songs of a type that were felt to be more up-to-date than the ballad-monger's old-fashioned wares. And the reduction of the stamp-duty from 4d. to 1d. in 1839 and its complete abolition in 1855 heralded the appearance of the cheap newspaper, which took over the journalistic functions of the street ballad. The canvas screens on which those ballad-mongers who were 'Standing' Patterers exposed their wares (like Silas Wegg in *Our Mutual Friend*, 1865) were still a common sight in London in the early and mid-Victorian periods. But in 1888 John Ashton wrote in his *Modern Street Ballads* that at that early date only one or two still remained in Gray's Inn Road, Faringdon Road and other London neighbourhoods. In the late Victorian period the street ballad was replaced by the music-hall song and the closely allied 'recitation piece' (of the sort produced by George R. Sims); later nineteenth-century broadsides are commonly mere reprints of such songs. None the less, genuine street ballads of a very degenerate type were still written and sold in the streets as late as the twentieth century on such occasions as the death of Edward VII in 1910[1] and President Wilson's visit to London in 1919.

However, the influence of the street ballad on literary poetry was by no means exhausted by the virtual disappearance of the ballad-monger from the streets. Hardy derives much of his strength from the form. His *Dark-Eyed Gentleman*, for instance, has precisely the same theme as *The Maid of Tottenham* (Part II, 110). Much of Rudyard Kipling's best verse obviously belongs to the street-ballad tradition (coming to him, doubtless, partly through G. R. Sims and the music-halls). W. B. Yeats used the Dublin street-ballad form magnificently in some of his poems on the Rebellion of 1916 (*Sixteen Dead Men* and *The Rose Tree*), and more recently W. H. Auden's interest in street ballads is seen not merely in his work as the anthologist of *The Poet's Tongue* and the *Oxford Book of Light Verse* but in a number of his own poems, such as '*O what is the sound that so thrills the ear*', *The Six Beggared Cripples*, *Miss Gee*,

1. See Part I, 36.

James Honeyman, or *Victor was a little baby* (*To the tune of Frankie and Johnny*). William Plomer, C. Day Lewis and Dylan Thomas (in *Under Milk Wood*) are other modern poets who have made effective use of the English street-ballad tradition. In Scotland, the parallel form was that of a hybrid product of folk song and suppressed street ballad (see above, p. 21), and its influence seems to be almost as strongly felt by modern Lallans poets as it was by Burns. The few sample Scots pieces included in this collection (in Part II) are mostly less respectable variants of poems in the official Burns canon (which, of course, does not include all that he actually wrote). They point to an un-tilled field which should prove most fruitful to the Burns critic.

Today, though its influence survives, the street ballad proper has disappeared entirely. Certain successors are to be found on matchboxes or in fugitive comic news-sheets (see specimens in the Appendix A), but these have little of the street-ballad vitality, and are even more liable to lose the metre or the thread of the story than the poorest nineteenth-century pieces. In ballads current orally in H.M. Forces, and elsewhere, more of the true spirit and something of the old form and idiom survives, but usually in a state of degeneration. The few samples included in the Appendix B, though by no means the worst to be found, show clearly enough that they carry to a conclusion the process which began in the nineteenth century, when the street ballad became *déclassé*. Comparing, for example, the probably seventeenth-century *Room for a Jovial Tinker* (Part II, 156) with the nineteenth-century *The Beverley Maid and the Tinker* (Part II, 177), we see at once that the story has become muddled and the language weaker. But a far greater degeneration reveals itself in *The Highland Tinker,* a present-day oral version of the same tale (Appendix B, 7). It is shorter, shows less skill in handling narrative, less feeling for words and less ingenuity of punning metaphor, and it confuses the merely obscene with the 'merry'. All the same, such ballads retain sufficient vitality and flexibility to serve as a reminder to modern poets of what they, and their audience, are in danger of losing with the disappearance of a genuine popular poetry.

PART I

GENERAL

ONE

HISTORICAL

I

A Ballade of the Scottyshe Kynge

BY JOHN SKELTON
(1513)

Kyng Jamy / Jamy your Joye is all go
Ye sommnoed our kynge why dyde ye so?
To you nothyng it dyde accorde
To sommon our kynge your soverayne lorde.
A kynge a somner it is wonder
Knowe ye not salt and suger asonder?
In your sommynge ye were to malaperte
And your harolde no thynge experte.
Ye thought we dyde it full valyauntolye
But not worth thre skippes of a pye.
Syr squyer galyarde ye were to swyfte
Your wyll renne before your wytte.
To be so scornefull to your alye
Your counseyle was not worth a flye.
Before the frensshe kynge / danes / and other
Ye ought to honour your lorde and brother.
Trowe ye syr James his noble grace
For you and your scottes wolde tourne his face
Now ye prode scottes of gelawaye   [*gelawaye =*
For your kynge may synge welawaye.   *Galloway*
Now must ye knowe our kynge for your regent
Your soverayne lorde and presedent
In hym is figured melchisedeche
And ye be desolate as armeleche.   [*armeleche =*
He is our noble champyon   *Amalek*

A kynge anoynted and ye be non,
Thrugh your counseyle your fader was slayne
Wherefore I fere ye wyll suffre payne
And ye proude scottes of dunbar
Parde ye be his homager
And suters to his parlyment
Ye dyde not your dewty therein.
Wyerfore ye may it now repent
Ye bere yourselfe som what to bolde

[*copholde* = copyhold

Therefore ye have lost your copholde
Ye be bounde tenauntes to his estate
Gyve up your game ye playe chekmate
For to the castell of norham
I understonde to soone ye cam.
For a prysoner now ye be
Eyther to the devyll or the trinite.
Thanked be saynte Gorge our ladyes knythe
Your pryd is paste adwe good nyght.
Ye have determyned to make a fraye
Our kynge than beynge out of the waye
But by the power and myght of god
Ye were beten with your owne rod.
By your wanton wyll sýr at a worde
Ye have lost spores, cote armure, and sworde
Ye had better to have busked to huntey ba⟨n⟩kes
Than in England to playe ony suche prankes
But ye had som wyle sede to sowe
Therefore ye be layde now full lowe,
Your power coude no longer atteyne
Warre with our kynge to meyntayne

[*naverne* = Navarre

Of the kynge of naverne ye may take hede
How unfortunately he doth now spede,
In double welles now he doeth dreme.
That is a kynge witou a realme
At hym example ye wolde none take
Experyence hath brought you in the same brake

54

Of the out yles ye rough foted scottes
We have well eased you of the bottes
Ye rowe ranke scottes and dro⟨n⟩ken danes
Of our englysshe bowes ye have fette your banes.
It is not syttynge in tour nor towne
A somner to were a kynges crowne
That neble erle the whyte Lyon,
Your pompe and pryde hath layde a downe
His sone the lorde admyrall is full good
His swerd hath bathed in the scottes blode
God save kynge Henry and his lordes all
And sende the frensshe kynge suche an other fall
   Amen / for saynt charyte
   And god save noble
     Kynge / Henry /
       The VIII.

2

Fragment of an Anti-Papist Ballad

(*c.* 1548)

There hartes ware so roted in the popes lawes
They be gane the last yere when they slew bodye:
All England rejoycethe at ther over throwse
For only the Lorde is our Kynges victorye.

They had falce prophets which brought thi⟨n⟩nges to passe
Cleane contrary to her owne expectacion;
Ther hope was for helpe in ther popishe masse
They wolde nedes have hanged up a reservacion.
The vicare of pon wdstoke with his congeracio⟨n⟩
Commanded them to sticke to their Idolatry
They had muche provi⟨s⟩ion and grete preperacion
Yet God hath gyven our Kynge the victorye.

They did robe and spoule all the kynges frendes,
They called them heritekes with spight & disdayne,
They roffled a space like Tirantes and Findes,
They put some in preson & sume to greate payne,
And sume fled awaie or else they had been slayne
As was William hilling that martir truly,
Which they killed at Sandford moure in the playne,
Where yet god hath given oure Kynge the victory.

They came to plūmo with the Kynges trusty towne.

3

A New Ballade of the Marigolde

(On the Accession of Mary I, 1553)

The God above, for man's delight,
Hath heere ordaynde every thing –
Sonne, Moone, and Sterres, shinyng so bright,
with all kinde fruites that here doth spring,
And Flowrs that are so flourishyng.
     Amonges all which that I beholde,
As to my minde best contentyng,
     I doo commende the Marigolde.

[*Veare = Spring*   In Veare first springeth the Violet;
The Primerose, then, also doth spred;
The Couslip sweete abroade doth get;
The Daisye gaye sheweth forth her hed;
The Medowes greene, so garnishèd,
     Most goodly (truly) to beholde,
For which God is to be Praisèd:
     Yet I commende the Marigolde.

The Rose that chearfully doth showe
At Midsomer, her course hath shee;
The Lilye white after doth growe;
The Columbine then see may yee;
The Joliflowre in fresh degree,
   with sundrie mo then can be tolde:
Though they never so pleasaunt bee,
   Yet I commende the Marigolde.

Though these which here are mencionèd
Bee delectable to the iye,
By whom sweete smelles are ministred,
The sense of man to satisfye,
Yet each as serveth his fantasye;
   wherefore to say I wyll be bolde,
And to advoide all flaterye,
   I doo commende the Marigolde.

All these but for a time doth serve,
Soone come, soone gone, so doth they fare,
At fervent heates and stormes thei sterve,   *[sterve = die*
Fadyng away, their staulkes left bare.
Of that I praise, thus say I dare,
   Shee sheweth glad cheare in heate and colde,
Moche profityng to hertes in care,
   Such is this floure, the Marigolde.

This Marigolde Floure, marke it well,
with Sonne dooth open, and also shut;
which (in a meanyng) to us doth tell
To Christ, God's Sonne, our willes to put,
And by his woorde to set our futte,
   Stiffly to stande, as Champions bolde,
From the truthe to stagger nor stutte,   *[stutte = stumble*
   For which I praise the Marigolde.

57

To Marie, our Queene, that Floure so sweete,
This Marigolde I doo apply,
For that the Name doth serve so meete,
And properlee, in eache partie,
For her enduryng paciently
   The stormes of such, as list to scolde
At her dooynges, with cause why,
   Loth to see spring this Marigolde.

She may be calde Marigolde well,
Of Marie (chiefe), Christes mother deere,
That as in heaven shee doth excell,
And Golde in earth, to have no peere:
So (certainly) shee shineth cleere,
   In Grace and honour double folde,
The like was never earst seene heere,
   Suche is this floure, the Marigolde.

Her education well is knowne,
From her first age how it hath wrought;
In singler Vertue shee hath growne,
And servyng God, as she well ought;
For which he had her in his thought,
   And shewed her Graces many folde,
In her estate to see her brought,
   Though some dyd spite this Marigolde.

Yf she (in faith) had erred a-misse,
which God, most sure, doth understande,
wolde hee have doone, as provèd is,
Her Enmies so to bring to hande?
No, be ye sure, I make a bande,
   For servyng him he needes so wolde
Make her to Reigne over Englande, –
   So loveth hee this Marigolde.

Her conversacion, note who list,
It is more heavenly then terraine,
For which God doth her Actes assist;
All meekenesse doth in her remaine:
All is her care, how to ordayne,
   To have God's Glorie here extolde;
Of Poore and Riche, shee is most fayne.
   Christ save, therfore, this Marigolde.

Sith so it is, God loveth her,
And shee, His Grace, as doth appeare;
Ye may be bolde as to referre
All doubtfulnesse as to her most cleare,
That, as her owne, in like maneare
   She wilth your welthes, both yong & olde,
Obey her, then, as your Queene deare,
   And say: Christ save this Marigolde.

Christ save her in her High Estate,
Therin (in rest) long to endure;
Christ so all wronges heere mitigate,
That all may be to his pleasure:
The high, the lowe, in due measure,
   As membres true with her to holde,
So eache to be thother's treasure,
   In cherishyng the Marigolde.

Be thou (O God) so good as thus
Thy Perfect Fayth to see take place;
Thy peace thou plant here among us,
That Errour may go hide his face,
So to concorde us in eache case,
   As in thy Courte, it is enrolde,
wee all (as one) to love her Grace,
   That is our Queene, this Marigolde.

God save the Queene
Quod   William Forrest, Preest
Imprinted in London in Aldersgate Street by Richard Lant.

4

A songe betwene the Quenes majestie and Englande

(On the Accession of Elizabeth I, 1558)

(E = England; B = Bessy, i.e. Queen Elizabeth)

E. Come over the born bessy / come over the born bessy
    Swete bessy come over to me
  And I shall the take / and my dere lady make
    Before all other that ever I see.

B. My thinke I hear a voice / at whom I do rejoyce
    and aunswer the now I shall
  Tel me I say / what art thou that bids me com away
    and soo earnestly doost me call.

E. I am thy lover faire / hath chose the to my heir
    and my name is mery Englande
  Therefore come away / and make no more delaye
    Swete bessie give me thy hande.

B. Here is my hand / my dere lover Englande
    I am thine both with mind and hart
  For ever to endure / thou maiest be sure
    Untill death do us two depart.

E. Lady this long space / have I loved thy grace
    more then I durste well saye
  Hoping at the last / when all stormes were past
    For to see this joyfull daye.

B. Yet my lover England / ye shall understand
    How fortune on me did lowre
  I was tombled and lost / from piller to post
    and prisoner in the Toure.

E. Dere Lady we do know / how that tirauntes not a fewe
    went about to seke thy bloude
  An contrarie to right / they did what they might
    That now bare two faces in one hood.

B. Then was I caried to Wodstock / & kept close under lock
    That no man mighte with me speake
  And against all reason / they accused me of treason
    and ⟨terribly⟩ thei did me threate.

E. O my lover faire / my dearling and mine heire
    Full lo⟨n⟩ge for the did I lament
  But no man durst speak / but thei wuld him threat
    and quickly make him repent.

B. Then was I delivered their hands / but was fain to put
    in bands
    and good suerties for my forthcomminge
  Not from my house to departe / nor nowhere els to
    sterte
    as though I had ben alway runninge.

E. Why dere Lady I trow / those mad men did not knowe
    That ye were doughter unto King Hary
  And a princesse of birth / one of the noblest on earth
    and sister unto Quene Mary.

B. Yes, yet I must forgeve / al such as do live
    if they will hereafter amend
  And for those that have gone / God forgive them
    everyone
    and his mercy on them extend.

E. Yet my lover dere / tell me now here
    For what cause had ye this punishmente

61

For the commons did not know / nor no man wuld
    them shew
  The chief cause of your imprisonment.

B. No nor thei themself / that wuld have decaid my welth
    But only by powre and abusion
  Thei culd not detect me / but that thei did suspect me
    That I was not of their religion.

E. Oh cruell tirauntes / and also monstrous giauntes
    That woulde such a swete blossome devour
  But the lorde of his might / defended the in right
    And shortened their arme and powre.

B. Yet my lover dere / marke me well here
    Though thei were men of the devill
  The scripture plainly saith / al thei that be of faith
    must nedes do good against evill.

E. Oh swete virgin pure / longe may ye endure
    To reigne over us in this lande
  For your workes do accord / ye are the handmaid of
    the lord
    For he hath blessed you with his hand.

B. My swete realme be obedient / to gods holy
    commaundement
    and my procedinges embrace
  And for that that is abused / shall be better used
    and that within shorte space.

E. Dere lady and Quene / I trust it shal be sene
    Ye shall reigne quietly without strife
  And if any traiters there be / of any kind or degre
    I pray God send them short life.

B. I trust al faithful herts / will play tru subjects parts
    Knowing me their Queen & true heir by right
  And that much the rather / for the love of my father
    that worthy prince King Henrie theight.

E. Therfore let us pray / to God both night and day
    Continually and never to sease
  That he wil preserve your grace / to reigne over us long
    space

BOTH
  All honor laud & praise, / be to the lord god alwaies
    Who hath all princes hartes in his handes
  that by his powre & might / he may give them a right
    For the welth of all christen landes.

Finis q. William Birche

God save the Quene

Imprinted at London by William Pickeringe / dwelling
under Saynt Magnus church.

5

Upon Sir Francis Drake's return from
his voyage about the world, and the
Queen's meeting him

(*c.* 1584)

Sir Francis, Sir Francis, Sir Francis is come;
Sir Robert, and eke Sir William his son,
And eke the good Earl of Huntington
Marched gallantly on the road.

Then came the Lord Chamberlain with his white staff,
And all the people began to laugh;
And then the Queen began to speak,
'You're welcome home, Sir Francis Drake.'

You gallants all o' the British blood,
Why don't you sail o' the ocean flood?
I protest you're not all worth a filbert
If once compared to Sir Humphrey Gilbert.

For he went out on a rainy day,
And to the new-found land found out his way,
With many a gallant fresh and green,
And he ne'er came home again. God bless the Queen.

6

Lord Willoughby

OR

A true relation of a Famous and Bloody Battel fought in
Flanders, by the noble and valiant Lord Willoughby, with
1500 English against 40,000 Spaniards, where the English
obtained a notable victory, for the glory and renown of our
Nation.

(c. 1586)

The fifteen day of *July*,
    with glistering speare and shield,
A famous fight in *Flanders*
    was foughten in the field:
The most couragious officers
    was *English* Captains three;
But the bravest man in Battel
    was brave Lord *Willoughby*.

The next was Captain *Norris*,
  a valiant man was he;
The other Captain *Turner*
  that from field would never flee:
With fifteen hundred fighting men,
  alas! there was no more,
They fought with forty thousand then
  upon the bloody shore.

'Stand to it, noble Pike-men,
  and look you round about;
And shoot you right, you Bow-men,
  and we will keep them out:
You Musquet and Calliver men,
  do you prove true to me,
I'le be the foremost man in fight',
  says brave Lord *Willoughby*.

And then the bloody enemy
  they fiercely did assail:
And fought it out most valiantly,
  not doubting to prevail:
The wounded men on both sides fell,
  most piteous for to see,
Yet nothing could the courage quell
  of brave Lord *Willoughby*.

For seven hours to all men's view
  this fight endured sore,
Until our men so feeble grew,
  that they could fight no more:
And then upon dead Horses
  full savourly they eat,
And drank the puddle water,
  for no better they could get.

THE SECOND PART

When they had fed so freely,
    they kneeled on the ground,
And praised God devoutly,
    for the favour they had found:
And bearing up their Colours,
    the fight they did renew,
And turning toward the *Spaniard*,
    five thousand more they slew.

The sharp steel-pointed Arrows,
    and Bullets thick did flye,
Then did our valiant Souldiers
    charge on most furiously
Which made the *Spaniards* waver,
    they thought it best to flee,
They fear'd the stout behaviour
    of brave Lord *Willoughby*.

Then quoth the *Spanish* General,
    'Come, let us march away,
I fear we shall be spoiled all,
    if that we longer stay:
For yonder comes Lord *Willoughby*,
    With courage fierce and fell,
He will not give one inch of ground,
    for all the Devils in Hell'.

And then the fearful enemy
    was quickly put to flight,
Our men pursued courageously,
    and rout their forces quite:
And at last they gave a shout,
    which echoed through the sky,
'God and St *George* for *England*!'
    the conquerors did cry.

This news was brought to *England*,
  with all the speed might be,
And told unto our gracious Queen,
  of this same Victory:
'O this is brave Lord *Willoughby*,
  my love hath ever won,
Of all the Lords of honour,
  'tis he great deeds hath done'.

For soldiers that were maimed,
  and wounded in the fray,
The Queen allowed a Pension
  of eighteen pence a day:
Besides, all costs and charges
  she quit and set them free,
And this she did all for the sake
  of brave Lord *Willoughby*

Then courage, noble English men,
  and never be dismaid,
If that we be but one to ten,
  we will not be afraid
To fight with foreign Enemies,
  and set our Country free,
And thus I end this bloody bout
  of brave Lord *Willoughby*.

7

A Joyfull new Ballad

Declaring the happie obtaining of the great Galleazo wherein
Don Pedro de Valdes was the chiefe, through the mightie
power and providence of God, being a speciall token of his
gracious and fatherly goodness towards us, to the great en-
couragement of all those that willingly fight in the defence
of his gospel and our good Queene of *England*.

To the Tune of Monseurs Almaigne

BY THOMAS DELONEY

(1588)

O Noble *England*,
   fall downe upon thy knee:
And praise thy God with thankfull hart
   which still maintaineth thee.
The forraine forces,
   that seekes thy utter spoile:
Shall then through his especiall grace
   be brought to shamefull foile.
With mightie power
   they come unto our coast:
To over runne our countrie quite,
   they make their brags and boast.
In strength of men
   they set their onely stay:
But we, upon the Lord our God,
   will put our trust alway.

Great is their number,
   of ships upon the sea:
And their provision wonderfull,
   but Lord thou art our stay.
Their armed souldiers
   are many by account:
Their aiders eke in this attempt,
   doe sundrie waies, surmount.
The Pope of *Rome*
   with many blessed graines:
To sanctify their bad pretense
   bestowed both cost and paines.
But little land,
   is not dismaide at all:

The Lord no doubt is on our side,
   which soone will worke their fall.

In happy houre,
   our foes we did descry:
And under saile with gallant winde
   as they cam passing by.
Which suddaine tidings,
   to *Plymmouth* being brought:
Full soone oure Lord high Admirall,
   for to pursue them sought.
And to his traine,
   coragiously he said:
Now, for the Lord and our good Queene,
   to fight be not afraide.
Regard our cause,
   and play your partes like men:
The Lord no doubt will prosper us,
   in all our actions then.

This great Galleazzo,
   which was so huge and hye:
That like a bulwarke on the sea,
   did seeme to each mans eye.
There was it taken,
   unto our great reliefe:
And divers Nobles, in which traine
   Don *Pietro* was the chiefe.
Strong was she stuft,
   with Cannons great and small:
And other instruments of warre,
   Which we obtained all.
A certaine signe,
   of good successe we trust:
That God will overthrow the rest,
   as he hath done the first.

Then did our Navie
   pursue the rest amaine:
With roaring noise of Cannons great;
   till they neere *Callice* came:
With manly courage,
   they followed them so fast:
Another mightie Gallion
   did seeme to yeeld at last.
And in distresse,
   for savegard of their lives:
A flag of truce they did hand out,
   with many mournfull cries:
Which when our men,
   did perfectly espie:
Some little Barkes they sent to her,
   to board her quietly.

But these false Spaniards,
   esteeming them but weake:
When they within their danger came,
   their malice forth did breake.
With charged Cannons,
   they laide about them then:
For to destroy those proper Barkes,
   and all their valiant men.
Which when our men
   perceived so to be:
Like Lions fierce they forward went,
   to quite this injurie.
And bourding them,
   with strong and mightie hand:
They kild the men untill their Arke,
   did sinke in *Callice* sand.

The chiefest Captaine,
   of this Gallion so hie:

Don *Hugo de Moncaldo* he
   within this fight did die.
Who was the Generall
   of all the Gallions great:
But through his braines, with pouders force,
   a Bullet strong did beat.
And manie more,
   by sword did loose their breath:
And manie more within the sea,
   did swimme and tooke their death.
There might you see
   the salt and foming flood:
Died and staind like scarlet red,
   with store of Spanish blood.

This mightie vessell,
   was threescore yards in length:
Most wonderfull to each mans eie,
   for making and for strength.
In her was placed,
   an hundreth Cannons great:
And mightily provided eke,
   with bread-corne wine and meat.
There were of Oares,
   two hundreth I weene:
Threescore foote and twelve in length,
   well measured to be seene.
And yet subdued,
   with manie others more:
And not a Ship of ours lost,
   the Lord be thankt therefore.

Our pleasant countrie,
   so fruitfull and so faire:
They doe intend by deadly warre.
   to make both poore and bare.

Our townes and cities,
    to rack and sacke likewise:
To kill and murder man and wife,
    as malice doth arise.
And to deflower
    our virgins in our sight:
And in the cradle cruelly
    the tender babe to smite.
Gods holy truth,
    they meane for to cast downe:
And to deprive our noble Queene,
    both of her life and crowne.

Our wealth and riches,
    which we enjoyed long:
They doe appoint their pray and spoile,
    by crueltie and wrong.
To set our houses
    a fier on our heades:
And cursedly to cut our throates,
    As we lye in our beds.
Our childrens braines,
    to dash against the ground:
And from the earth our memorie,
    for ever to confound.
To change our joy,
    to grief and mourning sad:
And never more to see the dayes,
    of pleasure we have had.

But God almightie
    be blessed evermore:
Who doth encourage Englishmen,
    to beate them from our shoare.
With roaring Cannons,
    their hastie steps to stay:

And with the force of thundering shot
  to make them flye away.
Who made account,
  before this time or day:
Against the walles of faire *London*,
  their banners to display.
But their intent,
  the Lord will bring to nought:
If faithfully we call and cry,
  for succour as we ought.

And you deare bretheren,
  which beareth Arms this day:
For safegarde of your native soile,
  marke well what I shall say.
Regarde your dueties,
  thinke on your countries good:
And feare not in defense thereof,
  to spend your dearest bloud.
Our gracious Queene
  doth greete you every one:
And saith, she will among you be,
  in every bitter storme.
Desiring you,
  true English harts to beare:
To God, and her, and to the land,
  wherein you nursed were.

Lord God almightie,
  which hath the harts in hand:
Of everie person to dispose
  defend this English land.
Bless thou our Soveraigne
  with long and happie life:
Indue her Councel with thy grace,
  and end this mortall strife.

Give to the rest,
   of Commons more and lesse:
Loving harts, obedient minds,
   and perfect faithfulnesse.
That they and we,
   and all with one accord:
On Sion hill may sing the praise,
   of our most mightie Lord.

London. Printed by Johne Wolfe, for Edward White, 1588.

8

The Winning of Cales

BY THOMAS DELONEY

(c. 1596)

Long the proud Spaniard
   advanced to conquer us,
Threatning our Country
   with fire and sword,
Often preparing
   their Navy most sumptuous,
With all the provision
   that *Spain* could afford,
Dub, a dub, dub,
   thus strikes their Drummes,
Tan ta ra ra, tan ta ra ra,
   English men comes.

To the Seas presently,
   went our Lord admirall,
With Knights couragious,
   and Captains full good,

The Earl of *Essex*,
  a prosperous Generall,
With him prepared,
  to passe the salt flood:
Dub a dub, etc.

At Plimouth speedily,
  take they ships valliantly:
Braver ships never
  were seen under sails:
With their fair coulers spred,
  and streamers ore their head:
Now bragging Spaniards
  take heed of your taile:
Dub a dub, dub, etc.

Unto *Cales* cunningly
  came we most happily
Where the Kings Navie
  securely did ride,
Being upon their backs,
  peircing their Buts of Sacks,
Ere that the Spaniard
  our comming descrid
Tan ta ra ra ra, English men comes
  bounce abounce, bounce abounce
Off went our Guns.

Great was the crying,
  running and riding,
Which at that season
  was made in that place;
Then Beacons were fired,
  as need then required:

To hide their great treasure,
  they had little space:
Alas they cryed,
  English men comes.

There might you see the Ships,
  how they were fired fast:
And how the men drowned
  themselves in the Sea,
There might you hear them cry,
  wail and weep piteously:
When as they saw no shift
  to escape thence away,
Dub a dub, etc.

The great *Saint Philip*,
  The pride of the Spaniards,
Was burnt to the bottom
  and sunk in the sea,
But the *Saint Andrew*,
  and eke the *Saint Matthew*,
We took in fight manly,
  and brought them away.
Dub a dub, etc.

The Earl of *Essex*,
Most valiant and hardy,
With horsemen and footmen,
  marcht towards the Town.
The enemies which saw them,
  full greatly affrighted,
Did fly for their safegard,
  and durst not come down.
Dub a dub, etc.

Now quoth the noble Earl,
  courage my Soldiers all,
Fight and be valiant,
  and spoyl you shall have,
And well rewarded all,
  from the great to the small:
But look that Women
  and Children you save,
Dub a dub, etc.

The Spaniard at that sight,
  saw 'twas in vain to fight:
Hung up their flags of truce,
  yeelding the Town:
We marcht in presently,
  decking the walls on hie,
With our English coulors,
  which purchast renown:
Dub a dub, etc.

Entring the houses then
  of the richest men,
For Gold and Treasure
  we searched every day:
In some places we did finde
  pies baking in the Ovens,
Meat at the fire roasting,
  and men ran away.
Dub a dub, etc.

Full of rich marchandize
  every shop we did see,
Damask and Sattins
  and velvet full faire:
Which souldiers measured out
  by the length of their swords

Of all commodities,
   each one had share.
Dub a dub, etc.

Thus Cales was taken,
   and our brave Generall
Marcht to the Market place,
   there he did stand:
There many prisoners
   of good account were tooke:
Many crav'd mercy,
   and mercy they found.
Dub a dub, etc.

When our brave Generall
   saw they delayed time,
And would not ransom
   the Towne as they said:
With their faire Wainscots,
   their Presses and Bedsteds,
Their Ioynt-stooles and Tables,
   a fire we made:
And when the town burnt in a flame,
With tan ta ra, tan ta ra ra,
From thence we came.

9

A Famous Sea-Fight

OR

A ⟨Bloo⟩dy Battell, which was fought between the *Spaniard* ⟨and t⟩he *Hollander*, beginning on the sixth day of the present month of *September,* 163⟨9⟩ being Friday; and continued for the most part till Sunday-noon fo⟨ll⟩owing: being neer 70 sail of the *Spaniards* when they begun, and ⟨b⟩ut 15 of the

Hollanders, till 12 sail more came to their ayd. The Relation you shall have in the insuing Dity, with what hapned in the ⟨th⟩ree dayes above-named.

To the Tune of 'Brave Lord Willoughby'

BY JOHN LOOKE

(1639)

Give ear you lusty Gallants,
   my purpose is to tell
⟨News of⟩ the bloody Battell
   ⟨whic⟩h late on Seas befell:
⟨Near⟩ our English coast it was,
   not far from *Dover* where
The *Dutchman* with the *Spaniard* met,
   whose greetings bitter were.

⟨T⟩his present month *September,*
   ⟨a⟩ Fleet from *Spain* there went
⟨With s⟩ouldiers then for *Dunkerck,*
   ⟨which to the⟩ King was sent:[1]

    ·   ·   ·

And on the Friday morning
   they did begin to fight,
Continuing the Battell
   untill that it was night:
Discharging of their roaring Guns,
   the victory for to gain,
Till two ships of the *Hollander*
   were sunk into the main.

But yet the valiant *Hollander,*
   which scorns at Sea to fly,
The next day with the *Spaniard*
   another bout did try:

   1. Twelve lines of text torn away here.

Where 12 sail more came to their ayd,
    and then in that same fight,
One of the *Spaniards* great Gallons,
    and two ships sunk e'er night.

And then the next day following,
    being the Sabbath, they
At two o'th clock i'th morning,
    began a bloody fray:
And then with stinging Bullets
    they did each other vex,
Till blood into the Ocean
    run streaming from the Decks.

THE SECOND PART TO THE SAME TUNE

[*Admirall* =
   flagship

The *Hollanders* great Admirall,
    the *Spaniard* boarded thrice;
(Had not the *Dutch-man* quench'd the same)
    it had been fired twice:
Three score and six great Ordnances
    the Admirall did bear;
Her Souldiers and her Seamen then
    above a thousand were.

Each side did their indeavour,
    for conquest of the day;
And for eight hours together
    there was a bloody fray:
Then slaughtred men on every side
    they over ship-board cast,
Not possible to number them,
    they threw them out so fast.

But in the *Spanish* Admirall,
  it is for certain known,
A hundred men were slain therein,
  and over ship-board thrown;
Abundance more in it besides,
  which under cure lyes;
Some maim'd, and some dismembred
  in lamentable wise.

And then the valiant *Hollander*,
  in signe of victory they
Did take one of the *Spaniards* ships
  and caried quite away.
At ten of the Clock i'th forenoon,
  the battell ended were,
For then the King of Englands ships
  towards them approched near.

But when the valiant *Dutchman*
  our English ships past by,
They bowd there Sails unto them;
  the *Spaniards* did deny.
But when as *Sir John Pennington*
  did see they were so proud,
He threatned them with Canon shot
  and then the *Spaniards* bowd.

The *Spaniard* in our English Coast
  being forced for to fly,
For harbour to the South foreland,
  where now at road they lye,
The *Hollander* not farre from thence
  doth wayt their comming out,
Being resolved before they goe
  to have the other bout.

No certain Number their is known,
   how many their is kill'd;
Though many hundreds on both sides
   their dearest bloud hath spild:
The *Spaniard* hath no cause to boast,
   the *Dutchmen* queld their pride:
And those that gained Credit most,
   was of the losing side.

God blesse our gracious King and Queen
   and our brave English fleet,
And give them victory on the seas,
   when they with foes do meet:
Defend them from ill sands and rocks,
   and Lord their battell fight
As thou didst for *Elisabeth*
   in the yeare 88.

Finis   John Looke

London. Printed for Fr. Grove, near the Sarazens head,
without Newgate.

10

The Famous Fight at Malago

OR

The Englishmen's Victory over the Spaniards

To the tune (its own) of 'Five Sail of Frigats
bound for Malago,' etc.

(c. 1656)

Come all you brave Sailors, that sails on the Main,
I'll tell you of a fight that was lately in *Spain*;

And of five Sail of Frigats bound to *Malago*,
For to fight the Proud *Spaniards*, our orders was so.

There was the *Henry* and *Ruby*, and the *Antelope* also,
The *Grey-hound*, and the *Bryan*, for fire-ships must go;
But so bravely we weighed, and played our parts,
That we made the Proud *Spaniards* to quake in their hearts.

Then we came to an anchor so nigh to the Mould,
'Methinks you proud *English* do grow very bold!'
But we came to an anchor so near to the Town,
That some of their Churches we soon battered down.

They hung out their Flag of Truce, for to know our
intent,
And they sent out their Long-boat, to know what we
meant,
But our Captain he answer'd them bravely, it was so,
For to burn all your Shipping, before we do go.

For to burn all our Shipping, you must us excuse,
'Tis not five Sail of Frigats shall make us to muse.
But we burnt all their Shipping, and their Gallies also;
And we left in the City full many a Widow.

Come then, says our Captain, let's fire at the Church,
And down came their Belfrey, which grieved them much;
And down came the Steeple, which standeth so high;
Which made the Proud *Spaniards* to the Nunnery fly.

So great a confusion we made in the Town,
That their lofty Buildings came tumbling down;
Their wives and their children, for help they did cry,
But none could relieve them, though danger was nigh.

The flames and the smoak so increased their woe,
That they knew not whither to run nor to go;
Some to shun the Fire leapt into the Flood,
And there they did perish in Water and Mud.

Our Guns we kept firing, still shooting amain,
Whilst many a Proud *Spaniard* was on the place slain;
The rest, being amazed, for succour did cry,
But all was in vain, they had no where to fly,

At length being forced, they thought it most fit,
Unto the brave *English*-men for to submit:
And so a conclusion at last we did make,
Upon such Conditions as was fit to take.

The *Spanish* Armado did *England* no harm,
'Twas but a Bravado, to give us alarm;
But with our five Frigats we did them bumbast,
And made them of *English*-men's Valour to taste.

When this noble Victory we did obtain,
Then home we returned to *England* again,
Where we were received with Welcomes of Joy,
Because with five Frigats we did them destroy.

II

The Lancashire Puritane

To the tune of 'Bonny Nell'

From Holy, Holy, Holy ones,
From faire Toombes fill'd with Rotten Bones,
To *Langton* home I do retire,

And leave th'Hottspurres of *Lancashire*:
  Where Sir Pelt-Pulpitt seemes all sprite,
  Being *Purus-putus* Hypocrite.

                                                                 [sprite = spirit

Where each redd Petticoate being vext
With Cooke-like skill can scumme a Text;
And imitate the Preachers prowesse,
Making a dish of Bible Brewesse:
  And new borne bratts can plainely tell
  What's done in Heaven, no Saint so well.

The Puritane for painted show
The Pharisee doth farre outgoe;
His tedious Praiers of ten miles long,
His faith then *Samson* much more strong:
  Though Looks and Gestures seeme all sprite,
  Hee's *Purus-putus* Hypocrite.

This pure demure, this spottles Swanne
Is fram'd of purer mould then Man;
Hee's dropp't from foorth some falling starre,
Which makes him passe vild Earth so faire:
  Or being above with good St. Paul,
  From Heavens third loft to Earth did fall.

And well Hee might. Since *Lucifer*
For Pride his onely *Signifer*
Was hurld from Heaven; In Puritanes
More Pride then in the Divell remaines:
  Like Himm Hee can turne Angell bright,
  Though *Purus-putus* Hypocrite.

Hee talks, Hee walks, Hee frames his looke,
Hee eates, drinks, sleeps, and all by booke;
Offer him Gold Hee doth abhorre itt,

Unlesse You can bring Scripture for itt:
    In all Hee's more then most Divine,
    And letts no Fart but under Line.

Hee killd his Catt (as most men say)
For mousing on the Sabbaoth day;
And *Hunt* his Hound did the Gallows clime
For Sleeping in the Sermon time:
    Hee loaths the Flesh but loves the Sprite,
    Hee's *Purus-putus* Hypocrite.

For with a Holy Sister meeting,
Hee gives her *William Thrust's* kind greeting;
And sowes his Holy Seed so fast,
That faire yong Ears peepe foorth att last:
    Which what from Sires and Sisters traine
    May prove a double Puritane.

When as prophane eies note him not,
Tricongius like Hee'l take his pott;
In publique (Lord!) how Hee exclaimes,
And taxeth Drunkards by their Names:
    A Devil in Secrett, Saint in Sight,
    Hee's *Purus-putus* Hypocrite.

Att Papists like a Curre hee'l snatch,
Himselfe being of the selfe same hatch;
Our Common Praier Hee holds in scorne,
And praies in private Night and Morne:
    Att those Hee jestingly will gybe,
    Which to our Church-Laws do subscribe.

They make an Idoll of the Masse,
Hee idolatizeth with a Lasse;
They kisse and cringe unto the Pax,

Hee to his Mistres bawdy Boxe:
  From Romanists in this Hee differs,
  They spend in Almes what Hottspurre coffers.

This *Cumane Asse* in *Lyons* skinne
His side Ears cannot keepe within;
Stripp't of his stol'n Plumes glorious show,
Within there's nought but *Aesops Crow*:
  Pluck off his Vizard, view him right,
  Hee is a bisconted Hypocrite.

[*bisconted* =
twice-turned (?)

12

An Essay on The Fleet riding in the Downes

(c. 1672)

I climb'd a Hill, whose *Summit* crown'd with Wood,
Seem'd as ambitious, to o're look the Flood,
And yield a Prospect; whence my wandring Eye
Might see our *Navy* in its Glory lye,
With wanton *Streamers* sporting in the Sky.
Whilst underneath in more Majestick forms,
Death is prepar'd to fly in Iron Storms.
Under their Canvas Wings Fate Broods; and here,
Glorious and Deckt for Triumphs, all appear;
The meanest Spirit would disdain to fear.
When Trumpets sound, the Cliffs repeat each strain,
And Golden Lyons dance upon the Main.
Thus rides our Fleet *Triumphant*, and outbraves
Neptune, and 's scaled squadrons on the waves:
Whilst he resigns his Trident, and does stand,
Expecting new commission from your hand.
Since with our *Ships* compar'd, you'd take his Whales
To be but Minows of the larger Scales.

Such a vast disproportion that they be
No more than are the Rivolets to th' Sea,
Compar'd to our *Ships*: you'd think again
The Isle of *Delos* floated on the Main;
Or that some Forrest 'gainst the Dutch were sent
As when the Normans first invaded *Kent*,
For to chastise these *Pyrats*, who of late
Out of our Merchantes Ruines rais'd their S⟨t⟩ate
And with rebellious Oak they brought from hence,
Thus propagate their wrong in recompence.
Trees bought of Traytors, when Rebellion stood
At Helm, and steer'd the State in storms of Blood.
Thus they new Crimes unto their former bring
Of bearing Arms against their *Native King*;
Forgetting, like the new-made States aboard,
What Country-Trees they were, or who their Lord.

    But what Blew Mists are those that do arise,
And with their various forms delude mine Eyes
'Tis the *French Fleet*, whose Flags such flowers display,
You'd think they'd gotten all the Spoils of *May*.
The *Flower-de-Lysses* from Sicambria came,
And to their Native Country make their Claim
Now let these fabulous Frogs their Murmures bring,
And croak in Desperation to *our King*;
Whilst our Great Monarch *Charles, as Jove*, they say,
Sends them a *Stork* to Rule o'er *Belgia*
May he go on, till his Resistless Powers
Do bring the *Lyon Couchant* under ours:
Where Horse-leech stomachs suck'd our *English blood*
And dy'd *Amboyna* in the Purple-Flood;
Which He'll avenge, that the Proud States may know,
His *Grandsire* was a King and Prophet too.[1]
Now may in spite of Storm *our Navy* stand
As safe at Sea, as once it did at Land;

[*abroad* (?)] *(marginal note, line 15)*

1. King James prophetically said his son's son should revenge the bloodshed at Amboyna. [Note in original broadside]

That we may finde the same Powers on the Main,
Secure *three Kingdoms* in the Oak again.

By J. D. of Grayes Inn
London. Printed by J. C. for R. Robinson, near
Grayes-Inne-Gate in Holborn, 1672.

13

On the Lord Mayor and Court of Aldermen, presenting the late King and Duke of York each with a Copy of their Freedoms, Anno Dom. 1674.

BY ANDREW MARVELL

The Londoners Gent to the King do present
  In a Box the City Maggot;
'Tis a thing full of weight, that requires the Might
  Of whole *Guild-Hall* Team to drag it.

Whilst their Church's unbuilt, and their Houses undwelt,
  And their Orphans want Bread to feed 'em;
Themselves they've bereft of the little Wealth they had left,
  To make an Offering of their Freedom.

O ye Addle brain'd Cits who henceforth in their Wits
  Would intrust their Youth to your heading;
When in Diamonds and Gold you have him thus enroll'd,
  You know both his Friends and his Breeding?

Beyond Sea he began, where such a Riot he ran,
  That every one there did leave him;
And now he's come o'er ten times worse than before,
  When none but such Fools would receive him.

89

He ne'er knew, not he, how to serve or be free,
　　Though he has past through so many Adventures;
But e'er since he was bound, (that is he was crown'd)
　　He has every Day broke his Indentures.

He spends all his Days in running to Plays,
　　When he should in the Shop be poring:
And he wasts all his Nights in his constant Delights,
　　Of Revelling, Drinking and Whoring.

Thro' out *Lumbard street* each Man he did meet,
　　He would run on the *Score* and *borrow*,
When they'd ask'd for their own, he was broke and gone,
　　And his Creditors left to Sorrow.

Though oft bound to the Peace, yet he never would cease,
　　To vex his poor Neighbours with Quarrels,
And when he was beat, he still made his Retreat,
　　To his *Cleavelands*, his *Nels*, and his *Carwels*.

Nay, his Company lewd, were twice grown so rude,
　　That had not Fear taught him Sobriety,
And the House been well barr'd with Guard upon Guard,
　　They'd robb'd us of all our Propriety.

Such a Plot was laid, had not *Ashley* betray'd,
　　As had cancell'd all former Disasters;
And your Wives had been Strumpets to his Highnesses
　　　Trumpet,
　　And Foot Boys had all been your Masters.

So many are the Debts, and the Bastards he gets,
　　Which must all be defray'd by *London*,
That notwithstanding the Care of Sir *Thomas Player*,
　　The Chamber must needs be undone.

His Words nor his Oath cannot bind him to Troth,
  And he values not Credit or History;
And though he has serv'd through two Prentiships now,
  He knows not his Trade nor his Mystery.

Then *London* Rejoyce in thy fortunate Choice,
  To have made him free of thy Spices;
And do not mistrust he may once grow more just,
  When he's worn of his Follies and Vices.

And what little thing is that which you bring
  To the Duke, the Kingdom's Darling;
Ye hug it and draw like Ants at a Straw,
  Tho' too small for the Gristle of Starling.

Is it a Box of Pills to cure the Kings Ills?
  (He is too far gone to begin it)
Or that your fine Show in Processioning go,
  With the Pix and the Host within It.

The very first Head of the Oath you him read,
  Shews you all how fit he's to Govern,
When in Heart (you all knew) he ne'er was nor will be
    true,
  To his Country or to his Soveraign.

And who could swear, that he would forbear
  To cull out the good of an Alien,
Who still doth advance the Government of *France*,
  With a *Wife* and *Religion Italian*?

And now, Worshipful Sirs, go fold up your Furrs,
  And Vyners turn again, turn again;
I see who e'ers freed, you for Slaves are decreed
  Until you *burn again, burn again*.

14

The History of Insipids

A LAMPOON 1676

I

Chast, pious, prudent, C[*harls*] the Second,
The Miracle of thy Restauration,
May like to that of *Quails* be reckon'd
Rain'd on the Israelitick Nation;
The wisht for Blessing from Heav'n sent,
Became their Curse and Punishment.

II

The Vertues in thee, C[*harls*] inherent,
Although thy countenance be an odd piece,
Proves thee as true a Gods Vicegerent
As e're was *Harry* with the Codpiece:
For Chastity and pious Deeds,

[*Henry IV of France*

His Grandsire *Harry*, C[*harls*] exceeds.

III

[*Henry VIII*

Our *Romish* Bondage breaker *Harry*,
Espoused half a dozen Wives,
C[*harls*] only one resolv'd to marry,
And other Mens he never [*swives*]
Yet hath he Sons and Daughters more,
Than e're had *Harry* by threescore.

IV

Never was such a Faiths Defender,
He like a politick Prince, and pious,

Gives liberty to Conscience tender,
And doth to no Religion tye us.
Jews, *Christians*, *Turks*, *Papists*, he'll please us,
With *Moses*, *Mahomet*, or J[*esus*].

['Declaration o
Liberty to
tender
Consciences'
1662, and 'of
Indulgence to'
1672

V

In all Affairs of Church or State,
He very zealous is, and able,
Devout at Prayers, and sits up late
At the Cabal and Council Table.
His very Dog at Council Board,
Sits grave and wise, as any Lord.

VI

Let C[*harls*] his Policy no Man flout,
The wisest Kings have all some Folly,
Nor let his Piety any doubt;
C[*harls*] like a Sovereign wise and holy,
Makes young Men judges of the Bench,
And B[*ishops*] some that love a Wench.

VII

His Fathers Foes he doth reward,
Preserving those that cut off's Head:
Old Cavaliers the Crown's best Guard,
He lets them starve for want of Bread.
Never was any King endow'd
With so much Grace and Gratitude.

VIII

Blood, that wears Treason in his Face,
Villain compleat, in Parson's Gown,
How much is he at Court in Grace
For stealing *Ormond*, and the Crown?

[*Thomas Blood
(?1618–80),
Irish adventurer*

93

Since Loyalty do's no Man good,
Let's steal the King and out-do *Blood*.

IX

A Parliament of Knaves and Sots,
Members by Name, you must not mention,
He keeps in Pay, and buys their Votes,
Here with a Place, there with a Pension
When to give Mony he can't cologue 'um,
He doth with Scorn prorogue, prorogue 'um.

[A system
introduced
during the
struggle over
the accounts of
the Dutch
War 1665–8

X

But they long since by too much giving,
Undid, betray'd, and sold the Nation;
Making their Memberships a Living,
Better than e're was Sequestration.
God give thee C[*harles*] a Resolution
To damn the Knaves by a Dissolution.

XI

Fame is not grounded on Success,
Though Victories were *Cæsar*'s Glory;
Lost Battels make not *Pompey* less,
But left them stiled great in Story.
Malitious Fate doth oft devise
To beat the Brave and fool the Wise.

XII

C[*harls*] in the first *Dutch* War stood fair,
To have been Sovereign of the Deep;
When *Opdam** blew up in the Air,
Had not his Highness gone to sleep.
Our Fleet slack'd Sails, fearing his waking,
The *Dutch* else had been in sad taking.

*[*Dutch admiral; naval*
action 13 June 1665

[James, Duke of York

XIII

The *Bergen* Business was well laid,
Though we paid dear for that Design:
Had we not three days parling staid,
The *Dutch* Fleet there, C[*harls*], had been thine.
Though the false Dane agree'd to sell 'um,
He cheated us, and saved *Skellum*.

[*Naval action August 1665*

['*rascaly scamp*' (O.E.D.).
Here, the Dutch treasure fleet

XIV

Had not C[*harls*] sweetly choos'd the States,
By *Bergen* Baffle grown more wise,
And made them Sh–t as small at Ratts,
By their rich *Smyrna* Fleets Surprise?
Had haughty *Holms* but call'd in *Spragg*,
Hands had been put into a Bag.

[= '*choused*', tricked(?)

[*Sir Robert Holmes, Sir
Edward Spragg, English naval
commanders*

XV

Mists, Storms, short Victuals, adverse Winds,
And once the Navies wise Division,
Defeated C[*harls*] his best Designs,
Till he became his Foes Derision.
But he had swing'd the *Dutch* at *Chattam*,
Had he had Ships but to come at 'um.

[*Ironic ref. to De Ruyter's
success of 1667*

XVI

Our *Blackheath* Host without dispute,
Rais'd (put on Board, why, no Man knows)
Must C[*harls*] have rendred absolute,
Over his Subjects or his Foes.
Has not the *French* King made us Fools,
By taking *Maestricht* with our Tools?

[*1673. An English contingent
served with Louis XIV's forces*

XVII

But C[*harls*] what could thy Policy be,
To run so many sad Disasters;

[*French naval commander,
aiding English fleet in 1672*

To join thy Fleet with false *D'Etrees*,
To make the *French* of *Holland* Masters?

[*Louise Renée de Keronalle,
the French mistress of Charles
II; Duke of York; the
Catholic Irish*

Was't *Carewell*, brother *James*, or *Teague*,
That made thee break the Triple League.

XVIII

[*Goldsmith and Lord Mayor of
London, erected statue of
Charles II in Woolchurch
Market on the site of the
present Mansion House*

Could *Robin Vyner* have foreseen
The glorious Triumphs of his Master
The Wool-Church Statue Gold had been,
Which now is made of Alabaster:
But Wise Men think had it been Wood,
T'were for a Bankrupt K[*ing*] too good.

XIX

Those that the Fabrick well consider,
Do of it diversly discourse;
Some pass their Censure of the Rider,
Others their Judgment of the Horse:
Must say the Steed's a goodly thing,
But all agree 'tis a Lewd K[*ing*].

XX

By the Lord Mayor and his grave Coxcombs,
Free-man of *London* C[*harls*] is made;
Then to *Whitehall* a Rich Gold Box comes,

[*See above st. XVII*

Which is bestow'd on the *French* Jade.
But wonder not it should be so, Sirs,

[*Charles II was made an
honorary member of the
Grocers' Company*

When Monarchs rank themselves with Grocers.

XXI

Cringe, scrape, no more ye City Fopps,
Leave off your Feasting and fine Speeches,
Beat up your Drums, shut up your shops,
The Courtiers then will kiss your Breeches.
Arm'd, tell the Popish Duke that Rules,
You'r Free-born Subjects, not *French* Mules.

XXII

New upstarts, Pimps, Bastards, Whores,
That Locust like devour the Land,
By shutting up the Exchequer Doors,
When thither our Mony was trapan'd.
Have rend'red C[*harls*] his Restauration,
But a small Blessing to the Nation.

XXIII

Then C[*harls*] beware of thy Brother Y[*ork*]
Who to thy Government gives Law;
If once we fall to the old Sport,
You must again both to *Breda*:
Where Spight of all that would restore you,
Grown wise by wrongs, we shall abhor you.

XXIV

If of all Christian Blood the Guilt
Cry loud for Vengeance unto Heaven;
That Sea by Treacherous *Lewis* spilt,
Can never be by God forgiven.
Worse Scourge unto his Subjects, Lord,
Than Pestilence, Famine, Fire or Sword.

XXV

That false rapacious Wolf of *France*;
The Scourge of *Europe*, and its Curse,
Who at his Subject's cry, does Dance,
And study how to make them worse.
To say such kings, Lord, rule by thee,
Were most prodigious Blasphemy.

XXVI

Such know no Law but their own Lust,
Their Subjects' Substance, and their Blood
They count it Tribute, due and just,
Still spent, and spilt, for Subjects good.
If such Kings are by God appointed
The D[*evil*] may be the L[*ord's*] Anointed.

XXVII

Such Kings curst be the Power and Name,
Let all the World henceforth abhor'um;
Monsters which Knaves Sacred proclaim,
And then like Slaves fall down before 'um.
What can there be in Kings Divine?
The most are Wolves, Goats, Sheep, or Swine.

XXVIII

[*Portland
Miscellany:
'a Brittish'*]

Then Farewel Sacred Majesty,
Let's pull all Brutish Tyrants down;
When Men are born, and still live free,
Here ev'ry Head doth wear a Crown.
Mankind like miserable Froggs,
Prove wretched, king'd by Storks and Loggs.

15

A Ballad upon the Popish Plot

Written by a Lady of Quality

BY JOHN GADBURY

(1679)

Whether you like my song or like it not,
It is the downfall of the Popish Plot;
With Characters of Plotters here I sing,
Who would destroy our good and gracious King;
Whom God preserve, and give us leave to hope
His Foes will be rewarded with a Rope.

To the tune of 'Packington's Pound'

I

Since Counterfeit Plots have affected this Age,
Being acted by Fools, and contrived by the Sage:
In City and Suburb, no man can be found,
But frighted with Fire-balls, their heads turned round.
    From Pulpit to Pot
    They talked of a Plot
Till their Brains were enslav'd and each man turn'd Sot.
  But let us to Reason and Justice repair;
And this Popish Bugbear will fly into Air.

II

A Politick Statesman of body unsound,
Who once in a Tree with the Rable set round;
Run Monarchy down in a Fanatick Rage,
And preach'd up Rebellion i' that credulous Age.
    He now is at work,
    With the Devil and Turk;

Pretending a Plot, under which he does lurk,
To humble the Miter, while he squints at the Crown,
Till fairly and squarely he pulls them both down.

THE SECOND PART TO THE SAME TUNE

III

He had found out an Instrument fit for the Devil;
Whose mind had been train'd up to all that was evil:
His Fortune sank low, and detested by many;
Kick't out at *St Omers*, not pitty'd by any.
    Some Whisperers fix'd him
    Upon this design;
And with promis'd Reward did him countermine
Though his Tale was ill-told, it served to give fire;
Dispis'd by the Wise, whil'st Fools did admire.

IV

The next that appear'd was a Fool-hardy knave,
Who had ply'd the High-ways, and to Vice was a Slave;
Being fed out of Basket in Prison forlorn;
No wonder that mony should make him forsworn.
    He boldly dares swear,
    What men tremble to hear;
And learns a false Lesson without any fear.
For when he is out, there's one that's in's place:
Relieves his invention, and quickens his Pace.

V

In a Country Prison another is found,
Who has cheated his Lord of One Thousand Pound;
He was freed from 's Fetters, to swear and inform,
Which very courageously he did perform.
    To avoid future Strife,
    He take's away Life,

To save poor Protestants from Popish knife;
Which has only one Edge to cut a Rogues Eares,
For abusing the People with needless fears.

VI

Another starts up and tels a false Tale,
Which strait he revoked his Courage being frail;
But to fortify one that needeth his Aid
Being tempted with mony which doth much perswade
    He swore he knew all
    That contrived the fall,
Of one who that day was seen neer to *White-Hall*,
Where he by the Treasurers powerfull Breath
More likely by far received his Death.

VII

A Gown-man most grave with Fanatical form,
With his scribling wit doth blow up this storm;
For Moth-eaten Records he worships the Devil,
Being now lodg'd at court he must become civil,
    He hunts all about
    And makes a Great Rout,
To find some Old Prophecy to help him out;
But his Friend that was hous'd with him at Fox-Hall,
Being joyn'd with Master still strengthens 'em all.

VIII

Then com's a crack'd Merchant with his shallow Brain.
Who first did lead up this stigmatiz'd train;
He since is grown useless, his Skill being small,
Yet at a dead lift, hee's still at their call.
    He hath pester'd the Press
    In ridiculous dress

In this scribling Age he could not do less;
But to so little purpose as plainly appears
With Pen he had as good fate picking his Ears.

IX

To end with a Prayer as now tis my Lot,
Confounded be Plotters, with their Popish Plot;
God bless and preserve our gracious good King,
That he may ne're feel the PRESBYTERS sting;
 As they brought his Father
 With rage to the Block,
So would they extirpate all the whole Stock:
But with their false Plots I hope they will end,
At Tyburn where th' Rabble will surely attend.

16

England's Darling

OR

Great Britain's Joy and Hope on that
Noble Prince James, Duke of Monmouth

Brave Monmouth, England's glory,
Hated of none but Papist and Tory,
May'st thou in thy Noble Father's love remain,
Who happily over this land doth Reign.

(c. 1679)

Young *Jemmy* is a Lad
 that's Royally descended,
With every Virtue clad,
 by every Tongue commended:

A true and faithful *English* heart,
   Great *Britain's* joy and hope,
And bravely will maintain their part,
   in spight of *Turk* and *Pope*.

Your *Jemmy* is a Lad
   that hates all base pretences;
No *Tory* masquerade,
   with Popish sham-pretences:
A Heart and Soul so great and just,
   Such Conduct and Command,
A Champion in his Countries' trust,
   Young *Jemmy* still will stand.

Young *Jemmy* is a youth
   who thinks it no transgression
To stand up for the Truth,
   and Protestant Profession:
And oh! he fights with such success,
   all mortal powers obey,
No god of War but must confess
   Young *Jemmy* bears the sway.

At *Jemmy's* powerful voice
   the Drums and Trumpets sounded;
And *England* did rejoyce,
   when *Jemmy's* fame abounded.
Of *Jemmy* the victorious name
   did through all *Europe* flie,
And all the nations did proclaim
   his matchless Gallantry.

In *Maestricht* and in *France*,
   in *Germany* and *Flanders*,
Young *Jemmy* did advance
   amongst the chief Commanders;

By Sea and Land his fame did fly,
    and all the Nations round
Of *Jemmy's* constant victory
    and valour did resound.

In *Scotland Jemmy's* hand
    dispers'd the *Whigg* and *Tory*,
And *Bothwell Bridge* will stand
    to his eternal glory.
There he the Rebels' force withstood,
    and did their Might oppose,
Both for the King and Countries' good,
    in spight of all his foes.

But oh! unhappy Fates!
    a curse on Pride and Malice;
The *Popish* plotting States
    have banish'd him the Palace.
They turn'd him out of grace of late,
    of dignity and fame,
And every mighty place of State;
    Yet *Jemmy's* still the same.

Maliciously they plot
    (against all sense and reason)
'Gainst *Shaftesbury* and *Scot*,
    to cloak their *Popish* Treason:
Tories and *Papists* all agree
    to blast his spotless fame;
But spight of all their policy,
    Young *Jemmy's* still the same.

For still to lose his blood
    young *Jemmy* does importune,
And for his Countries' good,
    to spend his Life and Fortune,

For to support the Church and State,
    our Liberties and Laws,
Against their Malice, Plots, and Hate,
    that wou'd our rights oppose.

Let all good men implore
    for *Jemmy's* Restauration,
Whose conduct must restore
    the ruines of our Nation:
That he to *Charles's* praise may live,
    our freedome to maintain,
When *Jemmy* shall his fame retrieve,
    and be in grace again.

17

England's Triumph

OR

The Subjects' Joy

(1679)

The King's most faithful Subjects we,
    indeed we are not dull,
We drink to shew our Loyalty,
    and to fill his Coffers full:
If all his Subjects drank like us,
    he would be richer far,
More powerful and more prosperous,
    then all the Eastern Monarchs are,
    then all the Eastern Monarchs are.

Then let us drink all day and night,
   give each a lusty bowl,
This is the ravishing Delight
   of every generous Soul:
Whilst others lye and soak in bed,
   and live but half their time,
 This Wine that lies within our head
   shall full preserve us in our prime,
   (shall full preserve us in our prime).

Instead of sleep, we'll spend the Night
   in singing of the praise
Of Wine that makes the Souldier fight,
   and gives the Poet bays;
That fills the veins with noble blood,
   though we be ne'r so mean,
Inspires what's either great or good,
   and turns rank Clowns to Gentlemen,
   (and turns rank Clowns to Gentlemen).

Let Souldiers fight, and Parsons preach,
   and schollars break their brains;
Fanaticks sweat and bawl to teach
   sedition for their gains;
Whilst others they do waste and pine,
   we still are sound at heart,
And if we have but spritely Wine,
   we'l drink and roar, and never part,
   we'l drink and roar, and never part.

Let Merchants still for treasures run,
   and cross the burning Line,
We have our Engins here at home,
   in every glass of Wine.
Each Carbuncle upon my Nose
   better then Jems doth shine,

My cheeks are fresh like to a Rose,
my heart is merry with brisk Wine,
my heart is merry with brisk Wine.

Let Doctors cure themselves of grief,
and each Apothecary,
We are sure to give our selves relief,
by drinking of Canary.
If melancholly disturbs the mind,
and makes our hearts full sad,
We know where we good Sack can find,
and that will make us brisk and glad,
and that will make us brisk and glad.

Our Wives the benefit will find
when we come home at night,
Good Wine does always make us kind,
and give them their delight.
Whilst that the sóber sot is dull,
in counting of his coyn,
And filling of his Coffers full,
our brains shall swim in Spanish Wine,
our brains shall swim in Spanish Wine.

If that a forrraign Foe should strive
our Country to invade,
One bowl of Sack would conquer five,
drunk by an *English* blade:
It makes 'em fight couragiously,
their country to defend,
They never shrink, nor fear to dye,
but hold out stoutly to the end,
but hold out stoutly to the end.

If that Consumption should us waste,
and make our bodies poor,

Then every morning Sack we taste
    which doth our health restore.
Around, around, let's drink about,
    the first Glass shall be mine,
Fill it up to th' brim, i'le drink it out,
    and sit and sing the praise of Wine,
    and sit and sing the praise of Wine.

Here's a health, here's a health to *England*'s King,
    whom God grant long to Raign!
Our drinking shall him tribute bring,
    let sectaries complain.
Wealth, honour and renown attend
    his Royal name always,
His Joys I wish may ne'r have end,
    but gain his subjects' love and praise,
    but gain his subjects' love and praise.

18

The Courtier's Health

OR

Merry Boys of the Times

(1681)

He that loves Sack doth nothing lack,
*   If he but Loyal be;*
He that deny's Bacchus' supplyes,
*   Shows meer Hypocrisie.*

Come Boyes, fill us a Bumper, we'l make the Nation roare,
She's grown sick of a *Rumper* that sticks on the old score.
Pox on *Phanaticks*, rout 'um, they thirst for our blood;
We'l Taxes raise without 'um, and drink for the Nation's
    good.

Fill the Pottles and Gallons, and bring the Hogshead in,
We'l begin with a Tallen – a Brimmer to the KING.

[*Tallen or*
Tallboy = *a*
kind of long
glass

Round around, fill a fresh one, let no man bawk his Wine,
We'l drink to the next in Succession, and keep it in the
    Right Line.
Bring us ten thousand glasses, the more we drink we'r
    a-dry;
We mind not the beautiful Lasses, whose Conquest lyes
    all in the eye.
  Charge the Pottles and Gallons, and bring the Hogshead in,
  We'l begin with a Tallen, a Brimmer to the King.

We Boyes are truly Loyal, for *Charles* we'l venture all,
We know his blood is Royal, his Name shall never fall.
But those who seek his ruine may chance to dye before
    him,
While we, that Sack are wooing, for ever will adore him.
  Fill the Pottles and Gallons, and bring the Hogshead in,
  We'l begin with a Tallen, a Brimmer to the King.

I hate those strange dissenters that strives to bawk a glass,
He that at all Adventures will see what comes to pass.
And let the Popish Faction disturb us if they can,
They ne'r shall breed distraction in a true-hearted man.
  Fill the Pottles and Gallons, and bring the Hogshead in,
  We'l begin with a Tallen, a Brimmer to the King.

Let the *Phanaticks* grumble, to see things cross their grain,
We'l make them now more humble, or ease them of their
    pain:
They shall drink Sack amain, too, or else they shall be
    choak't,
We'l tell 'um 'tis in vain, too, for us to be provok't.
  Fill the Pottles and Gallons, and bring the Hogshead in,
  We'l begin with a Tallen, 'a Brimmer to the King!'

He that denyes the Brimmer, shall banish'd be in this Isle,
And we will look more grimmer till he begins to smile:
We'l drown him in Canary, and make him all our own,
And when his Heart is merry, he'l drink to *Charles* in's
    Throne:
  Fill the Pottles and Gallons, and bring the Hogshead in,
  We'l begin with a Tallen, a Brimmer to the King!

Quakers and Anabaptist, we'l sink them in a glass;
He deals most plain and flattest that sayes he loves a Lass:
Then tumble down Canary, and let your brains go round,
For he that won't be merry, he can't at heart be sound.
  Fill the Pottles and Gallons, and bring the Hogshead in,
  We'l begin with a Tallen, a Brimmer to the KING!

19

A Carrouse to the Emperor, the Royal Pole,
and the much-wronged Duke of Lorrain

(*c*.1683)

Hark I hear the Cannons Roar,
Echoing from the *German* Shore,
And the joyful News comes o'er,
    that the *Turks* are all confounded:
Lorraine comes they run, they run!
Charge with your Horse thro' the grand Half-moon,
And give Quarter unto none,
    since *Starenberg* is wounded.

Close your Ranks, and each brave Soul
Fill a lusty flowing Bowl,
A Grand Carrouse to the *Royal Pole*,
    the Empire's brave defender:

Let no man leave his Post by stealth,
Plunder the Barbarous *Visier's* wealth,
We'l drink a Helmet full, th' Health
   Of Second *Alexander*.

Fill the Helmet once again,
To the Emperor's happy Reign,
And the much-wrong'd Duke *Lorrain*:
   but when they've beat the *Turks* home,
Not a Soul the Field will leave,
Till they do again retrieve
What the *Monsieur* does deprive,
   and fix him in his Dukedom.

Then will be the Schem of War,
When such drinking Crowns prepare;
Those that love the *Monsieurs*, fear
   their Courage will be shrinking:
Loyal Hearts inspir'd with *Hock*;
Who can form a Better Rock?
The *French* will never stand the shock,
   for all their Claret-drinking.

Mahomet was a senseless Dogg,
  A *Coffee-drinking* drowsie Rogue;
The use of the Grape, so much in vogue,
   to deny to those above him:
Had he allow'd the Fruits of the Vine,
And gave them leave to Carrouse in Wine,
They had freely past the *Rhine*,
   and conquer'd all before them.

Coffee Rallies no retreat,
Wine can only do the Feat,
Had their Force been twice as great,
   and all of *Janizaries*:

Tho' he had drank the *Danube* dry,
And all their Prophet could supply,
By his interest from the Skie,
    Brisk *Langoon* ne'r miscarry'd.

Infidels are now o'recome;
The most Christian *Turk* at home
Watch'd the Fate of *Christendom*,
    but all his hopes are shallow:
Since the *Poles* have led the Dance,
If *England's* Monarch will advance,
And if he'l send a Fleet to *France*,
    He's a *Whigg* that will not follow.

20

The Dutchess of Monmouth's Lamentation
for the Loss of her Duke

(c. 1684*)*

'Loyal Hearts of *London* City, Come, I pray, and sing my
  Ditty,
    Of my Love that's from me gone;
I am slighted and much sprighted, and am left alone to
  mourn.

'Was not that a dreadful thing, To make a Plot against the
  King,
    And his Royal Brother too?
I am vexed and perplexed, for my dear that prov'd untrue.

'A Hellish Plot there was contrived, and then at last they
  were devised
    To make it known unto the King,
How they had plotted and alloted a Murther then for to
  kill him.

'But *Shaftsbury* and his wits confounded, that had my
  Jemmy so be rounded
      For to Conspire against his King,
But God Direct and him Protect, that they may never
  Murther him.

'My Jemmy was a Subject Royal, But now has prov'd
  himself Disloyal';
      (Then she cryed out a main)
'My heart will break, for my Love's sake, Because he ne're
  will come again.

'*Jemmy* now is prov'd a Traytor, *Tony* and he were so sad
  Creatures,
      For to meddle so with things,
That were too high: proud *Shaftsbury*, For him to meddle
  so with Kings!

'*Shaftsbury* was wondrous witty, to ruin three Nations,
  more's the pitty!
      Of it he was very shy;
But he is fled, and is since dead, that did disturb true
  Monarchy.

'*Jemmy* once was Loyal-hearted, And would his Life soon
  apparted
      For his King and Nation's good;
He delighting all in fighting, Made his peace where 'ere he
  stood.

'*Shaftsbury*, he was a Rebbel, Unto the King he was uncivil,
      For all the Honour he did gain;
The King he slighted, and much spighted, And so he did
  his Royal Train.

'*Jemmy* was a Foe to no Man, Till wheedl'd in by *Shaftsbury*,
    Till at last he was forc'd to fly:
You know the Reason, 'twas for Treason, For disturbing
  Monarchy.

'The Horrid Plot that they were known, Then against the
  King and Crown,
    That makes my Heart to Bleed full sad,
For to hear my only dear were lately grown so very bad.

'All my joys are gone and blasted. I with grief am almost
  wasted,
    For my *Jemmy* that's to me dear.'
Then from her Eyes, with fresh supplies, down trickles
  many a brackish Tear.

'God bless the King and his Royal Brother, And keep us
  from such horrid murther,
    That were contriv'd by *Shaftsbury*
He was a Wretch fit for *Jack Ketch*; for disturbing of
  Monarchy!'

Now she ends her doleful story, Her Lamentation⟨'s⟩ laid
  before ye,
    She laments for her own Dear,
Then from her Eyes, with fresh supplies, down trickles
  many a brinish Tear.

21

A New Song

(Lilliburlero)

BY THOMAS, MARQUIS OF WHARTON (?)

(1688)

Ho Brother *Teague* dost hear de Decree,
Li-li Burlero Bullen a-la,
Dat we shall have a new Debittie
Li-li Bur-le-ro Bullen a la,
Le-ro, Le-ro, Le-ro, Le-ro, Li-li Bur-le-ro, Bullen a-la,
Le-ro, Le-ro, etc.

Ho by my Shoul it is a *T—t*
Lilli Burlero, etc.
And he will Cut all de *English* T—t,
Lilli, etc.
Lero, Lero, etc.
Lero, Lero, etc.

Though by my shoul de English do Prat,
Lilli, etc.
De Laws on dare side, and Christ knows what,
Lilli, etc.
Lero, Lero, etc.
Lero, Lero, etc.

But if Dispence do come from de Pope
Lilli, etc.
Weel hang *Magna Carta* and demselves in a Rope,
Lilli, etc.
Lero, Lero, etc.
Lero, Lero, etc.

And the good T—t is made a lord,
Lilli, etc.
And he with good Lads is coming aboard,
Lilli, etc.
Lero, Lero, etc.
Lero, Lero, etc.

Who! all in *France* have taken a swear,
Lilli, etc.
Dat day will have no Protestant h—r,
Lilli, etc.
Lero, Lero, etc.
Lero, Lero, etc.

O but why does he stay behind,
Lilli, etc.
Ho be my Shoul 'tis a Protestant wind,
Lilli, etc.
Lero, Lero, etc.

Now *T–l* is come ashore
Lilli, etc.
And we shall have commissions gillore,
Lilli, etc.
Lero, Lero, etc.

And he dat will not go to M—ss,
Lilli, etc.
Shall turn out and look like an Ass,
Lilli, etc.
Lero, Lero, etc.

Now now de Hereticks all go down,
Lilli, etc.
By *Christ* and St *Patrick* the Nation's our own,
Lilli, etc.
Lero, Lero, etc.

22

A New Song of an Orange

To the tune of, The Pudding

(1688)

Good People come buy
  The Fruit that I cry,
That now is in Season, tho' Winter is nigh;
  'Twill do you all good,
  And sweeten your Blood,
I'm sure it will please when you've once understood
                        'tis an *Orange*.

It's Cordial Juice,
  Does much Vigour produce,
I may well recommend it to every Mans use,
  Tho' some it quite chills,
  And with fear almost kills,
Yet certain each Healthy Man benefit feels
                        by an *Orange*.

To make Claret go down,
  Sometimes there is found
A jolly good Health, to pass pleasantly round;
  But yet, I'll protest,
  Without any Jest,
No Flavour is better then that of the taste
                        of an *Orange*.

Perhaps you may think
  To *Peters* they Stink,
Because from our Neighbors they'r brought over Sea
  Yet sure, 'tis presum'd,
  They may be perfum'd
By th' scent of good *cloves*, for they may be stuck
                        in an *Orange*.

If they'll Cure the Ayls
In *England* and *Wales*,
Whose Meat to their Stomachs long have not agreed,
Since we're subject to Cast,
Let's better the taste,
(Still being careful lest it Curdle at last)
                                        with an *Orange*.

Old Stories rehearse,
In Prose and in Verse,
How a *Welsh* child was found by loving of *cheese*
Let Sympathy shew,
How others can Spew,
When once they'r brought to the hated View
                                        of an *Orange*.

[*Mobile* = *mob*]

Tho' the Mobile Bawl,
Like the Devil and all,
For Religion, Property, Justice and Laws;
Yet in very good sooth,
I'll tell you the Truth,
There nothing is better to stop a Man's Mouth
                                        then an *Orange*.

We are certainly told,
That by *Adam* of old,

[*Bearns* = children]

Himself and his Bearns for an Apple was sold;
And who knows but his Son,
By Serpent sundone,
And many besides may at last loose their own
                                        for an *Orange*.

FINIS
Printed for R. G. 1688

118

23

The Lord Chancellours Villanies Discovered

OR

His Rise and Fall in the Four last Years

(1688)

I

Good People, I pray now attend to my Muse,
I'le sing of a Villain I cannot abuse,
The Halter and Axe no such men will refuse:
Sing hey brave Chancellor, oh fine Chancellor, delicate
    Chancellor, Oh.

II

'Tis he was the cause of the Nations dismay,
He hath e're been a Knave from his Birth to this day,
To see the sot hang'd we will make Holiday.
Sing hey brave etc.

III

And first I will show what he is in grain;
I care not a pin for the Boobie's disdain,
His deeds now in brief unto you I'le proclaim.
Sing hey brave etc.

IV

He was the Inventer of *Oate's* punishment
From *Newgate* to *Tyburn,* and thither he sent,
To have him well whipt he gave his consent.
Sing hey brave etc.

V

The good *Mr Cornish* did innocent dye,
And all by this Chancellours curst villany;
His Blood now from Heaven for Vengeance doth cry.
Sing hey brave etc.

VI

He was the first Author that opend his Jaws
To take off the *Test* and *Priviledge* Laws;
The beheading of *Russel*, 'twas he was the cause,
Sing hey brave etc.

VII

Then next to the West he hurried with speed,
To murther poor men, a very good deed,
He made many honest mens hearts for to bleed.
Sing hey brave etc.

VIII

The prisoners to plead to his Lordship did cry,
But still he made answer, and thus did reply,
We'l hang you up first, then after we'l try.
Sing hey brave etc.

IX

Against their Petitions he stopt up his Ears,
And still did create all their Doubts and their Fears,
He left the poor Widows and Children in Tears.
Sing hey brave etc.

X

He was the Inventer that first did promote
That place called the *Ecclesiastical Court*,
And thither he made the poor Clergy resort.
Sing hey brave etc.

XI

Of *Magdalen-College* he thought it most fit
To turn out the Fellows, a very fine Trick,
And place Father *Walker*, that curst Jesuite.
Sing hey brave etc.

XII

Then next to the *Tower* our Bishops he packt
And swore he had done a very good Act,
But now shall be try'd for the matter of Fact.
Sing hey brave etc.

XIII

And when that the Bishops were brought to be try'd,
To accept a Petition they humbly desir'd;
He swore he would prove it a Libel to be cry'd
Sing hey brave etc.

XIV

What can he say now the Parliament sits?
Alas! they will Vote him quite out of his Wits;
They'l make him run mad, or fall into Fits.
Sing hey brave etc.

XV

In Wapping he thought for to make his Escape,
A very good Jest, but I' faith it won't take,
His Head on the Bridge must be stuck on a stake;
Sing hey brave etc.

XVI

He many Seditious Lines penn'd,
And sent them to *P——* his Honest Friend
My Muse she grows weary, and thus she doth end.

With pox o' Chancellour, *villanous* Chancellour,
  Damnable Chancellour, *oh.*

24

Sir T. J.'s Speech to his Wife and Children

(1688)

I

Dear Wife, let me have a Fire made,
I'll tell you such News will make you all glad,
The life for another is scarce to be had,
  This it is to be Learned and Witty

II

First (Butler do you a glass of Wine bring,)
I'll tell you all the great Love of my King,
Which is a dainty, curious fine thing.
  This it is etc.

III

A Wise Learned Sergeant at Law I was made,
And a dainty fine Coif was put on my Head,
Which is heavier far than a hundred of Lead.
  This it is etc.

IV

But soon after this I was made the Recorder,
To keep the Worshipful Rabble in Order,
And wore a Red Goun with long Sleeves and Border.
  This it is etc.

V

What Justice I did, my dear Wife, you can tell;
Right or wrong I spar'd none, like the Divel in Hell;
But, Guilty or not, I sent all to *Bridewell*.
    This it is etc.

VI

Unless it were those that greased my Fist,
To them, I gave Licence to cheat whom they list,
(For 'twas only those that my *Mittimus* miss'd)
    This it is etc.

VII

But then the King dy'd, which caused such a pother;
So I went to condole with the new King, his Brother,
With *Sorrow* in one Hand, and *Grief* in the other.
    This it is etc.

VIII

For an Ignorant Judge I was call'd by the King
To the *Chequer-Court*, 'tis a wonderful thing,
Of which in short time the whole Nation did ring.
    This it is etc.

IX

By Great James I was rais'd the *Common-Please* Bench,
'Cause he saw I had exquisite Politick Sense,
Which his Wisdom perceiv'd in the Future Tense.
    This it is etc.

X

At *Sarum* Five hundred Pounds I have gotten,
To save Malefactors from swinging in Cotton,
For which they are hang'd, and now almost rotten.
    This it is etc.

XI

But now, my dear Love, comes the Cream of the Jest,
For the King would take off the *Oaths* and the *Test*;
Which I told all his people would be for the best.
    This it is etc.

XII

He had my Opinion, that 'twas in his Power
To destroy all the Laws in less than an hour,
For which I may chance to be sent to the *Tower.*
    This it is etc.

XIII

And now to *Magdalen* College I come,
Where we turn'd out most, but kept in some,
That a New College of Priests might have room
    This it is etc.

XIV

And so by that means we left the Door ope,
To turn out the Bishops and let in the Pope,
For which we have justly deserved a Rope.
    This it is etc.

25

The Death of Admiral Benbow

The Brother Tars Song

(*c.* 1702)

Come all you sailors bold
Lend an ear, lend an ear;

Come all you sailors bold lend an ear:
   'Tis of our admiral's fame,
   Brave Benbow call'd by name;
   How he fought on the main
You shall hear, you shall hear.

   Brave Benbow he set sail
   For to fight, for to fight;
Brave Benbow he set sail for to fight:
   Brave Benbow he set sail
   With a fine and pleasant gale,
   But his captains they turn'd tail
In a fright, in a fright.

   Says Kirby unto Wade
   I will run, I will run;
Says Kirby unto Wade I will run:
   I value not disgrace,
   Nor the losing of my place,
   My enemies I'll not face
With a gun, with a gun.

   'Twas the Ruby and Noah's Ark
   Fought the French, fought the French;
'Twas the Ruby and Noah's Ark fought the French:
   And there was ten in all,
   Poor souls they fought them all,
   They valued them not at all,
Nor their noise, nor their noise.

   It was our admiral's lot,
   With a chain-shot, with a chain-shot;
It was our admiral's lot, with a chain-shot:
   Our admiral lost his legs,
   And to his men he begs,
   Fight on, my boys, he says,
'Tis my lot, 'tis my lot.

While the surgeon dress'd his wounds,
   Thus he said, thus he said;
While the Surgeon dressed his wounds, thus he said:
   Let my cradle now in haste
   On the Quarter deck be plac'd,
   That my enemies I may face
'Til I'm dead, 'til I'm dead.

And there bold Benbow lay
   Crying out, crying out:
And there bold Benbow lay crying out:
   Let us tack about once more,
   We'll drive them to their own shore,
   I value not half a score,
Nor their noise, nor their noise.

Fowler, Printer, Salisbury

26

Jack Frenchman's Lamentation

An Excellent New SONG

To the Tune of I'll tell thee Dick, &c.

(*c.* 1708)

Ye Commons and Peers,
   Pray lend me your Ears,
I'll sing you a Song, (if I can,)
   How *Lewis Legrand*
   Was put to a Stand,
By the Arms of our Gracious Queen Anne.

How his Army so great
   Had a total Defeat,

And close by the river *Dender*;
  Where his Grand-Children Twain
  For fear of being slain,
Gallop'd off with the *Popish* Pretender.

  To a Steeple on high,
  The Battle to spy,
Up mounted these clever Young Men,
  But when from the Spire
  They saw so much Fire,
Most cleverly came down again.

  Then on Horseback they got
  All on the same Spot,
By Advice of their Cousin *Vendosme*;
  O Lord! cried out he
  Unto young *Burgundy*,
Would your Brother and you were at Home!

  While this he did say,
  Without more Delay
Away the Young Gentry fled;
  Whose Heels for that Work,
  Were much lighter than Cork,
Though their Hearts were as heavy as Lead.

  Not so did behave
  Young *Hannover* Brave
In this Bloody Field I assure ye:
  When his War-Horse was shot
  He valu'd it not,
But fought it on Foot like a Fury.

  [Full firmly he stood,
  As became his high-Blood,

Which runs in his Veins so blew;
   For this Gallant Young Man,
   Being a-kin to QUEEN ANNE,
Did as (were she a Man) she would do.]

   What a Racket was here,
   (I think 'twas last year,)
For a little misfortune in *Spain*?
   For by letting 'em win,
   We have drawn the *Putts* in,
To lose all they're worth this Campaign.

   Tho' *Bruges* and *Ghent*
   To *Monsieur* we lent,
With Interest they shall repay 'em;
   While *Paris* may sing
   With her sorrowful King,
Nunc dimittis, instead of *Te Deum*.

   From this Dream of Success,
   They'll awaken, we guess,
At the sound of great *Marleborough's* Drum:
   They may think, if they will,
   Of *Almanza* still,
But 'tis *Blenheim* wherever he comes.

   O *Lewis* perplex'd,
   What General next!
Thou hast hitherto chang'd in vain:
   He has beat 'em all round;
   If no new one's found,
He shall beat 'em over again.

   We'll let *Tallard* out,
   If he'll take t'other Bout;

And much he's improved let me tell ye,
   With *Nottingham* Ale
   At every Meal,
And good Beef and Pudding in's Belly.

   But as Losers at Play
   Their Dice throw away,
While the Winners do still win on;
   Let who will Command,
   Thou hadst better disband,
For, old Bully, thy Doctors are gone.

27

A New Song entitled the Warming Pan

(*c.* 1745)

When *Jemmy* the Second, not *Jemmy* the First,
With Vexations and Poxes, and Impotence Curs'd,
Saw the good Cause must end, which so well he began,
Swore the Church, since he cou'd not, should get him a son
   Derry down, down etc.

To work went the Church on her Majesty's Womb,
By her true Representations, Fryers from *Rome*;
But [though] they well warm'd, her true Catholic Mettle,
They never could make the Meat boil in the Kettle.
   Derry Down

But since it was determin'd an Heir must be got,
No matter from *Kettle*, from *Pan*, or from *Pot*;
In Mettles Fertile, the old *JESUITS* clan,
Produc'd a brave Boy, from a *Brass-Warming-Pan*
   Derry Down

But *Old England*, quite harrass'd with Papists before,
The *Brat* being Spurious, would sure bear no more;
But with little *Will's* help, kick'd the spawn of a *Fryer*,
From out of the *Warming Pan* into the Fire.
    Derry Down

Full many a Year, has that *Bastard* been Nurs'd,
By *Paris* and *Rome*, who engender'd him first;
And now they have sent to promote their old Plan,
The Son of the Son, of the *Brass-Warming-Pan*
    Derry Down

Oh! *Britains*, reflect, why you drove out the *One*!
And dread the same evils or worse in the *Son*;
Quick, to *Paris*, or *Rome* make your *Perkin* retire,
Or we're out of the *Warming-Pan*, into the *Fire*.
    Derry Down

Sure *Scotland* remembers, the direful Fate,
When they succour'd the *Warming-Pan's*, Father of late;
How many to *Tower*, and *Newgate*, were sent,
Some Heads were cut off, and too late did Repent.
    Derry Down

May all be serv'd so, that takes up the Cause,
For *Rome* or the D—l, make daily applause;
Let's firmly unite in the Protestant Case,
Drive *Pretender* to the D—l, keep K. *George* in his place.
    Derry Down

28

Victory

(*c.* 1805)

I am a youthful lady, my troubles they are great,
My tongue is scarcely able my grievance to relate,
Since I have lost my true love that was ever dear to me,
He is gone to plough the Ocean, on board the Victory.

Many a pleasant evening my love and I have met,
He clasp'd me round my slender waist, and gave me kisses
    sweet,
I gave to him my hand and heart, he vow'd he'd marry me,
But I did not know that my love would go on board the
    Victory.

My parents could not endure my love, because he was poor,
Therefore he did not presume to come within the door;
But had he been some noble lord, or man of high degree,
They ne'er had sent the lad I love, on board the Victory.

Thirteen of the pressgang did my love surround,
And one of the cursed gang, he laid bleeding on the ground,
My love was overpowered, but he fought most manfully,
Till he was obliged to yield, and go in the Victory.

Each night, when in my slumbers, I can't find any rest,
Love for my lad so dearly reigns within my burning breast,
Sometimes I dream I do enjoy my love's sweet company,
And closely locked in my arms, on board the Victory.

His teeth were white as ivory, his hair in ringlets hung,
His cheeks like blooming roses, all in the month of June,

He is lively, tall and handsome, in every degree,
My heart lies in his bosom, on board the Victory.

Here's success unto the Victory, and crew of noble fame,
And glory to the noble lord, bold Nelson, was his name,
In the battle of Trafalgar, the Victory cleared the way,
And my love was slain with Nelson upon that very day.

29

A New Song composed on the Death of
Lord Nelson

(*c.* 1805)

Come all you gallant seamen that unite a meeting,
    Attend to these lines I am going to relate,
And when you've heard them 'twill move you with pity,
    To hear how Lord Nelson he met with his fate;
For he was a bold and undaunted commander,
    As ever did sail on the ocean so wide,
He made both the French and the Spaniards surrender,
    By pouring always into them a broadside,
      Mourn, England, mourn, mourn and complain,
      For the loss of Lord Nelson who died on the main.

One hundred engagements he had been in, sir,
    And ne'er in his life was he known to be beat,
Tho' he'd lost an arm, likewise a right eye, sir,
    No power on earth ever could him defeat.
His age at his death it was forty and seven,
    And as long as I breathe his great praises I'll sing,
For the whole navigation to him was given,
    Because he was loyal and true to his king.
      Mourn, England, mourn, etc.

Like an undaunted hero, exposed to the fire,
   He gave his command, on the quarter-deck stood,
To hear of his actions you would much admire,
   To see the decks covered all with human blood.
From aloft to below where he was commanding,
   All by a French gun he received a ball,
And by the contents he got mortally wounded,
   And that was the cause of Lord Nelson's fall.
     Mourn, England, mourn, etc.

Then up steps the doctor in a very great hurry,
   And unto Lord Nelson these words he did say,
'Indeed then, my lord, I am very sorry
   To see you here lying and bleeding this way'.
'No matter, no matter whatever about me,
   My time it has come – I am almost at the worst,
But there's my gallant seamen fighting so boldly,
   Discharge of your duty unto them all first'.
     Mourn, England, mourn, etc.

Then with a loud voice he called out to his captain,
   'Pray let me, sir, know how the battle does go,
For I think our great guns continue to rattle,
   Though death is approaching I firmly do know'.
'The antagonist's ship is gone to the bottom,
   Eighteen we have captur'd and brought them on
     board,
Four more we have blown clean out of the ocean,
   And this is the news I have brought you, my lord'.
     Mourn, England, mourn, etc.

Come all you gallant seamen that unite in a meeting,
   Always let Lord Nelson's memory go round,
For it is your duty when you unite in a meeting,
   Because he was loyal and true to the crown.

So now to conclude, and to finish these verses,
   Here's God bless all seamen that speak for his good,
May the heavens go with you, and ten thousand blessings
   Still rest on the fleet and brave Collingwood.
     Mourn, England, mourn, etc.

30

The Battle of Navarino

(1827)

You've heard of the Turks and the Greeks,
For all Europe's been told their bad habits,
How they cut down each other like leeks,
And the Turks slaughter children like rabbits:
But John Bull could bear it no more,
Said he, you death dealers, I'll stop you,
And if you don't both soon give o'er,
I swear by St George, that I'll whop you.

But the Turks supposed John was in jest,
Or concluded he was but a Green-o,
So they mustered their fleet all the best,
And lay in the Port Navarino.
Death and famine they carried before't,
And shot the poor Grecians by flocks, Sir,
Said our Tars, 'We'll go join in the sport,
And bring down a few Turkey Cocks, Sir'.

Then our Admiral boldly went in,
Said he, 'Mr Turk, just a word here',
But they answered him with a foul grin,
And a dirty trick something like murder.
Then Codrington proudly arose,

Said he, 'Do they take us for dull logs?
Well, since they're determined on blows,
Go at 'em, my brave British bull dogs'.

Now the Turk thought our ships were his prey,
And hoped soon to take them in tow-a,
The Asia then led on the way,
The next came the brave ship Genoa!
The Tars then bang'd into the Turks,
As they do to all foes that would wrong us,
The Musselmen cried, 'Here's your works!
Oh Mahomet! The Devil's upon us'.

The French took a share in the fun,
The Russians proved willing and able,
In three hours the business was done,
And the turkeys dished up for the table.
They were cooked to their heart's full desire,
'Twas not a mere frizzle or toasting,
But it seems they'd too much of the fire,
And were d—ly burnt in the roasting.

Then success to our lads of true blue,
Be they found upon sea or on shore,
And hurrah for the staunch gallant crew
That manned the brave ship the Genoa!
While we fight in humanity's cause,
Success all our efforts must crown, Sir,
And the tyrant that treads on her laws,
May the first honest man knock him down, Sir.

31

The Glorious Victory of Navarino!

(1827)

Come all you British hearts of oak, and listen unto me,
While I relate the famous fight now crown'd with victory,
When the Turkish and Egyptian Fleet were taught the
    truth again,
That Britons still and ever will be champions on the main.

CHORUS

    Then drink a health to Codrington – to Codrington
      huzza'
    Who did destroy the Turkish fleet in Navarino Bay.

On the 20th of October the glorious work began,
Bold *Ibrahim* vainly boasted he'd slaughter ev'ry man,
But Codrington resolved the Asia should display
A bright example to the rest, and he would lead the way.

The Genoa and the Albion he placed by his side,
And near to him *De Rigney*, commander of th' Armide,
The Glasgow and the Cambrian the Dartmouth & the Rose
Were placed in fine order alongside of their foes.

The proud Egyptians vainly said our fleet by far outvies
The boasting little squadron that's mann'd by the allies,
Then fir'e into the Asia, a signal for the fray,
But instantly brave Codrington a broadside did display.

[Then fir'e misprint for 'they fire'?

O then it was a glorious sight, which Britons do admire.
From ship to ship most gallantly began a raking fire,
The Turkish and Egyptian fleet, by British tars employ'd,
Roll one by one until the whole completely was destroy'd.

Then Briton fill a bumper to the memory of the slain,
Who fell defending of our rights upon the stormy main,
To the French and Russian Admirals, who Codrington
   did aid,
And to the men on board each ship who courage have
   displayed.

Printed for R. Heppel, 113 Coleshill Street, Birmingham.

32

A New Hunting Song

(*c.* 1846)

Now those that are low spirited I hope won't think it wrong,
While I sing to you a verse or two of a new hunting song;
For the hunting season has set in, or else just now begun,
Our heroes all will have their fun with the dog and gun.

CHORUS

And a hunting they will go, will go,
And a hunting they will go, will go!
They'll use all means, and try all schemes,
For to keep the poor man low.

With one of our brave huntsmen, I'm going to commence,
His name it was bold Bonaparte, he was a man of sense;
He hunted off from Corsica upon a game of Chance,
And hunted until he became the Emperor of France.

The next huntsman was Wellington, he'd the best of luck,
He hunted from lieutenant, till he became a Duke,
His men did fight well for him, and did his honour gain,
He done his best endeavours to have their pensions taken.

As for our hero Nelson, he hunted well for fame,
He was as bold a huntsman as e'er hunted on the main;
And for his warlike valour, he always bore the sway,
Till a cannon ball caused his downfall, all in Trafalgar Bay.

Prince Albert to this country came hunting for a wife,
He got one whom he loved dear as his own life;
Oh yes, a blooming little Queen for to dandle on his knee
With thirty thousand pounds a year paid from this country.

O'Connell he went hunting all through old Ireland's vale,
And says he'll go on hunting until he gets repeal.
They swear they'll have a Parliament in Dublin once more,
And make the trade to flourish all round green Erin's shore.

John Frost in Wales a hunting went, and well knew how
    to ride,
He had a fine bred Chartist horse, but got on the wrong
    side,
If he had held the reins quite firm in his own hand,
They'd ne'er have hunted him into Van Diemans Land.

The Queen she went a hunting thro' Scotland and France,
She hunted foreign countries through to learn the Polka
    dance;
Bobby Peel, he's a huntsman bold, was never known to
    fail,
He hunted up the Income Tax, and then the Corn Law
    Bill.

They're hunting up the poor man, he's hunted every day,
And hawkers too, if they do not a heavy licence pay.
They won't allow the poor to bed, it is a crime to steal,
For the one there's the Union, for the other there's the gaol.

So to conclude my hunting song, I hope you'll all agree
While the poor are starved and hunted down, the rich will
   have their spree.
To complain is quite a crime, for poor you're to remain,
The Parson says, if you're content, Heaven you're sure to
   gain.

33

Queen Victoria

(1837)

Welcome now, VICTORIA!
Welcome to the throne!
May all the trades begin to stir,
   Now you are Queen of England;
For your most gracious Majesty,
May see what wretched poverty,
Is to be found on England's ground,
   Now you are Queen of England.

While o'er the country you preside,
Providence will be your guide,
The people then will never chide
   Victoria, Queen of England.
She doth declare it her intent
To extend reform in Parliament,
On doing good she's firmly bent,
   While she is Queen of England.

Says she, I'll try my utmost skill,
That the poor may have their fill;
Forsake them! – no, I never will,
   When I am Queen of England.

For oft my mother said to me,
Let this your study always be,
To see the people blest and free,
    Should you be Queen of England.

And now, my daughter, you do reign,
Much opposition to sustain,
You'll surely have, before you gain
    The blessings of Old England,
O yes, dear mother, that is true,
I know my sorrows won't be few,
Poor people shall have work to do,
    When I am Queen of England.

I will encourage every trade,
For their labour must be paid,
In this free country then she said,
    Victoria, Queen of England;
That poor-law bill, with many more,
Shall be trampled on the floor –
The rich must keep the helpless poor,
    While I am Queen of England.

The Royal Queen of Britain's isle
Soon will make the people smile,
Her heart none can the least defile,
    Victoria, Queen of England.
Although she is of early years,
She is possess'd of tender cares,
To wipe away the orphan's tears,
    While she is Queen of England.

With joy each Briton doth exclaim,
Both far and near across the main,
Victoria we now proclaim
    The Royal Queen of England;

Long may she live, and happy be,
Adorn'd with robes of Royalty,
With blessings from her subjects free,
    While she is Queen of England.

In every town and village gay,
The bells shall ring, and music play,
Upon her Coronation-day,
    Victoria, Queen of England.
While her affections we do win,
And every day fresh blessings bring,
Ladies, help me for to sing,
    Victoria, Queen of England.

34

A New Song on the Birth of the Prince of Wales

Who was born on Tuesday, November 9, 1841

There's a pretty fuss and bother both in country and in
    town,
Since we have got a present, and an heir unto the Crown,
A little Prince of Wales so charming and so sly,
And the ladies shout with wonder, What a pretty little boy!

He must have a little musket, a trumpet and a kite,
A little penny rattle, and silver sword so bright,
A little cap and feather with scarlet coat so smart,
And a pretty little hobby horse to ride about the park.

Prince Albert he will often take the young Prince on his
    lap,
And fondle him so lovingly while he stirs about the pap,
He will pin on his flannel before he takes his nap,
Then dress him out so stylish with his little clouts and cap.

He must have a dandy suit to strut about the town,
John Bull must rake together six or seven thousand pound,
You'd laugh to see his daddy, at night he homewards runs,
With some peppermint or lollipops, sweet cakes and sugar
    plums.

He will want a little fiddle, and a little German flute,
A little pair of stockings and a pretty pair of boots,
With a handsome pair of spurs, and a golden headed cane,
And a stick of barley sugar, as long as Drury Lane.

An old maid ran through the palace, which did the nobs
    surprize,
Bawling out, he's got his daddy's mouth, his mammy's
    nose and eyes.
He will be as like his daddy as a frigate to a ship,
If he'd only got mustachios upon his upper lip.

Now to get these little niceties the taxes must be rose,
For the little Prince of Wales wants so many suits of clothes,
So they must tax the frying pan, the windows and the
    doors,
The bedsteads and the tables, kitchen pokers, and the floors.

John Harkness, Printer, Church Street, Preston.

35

The Slave Chase

(c. 1850)

Set every stitch of canvas to woo the fresh'ning wind;
Our bowsprit points to Cuba, the coast lies far behind.
Filled to the hatches full, my boys, across the seas we go;

There's twice five hundred niggers in the stifling hold
   below.
'A sail! What say you, boys? Well – let him give us chase
A British man-of-war you say – well, let him try the race;
There's not a swifter vessel ever floated on the waves
Than our tidy little schooner well ballasted with slaves.'

Now stronger yet and stronger still came down the fiery
   breeze,
And ever fast and faster sped the strange ship on the seas,
Flinging each rude and bursting surge in glittering haloes
   back,
And bearing high to heaven aloft the English Union Jack!
'Now curses on that ensign,' the slaving captain said;
'There's little luck for slavers when the English bunting's
   spread.
But pack on sail and trim the ship; before we'll captured
   be
We'll have the niggers up, my boys, and heave them in
   the sea.'

Hoarse was the slaving captain's voice, and deep the oath he
   swore:
'Haul down the flag; that's shot enough, we don't want
   any more.'
Alongside dashed the cruiser's boat to board and seize the
   prize.
Hark to that rattling British cheer that's ringing to the
   skies!
'Up, up with the negroes speedily; up, up, and give them
   breath;
Clear out the hold from stem to stern: that noisome den is
   death;
And run aloft St George's Cross, all wanton let it wave,
The token proud that under it there never treads a slave.'

36

Elegy on Albert Edward the Peacemaker

(Edward VII)

(1910)

Roll out ye drums, peal organs' loudest thunder,
'Tis Albert Edward, Prince of Wales, the whole world
    mourns with wonder.
What's that you cry? He's more than King!
The friend of fifty years or so!
The comrade gay, the kindly hand, has gone to join the
    phantom band.
What's that you say? We've lost the King!
'Tis Albert Edward, Prince of Wales, whose corse is
    passing on its way.
    'God bless the Prince of Wales' –
Ah lack-a-day! our childhood's song!
Our manhood's happy memory!
On, on, through decades almost seven!
For fifty years the cynosure of all the ruling Powers.
Then, as the King, he quelled all storms and furies,
Bringing our history up to highest point of glory!
Which ranks him in a line with Harry Monmouth and the
    bold Black Prince.
For they both faced their foreign foe;
While he ne'er shunned the traitor's deadly pistol
Or chanced affray with malcontent assassin, –
Straight to the front went our brave Prince of Wales,
And faced his crowds in almost every clime;
Through divers countries in both hemispheres.
Our Nation's leader and the people's pride.
None higher stood, or grasped a mightier place
Than England's Edward, doughtiest of all his race.
We sing his praises, bearing on the flag

Which yet is sadly drooping half-mast high
From church and tower and castle far and nigh.
While all concur that yet in century's fame
There stands no higher, more beloved name
Than Albert Edward, Prince of Wales.
Renowned in every country, o'er all seas, far and wide,
On ocean's billows, and in calm spring tide,
To each and all a memory dear beside,
Which has by time and fealty firm been tried;
And when at last this record to a close we bring
A symphony of praises loud we sing
In faithful memory of our Peaceful King.

TWO

SOCIAL CRITICISM

37

London Lickpenny

(*London licpenye*)

I

In London there I was bent
I saw myselfe, where truth shuld be a-teynte
fast to westminstar ward I went
to a man of lawe, to make my complaynt
I sayd for maris love, that holy seynt   [*maris* = *Mary's*
have pity on the powre, that would procede   [*powre* = *poor*
I would give sylvar, but my purs is faynt
for lacke of money, I may not spede

II

As I thrast thrughe out the thronge
amonge them all, my hode was gonn
netheles I let not longe,   [*let* = *stayed*
To kyngs benche tyll I come
by fore a juge I kneled anon
I prayd hym for gods sake he would take hede
full rewfully to hym I gan make my mone
for lacke of money I may not spede

III

benethe hym sat clerks, a great Rowt
fast they writen by one assent
there stode up one and cryed round about
Richard Robert and one of Kent
I wist not wele what he ment

[*thike* =
hoarsely

he cried so thike there indede
there were stronge theves shamed & shent
but they that lacked money mowght not spede.

IV

[*thoo* =*then*

unto the comon place I yowde thoo
where sat one with a sylken houde
I dyd hym reverence as me ought to do
I tolde hym my case, as well as I coude

[*by norord and
by sorode* =*by
north and by
south*

and seyd all my goods by norord and by sorode
I am defraudyd with great falshed
he would not geve me a momme of his mouthe
for lacke of money, I may not spede.

V

Then I went me unto the Rollis
before the clerks of the chauncerie
there were many qui tollis
but I herd no man speke of me
before them I knelyd upon my kne
shewyd them myne evidence & they began to reade
they seyde trewer things might there nevar be
but for lacke of money I may not spede.

VI

In westminster hall I found one
went in a longe goune of Ray
I crowched I kneled before them anon
for marys love of helpe I gan them pray
as he had be wrothe, he voyded away
bakward, his hand he gan me byd
I wot not what thou menest gan he say
ley downe sylvar, or here thow may not spede.

VII

In all Westminstar Hall I could find nevar a one
that for me would do, thowghe I shuld dye
without the dores, were flemings grete woon
upon me fast they gan to cry
and sayd mastar what will ye copen or by
fine felt hatts, spectacles for to rede
of this gay gere, a great cause why
for lacke of money I might not spede.

VIII

Then to westminster gate I went
when the sone was at highe prime
Cokes to me, they toke good entent
called me nere, for to dyne
and proferyd me good brede ale and wyne
a fayre clothe they began to sprede
rybbes of befe, bothe fat and fine
but for lacke of money I might not spede.

[*Cokes = cooks*

IX

In to London I gan me to hy
of all the lond it bearethe the prise
hot pescods, one can cry
strabery rype, and chery in the ryse
one bad me come nere and by some spice
pepar and saffron they gan me bede
clove, grayns, and flowre of Rise
for lacke of money I might not spede

[*by = buy*
[*bede = offer*

X

Then into Chepe I gan me drawne
where I saw stond moche people
one bad me come nere, and by fine cloth of lawne

[umple = a kind
of linen stuff

paris thred, coton, and umple
I seyde there upon I could not skyle
I am not wont there to in dede

[heure = cap

one bad me by an heure, my hed to hele
for lacke of money I might not spede

XI

Then went I forth by london stone
Thrwghe out all canywike strete
drapers to me they called anon

[hete = promise

grete chepe of clothe, they gan me hete
then come there one, and cried hot shepes fete
Risshes faire and grene, an othar gan to grete

[melwell = cod

both melwell and makarell I gan mete
but for lacke of money I myght not spede

XII

Then I hied me into estchepe
one cried ribes of befe, and many a pie
pewtar pots they clatteryd in a heape
ther was harpe pipe and sawtry
ye by cokke, nay by cokke some began to cry
some sangen of Jenken and Julian, to get them selvs mede
full fayne I wold had of that mynstralsie
but for lacke of money I could not spede

XIII

[yode = went

Into Cornhill anon I yode
Where is much stolne gere amonge
I saw wher hange myne owne hode
that I had lost in westminstar among the throng

[lokes = looks
[kenned = knew

then I beheld it with lokes full longe
I kenned it as well as I dyd my crede
to by myne owne hode agayne, me thought it wrong
but for lacke of money I might not spede

XIV

Then came the Taverner, and toke my by the sleve
and seyd ser a pint of wyn would you assay
syr quod I it may not greve
for a peny may do no more than it may
I dranke a pint, and therefore gan pay
sore a hungred away I yede
for well london lykke peny for ones & aye
for lacke of money I may not spede

XV

Then I hyed me to byllingesgate
and cried wagge wagge yow hens
I praye a barge man for gods sake
that they would spare me myn expens
he sayd ryse up man, and get the hens
What winist thow I will do on the my almes dede
here skapethe no man, by nethe ij pens
for lacke of money I myght not spede

[*skapethe =
escapes*;
pens =pence

XVI

The⟨n⟩ I conveyed me into Kent,
for of the law would I medle no more
by caus no man to me would take entent
I dight me to the plowe, even as I ded before
Jesus save london, that in bethelem was bore
and every trew man of law god graunt hym souls med
and they that be othar, god theyr state restore
for he that lackethe money, with them he shall not spede
       Explicit london likke peny.

38

The Map of Mock-Begger Hall

with his scituation in the spacious Countrey, called
Anywhere

*To the Tune of 'It is not your Northerne Nanny': or
'Sweet is the Lasse that Loues Me'*

I Reade in ancient times of yore,
That men of worthy calling
Build almes houses and Spittles store,
Which now are all downe falling:
And few men seeke them to repaire,
Nor is there one among twenty,
That for good deeds will take any care,
    While mock begger hall stands empty.

Farme houses which their fathers built,
And Land well kept by tillage,
Their Prodigall sons have sold for gilt,
In every Towne and village,
To th' City and Court they doe resort
With gold and silver plenty,
And there they spend their time in sport,
    While mock beggers hall stands empty.

Young Landlords when to age they come,
Their rents they will be racking,
The tenant must give a golden sum,
Or else he is turn'd packing,
Great fines and double rent beside.
Or else they'l not content be,
It is to maintain their monstrous pride,
    While mock begger hall stands empty.

Their fathers went in homely frèes,
And good plain broad cloathes brèeches,
Their stockings with the same agrees.
Sow'd on with good strong stitches.
They were not then call'd gentlemen,
Though they had wealth great plenty,
Now every gul's growne worshipfull,
   While mock beggers hall stands empty.

No gold nor silver parchment lace
Was worne but by our Nobles
Nor would the honest harmlesse face,
Weare Ruffes with so many doubles,
Our bands were to our shirts sowne then,
Yet cloath was full as plenty,
Now one band hath more cloath than ten,
   While mock begger hall stands empty.

Now we are Apes in imitation,
The more indeed's the pitty,
The Country followes the City,
And ere one fashion is knowne throughout,
Another they will invent yée,
Tis all your gallant's study about,
   While mock beggers hall stands empty.

THE SECOND PART, TO THE SAME TUNE

Me thinks it is a great reproach,
To those that are nobly descended,
When for their pleasures cannot have a Coach,
Wherewith they might be attended,
But every beggerly Jack and Gill
That eat scant a good meale in twenty,
Must thorow the streets be jolted still,
   While mock begger hall stands empty.

There's some are rattled thorow the streets,
Probatum est, I tell it,
Whose names are wrapt in parchment sheets,
It grieves their hearts to spell it,
They are not able two men tu keepe,
With a Coachman they must content be,
Which at playhouse doores in his box lies asleep
  While mock begger hall stands empty.

Our Gentlewomen whose meanes is nothing
To that which they make shew of,
Must use all the fashions in their cloathing,
Which they can heare or know of,
They take much care themselves to decke,
That money is oft so scanty,
The belly is forc'd to complaine of the backe,
  While mock begger ⟨hall⟩ stands empty.

It may well be that some will muse,
Wherefore in this relation,
The name of Mock begger I doe use,
Without any explanation,
To cleare which doubt before I end,
Because they shall all content be,
To shew the meaning I doe intend
  Of mock begger hall still empty.

Some Gentlemen and Citizens have
In divers eminent places,
Erected houses rich and brave,
Which stood for the owners graces,
Let any poore to such a doore
Come, they expecting plenty,
They there may ask till their throats are sore,
  For mock begger hall stands empty.

Thus in these times we can perceive
Small charity comfort yielding,
For pride doth men of grace bereave,
Not onely in clothes but in building.
Man makes the senseless stones and bricks,
Which by heavens goodness lent be,
Expresse his pride by these vaine tricks,
  For mock begger hall stands empty.

  *Printed at London for Richard Harper, neere to
      the Hospital gate in Smithfield.*

39

The Poore Man Payes for All

  *This is but a dreame which here shall insue,
  But the Author wishes his words were not true.*

As I lay musing all alone
    upon my resting bed,
Full many a cogitation
    did come into my head:
And waking from my sleepe, I
    My dreame to mind did call:
Me thought I saw before mine eyes,
    how poore men payes for all.

I many objects did behold
    in this my frightfull Dreame,
A part of them I will unfold:
    and though my present Theame
Is but a fancy, you may say,
    yet many things doe fall
Too true alas! for at this day
    the poore man payes for all.

Me thought I saw (which caus'd my care)
   what I wish were a fable,
That poore men still inforced are
   to pay more then they are able:
Me thought I heard them weeping say,
   their substance was but small,
For rich men will beare all the sway,
   and poore men pay for all.

Me thought I saw how wealthy men
   did grind the poore men's faces,
And greedily did prey on them,
   not pittying their cases:
They make them toyle and labour sore
   for wages too too small;
The rich men in the tavernes rore,
   but poore men pay for all.

Me thought I saw an usurer old
   walke in his Fox-fur'd gowne,
Whose wealth and eminence controld
   the most men in the towne;
His wealth he by extortion got,
   and rose by others' fall,
He had what his hands earned not,
   but poore men pay for all.

Me thought I saw a Courtier proud
   goe swaggering along,
That unto any scarce allow'd
   the office of his tongue:
Me thought, wert not for bribery,
   his peacock's plumes would fall;
He ruffles out in bravery,
   but poore men pay for all.

Me thought I met, sore discontent,
   some poore men on the way,
I asked one whither he went
   so fast and could not stay.
Quoth he, I must goe take my Lease,
   or else another shall;
My landlord's riches doe increase,
   but poore men pay for all.

THE SECOND PART

Me thought I saw most stately wives
   goe jetting on the way,
That live delightfull idle lives
   and go in garments gay;
That with the moon their shapes doe change,
   or else they'l childe and brawle;
Thus women goe like monsters strange,
   and poore men pay for all.

Me thought I was i' th' countrey,
   where poore men take great paines,
And labour hard continually,
   onely for rich men's gaines:
Like th' Israelites in Egypt,
   the poore are kept in thrall;
The task-masters are playing kept,
   but poore men pay for all.

Me thought I saw poore Tradesmen,
   i' th' City and else-where,
Whom rich men keepe as beads-men,
   in bondage care and feare:
Thei'l have them worke for what they list,
   thus weakest go to the wall:
The rich men eate and drinke the best,
   but poore men pay for all.

Me thought I saw two Lawyers base
    one to another say,
We have had in hand this poore man's Case
    a twelvemonth and a day:
And yet wee'l not contented be
    to let the matter fall;
Beare thou with me, & Ile beare with thee,
    while poore men pay for all.

[*Oast = Host*

Me thought I saw a red-nose Oast,
    as fat as he could wallow;
Whose carkasse, if it should be roast,
    would drop seven stone of tallow:
He growes rich out of measure
    with filling measure small;
He lives in mirth and pleasure,
    but poore men pay for all.

And so likewise the Brewer stout,
    the Chandler and the Baker,
The Mault-man also, without doubt,
    and the Tobacco-taker:
Though they be proud, and stately growne,
    and beare themselves so tall;
Yet to the world it is well knowne
    that poore men pay for all.

Even as the mighty fishes still
    doe feed upon the lesse;
So rich men, might they have their will,
    would on the poore men ceaze:
It is a proverbe old and true –
    that weakest goe to th' wall,
Rich men can drink till th' sky looke blue,
    but poore men pay for all.

But now, as I before did say,
    this is but a Dreame indeed;
Though all dreames prove not true, some may
    hap right as I doe reade:
And if that any come to passe,
    I doubt this my Dreame shall;
For still 'tis found too true a case –
    that poore men pay for all.

40

The Downright Country-Man

OR

The Faithful Dairy Maid

⟨B⟩*ut mind how Country Lads do boast, whilst* Londoners *are blam'd,*
And Country Lasses praised most, while ours are Wags proclaim'd.

I am a downright Country-man, both faithful (aye) and
    true,
I'le live and dye so if I can, this I declare to you:
I study as I am at Plow, so shun all false deceit,
And you may plain discover now, *I am no London Cheat.*

Your *London* Cheats do go most fine, like Lords in their
    attire,
To swill their guts with Spanish Wine, it is their hearts'
    desire:
But it is very common, they do with the Vintners meet,
They'l get o' th' score, then run away, *just like a London*
    Cheat.

They oft pretend to be in Love, and ready for to dye,
Yea, vow to be just like the Dove, but know no Constancy;

Like Villains they the way do play, with every Lass they
    meet;
They plump them up, then run away, *this is a London*
    Cheat.

There is not one in Twenty but he wears his Sword by his
    side,
And walks with many an empty Gut, and ne'r will leave
    his Pride:
But when his brain is full of Wine, he'l stagger in the street,
And then picks up a Concubine, *to Pox the London Cheat.*

Then he for half a Crown will have, that which may make
    him rue,
A painted ⟨slave⟩ both fine and brave, perhaps the
    French-man too;
Thus he with his unwholsome flesh will be most brisk and
    sweet,
But see him once out of his dress, *he's like a London Cheat.*

But *London* City oft affords Females as bad as Men,
Who though they Hector with their swords, there is not
    one in ten
But has some pretty like Miss, to serve him at his need,
And every minute lends a Kiss, *this is a ⟨quean⟩ indeed.*

They'l vow for ever to be true, to them they do affect,
When Honesty is bid adieu what can you then expect?
No faith or troth is minded, when fools take so little heed,
For who so often clap their Men, *O these are whores indeed.*

Let honest men take so much care, that do inhabit *London*,
Of such false Girls to have a care, for fear they may be
    undone:
How many hundreds may be spoyl'd, if they do not take
    heed;

They who are so by Girls beguil'd, *do meet with ⟨Jades⟩ indeed.*

Why then give me the Country Lass, who honest is and true,
And yet may kiss upon the Grass, but nothing farther do:
She scorneth that her ⟨aimless⟩ deed should any mischief breed,
She takes delight in what is right, *and honest is indeed.*

See by the colours of their cheeks, they well and wholesome are;
While *London* Girls look green as Leeks, the Country Girls look fair;
Then old and young, I pray be ware, in Marrying take good heed,
Least you be brought into a snare *by cursed Jades indeed.*

See how the Rose and Lilly fair upon their cheeks do grow,
Mind how their breath perfumes the ayr, wherever they do go;
And what they touch im⟨m⟩ediately fresh odours on them breed:
They patterns are of constancy, *rare Country Girls indeed.*

Mind but the Girl that milks the Cow, how sweetly she doth sing,
She never knits an angry brow, but welcomes in the Spring,
And then, among the Butter flowers, she trips along the mead,
To pass away the tedious hours, *she's fair and Chaste indeed.*

41

The Old and the New Courtier

OLD COURTIER

An old song made by an old aged Pate,
Of an old worshipful gentleman, had a wealthy estate,
That kept an old house at a bountiful rate,
And an old Porter to relieve poor people at his gate,
  Like an old Courtier of the Queen's,
  And the Queen's old Courtier.

With an old Lady whose anger one word asswageth,
Who every Quarter paid his old Servants their wages,
Who never knew what belonged to Coachmen, Footmen,
  nor Pages,
But kept two and fifty men in Blew caps and badges.
  Like an old Courtier of the Queen's, etc.

With an old Study, stuff full of old learned books,
And an old Parson, you may know him by his looks;
And an old Butt'ry-hatch worn quite off the old hooks,
And an old Kitchin that maintain'd half a dozen old Cooks.
  Like an old Courtier of the Queen's, etc.

With an old Hall hung with Pikes, Guns, and Bows,
And old blades and Bucklers, had borne many shrowd
  blows,
With an old Freezadoe coat to cover his trunck hose,
With an old cup of Sherry to comfort his old nose.
  Like an old Courtier of the Queen's, etc.

With an old fashion, when Christmas was come,
To call in all his old neighbors with a Bagpipe or a Drum,
And good cheer enough to furnish out every old room,

And Beer and Ale would make a cat to speak, and a wise
   man dumb.
    Like an old Courtier of the Queen's, etc.

With an old Faulkner, a Huntsman, and a Kennel of
   Hounds,
That never Hauked nor hunted but in his grand-father's
   old grounds,
Who like a wise man kept himself in his own old bounds
And when he died gave each child a thousand old pounds.
    Like an old Courtier of the Queen's, etc.

But to his son and heir his lands he assign'd,
With an old will to charge him to keep the same bountiful
   minde,
To be good to his old Tenants, and to his old neighbours
   kinde,
But in the next ditty you shall hear how he was inclin'de.
    Like a new Courtier of the King's,
    And the King's new Courtier.

NEW COURTIER

With a new flourishing Gallant, who is newly come to his
   land,
Who keeps a brace of painted Creatures at his own
   command,
And can take up readily a thousand pounds on his new
   Bond,
And drink in a new Tavern, till he can neither go nor
   stand,
    Like a new Courtier of the King's, and the King's new
    Courtier.

With a new Lady whose face is beautiful and fair,
Who never knew what belong'd to house-keeping nor
care,
But purchas'd seven colour'd Fans to play with the wanton
ayr,
And seventeen new Dressings of other women's hair,
    Like a new Courtier of the King's, etc.

With a new study full of Pamphlets and playes,
With a new Chaplain, that drinks oftener than he prays,
With a new Butt'ry-hatch opens once in five or six days,
With a new *French* Cook to devise Cickshaws and toys,
    For the new Courtier of the King's, etc.

With a new Hall builded where an old Hall stood,
Hung round with new pictures, doe the poore little good,
With a new Shovel-board whereon never stood food,
With 22 fair Chimnies never burnt coals nor wood.
    For the new Courtier of the King's, etc.

With a new fashion when *Christmas* was drawing on,
Upon a new journey they must all to *London* be gon,
And leave none to keep house in the Country, but their
new man *John*,
Who relieves all his Neighbors with a great thump on the
back with a cold stone,
    Like a new Courtier of the King's, etc.

With a new Gentleman-Usher whose carriage is compleat,
With a new Coachman, and two footmen to carry up the
meat,
With a new waiting Gentlewoman whose dressing is very
neat,
Who when her Lady hath dined gives her fellows very
little meat,
    Like a new Courtier of the King's, etc.

With new titles of honor bought with his Grand-father's
   old gold,
For which most of his father's Mannors were all sold,
And that's one cause housekeeping is grown so cold,
Yet this is the new course most of our new Gallants hold,
    Like new Courtiers of the King's, and the King's new
      Courtiers.

Thus have you heard of the old Courtiers and the new,
And for the last I could wish never a word were true,
With these rude lines which I dedicate to you,
And these rude verses I present to your view,
    By the poor Courtier of the King's, and the King's poor
      Courtier.

42

All Things be Dear but Poor Mens Labour

OR

The Sad Complaint of Poor People

Being a true Relation of the dearness of all kind of Food, to
the great Grief and Sorrow of many Thousands in this Nation.
Likewise, the uncharitableness of Rich Men to the Poor. This
Song was begun at *Worcester,* the midle at *Shrewsbury,* the
end at *Coventry* by L.W.

   Kind Country-men listen I pray
      unto this my harmless Ditty,
   Observe these words which I shall say
      for it is true the mores the pitty;
   But chief to those that stand me by,
      whether stranger or my neighbour
   I think there's none that can deny
      all things are dear but poorman's labour

We find that Bread-Corn now is dear,
   in every Town throughout this Nation,
The Rich now poor men will not bear
   because Charity's out of fashion,
Poor men do work all day and night
   for that which in it hath small favour,
A Loaf of sixpence is but small
   all things etc.

Beef and Mutton is so dear
   a mans weeks wages cannot buy it,
   all things are dear who can deny it,
But poor mens labour is too cheap
   and Tra⟨d⟩ing's dead which makes times harder
That all their pains wont find them meat
   all things etc.

Cheese and Butter is so dear
   you know it better than I can tell ye
I⟨t⟩ would grieve a sto⟨n⟩y heart to hear
   the poor complain thus for their belly.
And trading still continues dead,
   with every one that is a trader,
That all their pains wont find them bread
   all things etc.

It makes my very heart to ake,
   to hear poor people thus complaining,
For all their care and pains they take,
   rich men are still the poor disdaining,
But let Rich Misers consider well
   the poor, and show to them some favour
Or else their soules will hang in Hell
   all things etc.

Is it not sad for Parents now
   to hear their children for bread crying,
And has it not for them to give
   although for food they lye a dying,
Poor little Babies they must fast
   although it grieves Mother and Father,
A bit of bread they cannot tast,
   all things etc.

To hear the many sad Complaints
   as I have heard in Town and City,
I think you'd cry as well as I,
   the Rich has for the Poor no pitty
For if they work now for Rich men
   there some, will keep their Wages from them
And make them run to and agan,
   Which makes the poor cry fye upon them.
   all things etc.

Farmers so covetous they be
   Their Corn they'l hoard for better profit
Although the Poor do fast we see,
   their grain they'l keep what ere comes of it.
Whole Ricks of Corn stands in their yards
   and scorns to show the Poor some favour
For some do swear they do not care
   if things be dear, but poor mans labour

A Rich man there was in Staffordshire,
   which is a knave, i'me sure no better
He hop'd to sell his Corn so dear ⟨as others⟩ do
    their Pepper,
When Wheat was sold for shillings ten
   he would not Thrash, Fan, nor yet rake it
Let poor despair he oft did swear
   heed keep it for a better market

Too many there is of such base men
   all England round in Town and City
They'l see the poor starve at their door
   before they'l shew them any pity;
For some will make poor man to work,
   all day and night for little favour,
For Rich men be cruel mee see
   all things be dear etc.

But thanks to God, Corn falls apace,
   and all things else that's for the belly,
Yet still it doth go bad with some
   although they work full hard I tell you,
Sixpence a day, is now the pay
   for a days work, and held a favour
This must maintain Wife and Babes
   all things etc.

So to conclude, lets be Content
   with what the Lord doth please to send us,
Let us our evil lives repent
   then in our woes God will defend us:
And let rich men be merciful
   unto the poor stranger or neighbour,
For all do know, unto their woe
   all things be dear but poor mens labour

43

An Excellent New Song Upon His Grace Our good Lord Archbishop of Dublin

By honest JO. one of His Grace's Farmers in Fingal

To the Tune of —

(1724)

BY JONATHAN SWIFT

I Sing not of the *Draper's* Praise, nor yet of *William Wood*;
But I sing of a *Famous Lord*, who seeks his *Country's* Good.
Lord WILLIAM'S Grace of *Dublin* Town, 'tis he that first
 appears,
Whose Wisdom and whose Piety, do far exceed his Years.
In ev'ry *Council* and *Debate* he stands for what is *Right*;
And still the *Truth* he will *Maintain*, what'er he loses by't.
And though some think him in the Wrong, yet still there
 comes a Season
When ev'ry one turns round about, and owns His Grace
 had Reason.
His *Firmness* to the *publick Good*, as one that knows it Swore,
Has lost His Grace for Ten Years past Ten thousand Pounds
 and more:
Then come the Poor and strip him so, they leave him not
 a Cross,
For he regards Ten thousand Pounds no more than
 Wood's Dross.
To beg his Favour is the Way new Favours still to win,
He makes no more to give ten Pounds than I to give a Pin.
Why, there's my Landlord now the *'Squire*, who all in
 Money wallows,
He would not give a Groat to save his Father from the
 Gallows.
A *Bishop* says the noble *'Squire*, I hate the very Name,

169

To have two thousand Pounds a Year, O 'tis a burning
    Shame!

Two thousand Pounds a Year, Good Lord! and I to have
    but Five.

And under him no Tenant yet was ever known to thrive.

Now from his Lordship's Grace I hold a little Piece of
    Ground,

And all the Rent I pay is scarce five Shillings in the Pound.

Then Master *Steward* takes my Rent, and tells me, honest
    Jo.

Come, you must take a Cup of Sack or two before you go.

He bids me then to hold my Tongue, and up the Money
    locks,

For fear my Lord should send it all into the poor Man's
    Box.

And once I was so bold to beg that I might see His Grace,

Good Lord! I wondred how I dar'd to look him in the
    Face.

Then down I went upon my Knees, his Blessing to obtain,

He gave it me, and ever since I find I thrive amain.

Then said my Lord, I'm very glad to see thee honest Friend,

I know the Times are something hard, but hope they soon
    will mend,

Pray never press your self for Rent, but pay me when you
    can,

I find you bear a good Report, and are an honest Man.

Then said his Lordship with a Smile, I must have
    LAWFUL *Cash*,

I hope you will not pay my Rent in that same *Wood*'s
    Trash.

God Bless your Grace I then reply'd, I'd see him hanging
    high'r,

Before I'd touch his filthy Dross, than is *Clandalkin* Spire.

To every Farmer twice a Week all round about the *Yoke*,

Our *Parsons* Read the *Draper's* Books, and make us honest
    Foke.

And then I went to pay the 'Squire and in the Way I
  found,
His Baily Driving all my Cows into the Parish Pound.
Why Sirrah said the Noble 'Squire, how dare you see my
  Face,
Your Rent is due almost a Week beside the Days of Grace.
And Yet the Land I from him hold is set so on the Rack,
That only for the Bishop's Lease 'twould quickly break my
  Back.
    Then God Preserve his Lordship's Grace, and make
      him live as long
    As did Methusalem of old, and so I end my SONG.

44

An Excellent New Song on a Seditious Pamphlet

To the Tune of 'Packington's Pound'

Written in the Year 1720

BY JONATHAN SWIFT

I

BROCADÓS and Damasks, and Tabbies, and Gawzes,
  Are, by Robert Ballentine, lately brought over,
With Forty Things more: now hear what the Law says,
  Whoe'er will not wear them is not the King's Lover.
      Though a Printer and Dean
      Seditiously mean
Our true Irish hearts from old England to wean;
We'll buy English Silks for our Wives and our Daughters,
In Spight of his Deanship and Journeyman Waters.

II

In England the dead in Woollen are clad,
  The Dean and his Printer then let us cry Fye on;

To be cloath'd like a Carcass would make a Teague mad,
 Since a living Dog better is than a dead Lyon.
   Our Wives they grow sullen
    At wearing of Wollen,
And all we poor Shopkeepers must our Horns pull in.
Then we'll buy *English* Silks, *&c.*

III

Whoever our Trading with *England* would hinder,
 To *inflame* both the Nations do plainly conspire,
Because *Irish* Linen will soon turn to Tinder,
 And Wool it is greasy, and quickly takes Fire.
   Therefore I assure ye,
   Our noble Grand Jury,
When they saw the Dean's Book they were in a great Fury;
They would buy *English* silks for their *Wives, &c.*

IV

This wicked Rogue *Waters*, who always is sinning,
 And before *Corum nobus* so oft has been call'd,
Henceforward shall print neither Pamphlets nor Linnen,
 And if Swearing can do't, shall be swingingly maul'd:
   And as for the Dean,
   You know whom I mean,
If the Printer will peach him, he'll scarce come off clean.
Then we'll buy *English* Silks for our Wives and our
 Daughters,
In Spight of his Deanship and Journeyman *Waters.*

45

A New Song, call'd The Red Wig

You good folks of Nottingham I would have you draw
 near,

172

And the feats of little Charly you quickly shall hear
Little Charley in his youth a wandering boy was he,
But now he's grown so great a man that an Overseer he be.

CHORUS

You poor folks of Nottingham I pray you draw near,
And the tricks of little Charley you quickly shall hear.

His father was a pauper and his uncle likewise.
And in Greasley workhouse the latter clos'd his eyes,
But Charley of late such a valiant man is grown,
He struts about the town like a toad upon his throne.

The poor in their new livery they look very fine,
And in the streets of Nottingham together they do shine
He's turn'd them up with scarlet to make himself look big,
So we'll join our mites together and buy him a red wig.

For to increase your sessments it is his daily plan,
And if you do not pay them he'll summons every man,
If you the poor rates my good people cannot pay,
Your goods to the workhouse he then will drag away.

By pinching his workmen and his runners likewise,
He had brought them to poverty and gain'd himself a
    prize,
By cheating the country with his one thread lace,
He has ruin'd the trade and brought the town disgrace.

And for that base action we will brand him with shame,
We will call him captain one-thread, that shall be his name;
The name of captain one-thread he richly deserves,
For all his base actions and knavish cards.

Little Charley and his colleagues I think are to blame,
For raising our sessments I'm sure it is a shame;
So now brother townsmen I will bid you farewell,
And wish little Charley and his colleagues safe in hell.

Ordoyne, Printer, Nottingham.

46

Good English Hospitality

BY WILLIAM BLAKE

This city & this country has brought forth many mayors,
To sit in state & give forth laws out of their old oak chairs,
With face as brown as any nut with drinking of strong ale;
Good English hospitality, O then it did not fail!

With scarlet gowns & broad gold lace would make a
    yeoman sweat,
With stockings roll'd above their knees & shoes as black
    as jet,
With eating beef & drinking beer, O they were stout &
    hale!
Good English hospitality, O then it did not fail!

Thus sitting at the table wide, the Mayor & Aldermen
Were fit to give law to the city; each eat as much as ten.
The hungry poor enter'd the hall, to eat good beef & ale.
Good English hospitality, O then it did not fail!

47

My Master and I

Says the master to me, is it true? I am told
Your name on the books of the Union's enroll'd,
I can never allow that a workman of mine
With wicked disturbers of peace should combine.

Says I to the master, it's perfectly true
That I am in the Union, and I'll stick to it too,
And if between Union and you I must choose
I have plenty to win and little to lose.

For twenty years mostly my bread has been dry,
And to butter it now I shall certainly try;
And tho' I respect you, remember I'm free,
No master in England shall trample on me.

Says the master to me, a word or two more,
We never have quarrelled on matters before,
If you stick to the Union, ere long I'll be bound,
You will come and ask me for more wages all round.

Now I cannot afford more than two bob a day
When I look at the taxes and rent that I pay,
And the crops are so injured by game as you see,
If it is hard for you it's hard also for me.

Says I to the master I do not see how
Any need has arisen for quarrelling now,
And tho' likely enough we shall ask for more wage
I can promise you we shall not get first in a rage.

48

An Ode to the Framers of the Frame Bill

BY LORD BYRON

(1812)

I

Oh well done Lord E[ldo]n! and better done R[yde]r!
  Britannia must prosper with councils like yours;
Hawkesbury, Harrowby, help you to guide her,
  Whose remedy only must *kill* ere it cures:
Those villains; the Weavers, are all grown refractory,
  Asking some succour for Charity's sake –
So hang them in clusters round each Manufactory,
  That will at once put an end to *mistake*.

II

The rascals, perhaps, may betake them to robbing,
  The dogs to be sure have got nothing to eat –
So if we can hang them for breaking a bobbin,
  'T will save all the Government's money and meat:
Men are more easily made than machinery –
  Stockings fetch better prices than lives –
Gibbets on Sherwood will heighten the scenery,
  Shewing how Commerce, how Liberty thrives!

III

Justice is now in pursuit of the wretches,
  Grenadiers, Volunteers, Bow-street Police,
Twenty-two Regiments, a score of Jack Ketches,
  Three of the Quorum and two of the Peace;
Some Lords, to be sure, would have summoned the Judges,

To take their opinion, but that they ne'er shall,
For LIVERPOOL such a concession begrudges,
  So now they're condemned by *no Judges* at all.

IV

Some folks for certain have thought it was shocking,
  When Famine appeals and when Poverty groans,
That Life should be valued at less than a stocking,
  And breaking of frames lead to breaking of bones.
If it should prove so, I trust, by this token,
  (And who will refuse to partake in the hope?)
That the frames of the fools may be first to be *broken*,
  Who, when asked for a *remedy*, sent down a *rope*.

49

The Framework-knitters Lamentation

Come now each gen'rous feeling heart,
  And lend an ear I pray:
From your abundance O impart,
  Relieve our wants to day.

Could you but see the flowing tear,
  Fall from each infants eye;
Methinks your hearts could not forbear,
  Your aid for their supply.

We labour hard from morn till night,
  For our and their defence;
We tug, and toil, with all our might,
  And only get twelve pence.

Then how can wife and children four,
  Be fed with this supply;

For when thats done they ask for more,
　But Ah! we must deny.

No heathen Savage, Jew, or Turk,
　Such hardships has to bear;
For Britons ne'er refus'd to work,
　And yet how hard we fare.

Methinks I see the gen'rous heart,
　Beat high within each breast;
And say my mite I will impart,
　To aid the poor distress'd.

Wightman, Printer, Sutton.

50

The Framework-knitters Petition

Could we obtain our food by work,
Wou'd labour like the hardy turk;
But all our hopes from thence are fled,
And we now pine for want of bread.

Our Children tho' to us most dear,
Must Die for want, we greatly fear;
Unless some human generous heart,
Some food for them to us impart.

Could you our habitations see,
The seats of abject misery;
We think you would afford your aid,
Till we return unto our trade.

On heaven and you we now depend,
And trust in you we've found a friend,
And what you give, God will re-pay,
Both here and in the Judgment day.

Written by C. Briggs, Sutton.
Wightman, Printer, Sutton.

51

The Times have Altered

(*c.* 1820)

Come all you swaggering farmers, whoever you may be,
One moment pay attention and listen unto me;
It is concerning former times, as I to you declare,
So different to the present times if you with them compare.

> *Chorus* – For lofty heads and paltry pride, I'm sure
> it's all the go,
> For to distress poor servants and keep their
> wages low.

If you'd seen the farmers wives 'bout fifty years ago,
In home-spun russet linsey clad from top to toe;
But now a-days the farmer's wives are so puffed up with
pride,
In a dandy habit and green veil unto the market they must
ride.
> *Chorus* – For lofty heads, etc.

Some years ago the farmer's sons were learnt to plough and
sow,

And when the summer-time did come, likewise to reap
   and mow;
But now they dress like Squire's sons, their pride it knows
   no bounds,
They mount upon a fine blood horse to follow up the
   hounds.

The farmer's daughters formerly were learnt to card and
   spin,
And, by their own industry, good husbands they did win;
But now the card and spinning-wheel are forced to take
   their chance,
While they're hopped off to a boarding-school to learn to
   sing and dance.

In a decent black silk bonnet to church they used to go,
Black shoes, and handsome cotton gown, stockings as white
   as snow,
But now silk gowns and coloured shoes they must be
   bought for them,
Besides they are frizzed and furbelowed just like a freizland
   hen.

Each morning when at breakfast, the master and the dame
Down with the servants they would sit, and eat and drink
   the same,
But with such good old things, they've done them quite
   away;
Into the parlour they do go with coffee, toast, and tea.

At the kitchen table formerly, the farmer he would sit,
And carve for all his servants, both pudding and fine meat,
But now all in the dining-room so closely they're boxed
   in,
If a servant only was to peep, it would be thought a sin.

Now, in those good old fashion'd times, the truth I do
  declare,
The rent and taxes could be spared, and money for to spare,
But now they keep the fashion up, they look so very nice,
Although they cut an outside show they are as poor as
  mice.

When Bonaparte was in vogue, poor servants could engage
For sixteen pounds a year, my boys, that was a handsome
  wage,
But now the wages are so low, and what is worse than all,
The masters cannot find the cash, which brings them to the
  wall.

When fifty acres they did rent, then money they could
  save,
But now for to support their pride, five hundred they must
  have;
If those great farms were taken and divided into ten,
Oh! we might see as happy days as ever we did then.

52

The Fine Old English Gentleman

New Version

TO BE SAID OR SUNG AT ALL CONSERVATIVE DINNERS

BY CHARLES DICKENS

(1841)

I'll sing you a new ballad, and I'll warrant it first-rate,
Of the days of that old gentleman who had that old estate;
When they spent the public money at a bountiful old rate

On ev'ry mistress, pimp, and scamp, at ev'ry noble gate,
    In the fine old English Tory times;
    Soon may they come again!

The good old laws were garnished well with gibbets, whips,
  and chains,
With fine old English penalties, and fine old English pains,
With rebel heads, and seas of blood once hot in rebel veins;
For all these things were requisite to guard the rich old
  gains
    Of the fine old English Tory times;
    Soon may they come again!

This brave old code, like Argus, had a hundred watchful
  eyes,
And ev'ry English peasant had his good old English spies,
To tempt his starving discontent with fine old English lies,
Then call the good old Yeomanry to stop his peevish cries,
    In the fine old English Tory times;
    Soon may they come again!

The good old times for cutting throats that cried out in
  their need,
The good old times for hunting men who held their fathers'
  creed,
The good old times when William Pitt, as all good men
  agreed,
Came down direct from Paradise at more than railroad
  speed. . . .
    Oh the fine old English Tory times;
    When will they come again!

In those rare days, the press was seldom known to snarl or
  bark,
But sweetly sang of men in pow'r, like any tuneful lark;
Grave judges, too, to all their evil deeds were in the dark;

And not a man in twenty score knew how to make his
    mark.
        Oh the fine old English Tory times;
        Soon may they come again!

Those were the days for taxes, and for war's infernal din;
For scarcity of bread, that fine old dowagers might win;
For shutting men of letters up, through iron bars to grin,
Because they didn't think the Prince was altogether thin,
        In the fine old English Tory times;
        Soon may they come again!

But Tolerance, though slow in flight, is strong-wing'd in
    the main;
That night must come on these fine days, in course of time
    was plain;
The pure old spirit struggled, but its struggles were in vain;
A nation's grip was on it, and it died in choking pain,
        With the fine old English Tory days,
        All of the olden time.

The bright old day now dawns again; the cry runs through
    the land,
In England there shall be dear bread – in Ireland, sword and
    brand;
And poverty, and ignorance, shall swell the rich and grand,
So, rally round the rulers with the gentle iron hand,
        Of the fine old English Tory days;
        Hail to the coming time!

53

The Bishop's See

The see, the see, the Bishop's see,
That ever wealthy Bishop's see,
Without a mark, without a bound,
It feeds on all the country round;
It grinds the farmers, eats the tithes,
And like an Incubus it lies,
I'm in the see, the Bishop's see,
I am where I would ever be,
With the rich above and the poor below,
The farmers sigh where'er I go,
However hard their lot may be
What matter, what matter,
    For I'm in the Bishop's see.

I love, oh! how I love the tithe,
To see the Church and Clergy thrive;
To loll at ease from morn till noon,
Within the splendid drawing room;
While the farmers plough and sow
To make my coffers overflow.
I never see the starving poor
But I love my Bishopric more and more,
And firmly cling to its well lin'd nest,
As a child would cling to its mother's breast,
For a mother it was and is to me,
For I was born in the Bishop's see.

The sky was black, and wet the morn,
In the noisy hour when I was born;
The tithe pig squall'd, the thunder roll'd,
The cattle bellowed in the fold;

And never was heard such a hubbub wild
As welcom'd to life the tithe fed child;
I've liv'd since then amidst care and strife
Full fifty years a lazy life,
With wealth to spend and power to range,
And never have sought or sigh'd for change,
And Death whene'er he comes to me
Shall come to the wealthy Bishop's see.

54

The Coal-Owner and the Pitman's Wife

(*c.* 1844)

A dialogue I'll tell you as true as my life,
Between a coal-owner and a poor pitman's wife.
As she was a-travelling all on the highway,
She met a coal-owner and this she did say,
   Derry down, down, down derry down.

'Good morning, Lord Firedamp,' this woman she said,
'I'll do you no harm, sir, so don't be afraid,
If you'd been where I've been the most of my life,
You wouldn't turn pale at a poor pitman's wife.'
   Derry down, down, down derry down.

'Then where do you come from?' the owner he cries.
'I come from hell,' the poor woman replies.
'If you come from hell, then come tell me right plain,
How you contrived to get out again'.
   Derry down, down, down derry down.

'Aye, the way I got out, the truth I will tell.
They're turning the poor folk all out of hell.

This is to make room for the rich wicked race,
For there is a great number of them in that place.
  Derry down, down, down derry down.

'And the coal-owners is the next on command
To arrive in hell, as I understand,
For I heard the old devil say as I came out,
The coal-owners all had received their rout.'
  Derry down, down, down derry down.

'Then how does the old devil behave in that place?'
'Oh sir, he is cruel to that rich wicked race.
He is far more crueller than you can suppose,
Even like a mad bull with a ring through his nose.
  Derry down, down, down derry down.

'If you be a coal-owner, sir, take my advice,
Agree with your men and give them a full price.
For if and you do not, I know very well,
You'll be in great danger of going to hell.
  Derry down, down, down derry down.

'For all you coal-owners great fortunes has made,
By those jovial men that works in the coal trade.
Now, how can you think for to prosper and thrive
By wanting to starve your poor workmen alive?'
  Derry down, down, down derry down.

'Good woman,' says he, 'I must bid you farewell.
You give me a dismal account about hell.
If this be all true that you say unto me,
I'll go home and with my poor men I'll agree.'
  Derry down, down, down derry down.

So all you gay gentlemen with riches in store,
Take my advice and be good to the poor.

And if you do this, all things will gan well,
And perhaps it will save you from going to hell.
  Derry down, down, down derry down.

So come ye poor pitmen and join heart and hand,
For when you're off work, all trade's at a stand.
In the town of Newcastle all cry out amain:
'Oh, gin the pits were at work once again!'
  Derry down, down, down derry down.

Well the pit gates are locked, little more I've to say,
I was turned out of my house on the thirteenth of May,
But it's now to conclude and I'll finish my song,
I hope you'll relieve me and let me carry on.
  Derry down, down, down derry down.

55

The Song of the Lower Classes

BY ERNEST JONES

*Music by John Lowry. This Song can also be sung to the air of
'The Monks of Old'*

(*c.* 1848)

We plough and sow – we're so very, very low,
  That we delve in the dirty clay,
Till we bless the plain – with the golden grain,
  And the vale with the fragrant hay,
Our place we know, – we're so very low,
  'Tis down at the landlord's feet:
We're not too low – the bread to grow,
  But too low the bread to eat.

Down, down we go, – we're so very low,
    To the hell of the deep sunk mines,
But we gather the proudest gems that glow,
    When the crown of a despot shines.
And whenever he lacks – upon our backs
    Fresh loads he deigns to lay:
We're far too low to vote the tax,
    But not too low to pay.

We're low – we're low – mere rabble, we know
    But, at our plastic power,
The mould at the lordling's feet will grow
    Into palace and church and tower.
Then prostrate fall – in the rich man's hall,
    And cringe at the rich man's door;
We're not too low to build the wall,
    But too low to tread the floor.

We're low – we're low – we're very very low,
    Yet from our fingers glide
The silken flow – and the robes that glow
    Round the limbs of the sons of pride.
And what we get – and what we give –
    We know, and we know our share;
We're not too low the cloth to weave,
    But too low the Cloth to wear!

We're low – we're low – we're very very low,
    And yet when the trumpets ring,
The thrust of a poor man's arm will go
    Thro' the heart of the proudest King.
We're low – we're low – our place we know,
    We're only the rank and file,
We're not too low – to kill the foe,
    But too low to touch the spoil.

56

The Durham Lock-Out

(1892)

In our Durham County I am sorry for to say,
That hunger and starvation is increasing every day,
For the want of food and coals, we know not what to do,
But with your kind assistance we will stand the struggle
  through.

I need not state the reason why we have been brought so
  low,
The masters have behaved unkind, which everyone will
  know;
Because we won't lie down and let them treat us as they
  like,
To punish us, they've stopped the pits and caused the
  present strike.

May every Durham colliery owner that is in the fault,
Receive nine lashes with the rod, and then be rubbed with
  salt,
May his back be thick with boils so that he may never sit,
And never burst until the wheels go round at every pit.

The pulley wheels have ceased to move which went so
  swift around,
The horses and the ponies too all brought from under-
  ground,
Our work is taken from us now, they care not if we die,
For they can eat the best of food, and drink the best when
  dry.

The miner and his wife too, each morning have to roam,
To seek for bread to feed the hungry little ones at home.
The flour barrel is empty now, their true and faithful
     friend,
Which makes the thousands wish today the strike was at an
     end.

We have done our very best as honest working men.
To let the pits commence again, we've offered to them ten.
The offer they will not accept, they firmly do demand
Thirteen and a half per cent, or let the collieries stand.

Let them stand or let them lie or do with them as they
     choose,
To give them thirteen and a half we ever shall refuse.
They're always willing to receive, but not inclined to give.
Very soon they won't allow a working man to live.

With tyranny and capital they never seem content,
Unless they are endeavouring to take from us per cent.
If it was due, what they request, we willingly would grant;
We know it's not, therefore we cannot give them what
     they want.

The miners of Northumberland we shall for ever praise,
For being so kind in helping us those tyrannising days.
We thank the other countries too, that have been doing the
     same,
For every man who hears this song will know we're not
     to blame.

THREE

MANNERS AND FASHIONS

57

Turners Dish of Lentten Stuffe

OR

A Galymaufery

To the Tune of 'Watton Townes end'

BY WILLIAM TURNER

(1612)

My Maisters all attend you,
  if mirth you love to heare:
And I will tell you what they cry,
  in London all the yeare.
Ile please you if I can,
  I will not be too long,
I pray you all attend a while,
  and lissen to my song.

The fish-wife first begins,
  nye Musckles lylly white:
Hearings, Sprats, or Pleace,
  or Cockles for delight.
Nye welflet Oysters:
  then she doth change her note,
She had need to hane her tongue by grease
  for she rattles in the throat.

For why they are but Kentish,
  to tell you out of doubt:

[*nye = any*

191

Her measure is to little,
   go beate the bottom out.
Halfe a Pecke for two pence,
   I doubt it is a bodge,
[bodge = half a peck
Thus all the citty over,
   the people they do dodge.

The wench that cries the Kitchin stuffe,
   I marvell what she ayle:
She sings her note so merry,
   but she has a dragle taile,
An empty Car came running,
   and hit her on the bum,
Downe she threw her greasie tub,
   and away that she did run.

But she did give a blessing,
   to some but not to all:
To beare a loade to Tyburne,
   and there to let it fall,
The miller with his golden thumbe,
   and his dusty necke:
If that he grind but two bushels,
   he needs must steale a peck.

The Weaver and the Tayler,
   cozens they be sure:
They cannot worke but they must steale,
[ure = use, practice
   to keepe their hands in ure,
For it is a common proverbe,
   throughout all the towne,
The Taylor he must cut three sleeves,
   for every womans gowne.

Marke but the Water man,
   attending for his fare:

Of hot and could, of wet and dry,
   he alwaies takes a share.
He carrieth bony lasses,
   over to the plaies,
And here and there he gets a bit,
   and that his stomake staies.

There was a slinging boy,
   did write to ride to Rumford:
When I go to my close stoole,
   I will put him in a comfort:
But what I leave behind,
   shall be no private gaine:
But all is one when I am gone,
   let him take it for his paine.

Ould shoes for new Broomes,
   the broome man he doth sing:
For hats or caps or buskins,
   or any ould Pooch rings.
⟨Buy⟩ a mat, a bed Mat,
   ⟨a pad⟩lock or a Pas,
A cover for a close stoole,
   a bigger or a lesse.

Ripe Chery ripe,
   the Coster-monger cries,
Pipins fine, or Peares,
   another after hies,
With basket on his head,
   his living to advance,
And in his purse a paire of Dice,
   for to play at Mumchance.

Hot Pippin pies,
   to sell unto my friends:

Or puding pies in pans,
   well stuft with Candles ends,
Will you buy any Milke,
   I heare a wench that cries,
With a paile of fresh Cheese and creame,
   another after hies.

Oh the wench went neately,
   my thought it did me good:
To see her cheery cheekes,
   so dimpled ore with blood,
Her wastecoate washed white:
   as any lilly flower,
would I had time to talke with her
   the space of halfe an houre.

Buy blacke, saith the blacking man
   the best that ere was seene:
Tis good for poore men Cittizens
   to make their shooes to shine,
Oh tis a rare comodity,
   it must not be for-got,
It will make them glister gallantly
   and quickly make them rot.

The world is ful of thredbare poets,
   that live upon their pen:
But they will write too eloquent,
   they are such witty men.
But the Tinker with his budget,
   and begger with his wallet,
And *Turners* turnd a gallant man,
   at making of a Ballet.

Imprinted at London for I. W.

58

The Journey into France

(*c.* 1623)

I came from *England* into *France*
Neither to learne to crindge, nor dance,
    Nor yett to ride, nor fence;
Not for to doe such things as those,
Who have return'd without a nose,
    They carried out from hence.

But I to Paris rode along,
Much like *John Dory* in the Song,
    Upon a holy tide:
I on an ambling nagg did gett,
I hope itt is not paid for yett,
    I spurr'd him on each side.

And to *St Denis* first wee came
To see the sights at *Nostredame*,
    The man that shews them snuffles:
Where who is apt for to beleive,
May see our Ladies right hand sleeve,
    And her old Pantofles.

Her Haire, her Milke, her very Gowne,
Which shee did weare in *Bethleem* Towne,
    When in the Inne shee lay:
Yet all the World know's that's a Fable,
For so good clothes ne're lay in Stable
    Upon a lock of Hay.

No Carpenter could by his trade,
Gaine so much wealth as to have made
    A Gowne of so rich stuffe:
Yet they (poore Fooles) thinke for Her creditt,
They must, beleive old *Joseph* did itt,
    'Cause Shee deserv'd enough.

There is the Lanthorne, which the *Jewes*
(When Judas ledd them foorth) did use,
    Itt weighs my weight downe right:
But to beleive itt you must thinke,
The *Jewes* did putt a candle in't,
    And then 'twas wondrous light.

There is one of the Crosses Nailes,
Which who so sees his Bonnett vailes,
    And if hee list may kneele:
Some say it's false, 'twas never so,
Yet feeling itt thus much I know,
    Itt is as true as Steele.

There's one Saint there hath lost his Toes,
Another his Head, but not his Nose,
    A Finger and a Thumbe:
Now when wee had seene these holy raggs,
Wee went to th'Inne and tooke our naggs,
    And so away did come.

Wee came to *Paris* on the *Seane*,
It's wondrous Faire, but nothing Cleane,
    'Tis *Europes* Greatest Towne:
How strong itt is I need not tell itt,
For all the world may easily smell itt,
    That walke itt upp and down.

There's many strange things for to see,
The Hospital, the Gallery,
    The Place Roiall doth excell:

The New bridge and the Statues there,
At *Nostre-Dame St Christopher,*
     The Steeple beares the Bell.

For Learning the University,
And for old Clothes the Frippery,
     The House the Queene did build:
St Innocents, whose Earth devoures,
Dead corps in foure and twenty houres,
     And there the King was kill'd.

The *Bastile,* and *St. Dennis* sheete,
The *Shateele* much like *London* Fleete,
     The *Arsenall,* no toy:
But if you'le see the prettiest thing,
Go to the Court and see the King,
     Itt is a hopefull boy.

Hee is by all his Dukes and Peeres,
Reverencd as much for Witt as Yeares,
     Nor must you thinke itt much:
For Hee with little switch doth play,
And can make fine durt pies of clay,
     Oh never King made such.

A Bird that can but catch a fly,
Or prate, doth please his Majesty,
     'Tis knowne to every one:
The *Duke de Guise* gave him a Parrett,
And hee had twenty canons for itt,
     For his new Galeon.

Oh that I e're might have the happ,
To get the Bird which in the Mapp
     Wee call the *Indian Ruck:*

I'de give itt Him, and looke to bee
As Great and Wise as *Luinee*,
      Or else I had ill luck.

Birds round about his chamber stand,
And hee them feeds with his owne hand,
      'Tis his humility:
And if they doe lack anything,
They may but whistle for the King,
      And hee comes presently.

Now for these vertuous parts hee must
Entitled bee *Lewis the Just*,
      Great Henries rightfull Heire:
When to his Stile to adde more words,
You may better call Him King of Birds,
      Instead of lost *Navarre*.

Hee hath beside a pretty firke,
Taught him by Nature for to worke
      In yron with great ease:
Sometimes unto his forge hee goes,
And there hee puffs and there hee blows,
      And makes both Locks and Keies.

Which putts a doubt in every one,
Whether hee were *Mars* or *Vulcans* sonne,
      Some few ⟨suspect⟩ his Mother:
Yet let them all say what they will,
I am resolv'd and will thinke still,
      As much the t'one as t'other.

His Queene's a pretty little Wench,
But borne in Spaine, speaks little French,
      Shee's ne're like to bee Mother:

For her incestuous house could not
Have any children but begott
     By Uncle or by Brother.

Now why should *Lewis* being so *Just*
Content himselfe to take his lust,
     On his Luina's mate:
And suffer his pretty little Queene,
From all her race that yett hath beene,
     So to degenerate.

'Twere Charity for to bee knowne,
To love others children as his owne,
     And keepe them; 'Tis no shame;
Unles that hee would greater bee,
Then was his Father King *Henry*,
     Who (men thought) did the same.

59

The Innocent Country-Maid's Delight

OR

A Description of the Lives of the Lasses of London

Some Lasses are nice and strange,
That keep shop in the *Exchange*,
    Sit pricking of clouts,
    And giving of flouts,
  And seldom abroad do range:
    Then comes the Green Sickness,
    And changes their likeness,
  And all for want of Sale;
But 'tis not so, with we that go,
Through frost and snow, when winds do blow,
  To carry the milking-payl.

Each Lass she will paint her face,
To seem with a comely grace,
    And powder their hair,
    To make them look fair,
  That Gallants may them embrace:
    But every morning,
    Before their adorning,
  They're far unfit for Sale;
But 'tis not so, etc.

The more to appear in pride,
They often in coaches ride,
    Drest up in their knots,
    Their jewels and spots,
  And twenty knick-knacks beside:
    Their Gallants embrace 'em,
    At length they disgrace 'em,
  And then they weep and wail;
But 'tis not so, etc.

There's nothing they prize above,
The delicate Charms of Love,
They kiss and they Court, they're right for the Sport,
No way like the Turtle-dove:
    For they are for any,
    Not one, but a many,
  At length they spoyl their Sale;
But 'tis not so, etc.

They feed upon Dainties fine,
Their Liquor is curious Wine,
If any will lend, they'l borrow and spend,
  And this is a perfect sign
    That they are for pleasure,
    Whilst wasting their treasure,
  And then they may to Jayl;
But 'tis not so, etc.

They sit at their windows all day,
Drest up like your Ladies gay,
They prattle and talk, but seldom they walk,
   Their Work is no more than play:
      They living so easy,
      Their Stomachs are squesie,
    They know not what they ail;
But 'tis not so, etc.

When e're they have been too free,
And happen with child to be,
The Doctor, be sure, is sent for to cure
   This two-legged tympany:
      And thus the physician
      Must hide their condition,
    For fear they spoyl their sale,
But 'tis not so, etc.

There's *Margery, Ciss* and *Prue,*
Right country girls and true,
Nay *Bridget* and *Jane,* full well it is known,
   They'l dabble it in the dew:
      They trip it together,
      And fear not the weather,
    Although both rain and hail:
Full well you know, away we go,
Through frost and snow, when winds do blow,
   To carry the milking-payl.

60

The Man in the Moon drinks Clarret

As it was lately sung at the Curtain, Holy-Well

Bacchus, the father of drunken Nowls,
Full Mazers, Beakers, Glasses, Bowls,
Greasie flapdragons, Flemish upsie freeze,
With health tap'd in arms, upon naked knees;
Of all his wines he makes you tasters,
So you tipple like bumbasters.
Drink till you reel, a welcome he doth give;
O how the boon claret, makes you live!
Not a painter purer colour shows
   Than what's laid on by claret,
Pearl and ruby doth set out the nose,
    When thin small beer doth mar it;
     Rich wine is good, it heats the blood,
    It makes an old man lusty,
     The young to brawl, and the Drawers call,
    Before being too much musty.
Whether you drink all or little,
Pot it so your selves to whittle:
   Then though twelve a Clock it be,
Yet all the way go roaring,
   If the band of Bills cry 'Stand!'
Swear that you must a ⟨-⟩ Who ⟨-ring⟩
   Such gambols, such tricks, such fegaries,
   We fetch, though we touch no canaries:
   Drink wine till the welkin roars,
   And cry out A pox of your Scores.

In wine we call for bawdy Jiggs,
Catzoes, rumbillows, whirligigs;
Campo get in Huff-Cup vain,

The devill in the places you ⟨'d⟩ wot were raign.
Brave wine it thus tickles our Heels,
Mull'd well in wine, none sorrow feels.
Our Moon man and his powder-beef mad crew
Thus caper through the liquor sweet turnip drew.
Round about, over tables and joint stools,
   Let's dance with naked rapiers:
Cut the fiddle strings, and then like fools
   Kick out the fum-fum scrapers.
There is no sound that cares can wound
   As lids of wine-pots clinking;
There's no such sport, when all amort,
   Men cry Let's fall to drinking.
O 'tis nappy Gear,
Would each belly was filled here,
   Herrings pickled must be tickled
Down to draw the liquor,
   The salt Sammon and fat Gammon,
Makes our wine drink quicker.
   Our Man in the Moon drinks Clarret,
   With powder-beef turnep and carret,
   If he doth so, why should not you
   Drink until the sky looks blew.

Hey for a turn thus above Ground,
O, my noddle too heavy doth weigh,
Metheglin, Perry, Sider, nor strong ale,
Are half so heavy, be they nere so stale.
Wine in our guts can never rumble,
Down, now and then, tho' it makes us tumble;
Yet, scrambling up, a drunkard feels no pain,
But crys Sirrah hoy, t'other pottle againe.
We can drink no more unlesse we have
   Full pipes of Trinnidado,
Gives us the best, it keeps our brains
   More warm than does freezado.

It makes us sing, and cry Hey ding,
   And laugh when Pipes lie broken,
For which to pay at going away,
   We scorn a Mustard token;
Never curse the saucy Score,
Outswear the bar You'll pay no more;
   In these daies he is no Gallant
That cannot puff and swagger;
   Though he dare not kill a sheep,
Yet out must flie his dagger:
   If then you do love my Hosts Clarret,
   Fat powder-beef, turnep, and carret,
   Come again and again,
   And still welcome, Gentlemen.

61

The Old Man's Wish

   The Old Man he doth wish for Wealth in vain,
     But he doth not the Treasure gain;
   For if with Wishes he the same could have,
     He would not mind nor think upon the Grave.

BY WALTER POPE

If I live to grow old (for I find I go down),
Let this be my fate in a Country Town;
Let me have a warm House, with a Stone at the Gate,
And a cleanly young Girl to rub my bald Pate:
   May I govern my passion with an absolute sway,
   And grow wiser and better, as my strength wears away,
   Without Gout or Stone, by a gentle Decay.

In a Country Town, by a murmuring Brook,
The Ocean at distance, on which I may look;
With a spacious Plain, without Hedge or Stile,
And an easy Pad-nagg to ride out a Mile:
   May I govern etc.

With a pudding on *Sunday*, and stout humming Liquor,
And Remnants of *Latine* to puzzle the Vicar;
With a hidden reserve of *Burgundy*-wine,
To drink the King's Health as oft as I dine:
   May I govern etc.

With *Plutarch*, and *Horace*, and one or two more
Of the best Wits that liv'd in the ages before;
With a dish of Roast Mutton, not Venison nor Teal,
And clean (tho' coarse) Linnen at every meal;
   May I govern etc.

And if I should have Guests, I must add to my Wish,
On *Frydays* a Mess of good buttered fish;
For full well I do know, and the truth I reveal,
I had better do so, then come short of a Meal:
   May I govern etc.

With Breeches and Jerkin of good Country Gray,
And live without Working, now my strength doth
   decay:
With a hog's-head of Sherry, for to drink when I please,
With Friends to be merry, and to live at my ease;
   May I govern etc.

Without Molestation may I spend my last Days,
In sweet Recreation, and sound forth the Praise
Of all those that are true to the King and his Laws,
Since it be their due, they shall have my Applause:
   May I govern etc.

With a country Scribe for to write my last Will,

[chousing = cheating

But not of the tribe that in chousing have skill:
For my easie Pad-nagg I'll bequeath to *Don John*,
For he's an arch wag, and a jolly old man:
 May I govern etc.

With Courage undaunted may I face my last Day;
And when I am dead, may the better sort say,
In the Morning when sober, in the Evening when
 mellow,
He is gone, and has left not behind him his Fellow:
 For he govern'd his passion with an absolute sway,
 And grew wiser and better as his strength wore away,
 Without Gout or Stone, by a gentle Decay.

62

Advice to the Ladies of London in the choice of their Husbands

To an excellent New Court Tune

Ladies of London, both wealthy and fair,
 Whom every Town Fop is pursuing,
Still of your Persons and Purses take care
 The greatest deceit lies in wooing.
From the first rank of the bonny brisk sparks,
 Their Vices I here will discover,
Down to the basest mechanick Degree,
 That so you may chuse out your Lover.

First for the Courtier, look to his Estate,
 Before he too far be proceeding;
He of Court Favours and Places will prate,
 And settlements make of his breeding:

Nor wear the yoak with dull Country Clown,
   Who, though they are fat in their Purses,
Brush you with Brissles and, toping full Fowl,   [broadside:
   Make Love to their Dogs and their Horses.   '*Fowls*'

But, above all, the rank Citizen hate;
   The Court or the Country chuse rather;
Would you have a Blockhead that gets an Estate,
   By the Sins of the Cuckold his Father?
The sneaking Clown intreaguing does mar,
   The apprentices huffing and ranting:
Cit. puts on his Sword when without Temple-Bar,
   To go to Whitehall a gallanting.

Let no spruce Officer keep you in awe,
   The Sword is a thing Transitory;
Nor be blown up by the Lungs of the Law,
   A World has been cheated before you:
Soon you will find your Captain grow bold,
   And then 'twill be hard to o'ercome him;
But if the Lawyer touch your Copy-hold,
   The Devil will ne'er get it from him.

Fly, like the Plague, the huffing brave Boys,
   That Court you with lying Bravadoes,
Tyring your senses with Bombast and Noise,
   And Stories brought from the Barbadoes.
And be sure ever shun the Doctor, that Fool,
   Who seeking to mend your Condition,
Tickles your Pulse, and peeps in your Close-stool,
   Then sets up ⟨for⟩ a famous Physitian.

Chuse not a spark that has known the town,
   Who makes it his Practice to Bully;
You'd better take up with a country clown,
   He'l make an officious cully.

You with a word may his Passion appease
  And make him a Cuckold at leasure,
Give him but money to live at his ease,
  You may follow Intregues at your Pleasure.

Neither admire much a man that is wise
  If e're you intend to deceive him,
He cunning plots and intreagues will devise
  And trap you, e're you shall perceive him;
Therefore beware that he never disclose
  Your tricks, if he do's he will slight you;
He'l keep a gay mistriss under your nose
  If it be but on purpose to spight you.

But if you'd thrive, and grow wealthy apace,
  Then marry a doting old sinner;
What if you view there Old Time in his face,
  You will by that bargain be winner.
You may have lusty Gallants good store,
  If you can produce but th' Guinea,
And those young coxcombs your face will adore
  If this don't please, old Nick is in you.

63

The Beau's Receipt for a Lady's Dress

Hang a small bugle cap on, as big as a crown,
Snout it off with a flow'r, vulgo dict, a Pompoun,

Let your powder be gay, and braid up your hair,
Like the mane of a colt to be sold at a Fair.
Like the mane etc.

A short pair of jumps, half an ell from your chin,
To make you appear as one just lying-in;
Before your brest pin a stomacher bib on,
Ragout it with curlets of silver and ribbon.

Your neck and your shoulders both naked should be,
A-la-mode de Vandyke, bloun with chevaux de frize,
Let your goun be a sack, blue, yellow or green,
And frizzle your elbous with ruffles sixteen.

Furl off your lawn apron with flounces in rows,
Puff and pucker up knots on your arms and your toes,
Make your petticoats short, that a hoop 8 yards wide
May decently shew how your garters are ty'd.

With fringes of knotting your dicky cabob,
On slippers of velvet set gold a-la-daube;
But mount on French heels when you go to a ball,
'Tis the fashion to totter, and show you can fall.
Throw modesty out from your manners and face,
A la-mode de francois, you're a bit for his grace.

64

The Lady's Receipt for a Beau's Dress

Since, Sir, you have made it your study to vex,
And audaciously laugh at the dress of our sex,
Pray don't be so blind at the faults of your own,
But let them, I say, in the next lines be shewn.

Instead of small caps, you must then add small wigs,
The tail of which mostly resembles a pig's;
Put a hat upon that and point it up high,
Just like to an arrow that's aim'd at the sky.

At the Corner of which, I pray don't forget,
Hang a tassel of silver, to make it compleat;
Let the stock be well plaited, in fanciful forms,
While a fine diamond heart, the shirt bosom adorns.

Let the sword-hilt be cover'd with ribbon good store,
Lest the roughness around make the tender hand sore;
Yet no need is for that, for they'll certainly fly
The place where they think any danger is nigh.

His coat is to be but a foot from his waist,
And fix'd as light too as if it were lac'd;
In his pocket a housewife and pin cushion place,
Nor forgetting a glass to show his sweet face.

With stockings of his silk, nothing less such can please,
Bind his legs round with silver an inch above knees,
Hang a tassel to that, or else it won't do,
And in length it must reach half way to his shoe.

His bright buckles of stone, of five guineas price,
To adorn his neat feet, and make him more nice:
Thus drest and equipt, tis plain to be seen,
He's not one jot better than monsieur Pantin.

65

London is a Fine Town

O London is a dainty place,
  A great and gallant city!
For all the Streets are pav'd with gold,
  And all the folks are witty.
And there's your lords and ladies fine,
  That ride in coach and six;
That nothing drink but claret wine,
  And talk of politicks.

And there's your beaux with powder'd clothes,
  Bedaub'd from head to chin;
Their pocket-holes adorned with gold,
  But not one sous within.
And there the English actor goes
  With many a hungry belly;
While heaps of gold are forc'd, God wot,
  On Signor Farinelli.

And there's your dames with dainty frames,
  With skins as white as milk;
Dressed every day in garments gay,
  Of satin and of silk.
And if your mind be so inclined
  To offer them your arm,
Pull out a handsome purse of gold,
  They can't resist the charm.

66

A New Song called The Curling of the Hair

You Ladies all that are in Fashion;
Both here and every where'o,
Who tells bright Beaus by love-sick Passion
By buckling of their Hair'o.
    Tal, la &c

The Ladies Maid well immitates,
The Mistress in the Fair'o,
The Footman with his Curling Irons,
To Buckle and Curl her Hair'o.

There's Mistress Betty, a beautiful Lady,
Her Fortune one hundred a Year'o,
She longs o'the Squire and begs of her Mamy
To Buckle and Curl her Hair'o.

The Mantua maker and modest Quaker,
They all must have a Share'o,
In hopes to get some lover True,
And charm some busy young Hair'o.

The Chimney Sweepers Daughter Sue,
She swears she'll drive up the Rear'o
And tho' she's neither stocking or shoe
She'll Buckle and Curl her Hair'o.

Te-re Re-re, my Rump-Itches
Te-re Re-re, where'o
Here and there and everywhere
And amongst the Tuft of Hair'o.

The Collier has a beautiful Daughter,
She swears she'll drive up the Rear'o
Tho' she has not a Smock to cover her garter
She'll Buckle and Curl her Hair'o.

There's Huge Matees and Sugar Loaf laps
With nice Clock Stockings a Pair-o;
And Hoops there are of a Monstrous size,
I long to stick a pin there'o.

I've got never a Penny of Money,
Nor never a Smock to wear'o;
Nor never a Rag to cover my C—
But one poor Tuft of Hair'o.

My Daddy left me twice Ten Pounds,
My Mammy a Horse and Mair'o
But never a lad that ever I found,
Was able to Curl my Hair'o.

67

The Dandy O

I'm a fashionable beau, just turn'd out the newest go,
So elegant, so exquisite, so handy O;
My tiptop stile of dress, my shape, my air, my face
All prove beyond compare that I'm a Dandy O.

A skeleton's the taste, five inches round the waist,
My body-belt tight buckled in so handy O,,
My pantaloon cossacks puff'd and swelled out like sacks,
I'm sure from head to toe I'm quite a Dandy O.

Now do but view my coat, for 'tis meet that you should
    know,
My bosom here so beautiful so handy O:
My hair quite flat at top, thick and bushy like a mop,
My neck a foot in length, I'm all the Dandy O.

My stays are lac'd so tight, that I'm forc'd to walk
    upright,
My chin pok'd out, my neck-cloth stiff and handy O,
My whiskers neatly trimm'd, and my hat so narrow
    rimm'd,
My spurs are all the kick, I'm quite a Dandy O.

You see I've got the swell of Bond-street and Pall Mall,
For quizzing all, and cutting some, so handy O.
I lounge from street to street, as my brother swells I
    meet,
Some stare, but all declare that I'm a Dandy O.

At op'ra, rout, and play, then I hear the ladies say,
'How stilish! lud, how handsome, how handy O,
He's got the Bond-street swing, I declare he's quite the
    thing,
Do, do but see! now is'nt he a Dandy O.'

Pretending not to hear, then I modestly draw near
My ribbon sport, my rings display, so handy O.
I read it in their eyes, and I hear it in their sighs,
The ladies all are dying for the Dandy O.

*W. Collard, printer, Bridewell-Lane, Bristol, and
Hotwell-road, where travellers, &c., may be supplied.*

FOUR

SOLDIERS, SAILORS, HIGHWAYMEN, AND POACHERS

68

The Maunding Souldier
OR
The Fruits of Warre is Beggery

Good, your worship, cast your eyes
Upon a Souldier's miseries;
Let not my leane cheekes, I pray,
Your bounty from a Souldier stay,
   but, like a Noble friend,
    some Silver lend,
and Jove shall pay you in the end:
    and I will pray that Fate
    may make you fortunate
in heavenly, and in Earth's, estate.

To beg I was not borne (sweet Sir)
And therefore blush to make this stirre;
I never went from place to place
For to divulge my wofull case:
    for I am none of those
    that roguing goes,
that, maunding, shewes their drunken
     blowes,
    which they have onely got
    while they have bang'd the pot
in wrangling who should pay the shot.

*[Maunding =
begging*

I scorne to make comparison
With those of Kent-street Garrison,

That in their lives nere crost the seas,
But still at home have lived at ease;
   yet will they lye and sweare,
   as though they were
men that had travel'd farre and neere;
   true souldiers' company
   doth teach them how to lye;
they can discourse most perfectly.

But I doe scorne such counterfaits
That get their meanes by base deceits:
They learne of others to speake Dutch;
Of Holland they'l tell you as much
   as those that have bin there
   full many a yeere,
and name the townes all farre and neere;
   yet they never went
   beyond Graves-end in Kent,
but in Kent-*street* their dayes are spent.

⟨They⟩ in Olympicke games have beene,
Whereas brave battels I have seene;
And where the Cannon use to roare
My proper spheare was evermore:
   the danger I have past,
   both first and last,
would make your worship's selfe agast;
   a thousand times I have
   been ready for the grave;
three times I have been made a Slave.

Twice through the bulke I have been shot;
My braines have boylèd like a pot:
I have at lest these doozen times

[They, broadside: But

216

Been blowne up by those roguish mines
   under a barracado,
   in a bravado,
throwing of a hand-grenado:
   Oh death was very neere,
   for it tooke away my eare,
and yet (thanke God) cham here, cham here.   *[cham = I am*

THE SECOND PART

I have uppon the Seas been tane
By th' Dunkerks, for the King of Spaine,
And stript out of my garments quite,
Exchanging all for canvis white;
   And in that poore aray
   For many a day
I have been kept, till friends did pay
   A ransome for release;
   And having bought my peace,
My woes againe did fresh increase.

There's no land-service as you can name
But I have been actor in the same;
In th' Palatinate and Bohemia
I served many a wofull day;
   At Frankendale I have,
   Like a Souldier brave,
Receiv'd what welcomes canons gave;
   For the honour of England
   Most stoutly did I stand
'Gainst the Emperour's and Spinolae's Band.

At push of Pike I lost mine eye;
At Bergen Siege I broke my thigh;
At Ostend, though I were a lad,

217

I laid about me as I were mad.
　Oh you would little ween
　That I had been
An old, old souldier to the Queene;
　But if Sir Francis Vere
　Were living now and here,
Hee'd tell you how I slasht it there.

Since that, I have been in Breda
Besieg'd by Marquesse Spinola;
And since that made a warlike dance
Both into Spaine, and into France;
　And there I lost a flood
　Of Noble blood,
And did but very little good:
　And now I home am come,
　With ragges about my bumme,
God bless you, Sir, from this poore summe!

And now my case you understand,
Good Sir, will you lend your helping hand,
A little thing will pleasure me,
And keepe in use your charity:
　It is not bread nor cheese,
　Nor barrell lees,
Nor any scraps of meat, like these;
　But I doe beg of you
　A shilling or two,
Sweet Sir, your purse's strings undoe.

I pray your worship, thinke on me,
That am what I doe seeme to be,
No rooking rascall, nor no cheat,

But a Souldier every way compleat;
   I have wounds to show
   That prove 'tis so;
Then, courteous good Sir, ease my woe;
   And I for you will pray
   Both night and day
That your substance never may decay.

69

The Souldiers Farewel to his Love

Being a Dialogue betwixt Thomas and Margaret

To a Pleasant New Tune

(1624)

THOMAS
   Margaret my sweetest, Margaret I must go.
MARGARET
   Most dear to me, that never may be so:
T. Ah, Fortune wills it, I cannot it deny.
M. Then know my love your Margaret must dye.

T. Not for the gold my Love that *Croesus* had,
   Would I once see thy sweetest looks so sad.
M. Nor for all that the which my eye did see,
   Would I depart my sweetest Love from thee.

T. The King commands, & I must to the wars.
M. Ther's others more enough may end the jars.
T. But I for one commanded am to go,
   And for my life I dare not once say no.

M. Ah marry me, and you shall stay at home,
   Full thirty weeks you know that I have gone.

T. There's time enough another for to take
   He'l love thee well, and not thy child forsake.

M. And have I doted on thy sweetest face?
   and dost infringe that which thou suedst in chase.
   Thy faith I mean but I will wend with thee.
T. It is too far for Peg to go with me.

M. I'le go with thee my Love both night and day.
   I'le bear thy sword, i'le run and lead the way.
T. But we must ride, how will you follow then,
   Amongst a Troop of us thats Armed men?

M. Ile bear the Lance, ile guide thy stirrop too,
   Ile rub the horse, and more then that ile do.
T. But Margarets fingers they are all too fine,
   To wait on me when she doth see me dine.

M. Ile see you dine, ile wait still at your back,
   Ile give you wine, or any thing you lack.
T. But youl repine when you shall see me have
   A dainty wench that is both fine and brave.

M. Ile love your wench, my sweetest, I do vow,
   I'le watch time when she may pleasure you.
T. But you will grieve to see me sleep in bed,
   And you must wait still in anothers stead.

M. I'le watch my love to see you sleep in rest,
   And when you sleep then I shall think me blest.
T. The time will come you must delivered be,
   If in the Camp it will discredit me.

M. I'le go from you before the time shall be,
   When all is well my love againe ile see.
T. All will not serve for Margaret must not go,
   Then do resolve my Love, what else to do.

M. If nought wil serve why then sweet love adieu.
      I needs must die, and yet in dying true.
T. Nay stay my love, for I love Margaret well,
      And here I vow with Margaret to dwell.

M. Give me your hand, your Margaret livs again.
T. Here is my hand, ile never breed thy pain.
M. I'le kiss my love in token it is so.
T. We will be wed, come Margaret let us go.

70

Saylors for my Money

A new Ditty composed in the praise of Saylors and Sea
affaires, breifly shewing the nature of so worthy a calling, and
effects of their industry,

To the Tune of 'The Joviall Cobbler'

BY MARTIN PARKER

Countrie men of *England*, who live at home with ease,
And little thinke what dangers are incident o' th' Seas:
Give eare unto the Saylor who unto you will shew
   His case, his case: *How ere the winde doth blow.*

He that is a Saylor must have a valiant heart,
For, when he is upon the sea, he is not like to start;
But must, with noble courage, all dangers undergoe:
   Resolve, resolve: *How e're the wind doth blow.*

Our calling is laborious, and subject to much ⟨care⟩;   [*care*:
But we must still contented be, with what falls to our   broadside,
   share.   *woe*
We must not be faint-hearted, come tempest, raine or
   snow,
   Nor shrinke: nor shrinke: *How e're the winde doth blowe.*

Sometimes on *Neptune's* bosome our ship is tost with
    waves,
And every minute we expect the sea must be our graves,
Sometimes on high she moŭteth, then falls againe as low:
  With waves: with waves: *When stormie winds do blow.*

Then with unfained prayers, as Christian duty bindes,
Wée turne unto ye Lord of hosts, with all our hearts and
    minds;
To Him we flie for succour, for He, we surely know,
  Can save: can save, *How ere the wind doth blow.*

Then He who breaks the rage, the rough and blustrous seas,
When His disciples were afraid, will straight ye stormes
    apease.
And give us cause to thanke, on bended knees full low:
  Who saves: who saves, *How ere the wind doth blow.*

Our enemies approaching, when wée on sea espie,
Wée must resolve incontinent to fight, although we die,
With noble resolution we must oppose our foe,
    In fight, in fight: *How ere the wind do⟨e⟩s blow.*

And when by God's assistance, our foes are put to th' foile
To animate our courages, wee all have share o' th' spoile.
Our foes into the ocean we back to back do throw,
    To sinke, or swimme, *How ere the wind doth blow.*

THE SECOND PART, TO THE SAME TUNE

Thus wée gallant Sea-men, in midst of greatest dangers,
Doe alwaies prove our valour, wée never are no changers:
But what soe ere betide us, wée stoutly undergoe,
    Resolv'd, resolv'd, *How ere the wind doth blow.*

If fortune doe befriend us, in what we take in hand,
Wée prove our selves still generous whē ere we come to
    land,
Ther's few yt shall out brave us, though neere so great in
    show,
    Wée spend, and lend, *How ere the wind doth blow.*

We travell to the *Indies,* from them we bring som spice,
Here we buy rich Merchandise at very little price.
And many wealthy prizes, we conquer from the foe:
    In fight: in fight, *How ere the wind doth blow.*

Into our native Country, with wealth we doe returne:
And cheere our wives and childrē, who for our absence
    mourne.
Then doe we bravely flourish, and where so ere we goe,
    We roare: we roare: *How ere the wind doth blow.*

For when we have received our wages for our paynes,
The Vintners and the Tapsters by us have golden gaines
We call for liquor roundly, and pay before we goe:
    And sing: and drink, *How ere the wind doth blow.*

Wée bravely are respected, when we walke up and downe,
For if wee méete good company, wee care not for a
    crowne,
Ther's none more free than saylors, where ere he come or
    goe,
    Tho' he'll roare o' th' shore, *How ere the winde doth blow.*

Then who would live in *England* and no⟨u⟩rish vice with
    ease,
When hée that is in povertie may riches get o' th' seas?
Let's saile unto the *Indies,* where golden grass doth grow:
    To sea, to sea, *How ere the wind doth blow.*

71

The Jovial Marriner

OR

The Sea-man's Renown

Sail forth, bold Sea-men, plough the liquid main;
Fear neither Storms nor Pirats, strive for gain;
Whilst others sleep at home in a whole skin,
Your brave adventures shall great honours win.

To the tune of 'I am a Jovial Batchelor', etc.

BY JOHN PLAYFORD

I am a Jovial Marriner, our calling is well known,
We trade with many a Foreigner to purchase high renown;
We serve our country faithfully, and bring home store of
    gold;
We do our business manfully, for we are free and bold;
  A Sea-man hath a valiant heart, and bears a noble minde;
  He scorneth once to shrink or start for any stormy wind.

'Tis known what hardships we endure abroad upon the
    seas,
Whilst others sleep at home secure, and spend their time
    in ease;
We seldom dare lie down to rest, lest danger should ensue;
Our heads with care is sore opprest: believe me it is true!
  A Sea-man hath a valiant heart, etc.

A cowardly spirit must not think to prove a Sea-man
    bold,
For to be sure he may not shrink in dangers manifold;
When Sea-fights happen on the main, and dreadful
    cannons rore,

Then all men fight, or else be slain, and Braggarts proud
    look poor.
    A Sea-man hath a valiant heart, etc.

'Tis Sea-men stout that doth deserve both honour and
    renown,
In perils great we may not swerve, though *Neptune* seem
    to frown;
If once his curled front we spy, drencht in the foamy brine,
Then each man doth his business ply, there's none that
    doth repine:
    A Sea-man hath a valiant heart, etc.

When angry billows brush the skye, most hideous to
    behold,
Then up our Ships are tost on high, and with the waves are
    roull'd;
When tempest fierce our sails doth tear, and rends the
    masts asunder,
O! then we have great cause to fear, or else it were a
    wonder:
    A Sea-man hath a valiant heart, etc.

Great Rocks which lye amongst the waves do threaten us
    with death,
And many Sea-men finde their Graves in sands which are
    beneath;
To see the masts of Ships appear, which hath been cast
    away,
Would make a Land-man dye for fear, 'tis best at home to
    stay.
    A Sea-man hath a valiant heart, etc.

Brave England hath been much inricht by art of
    Navigation;

H   225

Great store of wealth we home have fetched for to adorn
    our Nation:
Our Merchants still we do supply with Traffick that is rare,
Then Sea-men cast your caps on high, we are without
    compare.
    A Sea-man hath a valiant heart, etc.

Who should the Ladies' pallats please, with spices of the
    best,
If Sea-men all should take their ease, and stay at home to
    rest?
Our Gallants they would finde a want of silks to make
    them fine,
And tearing boyes no more would rant if once they wanted
    wine.
    A Sea-man hath a valiant heart, etc.

Our Land it would invaded be if Sea-men were not
    stout;
We let our friends come in yon sea, and keep our foes
    without;
Our privilege upon the seas we bravely do maintain,
And can enlarge it when we please in Royal *Charles* his
    Reign.
    A Sea-man hath a valiant heart, etc.

Such Countries as do lie remote doth tremble at our
    fame,
For we have taught them all to note 'tis *England* bears the
    name:
In foreign parts where ere we come our valour is well
    known,
What ere they be they dare not mumm, if we say all's our
    own:
    A Sea-man hath a valiant heart, etc.

When as our Ships with merchandize are safely come to
    shore,
No men like us under the skies to drink, to sing, and rore;
Good wine and beer we freely tope, until the ground
    look blew:
We value neither *Turk* nor *Pope*, we are a jovial crew.
    A Sea-man hath a valiant heart, etc.

We kiss our Wives when we return, who long for us did
    wait,
And he that's single needs not mourn, he cannot want a
    mate:
Young women still are wondrous kinde to Sea-men in
    their need;
And sure it shows a courteous minde to do a friendly deed.
    A Sea-man hath a valiant heart, etc.

With pretty courteous dainty knacks we please the
    females well,
We know what longing woman lacks, most surely we can
    tell;
A Sea-man is a Cock o' th' Game, young maidens find
    it true;
We never are so much to blame to let them want their due.
    A Sea-man hath a valiant heart, etc.

Thus, gallant Sea-men, I have spread abroad your high
    renown:
Which shall survive when you are dead, and gain a
    lasting Crown;
Your Praise to future ages shall most gloriously appear,
Then courage, noble Sea-men all, 'tis you I love most dear.
    A Sea-man hath a valiant heart, and bears a noble minde,
    He scorneth once to shrink or start for any stormy wind.

London. Printed for T. Passenger, on London Bridge.

72

Song

Written at Sea, in the first DUTCH WAR, 1665, the
Night before an Engagement.

BY CHARLES SACKVILLE, EARL OF DORSET

I

To all you ladies now at land
    We men at sea indite;
But first wou'd have you understand
    How hard it is to write;
The Muses now, and Neptune too,
We must implore to write to you,
    With a fa, la, la, la, la.

II

For tho' the Muses should prove kind,
    And fill our empty brain;
Yet if rough Neptune rouze the wind,
    To wave the azure main,
Our paper, pen, and ink, and we,
Roll up and down our ships at sea,
    With a fa, &c.

III

Then, if we write not by each post,
    Think not we are unkind;
Nor yet conclude our ships are lost
    By Dutchmen, or by wind:
Our tears we'll send a speedier way,
The tide shall bring 'em twice a day.
    With a fa, &c.

IV

The king with wonder, and surprize,
　　Will swear the seas grow bold;
Because the tides will higher rise,
　　Than e'er they us'd of old:
But let him know it is our tears
Bring floods of grief to Whitehall stairs.
　　With a fa, &c.

V

Should foggy Opdam chance to know　　　　　*[Dutch admiral*
　　Our sad and dismal story;
The Dutch wou'd scorn so weak a foe,
　　And quit their fort at Goree:
For what resistance can they find
From men who've left their hearts behind!
　　With a fa, &c.

VI

Let wind and weather do its worst,
　　Be you to us but kind;
Let Dutchmen vapour, Spaniards curse,
　　No sorrow we shall find:
'Tis then no matter how things go,
Or who's our friend, or who's our foe.
　　With a fa, &c.

VII

To pass our tedious hours away,
　　We throw a merry main;
Or else at serious ombre play;
　　But, why should we in vain
Each others ruin thus pursue?
We were undone when we left you.
　　With a fa, &c.

VIII

But now our fears tempestuous grow,
   And cast our hopes away;
Whilst you, regardless of our woe,
   Sit careless at a play:
Perhaps permit some happier man
To kiss your hand, or flirt your fan.
   With a fa, &c.

IX

When any mournful tune you hear,
   That dies in ev'ry note;
As if it sigh'd with each man's care,
   For being so remote;
Think then how often love we've made
To you, when all those tunes were play'd
   With a fa, &c.

X

In justice you cannot refuse,
   To think of our distress;
When we for hopes of honour lose
   Our certain happiness;
All those designs are but to prove
Ourselves more worthy of your love.
   With a fa, &c.

XI

And now we've told you all our loves,
   And likewise all our fears;
In hopes this declaration moves
   Some pity from your tears:
Let's hear of no inconstancy,
We have too much of that at sea.
   With a fa, la, la, la, la.

73

A Ballad

(1715)

'Twas when the seas were roaring
  With hollow blasts of wind;
A damsel lay deploring,
  All on a rock reclin'd.
Wide o'er the rolling billows
  She cast a wistful look;
Her head was crown'd with willows
  That tremble o'er the brook.

Twelve months are gone and over,
  And nine long tedious days.
Why didst thou, vent'rous lover,
  Why didst thou trust the seas?
Cease, cease, thou cruel ocean,
  And let my lover rest:
Ah! what's thy troubled motion
  To that within my breast?

The merchant, rob'd of pleasure,
  Sees tempests in despair;
But what's the loss of treasure
  To losing of my dear?
Should you some coast be laid on
  Where gold and di'monds grow,
You'd find a richer maiden,
  But none that loves you so.

How can they say that nature
  Has nothing made in vain;

231

Why then beneath the water
  Should hideous rocks remain?
No eyes the rocks discover,
  That lurk beneath the deep,
To wreck the·wand'ring lover,
  And leave the maid to weep.

All melancholy lying,
  Thus wail'd she for her dear;
Repay'd each blast with sighing,
  Each billow with a tear;
When, o'er the white wave stooping,
  His floating corpse she spy'd;
Then like a lily drooping,
  She bow'd her head, and dy'd.

74

Captain Death

(1757)

The muse with the hero's brave deeds being fired, –
For similar views had their bosoms inspired; –
For freedom they fought and for glory contend.
The muse o'er the hero still mourns as a friend;
Then oh! let the muse this poor tribute bequeath
To a true British hero, the brave Captain Death.

His ship was the Terrible, dreadful to see,
Each man was as gallantly brave as was he;
Two hundred and more were his good complement,
But sure braver fellows to sea never went:
Each man had determined to spend his last breath
In fighting for Britain and brave Captain Death.

A prize they had taken diminished their force,
But soon this good prize was lost on her course;
When the French man-of-war and the Terrible met,
A battle began with all horror beset.
No man was dismayed, – each as bold as Macbeth; –
In fighting for Britain and brave Captain Death.

Grenades, fire, and bullets were soon heard and felt,
A fight that the heart of Bellona would melt,
The rigging all torn, the decks filled with blood,
And scores of dead bodies were thrown in the flood; –
The flood, from the time of old Noah and Seth,
Ne'er bore the fellow of brave Captain Death.

But at length the dread bullet came wingèd with fate,
Our brave Captain dropt, and soon after his mate;
Each officer fell, and a carnage was seen,
That soon dyed the waves to crimson from green,
Then Neptune arose and pulled off his wreath,
Instructing a Triton to crown Captain Death.

Thus fell the strong Terrible, dreadfully bold,
But sixteen survivors the tale could unfold.
The French proved the victors, though much to their cost,
For many stout French were with Englishmen lost.
And thus said old Time, 'since good Queen 'Lizabeth
We ne'er saw the fellow of bold Captain Death'.

75

My Bonny Black Bess

Dick Turpin bold! Dick, hie away,
Was the cry of my pals, who were startled, I guess,
For the pistols were levelled, the bullets whizzed by,

As I leapt on the back of Black Bess.
Three Officers mounted, led forward the chase,
Resolv'd in the capture to share;
But I smil'd on their efforts, tho' swift was their pace,
As I urg'd on my bonny Black Mare.
So when I've a bumper, what can I do less,
   Than the memory drink of my bonny Black Bess?

Hark away, hark away! still onward they press,
As we saw by the glimmer of morn,
Tho' many a mile on the back of Black Bess,
That night I was gallantly borne;
Hie over, my pet, the fatigue I must bear
Well clear'd! never falter for breath,
Hark forward, my girl, my bonny Black Mare,
We speed it for life or for death.
But when I've a bumper, what can I do less,
   Than the memory drink of my bonny Black Bess?

The spires of York now burst on my view,
But the chimes, they were ringing her knell,
Halt! Halt! my brave mare, they no longer pursue,
She halted, she staggered, she fell!
Her breathing was o'er, all was hushed as the grave,
Alas! poor Black Bess, once my pride,
Her heart she had burst, her rider to save,
For Dick Turpin, she lived, and she died.
Then the memory drink of my bonny Black Bess,
Hurrah for poor bonny Black Bess!

A Shining Night

OR

Dick Daring, the Poacher

Honest regular work Dick Daring gave up,
And the day in the alehouse he spent o'er his cup
And to his pot companions he sung o'er his beer,
A shining night is my delight in the season of the year.

Tom Thoughtless too easy gave ear to his song,
Dick proposed he with him should one night go along,
And Tom gave consent for it rung in his ear.
A shining night, etc.

They jogged on together till Dick led him where,
Poor puss was caught fast in the too fatal snare
But the keepers were watching for they too would hear,
A shining night, etc.

The constables led them next morning at nine,
To the justice who laid upon each a smart fine
But unable to pay them to prison they bear,
For a shining night, etc.

In prison some months they there met with men,
More daring and wicked then they had been then
And e'en in the prison each other they'd cheer,
Oh! a shining night, etc.

Their time when expired together they sung.
And they swore and composed themselves into a gang,
And from snaring and tracing they got to steal deer,
For a shining night, etc.

But the gang was well known and the keepers all watch'd
And one in the act of deer stealing was catch'd
A hot fight ensued when they set at nought fear.
For a shining night etc.

A keeper was kill'd and his death bell was rung,
And Dick and Tom Thoughtless was ta'en tried and hung.
And the dreadful effects now too plainly appear,
On a shining night, etc.

Be advised then ye young be advised too ye old,
To soberness honesty, industry hold,
For stealing and murder may rise it is clear
From a shining night if 'tis our delight in the season of the
    year.

*Printed at J. Pitts Wholesale Toy and marble Warehouse
6, Great St Andrew Street, 7 dials.*

77

Van Dieman's Land

Come all you gallant poachers, that ramble void of care
That walk out on moonlight night with your dog, gun and
    snare,
The lofty hare and pheasants you have at your command,
Not thinking of your last career upon Van Dieman's Land.

Poor Tom Brown, from Nottingham, Jack williams, and
    Poor Joe,
we are three daring poachers, the country do well know.
At night we were trepann'd by the keepers hid in sand,
who for 14 years, transported us into Van Dieman's Land.

The first day that we landed upon that fatal shore
The planters they came round us full twenty score or more,
They rank'd us up like horses, and sold us out of hand
Then yok'd us unto ploughs, my boys, to plow Van
    Dieman's Land.

Our cottages that we live in were built of clod & clay,
And rotten straw for bedding, & we dare not say nay
Our cots were fenc'd with fire, we slumber when we can,
To drive away wolves & tigers upon Van Dieman's Land.

Its often when in slumber I have a pleasant dream
with my sweet girl a setting down by a purlin stream,
Thro' England I've been roaming with her at command
Now I awaken broken hearted upon Van Dieman's Land.

God bless our wives and families likewise the happy shore,
That isle of great contentment which we shall see no
    mor⟨e⟩
As for our wretched females, see them we seldom can,
There's twenty to one woman upon Van Dieman's Land.

There was a girl from Birmingham, Susan Summers was
    her name,
For fourteen years transported we all well know the same
Our planter bought her freedom, and married her out of
    hand
She gave to us good usage upon Van Dieman's Land.

So all young gallant poachers give ear unto my song
It is a bit of good advice, although it is not long
Throw by your dogs & snare, for to you I speak plain,
For if you knew our hardships you'd never poach again.

I. Catnach, Printer, 2 Monmouth Court, 7 Dials.

78

Lancashire Lads

It was last Monday morning as I have heard them say,
Our orders came that afternoon we were to march away,
Leaving many pretty fair maids crying alas what shall we
    do,
For the Lancashire lads are gone abroad alas what shall
    we do,
Says the mother to her daughter what makes you talk so
    strange,
For you to be a soldier's wife the wide world to range,
The soldiers they are rambling boys and have but little pay,
How can they maintain their wives out of thirteen pence
    a day,
Says the mother to her daughter, I'll have you close
    confin'd,
While the Lancashire lads are gone a broad while they
    march this time,
If you confine me seven long years and after set me free,
I'll search for my brave Lancashire lad when I've gain'd my
    liberty,
My love is clothed in scarlet and turned up with blue,
And every town that we go through we got sweethearts
    enough,
We get sweethearts enough brave boys, and girls to our
    mind,
But we'll ne'ver forget sweet Manchester and the girls we
    leave behind.

T. Bloomer, Printer, High Street, Birmingham.

79

Jimmy's Enlisted

OR

The Recruited Collier

Oh, what's the matter wi' you, my lass,
    An' where's your dashin Jimmy?
The sowdger boys have picked him up
    And sent him far, far frae me.

Last pay-day he set off to town,
    And them red-coated fellows
Enticed him in and made him drunk,
    And he'd better gone to the gallows.

The very sight o' his cockade,
    It set us all a-cryin;
And me, I fairly fainted twice,
    I thought that I was dyin.

My father would have paid the smart,
    And run for the golden guinea,
But the sergeant swore he'd kissed the book,
    And now they've got young Jimmy.

When Jimmy talks about the wars
    It's worse than death to hear him.
I must go out and hide my tears,
    Because I cannot bear him.

For aye he jibes and cracks his jokes,
    And bids me not forsake him.
A brigadier or grenadier,
    He says they're sure to make him.

As I walked over the stubble field,
    Below it runs the seam,
I thought o' Jimmy hewin there,
    But it was all a dream.

He hewed the very coals we burn,
    And when the fire I'se leetin,
To think the lumps was in his hands,
    It sets my heart to beatin.

So break my heart, and then it's ower,
    So break my heart, my dearie,
And I'll lie in the cold, cold grave,
    For of single life I'm weary.

80

The Soldier's Farewell to Manchester

In coming down to Manchester to gain my liberty
I saw one of the prettiest girls that e'er my eyes did see,
I saw one of the prettiest girls that e'er my eyes did see,
At the Angel Inn in Manchester, there lives the girl for me.

'Twas early in the morning by the break of the day,
I went to my love's fire-side my parting vows to pay,
I huddled her and cuddled her and bade her to lie warm,
She said, my jolly soldier do you mean me any harm.

To do you any harm my love is what I always scorn,
If I stay with you all night my dear I'll marry you next
    morn,
Before all of my officers these words I will fulfil,
She says my jolly soldier you may do just as you will.

On Thursday our rout did come, on Monday marched
    away,
The drums and bugle horns so sweetly did play,
Some hearts they are merry love, but mine was filled with
    woe,
Will you let me go along with you? No, no, my dear, no.

I'll go down unto your officers and fall upon my knees
Ten guineas I'll surrender, to buy my love's discharge,
But if that will not do my dear along with you I'll go,
Will you let me go along with you? No, hang me if I do.

If I see you stand sentry on a cold rainy day,
Your colour it will go my love your beauty will decay,
If I see you stand sentry, 'twill fill my heart with woe,
Stay at home my dearest Nancy, but still she answer'd no.

I'll go down to some nunnery and there I'll end my life,
I never will get married nor yet become a wife,
But constant and true hearted for ever will remain,
But I never will be married till my soldier comes again.

London. Printed and Published by H. Such,
177 (late 123) Union Street, Boro', – S.E.

FIVE

PORTENTS AND PRODIGIES

81

A Description of a Strange (and Miraculous) Fish

Cast upon the sands in the Meads, in the Hundred of *Worwell*, in the County Palatine of *Chester* (or *Chesshiere*). The certainty whereof is here related concerning the said Monstrous Fish.

To the Tune of 'Bragandary'

BY MARTIN PARKER

(*c.* 1636)

Of many marvels in my time
   I've heretofore,
But here's a stranger now in prime
   that's lately come on shore,
Invites my pen to specifie
What some (I doubt) will think a lie.
    O rare
    beyond compare,
  in England nere the like.

It is a fish, a monstrous fish,
   a fish that many dreads,
But now it is as we would wish,
   cast up o'th sands i'th meads,
In *Chesshire*; and tis certaine true,
Describ'd by those who did it view.
    O rare
    beyond compare,
  in England nere the like.

Full twenty one yards and one foot
   this fish extends in length,
With all things correspondent too't,
   for amplitude and strength:
Good people what I shall report,
Doe not account it fained sport.
     O rare
      beyond compare,
   in England nere the like.

It is almost five yards in height,
   which is a wondrous thing,
O mark what marvels to our sight
   our Potent Lord can bring.
These secrets *Neptune* closely keeps
Within the bosome of the deeps.
     O rare
      beyond compare,
   in England nere the like.

His lower jaw-bone's five yards long,
   the upper thrice so much,
Twelve yoak of oxen stout and strong,
   (the weight of it is such)
Could not once stir it out o'th sands
Thus works the All-creating hands.
     O rare
      beyond compare,
   in England nere the like.

Some have a project now in hand,
   (which is a tedious taske)
When the Sea turnes, to bring to Land
   the same with empty cask:
But how I cannot well conceive,

To each mans judgement that I leave.
 O rare
 beyond compare,
in England nere the like.

The lower jaw-bone nam'd of late,
 had teeth in't thirty foure,
Whereof some of them are in weight
 two pounds, or rather more:
There were no teeth i'th upper jaw,
But holes, which many people saw.
 O rare
 beyond compare,
in England nere the like.

THE SECOND PART, TO THE SAME TUNE.

His Pissle is in length foure yards,
 big as a man i'th wast,
This monster he who well regards,
 from th'first unto the last,
By every part may motives find,
To wonder at this wondrous kind.
 O rare
 beyond compare,
in England nere the like.

His Cods are like two hogsheads great,
 this seemeth past beleefe,
But men of credit can relate
 what I describe in briefe:
Then let's with charity confesse
Gods works are more then man can guesse.
 O rare, etc.

The tongue on't is so mighty large,
   I will it not expresse,
Lest I your credit over-charge,
   but you may easily guesse,
That sith his shape so far excels,
The tongue doth answer all parts else.
    O rare, etc.

A man on horseback as tis try'd
   may stand within his mouth,
Let none that hears it this deride,
   for tis confirm'd for truth:
By those who dare avouch the same,
Then let the Writer beare no blame.
    O rare, etc.

His nerves or sinewes like Bulls pissles,
   for riding rods some use:
Of Spermaceti there's some vessels:
   if this be the worst newes,
That of this monster we shall heare,
All will be well I doe not feare.
    O rare, etc.

Already sixteene tuns of Oyle
   is from this fish extracted,
And yet continually they boyle,
   no season is protracted:
It cannot be imagin'd how much
'Twill yeeld, the vastnesse on't is such.
    O rare, etc.

When he upon the sands was cast
   alive, which was awhile:
He yell'd so loud, that many (agast)
   heard him above six mile:

Tis said the Female fish likewise
Was heard to mourne with horrid cryes:
    O rare, etc.

The Mariners of *Chester* say
    a Herring-hog tis nam'd:
Whatere it be, for certaine they
    that are for knowledge fam'd,
Affirme, the like in ages past
Upon our Coast was never cast.
    O rare
    beyond compare
in England nere the like.

Printed at London for Thomas Lambert, at the sign of the
Hors-shoo in Smithfield.
There is a Book to satisfie such as desire a larger description thereof.

82

A Ballad of the Strange and Wonderful Storm of Hail

Which fell in *London* on the 18th of May 1680, which hurt
several men, killed many Birds, and spoiled many Trees;
together with other strange Accidents, the like never before
known in *England*.

To the Tune of 'Aim not too High'

Good Christians all attend unto my Ditty,
And you shall hear strange News from *London* City;
The like before I think you ne'r did hear,
Which well may fill our hearts with Dread and Fear.

Upon the Eighteenth of this present *May*,
A Tempest strange, pray mind me what I say:
So strange, I think the like was never known,
As I can hear of yet by any one.

Hail-stones as bigg as Eggs a pace down fell,
And some much bigger, as I hear some tell:
Who took them up as they lay on the ground,
And measur'd, they were found Eight Inches round.

And Fourteen Ounces two of them did Weigh,
As one who weigh'd them unto me did say:
It is so strange, and yet so very true,
The like before no mortal ever knew.

Much mischief by these Hail-stones there was done,
For in St. *Leonard Shorditch* there was one
Who as he was a dressing Hemp, 'tis said,
All on a sudden he was stricken dead.

His Child being by at this was terrifi'd,
My Father he is dead, the Child he cry'd:
At this Out-cry Neighbours came in amain,
And found the man as they supposed slain.

Great care was taken by his friends and Wife,
All Art they us'd to bring him unto Life:
So that at last they found that he had breath,
And God preserv'd him from that sudden death.

He in his Bed in trembling manner lies,
A stranger sight ne'r seen with mortal eyes:
His Hat was burnt, the Hair scorcht off his breast,
With Limbs struck lame, full sad to be exprest.

The very Fowls that flew up in the Air
Were stricken dead, it plainly doth appear:
Wings from their bodies parted by this Hail,
A Story true, although a dreadful Tale.

Trees of their Branches then was stripped quite,
Some people from their Houses put to flight:
Such terrours then possest the hearts of men,
The like I hope they'l never see agen.

Let all good people keep this in their minds,
He'l nothing lose who for his Sins repines:
For this I fear fore-runs some stranger things,
And's sent for warning by the King of Kings.

Who only knows what there is yet to follow,
And when the Grave each sinful man shall swallow
Repent in time and fit your selves for Death,
Then do not fear how soon you lose your breath.

Fitted for Death, you fitter are to Live,
Dispise not then this counsel which I give:
You do not know when Death shall give the stroke,
But that once done, your hearts is quickly broke.

He that's prepar'd, grim Death cannot affright,
What man doth fear what doth his heart delight:
A Christian true desires Dissolv'd to be,
That he may Live with God Eternally.

These things as judgements surely they are sent,
That all poor Sinners timely may Repent:
E're vengeance fall, for then 'twill be too late,
For to Deplore your Sinful wretched state.

But them who boldly say, There is no GOD,
Shall surely taste of his sharp scourging Rod:
Vengeance shall overtake them e're they know,
Into the Pit of Darkness they must go.

Printed for F. Coles, T. Vere, J. Wright, J. Clarke,
W. Thackeray, and T. Passinger.

83

Man's Amazement

It being a true Relation of one Thomas Cox, a Hackney-Coach-Man, to whom the Devil appeared on Friday the 31st of *October,* first in the likeness of a gentleman, seeming to have a role of Paper or Parchment in his hand, afterwards in the likeness of a Great Bear with glaring eyes, which so affrighted him, that it deprived him of all his Senses.

To the Tune of 'Digbys Farewell'

(*c.* 1684)

Good People attend now, and I will declare,
A wonder as strange as you ever did hear;
It hath been apparent to many ones view,
For though it is strange, yet 'tis certainly true;
The last of *October,* on Friday at night,
A strange apparition a Coachman did fright,
In such a strange manner the like was ne'r known,
As here by these lines shall plainly be shown.

That night near *White-Hall* he had took up a fair,
And then unto *Water-Lane* he did repair,
And when he had set his fare down in the Lane,
He drove to the end to return back again:

And as he was driveing then easily on
The Devil appear'd in the shape of a man,
And leaning against a great post he did stand,
With likeness of Parchment rol'd up in his hand.

He call'd to the Coach-man as it did appear,
The Coach-man Supposing he had been a Fare;
He stopped his horses and came down therefore
And stept to his Coach and then open'd the door,
He bid him to drive him to *Brides* Low Church yard,
The Coachman observ'd him with reverent regard;
For little he thought of that infernal sin,
And therefore to drive him he then did begin.

The Horses possest with a Habit of fear,
They snorted and startled as it did appear,
The Coachman his hat it fell of to the ground,
The night being dark it could not be found:
This gentleman told him though he did not see it
His hat it lay under his horses fore-feet;
There finding his hat and the words to be true,
He then was amazed to think how he knew.

But when he got into his Coachbox again,
His horses they startled and could not refrain,
Thus snorting and flouncing being frighted withal,
At length he came near to St *Brides* church-yard-wall
The coach-man came down from his box in a fright,
And said he would drive him no further that night:
The Devil he held out his hand and did say,
Here's mony enough I will bountiful pay.

Then as he did proffer to feel for his hand,
Yet there was no substance he could understand
Nor there was no mony the coach-man could see,
The Devils a lyar and so he will be,

Still he in the shape of a man did remain,
Till he from the coach had descended again;
The Coach-man he turning about to his fare,
He then did appear in the form of a Bear.

Which did both his heart and his sences surprize,
It staring upon him with great flaming eyes
And also did seem to make at him amain
But he with his whip lashed at it again,
And then he did seem to give back and retire,
And vanisht away in great flashes of fire,
O this was a sad and deplorable case,
The flashes did seem for to fly in his face.

He then stepped into his Coach-box straightway,
The horses run homeward without there delay,
The coach-man was speechless like one almost dead
But they took him down and convey'd him to bed
Where five or six days he did speechless remain,
But then at the length it returned again.
Now from his own mouth he hath made it appear,
And briefly declared the things mention'd here.

He has lost both the sence and the use of his Limbs,
Which is a great cut and a grief to his friends,
To see how he lyes in a languishing state,
Alas this affliction and sorrow is great:
To see how he lyeth and still doth remain,
'Tis fear'd that he ne'r will recover again,
He says if the Lord will his Limbs now restore,
He never will follow the calling no more.

There's many hath seen him from both far and near;
From whose just Relation the truth did appear,
Now in *Baldwins* Gardens there in Cradle Court,
This man still is living as hundreds report,

And those that will take but the pains for to go
A further Account of the truth you may know,
Yea from his own mouth he will freely unfold,
The sum and the substance of what I have told.

Printed of I. Dracen at the Angel in Guilt-spar Street.

SIX

CRIME AND PUNISHMENT

84

A Lementable New Ballad upon the Earle of Essex Death

To the Tune of 'The King's Last Goodnight'

(1601)

All yow that crye O hone! O hone!
  come now and sing O lord! with me.
For why? our Jewell is from us gonne,
  the valient Knight of Chivalrye.
Of rich and poore beloved was hee, –
  in tyme an honorable Knight –
Who by our lawes condemnd was he
  and late take *his last good-night*.

Count him not like to Sauit, or Campion,
  these traytrous men, or Babbinton,
Nor like the earle of Westmerlande,
  by whom a number were undoone.
He never yet hurt mother's sonne;
  his quarrell still maintainde the right;
Which makes the teares my cheekes downe runne
  when I thinke of *his last good-night*.

The *Portingals* can witnes be
  his dagger at *Lisbone* gate he flunge,
And, like a knight of chevalrye,
  his chane upon the gate he hunge,
Would god that he would thither come
  to fetch them both in order right,
Which thinge was by his honour doone;
  yet lately tooke *his last good-night*.

The *Frenchmen* they can testifye
   the towne of *Gourney* he tooke in,
And marched to *Roane* immediatlye,
   not caring for his foes a pinne:
With bullets he persed their skinne,
   and made them flye farre from his sight:
He, at that time, did credite winne;
   and nowe hath tane *his last good-night*.

And stately *Cales* can witnesse well,
   even by his proclamations right,
He did commaund them all straytlye
   to have a care of infants' lives,
That non should ravishe mayde nor wife,
   which was against their order right
Therefore they prayed for his longe life,
   which lately tooke *his last good-night*.

Would god that he had ne'ere *Ireland* knowne,
   nor set his feete in *Flaunders* ground,
The⟨n⟩ might we well injoyde our owne
   where nowe our Jewell will not be found;
Which makes our woes still to abound,
   trickling with salt teares in my sight,
To heare his name in our eares to sound –
   Lord *Devreux* tooke *his last good-night*.

Ashe-wenesday, that dismall daye,
   when he came forth of his chamber-dore,
Upon a Scaffold there he sawe
   his headsman standing him before.
The Nobles all that did deplore,
   sheading their salt teares in his sight.
He bade farwell to rich and poore,
   at his good-morrowe and *good-night*.

My Lords, (quoth he) yow stand but by,
  to see performance of the lawe;
It's I that have deserved to dy,
  and yeeldes my selfe unto the blowe.
I have deserved to dye, I knowe;
  but never against my cuntrye's right,
Nor to my Queene was never foe;
  upon my death, at my *good-night*.

Farwell, *Elizabeth*, my gracious Queene!
  God blesse thee and thy counsell all.
Farwell, my Knights of chyvalrye;
  far-well my souldiers, great and tall;
Farwell, the Commons, great and small.
  into the hands of men I light;
My lyfe shall make amends for all,
  For *Essex* bids the world *good-night*.

Farewell, deare wife, and children three;
  farewell, my yong and tender sonne.
Comfort yourselves; morne not for me,
  although your fall be nowe begun.
My tyme is come; the glasse is runne.
  Comfort yourselves in former light.
Seeing, by my fall, yow are undone,
  your father bids the world *good-night*.

Dericke! thow knowst, at statelye *Cales* I savde
  thy lyfe, lost for a rape there done,
Which thow thyselfe canst testyfye –
  thy owne hand three and twenty hung.
But now, thow seest, my tyme is come;
  by chaunce into thy hands I light.
Stricke out the blow, that I maye knowe
  thow *Essex* lovedst at his *good-night*.

When *England* counted me a Papist,
　the works of Papists I defye.
I never worshipe S⟨ain⟩ct nor angell in heaven,
　nor to the Virgin *Marye*, I;
But to CHRIST, which for my synnes did dye.
　Trickling with sad teares in his sight,
Sp⟨r⟩eading my armes to god on high,
　Lord JESUS receive my soule this night.

85

Sir Walter Rauleigh his Lamentation

*Who was beheaded in the Old Pallace at Westminster
the 29. of October 1618*

Courteous kind Gallants all,
　pittie me, pittie me,
My time is now but small,
　here to continue:
Thousands of people stay,
To see my dying day,
Sing I then welladay,
　wofully mourning.

Once in a gallant sort
　lived I, lived I,
Belov'd in Englands court
　graced with honours:
Sir *Walter Rauleighs* name
Had then a noble fame:
Though turned now to shame
　through my misdoing.

In youth I was too free
   of my will, of my will,
Which now deceiveth me
   of my best fortunes:
All that same gallant traine
Which I did then maintaine,
Holds me now in disdaine
   for my vaine folly.

When as Queene *Elizabeth*
   ruld this land, ruld this land,
I trode the honord path
   of a brave Courtier;
Offices I had store,
Heapt on me more and more,
And my self I in them bore
   proud and commanding.

Gone are those golden dayes
   woe is me woe is me:
Offences many waies
   brought unto triall,
Shewes that disloyaltie
Done to his Majestie,
Judgeth me thus to dye;
   Lord for thy pitie.

But the good graces heere
   of my King, of my King,
Shewd to me many a yeere
   makes my soule happie
In that his royall Grace
Gave me both time and space
Repentance to embrace:
   now heaven be praised.

Thirteen yeare in the tower
   have I lien, have I lien,
Before this appoynted houre
   of my lives ending:
Likewise such libertie
Had I unluckily,
To be sent gallantly
   out on a voyage.

But that same voyage then
   prov'd amis prov'd amis,
Many good gentlemen
   lost their good fortunes:
All that with me did goe
Had sudden overthrowe
My wicked will to shew
   gainst my deere Countrey.

When I returned backe,
   hoping grace, hoping grace,
The tower againe alacke
   was my abiding:
Where for offences past,
My life againe was cast
Woe on woe followed fast
   to my confusion.

It pleas'd my royall King
   thus to doe, thus to doe,
That his peeres should me bring
   to my lives judgement.
The Lieutenant of the tower
Kept me fast in his power,
Till the appointed houre
   of my remooving.

THE SECOND PART

To Westminster then was I
   garded strong, garded strong
Where many a wandring eye
   saw me convayed
Where I a Judgment had,
for my offences bad,
Which was to loose my head,
   there the next morning.

So to the Gatehouse there,
   was I sent, was I sent,
By knights and gentlemen,
   guarding me safely,
Where all that wofull night,
My heart tooke no delight:
Such is the heavie plight
   of a poore prisoner.

Calling then to my mind,
   all my joyes, all my joyes,
Whereto I was inclind,
   living in pleasures:
All those dayes past and gon,
Brings me now care and mone,
Being thus overthrowne,
   by mine owne folly.

When the sad morning came
   I should die, I should die:
O what a fright of shame:
   fild up my bosome:
My heart did almost breake,
when I heard people speake,
I shold my ending make
   as a vile traitor.

I thought my fortunes hard,
   when I saw, when I saw
In the faire pallace yard
   a scaffold prepared:
My loathed life to end:
On which I did ascend,
Having at all no friend
   there to grant mercy.

Kneeling downe on my knee,
   willingly, willingly,
Prayed for his Majestie
   long to continue:
And for his Nobles all,
With subjects great and small,
Let this my wofull fall
   be a fit warning.

And you that hither come
   thus to see, thus to see
My most unhappy doome:
   pittie my ending.
A Christian true I die:
Papistrie I defie,
Nor never Atheist I
   as is reported.

You Lords & knights also
   in this place, in this place
Some gentle love bestow
   pity my falling:
As I rose suddenly
Up to great dignitie,
So I deservedly
   die for my folly.

Farewell my loving wife
  woe is me, woe is me:
Mournefull wil bee thy life,
  Left a sad widdow.
Farewell my children sweet,
We never more shall meet
Till we each other greet,
  blessed in heaven.

With this my dying knell
  willingly, willingly
Bid I the world farewell
  full of vaine shadowes
All her deluding showes
brings my heart naught but woes
Who rightly feeles and knowes,
  all her deceivings.

Thus with my dying breath
  doe I kis, doe I kis,
This axe that for my death
  here is provided:
May I feele little paine,
when as it cuts in twaine,
what my life must sustaine,
  all her deceivings.

My head on block is laid,
  And my last part is plaid:
Fortune hath me betraid,
  sweet Jesus grant mercy.
Thou that my headsman art,
when thou list, when thou list,
Without feare doe thy part
  I am prepared:

Thus here my end I take
  farewel world, farewel world,
And my last will I make,
  climing to heaven;
For this my offence,
I die with true penitence,
Jesus receive me hence:
  farewell sweet England.

86

A Ballad

To the Tune of Bateman

BY SIR CHARLES SEDLEY

(1692)

You Gallants all, that love good Wine,
  For shame your Lives amend;
With Strangers go to Church, or Dine,
  But drink with an old Friend.

For with him tipling all the Night,
  You kiss, hugg, and embrace;
Whereas a Stranger, at first sight,
  May kill you on the Place.

There was a rich old Usurer,
  A gallant Son he had;
Who slew an ancient Barrister,
  Like a true mettled Lad.

All in that very House, where Saint
  Holds Devil by the Nose;
These Drunkards met to Roar, and Rant,
  But quarrell'd in the close.

The Glass flew chearfully about,
   And drunken Chat went on;
Which Troops had fail'd, and which were stout,
   When *Namur* wou'd be won.

A learned Lawyer, at the last,
   No Tory, as I'm told,
Began to talk of Tyrants past,
   In Words both sharp and bold.

He toucht a little on our Times,
   Defin'd the Power of Kings,
What were their Vertues, what their Crimes,
   And many dangerous Things.

A Stranger that sat silent by,
   And scarce knew what he meant,
O'recome with Wine and Loyalty,
   Did thus his Passion vent:

I cannot bear the least ill Word,
   That lessens any King;
And the bold Man shall feel my Sword;
   At that their Friends stept in.

The Quarrel seem'd a while compos'd,
   And many Healths there past,
But one to Blood was ill dispos'd,
   As it appear'd at last.

The Counsellor was walking Home,
   Sober, as he was wont,
The young Man after him did come,
   With Sword, that was not blunt.

A Blow there past, which no Man saw,
　From Cane of Lawyer bold;
The young Man did his Weapon draw,
　And left the Lawyer cold.

Which Cane held up, in his Defence,
　Was judg'd a Weapon drawn:
What needs there farther Evidence,
　Th'Assault was very plain.

At *Hixes*'s Hall, by Jury grave,
　It was Man-slaughter found;
O what wou'd it have cost to have
　A Pardon from the Crown.

Then learn, my honest Country-men,
　To take yourselves the Pence;
Wisely prevent the Courtier's Gain,
　And save us that Expence.

Ye Gallants all, take heed how you
　Come to untimely Ends;
Justice has bid the World adieu,
　And dead Men have no Friends.

87

Clever Tom Clinch going to be hanged

Written in the Year 1726

BY JONATHAN SWIFT

As clever *Tom Clinch*, while the Rabble was bawling,
Rode stately through *Holbourne*, to die in his Calling;
He stopt at the *George* for a Bottle of Sack,

And promis'd to pay for it when he'd come back.
His Waistcoat and Stockings, and Breeches were white,
His Cap had a new Cherry Ribbon to ty't.
The Maids to the Doors and the Balconies ran,
And said, lack-a-day! he's a proper young Man.
But, as from the Windows the Ladies he spy'd,
Like a Beau in the Box, he bow'd low on each Side;
And when his last Speech the loud Hawkers did cry,
He swore from his Cart, it was all a damn'd Lye.
The Hangman for Pardon fell down on his Knee;
Tom gave him a Kick in the Guts for his Fee.
Then said, I must speak to the People a little,
But I'll see you all damn'd before I will *whittle*.
My honest Friend *Wild*, may he long hold his Place,
He lengthen'd my Life with a whole Year of Grace.
Take Courage, dear Comrades, and be not afraid,
Nor slip this Occasion to follow your Trade.
My Conscience is clear, and my Spirits are calm,
And thus I go off without Pray'r-Book or Psalm.
Then follow the Patience of clever *Tom Clinch*,
Who hung like a Hero, and never would flinch.

88

Confession and Execution of William Corder, the Murderer of Maria Marten

(1828)

Since the tragical affair between Thurtell and Weare, no event had occurred connected with the criminal annals of our country which has excited so much interest as the trial of Corder, who was justly convicted of the murder of Maria Marten on Friday last.

THE CONFESSION

'Bury Gaol, August 10th, 1828. – Condemned cell.
'Sunday evening, half-past Eleven.

'I acknowledge being guilty of the death of poor Maria Marten, by shooting her with a pistol. The particulars are as follows: – When we left her father's house, we began quarrelling about the burial of the child: she apprehended the place wherein it was deposited would be found out. The quarrel continued about three quarters of an hour upon this sad [sic] and about other subjects. A scuffle ensued, and during the scuffle, and at the time I think that she had hold of me, I took the pistol from the side pocket of my velveteen jacket and fired. She fell, and died in an instant. I never saw her even struggle. I was overwhelmed with agitation and dismay: – the body fell near the front doors of the floor of the barn. A vast quantity of blood issued from the wound, and ran on to the floor and through the crevices. Having determined to bury the body in the barn (about two hours after she was dead [sic]. I went and borrowed a spade of Mrs. Stow, but before I went there I dragged the body from the barn into the chaff-house, and locked the barn. I returned again to the barn, and began to dig a hole, but the spade being a bad one, and the earth firm and hard, I was obliged to go home for a pickaxe and a better spade, with which I dug the hole, and then buried the body. I think I dragged the body by the handkerchief that was tied round her neck. It was dark when I finished covering up the body. I went the next day, and washed the blood from off the barn-floor. I declare to Almighty God I had no sharp instrument about me, and no other wound but the one made by the pistol was inflicted by me. I have been guilty of great idleness, and at times led a dissolute life, but I hope through the mercy of God to be forgiven.

William Corder.'

Witness to the signing by the said William Corder,

John Orridge.

Condemned cell, Eleven o'clock, Monday morning,

August 11th, 1828.

The above confession was read over carefully to the prisoner in our presence, who stated most solemnly it was true, and that he had nothing to add to or retract from it. — W. Stocking, chaplain; Timothy R. Holmes, Under-Sheriff.

THE EXECUTION

At ten minutes before twelve o'clock the prisoner was brought from his cell and pinioned by the hangman, who was brought from London for the purpose. He appeared resigned, but was so weak as to be unable to stand without support; when his cravat was removed he groaned heavily, and appeared to be labouring under great mental agony. When his wrists and arms were made fast, he was led round twards [sic] the scaffold, and as he passed the different yards in which the prisoners were confined, he shook hands with them, and speaking to two of them by name, he said, 'Good bye, God bless you'. They appeared considerably affected by the wretched appearance which he made, and 'God bless you!' 'May God receive your soul!' were frequently uttered as he passed along. The chaplain walked before the prisoner, reading the usual Burial Service, and the Governor and Officers walking immediately after him. The prisoner was supported to the steps which led to the scaffold; he looked somewhat wildly around, and a constable was obliged to support him while the hangman was adjusting the fatal cord. There was a barrier to keep off the crowd, amounting to upwards of 7,000 persons, who at this time had stationed themselves in the adjoining fields, on the hedges, the tops of houses, and at every point from which a view of the execution could be best obtained. The prisoner, a few moments before the drop fell, groaned heavily, and would have fallen, had not a second constable caught hold of him. Everything having been made ready, the signal was given, the fatal drop fell, and the unfortunate man was launched into eternity. Just before he was turned off, he said in a feeble tone, 'I am justly sentenced, and may God forgive me.'

THE MURDER OF MARIA MARTEN
BY W. CORDER

Come all you thoughtless young men, a warning take by
 me,
And think upon my unhappy fate to be hanged upon a tree;
My name is William Corder, to you I do declare,
I courted Maria Marten, most beautiful and fair.

I promised I would marry her upon a certain day,
Instead of that, I was resolved to take her life away.
I went into her father's house the 18th day of May,
Saying, my dear Maria, we will fix the wedding day.

If you will meet me at the Red-barn, as sure as I have life,
I will take you to Ipswich town, and there make you my
 wife;
I then went home and fetched my gun, my pickaxe and
 my spade,
I went into the Red-barn, and there I dug her grave.

With heart so light, she thought no harm, to meet him she
 did go
He murdered her all in the barn, and laid her body low:
After the horrible deed was done, she lay weltering in her
 gore,
Her bleeding mangled body he buried beneath the
 Red-barn floor.

Now all things being silent, her spirit could not rest,
She appeared unto her mother, who suckled her at her
    breast;
For many a long month or more, her mind being sore
    oppress'd,
Neither night or day she could not take any rest.

Her mother's mind being so disturbed, she dreamt three
    nights o'er,
Her daughter she lay murdered beneath the Red-barn floor;
She sent the father to the barn, when he the ground
    did thrust,
And there he found his daughter mingling with the dust.

My trial is hard, I could not stand, most woeful was the
    sight,
When her jaw-bone was brought to prove, which pierced
    my heart quite;
Her aged father standing by, likewise his loving wife,
And in her grief her hair she tore, she scarcely could keep
    life.

Adieu, adieu, my loving friends, my glass is almost run,
On Monday next will be my last, when I am to be hang'd;
So you, young men, who do pass by, with pity look on me,
For murdering Maria Marten, I was hang'd upon the tree.

89

'A Ballad from the Seven Dials Press . . .'

*together with 'the "gag" and "patter" of a man formerly well-
known as " Tragedy Bill"'*

'Now, my friends, here you have, just printed and published, a full, true, and pertickler account of the life, trial,

character, confession, behaviour, condemnation, and hexecution of that unfortunate malefactor, Richard Wilbyforce,
who was hexecuted on Monday last, for the small charge of
one ha'penny, and for the most horrible, dreadful, and
wicked murder of Samuel – I means Sarah Spriggens, a
lady's maid, young, tender, and handsome. You have here
every pertickler, of that which he did, and that which he
didn't. It's the most foul and horrible murder that ever
graced the annals of British history(?) Here, my customers,
you may read his hexecution on the fatal scaffold. You may
also read how he met his victim in a dark and lonesome
wood, and what he did to her – for the small charge of a
ha'penny; and, further, you read how he brought her to
London, – after that comes the murder, which is worth all
the money. And you read how the ghost appeared to him
and then to her parents. Then comes the capture of the
willain; also the trial, sentence, and hexecution, showing
how the ghost was in the act of pulling his leg on one side,
and the 'old gentleman' a pulling on the other, waiting for
his victim (my good friends excuse my tears!) But as
Shakespeare says, 'Murder most foul and unnatural', but
you'll find this more foul and unnatural than that or the
t'other – for the small charge of a ha'penny! Yes, my customers, to which is added a copy of serene and beautiful
werses, pious and immoral, as wot he wrote with his own
blood and skewer the night after – I mean the night before
his hexecution, adressed to young men and women of
all sexes – I beg pardon, but I mean classes (my friends
its nothing to laugh at), for I can tell you the werses is
made three of the hard-heartedest things cry as never
was – to wit, that is to say, namely – a overseer, a
broker, and a policeman. Yes, my friends, I sold twenty
thousand copies of them this here morning, and could
of sold twenty thousand more than that if I could of but
kept from crying – only a ha'penny! – but I'll read the
werses.

'Come all you blessed Christians dear,
  That's a-tender, kind, and free,
While I a story do relate
  Of a dreadful tragedy,
Which happened in London town,
  As you shall all be told;
But when you hear the horrid deed
   'Twill make your blood run cold. –
    For the small charge of a ha'penny!

''Twas in the merry month of May,
  When my true love I did meet;
She look'd all like an angel bright,
  So beautiful and sweet.
I told her I loved her much,
  And she could not say nay;
'Twas then I strung her tender heart,
  And led her all astray. –
    Only a ha'penny!

'I brought her up to London town,
  To make her my dear wife;
But an evil spirit tempted me,
  And so I took her life!
I left the town all in the night,
  When her ghost in burning fire,
Saying, "Richard", I am still with you,
  Whenever you retire. –
    Only a ha'penny!

'And justice follow'd every step,
  Though often I did cry;
And the cruel Judge and Jury
  Condemned me for to die.
And in a cell as cold as death,
  I always was afraid,

For Sarah she was with me,
Although I killed her dead. –
For the small charge of a ha'penny!

'My tender-hearted Christians,
Be warned by what I say,
And never prove unkind or false
To any sweet la'-dy. [*sic*]
Though some there, who wickedness
Oft leads 'em to go astray;
So pray attend to what you hear.
And a warning take I pray.'

90

Farewell to the World of Richard Bishop

Who now lies under sentence of Death in Maidstone Gaol,
For the Murder of Alfred Cartwright.

In Maidstone Gaol, I am lamenting,
I am borne down with grief and pain,
I for my deeds am now repenting,
I shall Sydenham never see again;
I have been tried for wilful murder,
No power on earth can me now save,
I am doomed to die, my time's approaching,
And I must lie in a silent grave.

Now I, alas! must die for murder,
Oh, how awful is my doom,
Richard Bishop, one and twenty,
In youth and vigour, health and bloom.

Alfred Cartwright was my neighbour,
   We both at Forest Hill did dwell,
Alfred, servant was at the Swiss Cottage,
   Where he was respected well;
I went with others to annoy him,
   It was upon that fatal night,
Ere he returned from his day's labour,
   Unto his home and loving wife.

I never did intend to kill him,
   Why should I my neighbour slay,
He never gave me any reason,
   To take his youthful life away?
I was given in charge, and in a passion,
   I drew the awful, deadly knife,
And plunged it in poor Alfred's body,
   And there deprived him of his life.

The solemn funeral of my victim,
   Caused consternation miles around,
Thousands flocked from every quarter,
   The funeral dirge did mournful sound;
Poor Alfred, to his grave respected,
   Proceeded by a solemn band,
And I must die upon the gallows,
   A wicked and degraded man.

Farewell, vain world, I now must leave you,
   Farewell, my friends and neighbours all,
Around Forest Hill no more you'll see me,
   The hangman's voice on me does call;
Saying, Richard Bishop, now be ready,
   To die upon the fatal tree,
Oh, aged only one and twenty,
   What a dreadful sight to see.

Poor Alfred's friends, will you forgive me,
    His father, mother, tender wife,
I him did kill, his blood did spill,
    And I pay a forfeit with my life?
And God, look down from heaven upon me,
    Forgive the crime that I have done.
I see grim death standing before me,
    Saying, Richard Bishop's glass is run.

Oh, pray, young men, by me take warning,
    Remember me and what I done,
Ponder, yes, oh! and consider,
    Let passion you not overcome;
I did the deed in the heighth of passion,
    I had no animosity.
Little thought my tender parents,
    I should die upon a gallows tree.

When the Judge did pass the awful sentence
    Saying, Richard Bishop, you must die,
For the murder of young Alfred Cartwright,
    On Maidstone's tree so awful high;
Oh think, dear friends, what was my feelings,
    Sad and wretched and forlorn,
Doomed at the age of one and twenty,
    To die a dreadful death of scorn.

SEVEN

RELIGION

91

To Pass the Place where Pleasure is

(1561/2)

To passe the place where pleasure is,
　　it ought to please our fantasie;
If that the pleasure be amis
　　and to godes word plaine contrarie;
　　　　or eles we sinne, we sinne,
　　　　and hell we winne, –
　　　　great paine there-in,
　　　　all remedie gone
　　　　　　except in *Christ* alone, alone.

The lives that we long livèd have
　　in wantonnesse and jolitie,
Although the⟨y⟩ seeme and show full brave,
　　yet is their end plaine miserie.
　　　　Let us therefore, therefore,
　　　　now sinne noe more,
　　　　but learne this lore:
　　　　all remedie gone
　　　　　　except in *Christ* alone, ⟨alone⟩.

And say we then, with *Salomon*,
　　that bewtie is but vanitie,
Yet they that feare the lord alone
　　shall sure enjoy felicitie.
　　　　For this may wee, may we,
　　　　perceive and see

most true to be:
all remedie gone
except in *Christ* alone, alone.

Our perfett trust and confidence
   must fixèd be on *Christ* onelie,
Serveinge our lord with pure pretence,
   and shunning all hipocrisie, –
      which might us draw, us draw,
      from godes true law,
      marke well this saw:
      all remedie gone
         except in *Christ* alone, alone.

If godes true word, by preaching plaine,
   might anie wise us certiefie,
We should not, then, so blind remaine,
   but should imbrace the verietie;
      for why? – the word, the word,
      of god our lord
      doth well record,
      all remedie gone
         except in *Christ* alone, alone.

Our faithfull frendes, the pastors pure,
   doe give us councell, certainlie,
From wickednesse, for to be sure,
   to leave our fooleish fantasie, –
      which is the springe, the springe,
      that doth us bring
      to eich ill thing:
      all remedie gone
         except in *Christ* alone, alone.

What wisdome have our wicked wittes
   to worke all thinges untowardlie;

What reason restes in such fond fittes
   to cause things chance so frowardlie?
     Therefore betime, betime,
     leave we our crime
     and learne this rime:
     all remedie gone
     except in *Christ* alone, alone.

92

A Song made by F. B. P.

To the Tune of 'Diana'

Hierusalem, my happie home,
   when shall I come to thee?
When shall my sorrowes have an end?
   thy joyes when shall I see?

O happie harbour of the saintes,
   O sweete and pleasant soyle,
In thee noe sorrow may be founde,
   noe greefe, noe care, noe toyle.

In thee noe sickenesse may be seene,
   noe hurt, noe ache, noe sore:
There is noe death nor uglie devill,
   there is life for evermore.

Noe dampishe mist is seene in thee,
   noe could nor darksome night;
There everie soule shines as the sunne,
   there god himselfe gives light.

There lust and lukar cannot dwell,
　　there envie beares noe sway;
There is noe hunger, heate, nor coulde,
　　but pleasure everie way.

Hierusalem, Hierusalem,
　　god grant I once may see
Thy endlesse joyes, and of the same
　　partaker aye to bee.

Thy wales are made of precious stones;
　　thy bulwarkes, diamonds square;
Thy gates are of right Orient pearle,
　　exceedinge riche and rare.

Thy terrettes and thy Pinacles
　　with Carbuncles doe shine;
Thy verie streetes are paved with gould,
　　surpassinge cleare and fine.

Thy houses are of Ivorie,
　　thy windoes Cristale cleare;
Thy tyles are mad(e) of beaten gould, –
　　O god, that I were there!

Within thy gates nothinge doeth come
　　that is not passinge cleane;
Noe spider's web, noe durt, noe dust,
　　no filthe may there be seene.

Ay my sweet home, *hierusaleme,*
　　would god I were in thee;
Would god my woes were at an end,
　　thy joyes that I might see!

Thy saintes are crown'd with glorie great,
   they see god face to face;
They triumph still, they still rejoyce,
   most happie is their case.

Wee that are heere in banishment
   continuallie doe mourne;
We sighe and sobbe, we weepe and weale,
   perpetually we groane.

Our sweete is mixt with bitter gaule,
   our pleasure is but paine,
Our joyes scarce last the lookeing on,
   our sorrowes still remaine;

But there they live in such delight,
   such pleasure, and such play,
As that to them a thousand yeares
   doth seeme as yeaster-day.

Thy Viniardes and thy Orchardes are
   most beutifull and faire,
Full furnishèd with trees and fruites,
   most wonderfull and rare.

Thy gardens and thy gallant walkes
   continually are greene;
There gro⟨w⟩es such sweete and pleasant flowers
   as now where eles are seene.

There is nector and Ambrosia made,
   there is muske and Civette sweete;
There mainie a faire and daintie drugge
   are troden under feete.

There Cinomon, there sugar, gro⟨w⟩es;
   there narde and balme abound.

What tounge can tell or hart conceive
  the joyes that there are found?

Thy happy Saints (Jerusalem)
  doe bathe in endlesse blisse;
None but those blessèd soules can tell
  how great thy glory is.

Quyt through the streetes with silver sound
  the flood of life doe flowe;
Upon whose bankes, on everie syde,
  the wood of life doth growe.

There trees for evermore beare fruite,
  and evermore doe springe;
There evermore the Angels sit,
  and evermore doe singe.

There *David* standes, with harpe in hand,
  as maister of the Queere.
Tenne thousand times that man were blest
  that might this musique heare.

Our Ladie singes *magnificat*,
  with tune surpassinge sweete,
And all the virginns beare their partes,
  sitinge above her feete.

Te Deum doth sa⟨i⟩nt *Ambrose* singe,
  saint *Augustine* dothe the like;
Ould *Simeon* and *Zacharie*
  have not their songes to seeke.

There *Magdalene* hath left her mone,
  and cheerefullie doth singe,
With blessèd saintes whose harmonie
  in everie streete doth ringe.

Hierusalem, my happie home,
  would god I were in thee;
Would god my woes were at an end,
  thy joyes that I might see!

93

Here followeth the Songe of the Death of Mr Thewlis

To the Tune of 'Daintie, come thou to mee'

(1616)

O god above, relent,
  and lissten t⟨o⟩ our cry;
O *Christ,* our wooes prevent,
  let not thy Children die!

As at th' assyses late,
  good proofe, too much, we see,
Thy lambes their lyms have lost,
  through Tyrantes' Cruelltie.

One *Thewlis* is the man
  which makes me call and cry;
Come helpe me all that can
  of *Christ* to beg mercie!

His courage myld and meeke,
  and his most comlie glee,
His answere not to seeke,
  in middes of misserie, –

In a dungeòn he was cast,
  amonge the theeves to lye.

Of all meates he did tast
   which came to fellons' fee.

And in th' assyses weeke,
   in *lent*, arainde was he;
Where frendes and kinsfolks were
   to see his constancie.

Best preachers in the land –
   by name on parson *Lie*;
Noe better can be found
   within the Counterie –

Three suerall daies did tempt
   to try his constancie;
The judge beinge present there,
   with all his companie.

To all thinges they demande,
   he answeres Cheerfullye;
His answere there was sound
   in all contraversie.

As they were apt to move
   from poynt to poynt, trulie
He did not them reproove,
   but answered quyetlie.

When they could not preveile
   to wrest his constantie,
They did him treator call,
   and said that he should die.

Then smylinglie he said,
   with sweete and pleasant glee:
'Noe treason I have wrought,
   nor wicked Treacherie.

'Noe Treason I have done
 against king nor Countrie;
Christ Jesus, godes owne sonne,
 a witnes take for mee.

'It is for his deere sake,
 his Church both meeke and free,
That I doe undertake
 a true *Catholi⟨ke⟩* to dye;

'It is for his deere sake,
 that gave his life for me,
My Crosse I undertake,
 his spouse to glorifie.'

Then they gave him a note:
 th' effecte did signifie
That he must take the oeth,
 or eles prepare to dye.

Then answered he and said:
 'for dutie temperall,
I anye oeth will take,
 whensoever you doe call.

'For other oath,' quoth he,
 'I uterlie denye.
God save our king and queene,
 and send them meekle joy!'

According to the law,
 death sentance then had hee;
And, as all people knowe,
 he took it patientlie.

On *fryday* in the morne,
    attemptèd sore was hee;
They wilde him to reforme
    and take the king's mercie.

His kinsfolke, in like cause,
    did proffer gould and fee,
If his faith hee would refuse,
    a *Protestant* to bee.

He gave them hartie thankes,
    and tould them, Cheerfullie,
His life they should not crave –
    a *Protestant* to bee.

In wrastinge of⟨f⟩ his bondes
    somewhat too hastilie,
They hurt his tender leggs,
    whereat they seem'd sorie.

Then smylinglie he said:
   'Forbeare to mourne for mee!
Smale hurts doe little greeve,
    when great on⟨e⟩s are soe nye.

'I thanke my saviour sweete
    from these bondes I am free;
Soe soone I hope I shalle
    from all extremitie.

'By afflixtions god doth proove
    who his true Children bee;
Christ Jesus this can remoove,
    in the twinklinge of an eye!'

They forst him to the Church,
   in spite of his bodie,
Where he full myldlie sate,
   for all their crueltie.

Then did he aske the Sheriffe
   his breedren for to see,
With them to take his leave
   before he went to dye.

The sheriffe gave consent –
   he thankt him hartelie.
He to his breedren went
   with humble Curtesie.

Then did he frendlie leave
   of all his breethren take;
Sayinge, 'doe you not greeve,
   nor mourne not for my sake;

'For it's godes blessèd will
   that I must leade the way;
But be you constant still,
   and I will for you pray.'

And then with watterie Cheekes,
   they parted mournfullie;
His gesture little shranke –
   such was his constantsie.

Another Constante wight,
   which I had neare forgot,
Was constant day and night,
   and thankfull for his lot; –

On⟨e⟩ *wrennall* was he cal'd,
  a lay-man happie he,
They both prepar'd themselves
  on hurdle for to lye.

And thus these faithfull wightes
  soe myldlie fram'd the same:
The father and the sonne
  thus hath their journey tane.

My muse beginns to faint,
  and greefe me overflowe;
But of these martered saintes,
  the second part shall showe.

THE SECOND PART

As *Thewles* past the way,
  the poorest he did spye;
He gave that money he had lefte
  their wantes for to supplye.

O god above, relent,
  and listen to our crye;
Sweet *Christ*, thy spouse defend
  from tyrantes' crueltie!

To Th' execution place,
  the⟨y⟩ beinge thither drawne,
Present before their face
  was fier one cruell flame.

Then did they them attempt
  their faith for to denye;
Sainge they must be hangde
  and buried cruellie.

Then, smylinge, *Thewles* said:
  'If that the worst may bee,
Our saviour *Christ* hath paid
  farre greatter paines for me!'

Then myldlie they preparde
  to Th' execution place.
Three fellones they did see
  hanged before their face.

And at the ladder foote,
  where manie people stoode,
He held them with dispute,
  while ever they would abyde.

Then did they profer them
  part of the oath to take, –
And they should not be slaine,
  such frendshippe they would make.

But all could not preveale
  their mindes for to remove;
Nor once their courage quaile,
  soe constant was their love.

With Crosse and signes soe meeke,
  the ladder he did take;
Where manie a watterie eye
  appearèd for his sake.

A hundred poundes was there
  for his life offered free,
If he would yet consent
  a *protestant* to bee.

Then, smylingely, he said:
   'That ransome I denye;
That may noe way be paid
   but by death eternally.

'I thanke you for your loves, –
   your good will all I see, –
But I must take the Crosse
   that *Christ* hath lefte for me.'

Then willingly he did
   himselfe most readie make;
He proferred to unbare,
   and his Cloath of ⟨f⟩ to take.

A cap as white as snowe
   over his face pul'd hee;
His hat he threw him froe,
   and purse away gave he.

The hangman plaid his part,
   as he did him command;
Three stroakes upon his brest,
   he gave with his right hand.

The father beinge gone,
   the Child did after hye;
Without all show of mone
   he suffered willingly.

At first the rope did breake,
   which parson *Lee* did see;
He said it was godes will,
   to shew him such mercie.

The⟨y⟩ profered him the oath,
  which he did still denye.
'This night I hope we boath
  shall sup in heaven hye.'

The people moov'd and blusht,
  both hye and low degree,
And said they thought noe lesse
  but he should savèd bee.

When that the rope was cut,
  and quartered he should be,
The hangman did denye,
  and then a-way went hee.

The sheriffe did him oppresse
  with great extremitie,
And said: 'either thou or I
  must doe this butcherie'.

When *Thewles* was unbarde,
  a vision there was seene:
Out of his mouth appear'd
  of couller bright and sheene;

Most lyke the glorious sunne,
  shyninge in clearest skye,
Downe over his bodie ranne,
  and vanish from their eye.

The butcher play'd his part,
  his bodie he did goare;
And sure the hardest hart
  did much his death deplore.

A hundred handcarchaffes
 with his sweete blood was dight,
As Reliques for to we(a)re
 for this said blessèd wight.

Then were his quarteres set
 upon the Castell hye,
Where hapt as strange a thinge
 as ever man did see.

A flight of Ravens came,
 and pykèd flesh from banes;
In the Church-yarde the⟨y⟩ did light,
 and scrapèd there deepe holes!

O Christian hartes, relent;
 prepare your soules to save –
When fethered foules shall help
 for us to make a grave!

O happie marterèd saintes,
 to you I call and crye,
To helpe us in our wantes
 and begge for us mercie!

O *Christ*, that suffered death,
 thy spouse for to defend,
Lyke co⟨n⟩stansie till death
 and in heaven be our end!

94

The Pilgrim Song

BY JOHN BUNYAN

(1684)

Who would true Valour see,
Let him come hither;
One here will Constant be,
Come Wind, come Weather.
There's no *Discouragement*,
Shall make him once *Relent*,
His first avow'd *Intent*,
To be a Pilgrim.

Who so beset him round,
With dismal *Stories*,
Do but themselves Confound;
His Strength the *more is*.
No *Lyon* can him fright,
He'l with a *Gyant Fight*,
But he will have a right,
To be a Pilgrim.

Hobgoblin, nor foul *Fiend*,
Can *daunt* his Spirit:
He knows, he *at the end*,
Shall Life Inherit.
Then Fancies fly away,
He'll fear not what men say,
He'll labour Night and Day,
To be a Pilgrim.

PART II

AMATORY

ONE

RURAL

95

The Jolly Beggar

BY JAMES V OF SCOTLAND (?)

There was a jolly beggar, and a begging he was born.   [*born = set forth*
And he took up his quarters into a land 'art town,   [*land 'art town*
   And we'll gang nae mair a roving   *= country*
     Sae late into the night,   *farm-steading*
   And we'll gang nae mair a roving, boys,
   Let the moon shine ne'er so bright.

He wad neither ly in barn, nor yet wad he in byre;
But in ahint the ha'door, or else afore the fire.   [*ahint = behind*
   And we'll gang nae mair a roving
     Sae late into the night,
   And we'll gang nae mair a roving, boys,
   Let the moon shine ne'er so bright.

The beggar's bed was made at e'en wi' good clean straw
   and hay,
And in ahint the ha'door, and there the beggar lay.
   And we'll gang nae mair a roving
     Sae late into the night,
   And we'll gang nae mair a roving, boys,
   Let the moon shine ne'er so bright.

Up raise the goodman's dochter and for to bar the door,
And there she saw the beggar standin' i' the floor.
   And we'll gang nae mair a roving
     Sae late into the night,

And we'll gang nae mair a roving, boys,
Let the moon shine ne'er so bright.

He took the lassie in his arms, and to the bed he ran,
[hooly =   'O hooly, hooly wi' me, sir, ye'll waken our goodman.'
cautiously   And we'll gang nae mair a roving
                     Sae late into the night,
                 And we'll gang nae mair a roving, boys,
                 Let the moon shine ne'er so bright.

The beggar was a cunnin' loon, and ne'er a word he spake,
[crack = talk   Until he got his turn done, syne he began to crack.
                 And we'll gang nae mair a roving
                     Sae late into the night,
                 And we'll gang nae mair a roving, boys,
                 Let the moon shine ne'er so bright.

'Is there ony dogs into this town? maiden, tell me true.'
[hinny =honey   'And what was ye do wi' them, my hinny and my dow?'
dow =dove   And we'll gang nae mair a roving
                     Sae late into the night,
                 And we'll gang nae mair a roving, boys,
                 Let the moon shine ne'er so bright.

[pocks =bags   'They'll rive a' my meal pocks, and do me meikle
                     wrang.'
                 'O dool for the doing o't! are ye the poor man?'
                 And we'll gang nae mair a roving
                     Sae late into the night,
                 And we'll gang nae mair a roving, boys,
                 Let the moon shine ne'er so bright.

Then she took up the meal pocks, and flang them o'er the
    wa';
'The deil gae wi' the meal pocks, my maidenhead, and a'!'
    And we'll gang nae mair a roving
        Sae late into the night,

298

And we'll gang nae mair a roving, boys,
Let the moon shine ne'er so bright.

'I took ye for some gentleman, at least the laird of Brodie;
O dool for the doing o't! are ye the poor bodie?'   [*dool = woe*
  And we'll gang nae mair a roving
    Sae late into the night,
  And we'll gang nae mair a roving, boys,
  Let the moon shine ne'er so bright.

He took the lassie in his arms, and gar her kisses three,
And four and twenty hunder merk to pay the
    nurice-fee.   [*nurice-fee =*
  And we'll gang nae mair a roving   *wet-nurse fee*
    Sae late into the night,
  And we'll gang nae mair a roving, boys,
  Let the moon shine ne'er so bright.

He took a horn frae his side, and blew baith loud and shrill,
And four and twenty belted knights came skipping o'er
    the hill.
  And we'll gang nae mair a roving
    Sae late into the night,
  And we'll gang nae mair a roving, boys,
  Let the moon shine ne'er so bright.

And he took out his little knife, loot a' his duddies fa';   [*duddies = rags*
And he was the brawest gentleman that was amang them a'.
  And we'll gang nae mair a roving
    Sae late into the night,
  And we'll gang nae mair a roving, boys,
  Let the moon shine ne'er so bright.

The beggar was a cliver loon, and he lap shoulder height:
'O, ay for sicken quarters as I gat yesternight!'   [*sicken = such*

And we'll gang nae mair a roving
   Sae late into the night,
And we'll gang nae mair a roving, boys,
Let the moon shine ne'er so bright.

96

The Complaint of a Lover Forsaken of his Love

A poore soule sate sighing by a sicamore tree,
   O willow, willow, willow;
His hand on his bosome, his head on his knee,
   O willow, willow, willow;
   O willow, willow, willow;
Sing, O the greene willow shall be my garland.

He sigh'd in his singing, and, after each groane,
'Adue to all pleasure, my true love is gone.

Oh, false is she turned; untrue she doth prove;
She renders me nothing, but hate for my love.

Oh, pitty me' (cried he), 'you lovers each one,
Her heart's hard as marble, she rues not my moane.'

The cold streames ran by him, his eyes wept apace,
The salt teares fell from him, which softned the stone.

'Let no body blame me, – her scornes I doe prove, –
She was borne to be false, and I dye for her love.

O that beauty should harbour a heart that's so hard, –
My true love rejecting without all regard!

Let Love no more boast him, in pallace or bowre,
For women are trothlesse and fleet in an houre.

But what helps complaining? in value I complaine;
I must patiently suffer her scorne and disdaine.

Come, all you forsaken, and sit downe by me,
He that plaineth of his false love, mine's falser than she.

The willow wreath weare I since my love did fleet;
A garland for lovers forsaken most meet.'

THE SECOND PART

'Low layde by my sorrow, begot by disdaine,
Against her, too cruel, still, still I complaine:

O Love too injurious! to wound my poore heart,
To suffer her triumph, and joy in my smart.

O willow, willow, willow, the willow garland,
So hang it, friends ore me in grave where I lye:

In grave where I rest me, hang this to the view
Of all that do know her, to blaze her untrue:

With these words ingraven, as epitaph meete,
"Heere lyes one drunke poyson for potion most sweete."

Though she thus unkindly have scorned my love,
And carelessly smiles at the sorrows I prove;

I cannot against her unkindly exclaime,
Cause once well I lovde her and honourede her name:

The name of her sounded so sweet in mine eare,
It raisde my heart lightly – the name of my deare.

As then 'twas my comfort, it now is my griefe,
It now brings me anguish; then, brought me reliefe.

Farewel, faire false-hearted, plaints end with my breath,
Thou dost loth me, – I love thee, though cause of my death.'

97

On Dulcina

BY SIR WALTER RALEGH (?)

As at noone *Dulcina* rested,
 In her sweet and shady bower,
Came a shepheard and requested,
 In her lapp to sleep an houre;
  But from her look,
  A wound he took
So deep, that for a further boon,
  The Nimph he prayes,
  Whereto she sayes,
Foregoe me now, come to me soone.

But in vaine did she conjure him,
 To depart her presence so,
Having a thousand tongues to allure him,
 And but one to bid him go.
  Where lips invite,
  And eyes delight,
And cheeks as fresh as rose in *June*
  Perswade to stay,
  What boots her say,
Foregoe me now, come to me soon.

Words whose hopes might have injoin'd
　　Him to let *Dulcina* sleep,
Could a mans love be confin'd,
　　Or a mayd her promise keep;
But he her waste,
　　Still holds as fast,
　　As she was constant to her Tune,
　　　　And still she spake,
For *Cupid's* sake,
　　　　　Foregoe me now, come to me soon.

He demands what time or pleasure,
　　Can there be more soon than now?
She sayes Night gives love that leasure,
　　That the Day doth not allow.
The Sun's kind sight,
　　Forgives delight,
　　　　Quoth he, more easily than the Moon.
And *Venus* playes: he told, she sayes,
　　　　　Foregoe me now, come to me soon.

[he told: 'be bold', Percy Folio MS.

But no promise nor profession,
　　From his hands could purchase scope;
Who would sell the sweet possession
　　Of such beauty for a hope?
Or for the sight of ling'ring night,
　　Foregoe the present Joyes of Noon,
Though ne'er so faire, her speeches were,
　　　　　Foregoe me now, come to me soon.

How at last agreed these lovers,
　　He was faire, and she was young,
Tongue may tell what eye discovers,
　　Joyes unseen are never sung.

Did she consent,
Or he relent,
Accepts he night, or grants she noon,
Left he her mayd, or not? she said
Foregoe me now, come to me soon.

98

A New Courtly Sonnet of the Lady Greensleeves

Greensleeves was all my joy,
Greensleeves was my delight;
Greensleeves was my heart of gold,
And who but Lady Greensleeves.

Alas, my Love! ye do me wrong
To cast me off discourteously;
And I have loved you so long,
Delighting in your company.
Greensleeves was all my joy, &c.

I have been ready at your hand,
To grant whatever you would crave;
[Waged = risked] I have both waged life and land,
Your love and goodwill for to have.
Greensleeves was all my joy, &c.

I bought thee kerchers to thy head,
That were wrought fine and gallantly;
I kept thee both at board and bed,
Which cost my purse well favouredly.
Greensleeves was all my joy, &c.

I bought thee petticoats of the best,
The cloth so fine as fine might be;

I gave thee jewels for thy chest,
  And all this cost I spent on thee.
    Greensleeves was all my joy, &c.

Thy smock of silk, both fair and white,
  With gold embroidered gorgeously;
Thy petticoat of sendal right;
  And thus I bought thee gladly.
    Greensleeves was all my joy, &c.

[*Sendal=a fine silk*

Thy girdle of gold so red,
  With pearls bedecked sumptuously;
The like no other lasses had,
  And yet thou wouldst not love me.
    Greensleeves was all my joy, &c.

Thy purse and eke thy gay gilt knives,
  Thy pincase gallant to the eye;
No better wore the burgess wives,
  And yet thou wouldst not love me.
    Greensleeves was all my joy, &c.

Thy crimson stockings all of silk,
  With gold all wrought above the knee;
Thy pumps as white as was the milk,
  And yet thou wouldst not love me.
    Greensleeves was all my joy, &c.

Thy gown was of the grassy green,
  Thy sleeves of satin hanging by,
Which made thee be our harvest queen,
  And yet thou wouldst not love me.
    Greensleeves was all my joy, &c.

Thy garters fringed with the gold,
　And silver aglets hanging by,
Which made thee blithe for to behold,
　And yet thou wouldst not love me.
　　Greensleeves was all my joy, &c.

My gayest gelding I thee gave,
　To ride wherever liked thee;
No lady ever was so brave,
　And yet thou wouldst not love me.
　　Greensleeves was all my joy, &c.

My men were clothed all in green,
　And they did ever wait on thee;
All this was gallant to be seen,
　And yet thou wouldst not love me.
　　Greensleeves was all my joy, &c.

They set thee up, they took thee down,
　They served thee with humility;
Thy foot might not once touch the ground,
　And yet thou wouldst not love me.
　　Greensleeves was all my joy, &c.

For every morning when thou rose,
　I sent thee dainties orderly,
To cheer thy stomach from all woes,
　And yet thou wouldst not love me.
　　Greensleeves was all my joy, &c.

Thou couldst desire no earthly thing
　But still thou hadst it readily;
Thy music still to play and sing,
　And yet thou wouldst not love me.
　　Greensleeves was all my joy, &c.

And who did pay for all this gear
   That thou didst spend when pleased thee?
Even I that am rejected here,
   And thou disdain'st to love me.
     Greensleeves was all my joy, &c.

Well, I will pray to God on high,
   That thou my constancy mayst see,
And that yet once before I die,
   Thou wilt vouchsafe to love me.
     Greensleeves was all my joy, &c.

Greensleeves, now farewell! adieu!
   God I pray to prosper thee;
For I am still thy lover true.
   Come once again and love me.
     Greensleeves was all my joy,
       Greensleeves was my delight;
     Greensleeves was my heart of gold,
       And who but Lady Greensleeves.

99

Phillida Flouts Me

OR

The Country Lover's Complaint

Who does by all means for to win his Love,
But she doth scorn him, and disdainful prove;
Which makes him for to sigh, lament and cry,
He fears for Phillida that he shall dye

Oh! what a plague is Love! How shall I bear it?
She will unconstant prove, I greatly fear it:
It so torments my mind, that my strength faileth,

She wavers with the wind, as the ship saileth.
  Please her the best you may,
  She looks another way,
  Alas and well-a-day!
    Phillida flouts me.

At the Fair yesterday, she did pass by me;
She lookt another way, and would not spy me.
I woo'd her for to dine, I could not get her;
Dick had her to the wine : he might intreat her!
  With *Daniel* she did dance,
  On me she would not glance,
  Oh thrice unhappy chance!
    Phillida flouts me.

Fair Maid, be not so coy, do not disdain me;
I am my mother's joy : Sweet, entertain me!
Shee'l give me, when she dyes, all things that's fitting,
Her Poultry and her Bees, and her Geese sitting;

[*Mallerds*=   A paire of *Mallerds* beds
eider-down   And barrel full of shreds.
  And yet, for all these goods,
    Phillida flouts me!

Thou shalt eat curds and cream, all the year lasting,
And drink the chrystal stream, pleasant in tasting;

[*Wig*=*a small*   Wig and whey till thou burst, and Bramble Berries;
cake   Pye-lid and pasty-crust, Pears, Plums and Cherries.
  Thy raiment shall be thin,
  Made of a weather's skin;
  All is not worth a Pin :
    Phillida flouts me!

Cupid hath shot his Dart, and hath me wounded,
It pricked my tender heart, and ne'er rebounded :
I was a fool to scorn his Bow and Quiver,

308

I am like one forlorn, sick of a Feaver:
  Now I may weep and mourn,
  Whilst with Love's flames I burn,
  Nothing will serve my turn,
    Phillida flouts me.

I am a lively Lad, howe'er she take me,
I am not half so bad as she would make me.
Whether she smile or frown, she may deceive me;
Ne'r a girl in the Town but fain would have me.
  Since she doth from me flye,
  Now I may sigh and dye,
  And never cease to cry
    Phillida flouts me!

In the last moneth of *May*, I made her posies,
I heard her often say that she loved Roses;
Cowslips and Jilli-flowers, and the white Lilly,
I brought to deck the bowers, for my sweet *Philly*,
  But she did all disdain,
  And threw them back again,
  Therefore it's flat and plain,
    Phillida flouts me.

Fair Maiden, have a care, and in time take me;
I can have those as fair, if you forsake me,
For *Doll* the dairy-maide laught at me lately,
And wanton *Winifred* favours me greatly.
  One cast milk on my clothes,
  T'other plaid with my nose;
  What wanton toys are those?
    Phillida flouts me.

I cannot work and sleep, all at a season;
⟨Love⟩ wounds my heart so deep, without all reason.

I fade and pine away, with Grief and sorrow,
I fall quite to decay, like any shadow.
  I shall be dead, I fear,
  Within a thousand year,
  All is for grief and care:
    Phillida flouts me.

She hath a cloute of mine, wrought with good *Coventry*,
Which she keeps for a sign of my Fidelity.
But in faith, if she frown, she shall not weare it:
I'll give it *Doll* my maid, and she shall tear it.
  Since 'twill no better be,
  I'le bear it patiently,
  Yet all the world may see
    Phillida flouts me!

100

The Happy Husbandman

OR

Country. Innocence

My young *Mary* do's mind the Dairy,
While I go a Howing and Mowing each Morn;
Then hey the little Spinning-Wheel
Merrily round do's reel,
  while I am singing amidst the corn:
Cream and kisses both are my delight,
She gives me them, and the joys of night;
She's soft as the Air, as Morning fair,
Is not such a maid a most pleasing sight?

While I whistle, she from the Thistle
Does gather Down for to make us a Bed,

And then my little Love does lie
All the Night long, and dye
  in the kind arms of her nown dear *Ned*;
There I taste of a delicate spring,
But I mun not tell you, nor name the thing,
To put you a Wishing, and think of Kissing,
For Kisses cause sighs, and young Men shou'd sing.

Sedge and rushes, and tops of Bushes
Shall thatch our Roof, and shall strow all our Floar,
And then the pritty Nightingales
Will fly from Groves and Dales
  to live with us, and we'll ne'er be Poor:
Little Lambkins whenever they dye
Will bequeth new blankets to thee and I,
Our quilts shall be roses, which *June* disposes;
So warm and so sweet my young Love shall lie.

Fountains pure shall be thy ewer
To sprinkle water upon thy fair face;
And near the little flock shall play
All the long Summer's Day;
  gentle white lambs will adorn the place.
Then at night we'll hie home to our hive,
And (like bees) enjoy all the sweets alive:
We'll taste all Love's treasure, and enjoy that Pleasure,
While others for Fame and for Greatness strive.

No man's frowns are on the Downs,
For truly there we most freely may sing,
And kiss the pretty *Nancies*,
While Changes and Chances
  amuse all the Great, and Disturbance bring,
We will with our young Lambs go to Bed,
And observe the Lives that our Fathers led;
We'll mind not Ambition, nor sow Sedition,
And leave State-affairs to the State-man's head.

Oaten Reeds (those humble Weeds)
Shall be the Pipes upon which we will play,
And on the merry Mountain,
Or else by a fountain
   we'll merrily pass the sweet time away:
Sure no mortal can blame us for this.
And now mark the way of your *London* Miss,
She masters your breeches, and takes your riches,
While we have more joys by a harmless kiss.

No youth here need Willow wear,
No beauteous maid will her Lover destroy:
The gentle little Lass will yield
In the soft Daisy Field,
   freely our pleasures we here enjoy:
No great Juno we boldly defie,
With young Cloris' cheeks or fair Celia's eye;
We let those things alone, and enjoy our own,
Every Night with our Beauties lie.

101

Flora's Lamentable Passion

Crown'd with Unspeakable Joy and Comfort

Flora she did sore lament, her Spirit did decay;
Strephon fill'd her with content, and cast all Grief away.

Flora, 's in her Grove she lyed, sighing, panting, thus she
cryed,
   Strephon, thou art fled from me;
O my Swain 1 may complain, for thou dost prove unkind
I see.

I was ever chaste and Loyal, O, it is a grievous tryal,
　　that we should separated be:
Cupid's Dart hath pierc'd my heart, alas my joys are fled
　from me.

Here I sit in grief afflicted, by my love I am rejected,
　　sorrows hath compast me round:
Insulting Death, come stop my breath, and let not grief
　in me abound.

The pretty little lambs lamented, seeming to be
　discontented,
　　hearing of her make this moan;
Quoth she, My pain I can't contain, for all my joys from
　me are flown.

He a thousand times hath kist me, and as many times has
　blest me,
　　calling me his only joy;
But now I find he proves unkind, which doth my
　comforts quite destroy.

With sweet language thou did'st woe me, and with
　comforts did'st indue me,
　　yet thou proved'st most false I see;
Remember now thy former vow, which thou did'st make
　in secresie.

I was never false and fickle! Down her cheeks the tears
　did trickle,
　　and her colour waxed pale.
With complaint her heart did faint; quoth she, I find
　my spirits fail.

Strephon's ANSWER to *Flora's* COMPLAINT

In the midst of all her trouble *Strephon* did her joys
redouble,
    with a sweet oblieging way;
He did her greet, quoth he, My sweet, my Love is fixt
from all decay.

Floras I do dearly love thee, I esteem no one above thee,
    thou shalt have thy heart's delight.
Then her's my hand, do thou command, and I will serve
thee day and night.

Though I seemed to be parted, yet I am more loyal
hearted,
    my Love is linked unto thee;
Take hand and heart, we'l never part, thou art my life
and liberty.

Floras, I in heart adore thee, I prefer no one before thee,
    thou hast a sweet obliging Eye;
I'le ne'er be cruel to my jewel, but be faithful till I dye.

Do not think that I will slight thee, I endeavour to
delight thee,
    nothing shall my love annoy;
I will nourish, and will cherish, my sweet *Floras,* my
true joy.

102

The Wandering Maiden

OR

True Love at Length United

She search'd the Hills and Mountains round
  in grief and discontent,
At length her dearest Love she found,
  for whom she did lament:
Then all her tears, and sighs, and fears,
  was turned into bliss,
And in his arms, a thousand charms,
  she sealed with a kiss.

Over hills and high mountains
  long time have I gone,
Ah! and down by the fountains,
  by my self all alone:
Through bushes and briers
  being void of all care,
Through perils and dangers,
  for the loss of my dear.

I am forced and droven
  unconstant to prove,
I am forced and droven
  away from my love,
I am forced and droven
  from him quite away,
By reason I am bound, love,
  and needs must obey.

Through the shade will I wander,
  I can do no less,
For the grief I lye under
  no one can express:

315

Neither terror nor danger,
  I ever will fear,
For I will be a ranger
  to find out my dear.

I'll go to some desert,
  and mourn for my dear,
And a bunsh of green willows
  I vow for to wear:
And instead of love's token,
  my self I'll maintain,
I'll go to some desert,
  and I may come again.

For true love is a tryal,
  beyond all compare,
And without all denial
  my life will ensnare;
He is gone, and doth leave me,
  in much discontent,
For his absence doth grieve me,
  in tears I lament.

Sure if I cannot find him,
  I well may agree,
That the fates have design'd him
  my ruin to be:
Ah! sweet *Cupid* befriend me,
  and grant my desire,
Or kind Death now come end me
  that I may expire.

Then her tears they were flowing,
  down from her fair eyes,
But her love little knowing
  her sorrowful cries;

Yet at length when he heard,
  how she did lament,
He then quickly appeared
  to her hearts content.

THE MANN'S REPLY

My dear love, cease thy weeping,
  now listen to me,
For waking and sleeping,
  my heart is with thee;
My love, let nothing grieve thee,
  dear, do not complain,
For I never will leave thee,
  while life doth remain.

Then these lovers embraced
  in each others arms.
Their affections was placed
  in sweet loving charms:
Thus they both was united,
  and free from annoy,
Ah! she is delighted,
  with her only joy.

Then her trouble was ended,
  her grief did expel,
She in love was befriended,
  and then all was well;
For in him such a blessing,
  at length she hath found,
That beyond all expressing,
  her joys did abound.

103

The Shepheard and the Milkmaid

I'le tell you a Tale of my Love and I,
   How we did often a milking goe;
And when I look't merrily, then she would cry,
   And still in her fits she would use me so.
At last I plainly did tell her my mind,
   And then she began to love me;
I ask'd her the cause of her being unkind?
   She said, It was only to prove me!

I then did give her a kiss or two,
   Which she return'd with interest still;
I thought I had now no more to do.
   But that with her I might have my will.
But she, being taught by her crafty Dad,
   Began to be cautious and wary;
And told me, When I my will had had,
   The Divell a bit I would marry.

So marry'd we were, and when it was o'er,
   I told her plain, in the Parsonage Hall,
That if she had gi'n me my will before,
   The Divell a bit I'de a marry'd at all.
She smil'd, and presently told me her mind:
   She had vow'd she'd never do more so,
Because she was cozen'd (in being too kind)
   By three or four men before so.

104

The Coy Shepherdess

OR

Phillis and Amintas

Fair Phillis in a wanton posture lyes,
Not thinking to be seen by mortall eyes
Till accidentally Amintas came,
And see her lye, which made her blush for shame;
He cast himself down by her on the hay,
And won her love before he went away.

Phillis on the new made hay
On a pleasant Summers day
She in wanton posture lay
   thinking no Shephard nigh her
Till *Amintas* came that way
   and threw himself down by her.

At first she was amaz'd
And with blushes on him gaz'd
Her beauty bright did him invite
   her shape he did admire,
Her wanton dress could do no less,
   then set his heart on fire.

Then Amintas mildly said,
Phillis be not now afraid
But entertain, thy shepherd swain,
   now we are met together,
Then I shall prize thy sparkling eyes
   that did invite me hither.

I have rang'd the plains about
For to find my Phillis out

My flocks I left, of joys bereft,
  whilst I for thee did languish;
Tis in thy will my heart to fill
  with joy or else with anguish.

Then fair Phillis frowning said,
My privacy thou hast betraid;
Therefore be gone, let me alone,
  do not disturb my pleasure,
Nor do not move thy sute of love,
  but leave me to my leasure.

Never yet did Shepheards Swain
On this smooth Sicilian plain
Once dare to move my deep disdain
  by such like bold intrusion,
Then cease thy suit, 'tis but in vain
  I scorn such fond delusion.

When Amintas see her frown
Hoping still his joys to crown
Quoth he my dear, as I am here
  I like not this behaviour;
Tis lovers bliss, to toy and kiss
  it wins a maidens favor.

Let us like the Ivy twine
And our loves in one combine
Grim *Pluto* loved *Proserpine*
  her beauty did him fetter;
When thou art mine and I am thine,
  I'le please thee ten times better.

Fye for shame fond boy, she said,
Im resolv'd to live a Maid,

Thou art too young, to do me wrong
   be not so bold to venture,
Whilst he poor youth, to speak the truth,
   still aimed at the center.

Phillis blusht as red as blood
When his mind she understood
His bold intent for to prevent,
   she us'd her best endeavor,
His resolution it was bent
   for he was loath to leave her.

Hotly he persued the Game,
Whilst his heart was on a flame
She cry'd Pish nay fye for shame
   in faith you shall not do it
But the youth her overcame
   and eagerly fell to it.

Thus she strived all in vain
Whilst she felt a pleasing pain,
Yet he by no means would refrain
   but kindly did imbrace her,
He kist his love and told her plain
   he never would disgrace her.

In great rage she flung away
Tumbling ore the new-made hay
Whilst he ashamd & breathless ⟨lay;⟩
   although he then displeas'd ⟨her,⟩
He rally'd and renewd the fray,
   and manfully appeas'd her.

Thus they spent this christal day
in such wanton sports and play,

Amintas there, imbrac'd his Dear,
    and bid her be lighthearted;
But night being come they hasted home,
    and kindly kist and parted.

105

There was a Brisk Girle

There was a brisk Girle both bonny & browne
She corted her sweet hart in our Towne
She lad by her weerke her wheele and yearne
Too followe her Love in ye farmers barne
Quoth she if you'le be maryed
Weele hey to ye Parsons and then to bed
My virgins treasure Ile give thee ned
That is to be plaine my maidenhead.

You know yt my Love is a flame of fire
And Burns when itt Cannott obtane my desire
My Beauty is now in itts Blooming prime
and I cannot nor will nott dellay ye time
I Lonng to tastt those tender Joys
Those softe kisses and wanton toys
Thatt every Lasse in her wedding injoys:
Whilst Ladds with young Lasses get Lusty boys.

A Garland of Roses my Love shall weare
And Ile give him a loke of my Cole Black hair
At every wake my Love Ile treate
and give him kind kisses as dreame Boats Sweet
Thou shalt Be my Buck and Ile Be thy doe
Ile Mile and thou shalt mow
Ile Card and Ile Spin whileste you harrow & sow
And Call uponn Dobbin with hey Jee hoh:

I pray thee deare nell Lett Clout my shoun   [*Shoun=shoes*
And wee will be maryed be fore itt be nowne   [*Nowne=noon*
Ile goe to ye Church a Licanse Bring
Ile gee ye to Ride on my paceing Rone
With ye gray Pilling I Lentte to Jone   [*Pilling=
pillion

Ah woese my poore Jugge, howe will she mack mone   *Jugge=Joan*
Since fate had designed her to Ley alone.

106

The Merry Hay-Makers

OR

Pleasant Pastime between the Young-men and Maids, in the Pleasant Meadows

In our Country, in our Country
    Where Rufferlers was a raking;   [*Rufferlers=*
And the rarest pastime that ever you see,   *boisterous*
    was when Hay-cocks they were a making, *to be*   *people*

There's *Timmy*, and *Tommy*, with bottle and bag,
    as soon as the Lasses beheld them,
Because they did not give them what they did lack,
    adzuggers they swore they would geld 'em, *to be*

And did you not know one *Vulking* the Smith,
    and Mary that went to the Dairy;
O give me quoth she, a thing that is stiff,
    and make me look Buxom and Airy, *to be*

And down in a Dale was tumble down *Dick*
    with *Mary*, and *Sarah*, and *Susan*,
They being in haste for to play the old trick,
    they leap'd into bed with their shooes on, *to be*

And some they Fork, and some they will Rake
    when merrily they were a quaffing.
And if you had seen how *Jones* Buttocks did wag
    'twould a broke a Man's side out of laughing, *to be*

Young *Bridget* came next, and plaguily vext,
    with fury she fell upon *Robin.*
His Clater-de-vengeance adzuggers she claw'd,
    'cause he with young Kate had been bobing, *to be*

With that he made bold with speed to take hold
    of Bridget's young Chitter-de-widgeon,
He threw her along but did it no wrong;
    because it was just upon fledging, *to be.*

Her Mother came by, and as she drew nigh,
    the sight put her into a laughter,
His Buttocks she bang'd and bid him be hang'd,
    for playing the fool with her Daughter, *to be*

The Men and the Maids, they love their Comrades,
    above any Paltry Riches,
Quoth *Nancy* to *Dick* adzuggers i'm sick
    for something thou hast in thy Breeches, *to be.*

What sayst thou me so, then to it we'll go,
    thou shalt have thy earnest desire;
For thou art the Lass, I swear by the Mass,
    which I above all do admire, *to be.*

At making of Hay they frolick and play
    as you may observe by this Ditty,
And when they are crack'd, away they are pack'd,
    for Virgins, away to the City, *to be.*

107

A Pleasant New Court Song

Between a yong Courtier and a Country Lasse

Upon a Summer's time,
   in the middle of the morne,
A bonny Lasse I spide,
   the fairest ere was borne;
Fast by a standing poole,
   within a meddow greene,
She laide herselfe to coole,
   not thinking to be seene.

She gathered lovely flowers,
   and spent her time in sport,
As if to Cupid's bowers
   she daily did resort.
The fields afford content
   unto this maiden kinde,
Much time and paines she spent
   to satisfy her minde.

The Cowslip there she cropt,
   the Daffadill and Dazie;
The Primrose lookt so trim,
   she scorned to be lazie:
And ever as ⟨s⟩he did
   these pretty posies pull,
She rose and fetcht a sigh,
   and wisht her apron full.

I hearing of her wish,
   made bold to step unto her;

Thinking her love to winne,
    I thus began to wooe her: –
Faire maide, be not so coy,
    to kisse thee I am bent.
O fie, she cride, away!
    yet, smiling, gave consent.

Then did I help to plucke
    of every flower that grew;
No herbe nor flower I mist,
    but only Time and Rue.
Both she and I tooke paines
    to gather flowers store,
Untill this maiden said,
    kinde sir, Ile have no more.

Yet still my loving heart
    did proffer more to pull;
No sir, quoth she, ile part,
    because mine apron's full.
So, sir, ile take my leave,
    till next we meet againe:
Rewards me with a kisse,
    and thanks me for my paine.

108

The Wooing Rogue

Come live with me and be my Whore,
And we will beg from door to door
Then under a hedge we'l sit and louse us,
Until the Beadle come to rouse us
And if they'l give us no relief,
    Thou shalt turn Whore and I'l turn Thief.
    Thou shalt turn Whore and I'l turn Thief.

If thou canst rob, then I can steal,
And we'l eat Roast-meat every meal:
Nay, we'l eat white-bread every day
And throw our mouldy crusts away,
And twice a day we will be drunk,
  And then at night I'l kiss my Punk,
  And then at night I'l kiss my Punk.

And when we both shall have the Pox,
We then shall want both Shirts and Smocks,
To shift each others mangy hide,
That is with Itch so pockifi'd;
We'l take some clean ones from a hedge,
  And leave our old ones for a pledge.
  And leave our old ones for a pledge.

[*to shift = to change (of clothes*)

109

Young Coridon and Phillis

BY SIR CHARLES SEDLEY (?)

Young Coridon and Phillis
  Sate in a Lovely Grove;
Contriving Crowns of Lillies,
  Repeating Tales of Love:
And something else, but what I dare not name.

But as they were a Playing,
  She oagled so the Swain;
It sav'd her plainly saying
  Let's kiss to ease our Pain:
And something else, but what I dare not name.

A thousand times he kiss'd her,
   Laying her on the Green;
But as he farther press'd her,
   Her pretty Leg was seen:
And something else, but what I dare not name.

So many Beauties removing,
   His Ardour still increas'd;
And greater Joys pursuing,
   He wander'd o'er her Breast:
And something else, but what I dare not name.

A last Effort she trying,
   His passion to withstand;
Cry'd, but it was faintly crying,
   Pray take away your Hand:
And something else, but what I dare not name.

Young Coridon grown bolder,
   The Minute would improve;
This is the time he told her,
   To shew you how I love;
And something else, but what I dare not name.

The Nymph seem'd almost dying,
   Dissolv'd in amorous heat;
She kiss'd and told him sighing,
   My Dear your Love is great:
And something else, but what I dare not name.

But Phillis did recover
   Much sooner than the Swain;
She blushing ask'd her Lover,
   Shall we not kiss again:
And something else, but what I dare not name.

Thus Love his Revels keeping,
  'Til Nature at a stand;
From talk they fell to Sleeping,
  Holding each others Hand;
And something else, but what I dare not name.

110

The Maid of Tottenham

As I went to *Totnam*
Upon a Market-day,
There met I with a faire maid
Cloathed all in gray,
Her journey was to *London*
With Buttermilk and Whay,
  To fall down, down, derry down,
    down, down, derry down,
    derry, derry dina.

God speed faire maid quoth one,
You are well over-took;
With that she cast her head aside,
And gave to him a look.
She was as full of Leachery
As letters in a book.
  To fall down, down, derry down,
    down, down, derry down,
    derry, derry dina.

And as they walk'd together,
Even side by side,
The young man was aware
That her garter was unty'd,
For feare that she should lose it,

Aha, alack he cry'd,
Oh your garter that hangs down!
  To fall down, down, derry down,
    down, down, derry down,
    derry, derry dina.

Quoth she, I do intreat you
For to take the pain
To do so much for me,
As to tye it up again.
That will I do sweet heart, quoth he,
When I come on yonder plain.
  With a down, down, derry down,
    down, down, derry down,
    derry, derry dina.

And when they came upon the plain
Upon a pleasant green,
The fair maid spread her legs abroad.
The young man fell between,
Such tying of a Garter
I think was never seen.
  To fall down, down, derry down,
    down, down, derry down,
    derry, derry dina.

When they had done their businesse,
And quickly done the deed,
He gave her kisses plenty,
And took her up with speed.
And what they did I know not,
But they were both agreed.
  To fall down together, down
    down, down, derry down,
    down, down, derry dina.

She made to him low curtsies
And thankt him for his paine,
The young man is to High-gate gone⟨,⟩
The maid to *London* came
To sell off her commodity
She thought it for no shame.
   To fall down together, down
      down, down, derry down,
      down, down, derry dina.

When she had done her market,
And all her money told
To think upon the matter
It made her heart full cold⟨:⟩
But that which will away, quoth she,
Is very hard to hold.
   To fall down together, down
      down, down, derry down,
      down, down, derry dina.

This tying of the Garter
Cost her her Maidenhead,
Quoth she it is no matter,
It stood me in small stead,
But often times it troubled me
As I lay in my bed.
   To fall down together, down
      down, down, derry down,
      down, down, derry dina.

III

The Mourning Conquest

OR

The Woman's sad Complaint, and doleful Cry
To see her Love in Fainting fits to lye

As I did walk abroad one time
   I chanced for to see,
A Young-man and a Maid, but
   they did not know of me:
She being in the vain then,
   chuckt him under the Chin,
And smiling in his face, she said,
   Alas poor thing

The Young-man very bashful was,
   but had a good intent,
He lov'd the Maid with all his heart,
   but knew not what she meant:
And much ado she had poor heart,
   this young man for to bring
Unto her bow, which made her cry,
   Alas poor thing

She by his loving Complements,
   did undertake and find,
That she might safely let him go,
   and understand her mind:
Pretending for to stumble,
   on the ground her self did fling,
And said, sweet-heart, I fell by chance,
   Alas poor thing

I could not choose but laugh to see
   these two so close imploy'd,
The Young-man was contented, and
   the maid was overjoy'd:
Expressing of her love, she
   did closely to him cling
But finding him begin to fail,
   Alas poor thing

It was not long before this young-man
   was tir'd with this sport,
He laid him down to rest awhile,
   he took his breath full short:
She turn'd about and kiss'd him, and
   did closely to him cling,
Sweet-heart (quoth she) how dost thou now,
   Alas poor thing

But finding him in fainting fits,
   She then began to weep,
And with her hands she rubb'd his joynts,
   to keep this youth from sleep:
Quoth she, sweet-heart, thy weakness makes
   my very heart to sting,
Come fie for shame, rouse up thy self,
   Alas poor thing

And coming to himself again,
   his face lookt wondrous wan,
Wishing he were as strong, as when
   he first with her began;
And in a rage he swore, he thought
   no Woman e're could bring
A man so weak, which made him cry
   Alas poor thing

Quoth she, sweet-heart, the soldier that
   doth venture in the field,
Although at first repulsed, yet
   the day they will not yield.
But face about, and Charge again,
   and take the other fling,
Ile do my best to second thee,
   Alas poor thing

Poor heart, she said what in her lay,
   this Young-mans heart to cheer,
By kissing him and calling him,
   Her Honey and her Dear,
But finding of his Courage,
   so sadly for to hing,
Down she fell again and cry'd
   Alas poor thing

[*hing = hang*

So to conclude, I saw this youth,
   most fairly beat in field:
The stout'st heart that ever drew,
   is sometimes forc'd to yield,
And to put up his Blade again,
   there sadly for to hing,
And leave his foe to sigh and cry
   Alas poor thing

112

The Sound Country Lass

These *London* Wenches are so stout,
   They care not what they do;
They will not let you have a Bout,
   Without a Crown or two.

They double their Chops, and Curl their Locks,
   Their Breaths perfume they do;
Their tails are pepper'd with the Pox,
   And that you're welcome to.

But give me the Buxom Country Lass,
   Hot piping from the Cow;
That will take a touch upon the Grass,
   Ay, marry, and thank you too.

Her Colour's as fresh as a Rose in *June*
   Her Temper as kind as a Dove;
She'll please the Swain with a wholesome Tune,
   And freely give her Love.

113

A Ballad of the Courtier and the Country Clown

Your Courtiers scorn we Country Clowns,
   We Country Clowns care not for Court;
But we'll be as merry upon the Downs,
   As you are at Midnight with all your Sport.
      With a Fadding, etc.

You Hawk, you Hunt, you lie upon Pallets,
   You Eat you Drink, the Lord knows how;
We sit upon Hillocks, and pick up our Sallets,   [*Sallets = salads*
   And drink up a Sillibub under a Cow.
      With a Fadding, etc.

Your Masques are made for Knights and Lords,
   And Ladies that go fine and gay;
We Dance to such Musick the Bag-pipe affords,
   And trick up our Lasses as well as we may.
      With a Fadding, etc.

Your Cloaths are made of Silk and Sattin,
    And ours are made of good Sheeps Grey;
You mix your Discourses with pieces of *Latin*,
    We speak our English as well as we may.
        With a Fadding, etc.

Your Chambers are hung with Cloth of *Arras*,
    Our Meadows bedeck'd as fine as may be;
And from our Sport you never shall bar us,
    Since *Joan* in the Dark, is as good as my Lady.
        With a Fadding, etc.

Your Courtiers clip and cull upon Beds,
    We Jumble our Lasses upon the Grass;
And when we have gotten their Maiden-heads,
    They serve to make a Courtier's Lass.
        With a Fadding, etc.

You Dance Courants and the *French* Braul,
    We Jig the Morris upon the *Green*;
And we make as good sport in a Country-Hall,
    As you do before the King and the Queen.
        With a Fadding, etc.

Then Ladies do not us disdain,
    Although we wear no gaudy Cloaths;
You'll find as much Pith in a Country Swain,
    When he plucks up your gay Embroider'd Cloaths.
        With a Fadding, etc.

114

The Green-Gown

Pan leave Piping, the Gods have done Feasting,
   There's never a Goddess a Hunting to Day:
Mortals marvel at Coridon's Jesting,
   That gives the assistance to entertain May.
The Lads and the Lasses, with Scarfs on their Faces,
   So lively as passes, trip over the Downs:
Much Mirth and Sport they make, running at
      Barley-break;
   Lord what haste they make for a Green-gown!

John with Gillan, Harry with Frances,
   Meg and Mary, with Robin and Will,
George and Margery lead all the Dances,
   For they were reported to have the best Skill:
But Cicily and Nancy, the fairest of many,
   That came last of any, from out of the Towns,
Quickly got in among the midst of all the Throng,
   They so much did long for their Green-gowns.

Wanton Deborah whispered with Dorothy,
   That she would wink upon Richard and Sym,
Mincing Maudlin shew'd her Authority,
   And in the Quarrel would venture a Limb.
But Sibel was sickly, and could not come quickly,
   And therefore was likely to fall in a Swoon,
Tib would not tarry for Tom, nor for Harry,
   Lest Christian should carry away the Green-gown.

Blanch and Bettrice, both of a Family,
   Came very lazy lagging behind;
Annise and Aimable noting their Policy,
   Cupid is cunning, although he be blind:

[*passes* = a dance step(?), or '*pacers*'(?)]

But Winny the Witty, that came from the City,
  With Parnel the Pretty, and Besse the Brown;
Clem, Joan, and Isabel, Sue, Alice and bonny Nell,
  Travell'd exceedingly for a Green-gown.

Now the Youngsters had reach'd the green Meadow,
  Where they intended to gather their May,
Some in the Sun-shine, some in the Shadow,
  Singled in Couples did fall to their Play;
But constant Penelope, Faith, Hope and Charity,
  Look'd very modestly, yet they lay down;
And Prudence prevented what Rachel repented,
  And Kate was contented to take a Green-gown.

Then they desired to know of a truth,
  If all their Fellows were in the like Case,
Nem call'd for Ede, and Ede for Ruth,
  Ruth for Marcy, and Marcy for Grace;
But there was no speaking, they answer'd with squeaking,
  The pretty Lass breaking the head of the Clown;
But some were Wooing, while others were doing,
  Yet all their going was for a Green-gown.

Bright Apollo was all this while peeping,
  To see if his Daphne had been in the Throng,
But missing her hastily downwards was creeping,
  For Thetis imagin'd he tarried too long:
Then all the Troop mourned and homeward returned,
  For Cynthia scorned to smile, or to frown;
  Thus they did gather May, all the long Summer-day,
  And at Night went away with a Green-Gown.

115

'*A Shepherd kept Sheep on a Hill so High*'

BY T. D'URFEY

A Shepherd kept Sheep in a Hill so high, fa, la, la, etc.
And there came a pretty Maid passing by, fa, la, etc.
Shepherd, quoth she, dost thou want e'er a Wife,
No by my troth I'm not weary of my Life, fa, la, la, etc.

Shepherd for thee I care not a Fly, fa, la, la,
For thou'st not the Face with a fair Maid to lie, fa, la,
How now my Damsel, say'st thou me so,
Thou shalt tast of my bottle before thou dost go, fa, la.

Then he took her and laid her upon the Ground, fa, la,
And made her believe that the World went round, fa, la,
Look yonder my Shepherd, look yonder I spy,
There are fine pretty Babies that dance in the Sky, fa, la.

And now they are vanisht, and now they appear, fa, la,
Sure they will tell Stories of what we do here, fa, la, la,
Lie still my dear Chloris, enjoy thy Conceit,
For the Babes are too young and too little to prate, fa, la, la.

See how the Heavens fly swifter than Day, fa, la, la,
Rise quickly, or they will all run away, fa, la, la,
Rise quickly my Shepherd, quickly I tell ye,
For the Sun, Moon and Stars are got all in my Belly, fa, la.

O dear, where am I? pray shew me the way, fa, la, la,
Unto my Father's House hard by, fa, la, la,
If he chance to Chide me for staying so long,
I'll tell him the fumes of your Bottle were strong, fa, la, la.

And now thou hast brought my Body to shame, fa, la.
I prithee now tell me what is thy Name, fa, la, la,
Why Robin in the Rushes my Name is, quoth he,
But I think I told her quite contrary, fa, la, la.

Then for Robin in the Rushes, she did enquire, fa, la, la,
But he hung down his Head, and he would not come nigh
    her, fa, la, la,
He wink'd with one Eye, as if he had been Blind,
And he drew one Leg after a great way behind, fa, la, la.

116

Have-at a Venture

The powers of love so powerful are,
What mortal can withstand,
Or, who can say oppose they dare
Where Cupid *bears command*
This Damsel quickly she did yield
The youngsters skill to try,
The twinkling Archer won the Field,
And then she down did lye

A Country Lad and bonny Lass
    they did together meet
And as they did together pass
    thus he began to greet!
What I do say I may mind well,
    and thus I do begin:
If you would have your Belly swell
    Hold up, and i'l put in

Oh! Sir, (quoth she) I love the sport,
    Yet am afraid to try,
And for your love, I thank you for't,
    find but conveniency:

My mind I'le tell you by and by,
   your love my heart doth win,
And presently I down will lye,
   Oh! then Boy push it in.

He clasp'd this Damsel round the wast
   and softly laid her down,
Yea wantonly he her imbrac'd
   and her delights did Crown:
Thrust home (quoth she) my brisk young Lad,
   'Tis but a venial sin,
For I should soon have run quite mad
   had you not put it in.

The sport he did so close pursue
   that he was quickly tired;
But when he did her beauty view
   his heart again was fired:
He came on with such fresh supplies,
   he did her favour win,
And finding Babies in her eyes,
   he bravely thrust it in.

What pleasure is there like to this,
   this Damsel then did cry,
I've heard them talk of lovers bliss,
   O! what a foole was I
So long to live a maid, ere I
   did this same sport begin;
This death I now could freely dye:
   I prithee thrust it in.

She held this youngster to his task
   till he began to blow;
Then at the last he leave did ask
   and so she let him go:

Then down he panting lay awhile,
    and rouzing up agen
She charm'd him with a lovely smile
    again to put it in.

To work he went most earnestly,
    her fancy to fulfill;
Till at the last she loud did cry,
    I do't with such good will,
I pleasure feele in e'ry vein;
    my joys do now begin,
Oh Dearest quickly to't again
    and stoutly thrust it in

She seem'd at last to be content,
    and glad at heart was he,
His youthful strength was almost spent,
    so brisk a Lass was she:
He vow'd he never was so match'd,
    nor ne'r shall be agen:
And for that time they both dispatch'd,
    though he had put it in.

But when she from him parted was
    Thus she began to cry,
Was ever any wanton Lass
    in such a case as I:
He that hath got my Maiden-head
    I ne'r shall see again,
And now my heart is almost dead,
    to think he put it in

But yet it had the sweetest taste
    that ever mortal knew,
Our time we did not vainly waste,
    believe me this is true:

Should I e're see my bonny Lad,
  I'd venture once again,
And let the world account me mad,
  again I'le put it in

117

A Ballad of Andrew and Maudlin

Andrew and *Maudlin*, *Rebecca* and *Will*,
  Margaret and *Thomas*, and *Jockey* and *Mary*;
Kate o' th' Kitchin, and *Kit* of the Mill,
  Dick the Plow-man, and *Joan* of the Dairy,
To solace their lives and to sweeten their Labour,
All met on a time with a Pipe and a Tabor.

Andrew was Cloathed in Shepherd's Grey;
  And *Will* had put on his Holiday Jacket;
Beck had a Coat of *Popin-jay*,
  And *Madge* had a Ribbon hung down to her Placket;   [*Placket* =
Meg and *Mell* in Frize, Tom and Jockey in Leather,   opening of
And so they began all to foot it together.   petticoat

Their Heads and their Arms about them they flung,
  With all the Might and Force they had;
Their Legs went like Flays, and as loosely hung,
  They cudgel'd their Arses as if they were Mad;
Their Faces did shine, and their Fires did kindle,
While the Maids did trip and turn like a Spindle.

Andrew chuck'd *Maudlin* under the Chin,   [*Furmity* =
  Simper she did like a Furmity Kettle;   'frumenty':
The twang of whose blubber lips made such a din,   dish of wheat
  As if her Chaps had been made of Bell-metal: boiled in milk
Kate Laughed heartily at the same smack,   and seasoned
And loud she did answer it with a Bum-crack.

At no *Whilsum-Ale* there e'er yet had been,
　　Such Fraysters and Friskers as these Lads and Lasses;
From their Faces the Sweat ran down to be seen,
　　But sure I am, much more from their Arses;
For had you but seen't, you then would have sworn,
You never beheld the like since you were Born.

Here they did fling, and there they did hoist,
　　Here a hot Breath, and there went a Savour;
Here they did glance, and there they did gloist,
　　Here they did Simper, and there they did Slaver;
Here was a hand, and there was a Placket,
Whilst, hey! their Sleeves went Flicket-a-flacket.

The Dance being ended, they Sweat and they Stunk,
　　The Maidens did smirk it, the Youngsters did Kiss'em,
Cakes and Ale flew about, they clapp'd hands and drunk;
　　They laugh'd and they gigl'd until they bepist 'em;
They laid the Girls down, and gave each a green Mantle,
While their Breasts and their Bellies went Pintle a Pantle.

118

A Pastoral

BY G. A. STEVENS

(1782)

By the side of a green stagnate pool,
　　Brick-dust Nan she sat scratching her head,
Black matted locks frizzl'd her skull,
　　As bristles the hedge-hog bespread;
The wind toss'd her tatters abroad,
　　Her ashy-bronz'd beauties reveal'd:
A link-boy to her through the mud,
　　Bare-footed flew over the field.

As vermin on vermin delight,
  As carrion best suits the crow's taste,
So beggars and bunters unite
  And swine like on dirt make a feast;
To a Hottentot offals have charms,
  With garbage their bosoms they deck;
She sluttishly open'd her arms,
  He filthily fell on her neck.

[bunters =
female
rag-pickers

On her flabby breast one hand he plac'd.
  No towels those breasts ever teaze.
T'other fist grip'd her stays-wanting-waist,
  Like ladies she dress'd for her ease;
Jack drew forth his quid, and he swore,
  Then his lower lip, charg'd to the brim,
He scoul'd like a lewd grunting boar,
  And squinting, she leer'd upon him.

'Oh, my love, tho' I cannot well jaw,'
This plyer at playhouse began,
'Not tobacco's so sweet to the chaw,
  As to kiss is the lips of my Nan:'
'Oh! my Jack,' cries the mud-colour'd she,
  And gave him such rib-squeezing hugs,
'In a dust-hole I'll cuddle with thee,
  Aye, blast me! tho bit by the bugs.'

[chaw =chew

Full as black as themselves, now the sky
  To the south of the hemisphere lour'd,
To finish love's feast in the dry,
  To a stable they hastily scour'd;
While hungry rats round them explor'd,
  And cobwebs their canopy grace,
Undaunted on litter they snor'd,
  Fatigu'd with dirt, drink, and embrace.

119

Green Grow the Rashes

Green grow the rashes, O
  Green grow the rashes, O;
The sweetest bed that e'er I got,
  Was the bellies o' the lasses, O

'Twas late yestreen I met wi' ane
[*printed as 'wow'*   And vow but she was gentle, O;
[*gravat = cravat* Ae hand she put to my gravat
[*pintle = bolt (equivocal)* The tither to my p—t—e, O

Green grow &c.

[*fly'd = scared* I dought na speak, yet was na fly'd,
[*duntie, duntie* My heart play'd duntie, duntie, O.
= *pitter-patter* A' ceremonie laid aside,
  I fairly found her c—t—ie, O.

Green grow &c.

120

Gie the Lass her Fairin'

BY ROBERT BURNS

O gie the lass her fairin', lad,
  O gie the lass her fairin',
An' something else she'll gie to you,
  That's wallow worth the wearin';
Syne coup her o'er amang the creels,
  When ye hae ta'en your brandy,

The mair ye bang, the mair she squeals,
  An' hey for houghmagandie.

Then gie the lass her fairin', lad,
  O gie the lass her fairin',
An' she'll gie you a hairy thing,
  An' of it be na sparin';
But lay her o'er amang the creels,
  An' bar the door wi' baith your heels,
The mair she gets, the mair she squeals,
  An' hey for houghmagandie.

*[hough-
magandie=
fornication*

121

Sweet Robinette

Sweet sweet Robinette all the shepherds do declare,
They never yet saw so enchanting a fair;
The swains all admire her, no mortal, as yet
Has e'er seen a girl like my sweet Robinette.

Her eyes are attracting, her cheeks they disclose
The beautiful tint of the pale blushing rose,
The nymphs full of envy do nothing but fret,
To see all the swains sigh for sweet Robinette.

All nature seems pleas'd as she trips it along,
Her smiles make the lark swell his rapturous song;
The shepherds their cares and their labours forget,
To gaze on the charms of my sweet Robinette.

So gentle her manners they soften the sage,
She's the May-day of youth and the summer of age;
I love her, adore her, I'll venture a bet,
You ne'er saw a girl like my sweet Robinette.

122

Blue Ey'd Mary

In a cottage embosom'd within a deep shade
Like a rose in the desert oh view the sweet maid.
Her aspect all sweetness all plaintive her eye
And a bosom for which e'en a monarch might sigh
Then in a neat Sunday gown see her met by the squire
All attraction her countenance his all desire.
He accosts her she blunders he flatters she smiles
And soon blue ey'd Mary's seduced by his wiles
Now drops of contrition her pillow wet o'er
But the sleet when once stain'd knows whiteness no more
The aged folks whisper the maidens look shy
To town the squire presses how can she deny.
There behold her in lodging she dresses in style
[Hoil = Public places frequents sighs no more but reads Hoil,
E. Hoyle's Learns to squander they quarrel his love turns to hate,
book on whist, And soon blue ey'd Mary is left to her fate
1st edn 1742 Still of beauty possess'd and not void of shame
With a heart that recoils at the prostitute name
She tries for a service her character is gone
And for skill at her needle at last tis unknown,
Pale want now approaches the pawnbrokers near
And her trinkets and clothes one by one disappear
Till at length sorely pinn'd and quite desperate grown
The poor blue ey'd Mary is forc'd on the town
In a brothel next see her trick'd to allure
And all ages all humours compell'd to endure
Compell'd tho disgusted to wheedle and feign,
With an aspect all smiles and a bosom all pain
Now caress'd now insulted now flatter'd now scorn'd
And by ruffians and drunkards oft wantonly spurn'd
The worst of all misery she's doom'd to endure
For the blue ey'd Mary is now an impure

While thus the sharp arrow sinks deep in my soul
She flies for relief to that traitor the bowl,
Grows stupid and bloated and lost to all shame
Whilst a dreadful disease is pervading her frame,
Now with eyes dim and languid the once blooming maid
In a garret on straw faint and helpless is laid
Oh! mark her pale cheeks see her scarce take her breath
And lo! her blue eyes are now sealed in death.

123

The Frolicksome Farmer

'Tis of a brisk young Farmer, in —shire did dwel,
He kept a buxom Dairy-maid, as I for truth do tell
She was both tall and handsome, and pleasing to his mind
Which made him to slight his wife, as you shall quickly
    find.

It happened on a certain time he did to market go,
But little did his wife think he meant to serve her so
Twas near the hour of 12 that night, ere he went home
    again
When he found the buxom Dairy-maid waiting to let
    him in.

He said, charming Betsey, I'll tell unto thee this night
Its long I have admired thee, thy beauty so bright,
Here's half-a-crown, my pretty maid, I'll give unto thee,
Each market night when I come home, and be kind to me.

Long time both master and dairy-maid kept up this game
Until at length his jealous wife suspected the same;
She said I'll find out their tricks, if the harlot she's play'd
To the d— I'll soon kick him and his fine Dairy-maid.

As it happen'd he to market went upon a certain day,
When night came the mistress unto her maid did say,
Now that your work is done you may go up to bed,
For your master's coming home I'll sit up in your stead.

About the hour of 12 that nigh[t] unto the door he came,
The mistress thought, but nothing spoke, I'll find out same;
The kitchen being very dark, unto his wife he said,
My dear sit upon my knee, thinking 'twas the maid.

When that was past and over, he then without delay,
In his wife's hand slipt half-a-crown and to her did say,
Dear Betsey now go to bed, as fast as you can hie,
And at the fair a nice new gown for you I will buy.

Then the mistress to her room so quietly did creep,
When her husband came to bed she sham'd fast asleep;
They laid, but never spoke until the morning came,
And when they at breakfast met, she began the game.

O Betsey here's half-a-crown last night was giv'n for you
Put it safe in your pocket, for I'm sure its your due,
Besides your kind master, the first time he goes to town,
Did promise me last night he'd buy you a new gown.

Betsey then got discharged, and knew the reason why
The Farmer from his angry wife was forced to fly,
So all you cunning husbands that stay out late at night,
Be always sure when you come to choose the candle light.

124

Squire and Milkmaid

OR

Blackberry Fold

It's of a rich squire in Bristol doth dwell,
There are ladies of honour that love him well,
But all was in vain, in vain was said,
For he was in love with a charming milkmaid.

As the squire and his sister did sit in the hall,
And as they were talking to one and to all,
And as they were singing each other a song,
Pretty Betsy, the milkmaid, came tripping along.

Do you want any milk? pretty Betsy did say,
O yes, said the squire; step in, pretty maid.
It is you, fair body, that I do adore,
Was there ever a body so wounded before?

O, hold your tongue, squire, and let me go free,
Do not make your game on my poverty;
There are ladies of honour more fitter for you,
Then I, a poor milkmaid, brought up from the cows.

A ring from his finger he instantly drew,
And right in the middle he broke it in two;
And half he gave to her, as I have been told,
And they both went a walking to Blackberry Fold.

O Betsy, O Betsy, let me have my will,
So constant a squire I'll prove to you still;
And if you deny me, in this open field,
Why, the first time I'll force, and make you to yield.

With hugging and struggling, poor Betsy got free,
Saying, you never shall have your will of me;
I'll protect my own virtue, as I would my life,
And drew from her bosom a large dagger knife.

Then with her own weapon she run him quite through,
And home to her master like lightning she flew,
Saying, O, my dear master, with tears in her eyes,
I have wounded the squire, and I'm afraid dead he lies.

The coach was got ready, the squire brought home,
The doctor was sent for to heal up the wound,
Poor Betsy was sent for – the gay maiden fair –
Who wounded the squire, drove his heart in a snare.

The parson was sent for, this couple to wed,
And she did enjoy the sweet marriage bed;
It's better to be honest if ever so poor,
For he's made her his lady instead of his whore.

125

Don't Be Foolish Pray

Young Hodge met Mog the miller's maid,
   Who long his suit denied,
And half inclined and half afraid,
   Scratch'd his rough head and cried:
Now Molly while I love you so,
   Why still our joys delay,
Come dang it, to the parson go,
   And don't be foolish pray.

Sweet Moggy with an artful blush,
 That sham'd the rose's hue,
Look'd round, and cried to Hodge 'hush hush
 Speak softly, softly do:
We shall be overheard I know,
 The mill don't work to day
Be quiet, Hodge my hand let go,
 Now don't be foolish pray.'

Poor Hodge, thus chid, at a stand,
 And cried, – 'Well then, good bye.
I'se go to give to Sue my hand,
 Since thee do cast off I,
Me cast you off, cries Moggy 'no,
 The mill don't work to day;
And so dear Hodge, to church let's go,
 And don't be foolish pray.'

126

The Lovely Village Fair

OR

I dont mean to tell you her name

To my village fair no lass can compare
 For innocence and native grace,
She boasts not of wealth, though the pure bloom of health
 Shews forth in her beautiful face:
Such a form ne'er was seen as she tripp'd o'er the green,
 And her heart free from guile and from scheme.
She lives near the mill at the top of the hill,
 But I don't mean to tell you her name.

Her luxuriant hair, so bewitchingly fair
   As it sportively plays in the wind:
Her bright beaming eye, like the blue of the sky,
   Is an emblem so pure of her mind.
The sound of her voice makes my fond heart rejoice,
   My love, O what mortal can blame?
She lives near the mill at the top of the hill
   But I don't mean to tell you her name.

The lord and the squire, altho' they rank higher,
   Endeavour her favour to gain;
Let them try how they may, she still will say nay,
   And they'll find all their labour in vain.
It was but last night, as we walk'd by moonlight,
   She owned she for me felt love's flame:
She lives near the mill at the top of the hill,
   But I don't mean to tell you her name.

How happy I'll be when united I see
   Myself with this beauteous fair;
When to me she'll impart both her hand and her heart,
   No bliss with my joys can compare.
When in wedlock we join, our hearts will combine,
   And Cupid our love will inflame,
While we sport round the hill, and she lives near the mill,
   And that day I will tell you her name.

127

Shocking Rape and Murder of Two Lovers

Showing how John Hodges, a farmer's son, committed a rape upon Jane Williams, and afterwards Murdered her and her lover, William Edwards, in a field near Paxton.

This is a most revolting Murder. It appears Jane Williams was keeping company, and was shortly to be married to William Edwards, who was in the employment of Farmer Hodges. For some time a jealousy existed in John Hodges, who made vile proposals to the young girl, who although of poor parents was strictly virtuous. The girl's father also worked on farmer Hodges's estate. On Thursday last she was sent to the farm to obtain some things for her mother, who was ill; it was 9 o'clock in the evening when she set out, a mile from the farm. Going across the fields she was met by the farmer's son, who made vile proposals to her, which she not consenting to, he threw her down, and accomplished his vile purpose. In the meantime her lover had been to her house, and finding she was gone to the farm, went to meet her. He found her in the field crying, and John Hodges standing over her with a bill-hook, saying he would kill her if she ever told. No one can tell the feelings of the lover, William Edwards. He rushed forward, when Hodges, with the hook, cut the legs clean from his body, and with it killed the poor girl, and then run off. Her father finding she did not return, went to look for her; when the awful deeds were discovered. Edwards was still alive, but died shortly afterwards from loss of blood, after giving his testimony to the magistrates. The farmer's son was apprehended, and has been examined and committed to take his trial at the next Assizes.

Thousands of persons followed the unfortunate lovers to the grave, where they were buried together.

COPY OF VERSES

Jane Williams had a lover true
    And Edwards was his name,
Whose visits to her father's house,
    Had welcome now became.

In marriage soon they would be bound,
    A loving man and wife,
But John Hodges, a farmer's son,
    With jealousy was rife.

One night he met her in the field,
    And vile proposals made;
How can I do this wicked thing;
    Young Jane then weeping said.

He quickly threw her on the ground,
    He seized her by surprise,
And did accomplish his foul act,
    Despite her tears and cries.

Her lover passing by that way,
    Discovered her in tears,
And when he found what had been done
    He pulled the monster's ears.

Young Hodges with the bill-hook,
    Then cut young Edwards down:
And by one fatal blow he felled
    Jane Williams on the ground.

There side by side the lovers lay
    Weltering in their blood:
Young Jane was dead, her lover lived,
    Though ebb'd away life's flood.

Old Williams sought his daughter dear,
    When awful to relate,
He found her lifeless body there,
    Her lover's dreadful fate.

Now in one grave they both do lie,
   These lovers firm and true,
Who by a cruel man were slain,
   Who'll soon receive his due.

In prison now he is confined,
   To answer for the crime.
Two lovers that he murdered,
   Cut off when in their prime.

TWO

URBAN

128

Fain would I have a prettie thing to give
unto my Ladie

Fain would I have a prettie thing,
　To give unto my Ladie:
I name no thing, nor I mean no thing,
　But as prettie a thing as may bee.

Twenty journeys would I make,
　and twenty waies would hie me,
To make adventure for her sake,
　to set some matter by me:

But I would faine have a prettie thing, etc.,
I name no thing, nor I mean no thing, etc.

Some do long for prettie knackes,
　and some for straunge devices:
God send me that my Ladie lackes,
　I care not what the price is,
　　Thus faine, etc.

Some goe here, and some go there,
　where gazes not be geason;
And I goe gaping everywhere,
　but still come out of season
　　Yet faine, etc.

[*geason = rare,*
scarce

359

I walk the town and tread the streete,
   In every corner seeking,
The pretty thing I cannot meete,
   That's for my Ladies liking.
     Fain, etc.

The Mercers pull me going by,
   the Silkie wives say, What lack ye?
The thing you have not, then say I,
   ye foolish fooles, go pack ye.
     But fain, etc.

[Cheape =
Cheapside

It is not all the Silk in Cheape,
   nor all the golden treasure,
Nor twenty Bushels on a heape,
   can do my Ladie pleasure.
     But fain, etc.

The Gravers of the golden shows
   with Juelles do beset me;

[Shemiters =
   seamsters
[Let = hamper

The Shemiters in the shops that sews,
   They do no thing but let me.
     But fain, etc.

But were it in the wit of man
   by any meanes to make it,
I could for Money buy it than,
   and say, faire Lady, take it.
     Thus, faine etc.

O lady, what a lacke is this,
   That my good willing misseth
To find what prettie thing it is
   That my good Lady wisheth.

Thus fain would I have had this prettie thing
   to give unto my lady;
I said no harm, nor I meant no harm,
   But as pretty a thing as may be.

129

A Pleasant New Ballad of Two Lovers

'Complaine my lute, complaine on him
   that stayes so long away;
He promis'd to be here ere this,
   but still unkind doth stay,
But now the proverbe true I finde,
Once out of sight, then out of minde:
   Hey how my heart is full of woe!

'Peace, Lyer, peace! it is not so,
   he will by and by be here;
But every one that is in love
   thinkes every houre a yeere.
Harke, harke, me thinks I heare one knocke;
Run quickly then, and turne the locke,
   Then, farwell all my care and woe!

'Come, gallant, now, come, loyterer!
   for I must chide with thee;
But yet I will forgive thee once,
   come, sit thee downe by mee.'
'Faire lady, rest yourselfe content;
I will indure your punishment,
   And then we shall be friends againe.

'For every houre that I have stayd
   so long from thee away,
A thousand kisses will I give;
   receive them, ready pay.
And if we chance to count amisse,
Againe wee'le reckon every kisse;
   For he is blest that's punisht so.

'And if those thousand kisses then
   we chance to count aright,
We shall not need to count againe
   till we in bed doe light:
And then be sure that thou shalt have
Thy reckoning just as thou shalt crave;
   So shall we still agree as one.'

And thus they spent the silent night
   in sweet delightful sport,
Till Phoebus, with his beames so bright,
   from out the fiery port
Did blush to see the sweet content
In sable night so vainely spent
   Betwixt these Lovers two.

And then this gallant did perswade
   that he might now be gone:
'Sweet-heart,' quoth he, 'I am afraid
   that I have stayd too long.'
'And wilt thou then be gone?' quoth she,
'And wilt no longer stay with me?
   Then welcome all my care and woe.'

And then she tooke her lute in hand,
   and thus began to play;
Her heart was faint, she could not stand,
   but on her bed she lay:

'And art thou gone, my love?' quoth she,
'Complaine, my lute, complaine with me,
    Until that he doth come againe.'

130

Come Turn to Mee, Thou Pretty Little One

Sweet if thou wilt be
As I am to thee,
Then by *Cupid's* mother,
I have vow'd to have
    none other she:
Then turn to me, thou pretty little one,
    And I will turn to thee.

Those bright eyes of thine
Which so dazzle mine,
Like the stars of Heaven,
Which do keep their even
    course and shine:
Then let us in conjunction meet
    and both our loves combine.

If that lovely Face
Will to mine give place,
That with love's devotion
We may use the motion
    of imbrace:
Then sit thee down, my pretty little one,
    and let us love a space.

What hurt is this,
For to take a kisse?
    If it may be granted;

I that long have wanted
    such a blisse;
Then be not sparing of a few,
    whereas such plenty is.

If thy breasts do pant
For the milk they want,
Every Hill and Mountain
To supply each Fountain,
    be not scant:
Then give to me thy lilly white hand,
    and I thee mine will grant.

If so be that I
May but thee come nigh,
The Vine and Elm shall never
Joyn more close together
    than will I.
Then shew thy fruits, my amorous joy,
    and I'll with love supply.

If that thou dost crave
Silks and Garments brave,
Or what rich attyre
Could thy heart desire
    to receive:
Declare to me, thou pretty little one,
    thou canst but ask and have.

From the *Indies* far,
Where rich Jewels are,
I will bring thee treasure
Far beyond all measure
    and compare:
Then be not coy my pretty little one,
    for I no cost will spare.

Sweet-heart, for thy sake,
I will never make
Choice of any other;
Then by *Cupid's* Mother,
　　freely speak:
It's at thy choice, my dearest Love,
　　either to leave or take.

I Thy Marygold,　　(*She replies*)
Wrapt in many fold,
Like the golden Clyent,
To the Sun supplient,
　　shew it's gold:
Display the beams, my glorious Sun,
　　and I'le to thee unfold.

Those bright locks of hair　　(*He answers*)
Spreading o'er each ear,
Every crisp and curle,
Far more rich then pearl,
　　doth appear:
Then be thou constant in thy love,
　　and I will be thy Dear.

Till I have possest
Thee whom I love best,
I have vow'd for ever
In thy absence never
　　to take rest:
Deny me not, thou pretty little one,
　　In whom my hopes are blest.

If a kisse or two　　(*She replies*)
Can thee a favour do,
Were it more then twenty,

Love's indu'd with plenty;
   Lovers know:
For thy sweet sake a thousand take,
   for that's the way to wooe.

It doth grieve my heart
From thee for to part;
It is to me more pleasant
Ever to be present
   where thou art:
Yet in the absence of a friend,
   my love shall never start.

As to me thou art kind,
Duty shall mee bind
Ever to obey thee,
Reason so doth sway mee
   to thy mind:
Thou hast my heart where e're thou art,
   although I stay behind.

In thy bed or bark,
I will be thy mark;
Couples yet more loving
Never had their moving
   from the Ark:
Welcome to mee, my onely joy,
   all times be it light or dark.

131

The London Prentice

A Worthy *London* Prentice,
   Came to his Love by Night;

The Candles were lighted,
    The Moon did shine so bright:
He knocked at the Door,
    To ease him of his Pain;
She rose and let him in Love,
    And went to Bed again.

He went into the Chamber,
    Where his true Love did lye;
She quickly gave consent,
    For to have his Company:
She quickly gave consent,
    The Neighbours peeping out;
So take away your Hand,
    Love let's blow the Candle out.

I would not for a Crown Love,
    My Mistress should it know;
I'll in my Smock step down Love,
    And I'll out the Candle blow;
The Streets they are so nigh,
    And the People walk about;
Some may peep in and spy Love,
    Let's blow the Candle out.

My Master and my Mistress,
    Upon the Bed do lye;
Injoying one another,
    Why should not you and I:
My Master kiss'd my Mistress,
    Without any fear or doubt;
And we'll kiss one another,
    Let's blow the Candle out.

I prithee speak more softly,
    Of what we have to do;

Least that our noise of Talking,
   Should make our Pleasure rue:
For kissing one another,
   Will make no evil rout;
Then let us now be silent,
   And blow the Candle out.

But yet he must be doing,
   He could no longer stay;
She strove to blow the Candle out,
   And push'd his Hand away:
The young Man was so hasty,
   To lay his Arms about;
But she cryed I pray Love,
   Let's blow the Candle out.

As this young Couple sported,
   The Maiden she did blow;
But how the Candle went out,
   Alas I do not know!
Said she I fear not now, Sir,
   My Master nor my Dame;
And what this Couple did, Sir,
   Alas I dare not Name.

132

The Suburbs is a Fine Place

The Suburbs is a fine Place belonging to the City,
It has no Government at all, alack the more the Pity;
A Wife, a silly Animal, esteemed in that same Place,
For there a Civil Woman's now asham'd to shew her
  Face:

The Misses there have each Man's Time, his Money, nay,
   his Heart,
Then all in all, both great and small, and all in ev'ry Part.

Which Part it is a thorough-fair so open and so large,
One well might sail through ev'ry Tail even in a western
   Barge;
These Cracks that Coach it now, when first they came
   to Town,
Did turn up Tail for a Pot of Ale in Linsey Wolsey
   Gown.

The Bullies first debauch'd 'em, in Baudy Covent-Garden,
That filthy place, where ne'er a Wench was ever worth a
   Farthing;
And when their Maiden-heads are sold to sneaking Lords,
Which Lords are Clapt at least nine-fold for taking of
   their Words.

And then my Lord, that many tries, she looks so Innocent,
Believing he Infected her, he makes a Settlement;
These are your Cracks, who skill'd in all kind of Debauches,
Do daily piss, spue, and whore, in their own glass Coaches.

Now Miss turn⟨s⟩ Night-walker, till Lord-Mayor's Men
   she meets,
O'er Night she's Drunk, next Day she's finely flogged thro'
   London streets;
After their Rooms of State are chang'd to Bulks or Coblers
   Stalls,
'Till Poverty and Pox agree, they dying in Hospitals.

This Suburbs gallant Fop that takes delight in Roaring,
He spends his time in Huffing, Swearing, Drinking, and in
   Whoring;
And if an honest Man and his Wife meet them in the Dark,
Makes nothing to run the Husband through to get the
   name of Spark.

But when the Constable appears, the Gallant, let me tell ye,
His Heart defiles his Breeches, and sinks into his Belly;
These are the silly Rogues that think it fine and witty,
To laugh and joak at Aldermen, the Rulers of the City.

They'd kiss our Wives, but hold, for all their plotting Pates,
While they would get us Children, we are getting their
    Estates;
And still in vain they Court pretending in their Cares,
That their Estates may thus descend unto the Lawful Heirs.

Their Play-houses I hate, are Shops to set off Wenches,
Where Fop and Miss, like Dog and Bitch, do couple under
    Benches;
That I might advise the chiefest Play-house monger,
I have a Sister of my own both Handsomer and Younger.

She lives not far off in the Parish of St. Clements,
She never liv'd in Cellar nor sold Oranges and Lemons:
Then why should Play-house Trulls with Paint and such
    Temptations,
Be an Eye sore to me and more to the best part o'th' Nation.

Now you that all this while have listened to my Dity,
With streightened Hands pray drink a Health unto this
    noble City:
And let us pray to Jove, these Suburbs folks to mend,
And having now no more to say, I think it fit to end.

133

The Merry Hoastess

OR

*A pretty new Ditty, composed by an Hoastess that lives in
    the City:
To wrong such an Hoastess it were a great pitty,
By reason she caused this pretty new Ditty.*

Come all that loves good company
    and hearken to my Ditty;
'Tis of a lovely hoastess fine,
    that lives in London City:
Which sells good Ale, nappy and stale,
    and alwayes thus sings she,
*My Ale was tunn'd when I was young,
    and a little above my knee.*

[*nappy and
stale=heady,
strong*

Her ale is lively, strong and stout,
    if you please but to taste;
It is well brew'd, you need not fear,
    but I pray you make no waste;
It is lovely brown, the best in town,
    and alwayes thus sings she:
My Ale was etc.

The gayest lady with her fan
    doth love such nappy Ale;
Both City Maids, and Countrey Girles
    that carries the milking Pail;
Will take a touch, and not think much,
    to sing so merrily,
My Ale was etc.

Both Lord and Esquire hath a desire
    unto it night and day;
For a quart or two, be it old or new,
    and for it they will pay:
With pipe in hand they may her command
    to sing most merrily:
My Ale was etc.

You'r welcome all, brave Gentlemen,
    if you please to come in;
To take a cup I do intend,
    and a health, for to begin;
To all the merry joval blades,
    that will sing for company:
My Ale was etc.

Here's a Health to all brave English men
    that loves this cup of Ale;
Let every man fill up his Can,
    and see that none do fail,
'Tis very good to nourish the blood,
    and make you sing with me,
My Ale was etc.

THE SECOND PART

The bonny Scot will lay a plot
    to get a handsom tutch
Of this my ale, so good and stale;
    so will the cunning Dutch:
They will take a part, with all their heart,
    to sing this tune with me,
My Ale was etc.

It will make the Irish cry a hone,
   if they but take their fill;
And put them all quite out of tune,
   let them use their chiefest skill:
So strong and stout, it will hold out
   in any company;
For my Ale was tunn'd when I was young,
   and a little above my knee.

The Welch-man on Saint David's Day
   will cry, Cots plutter a nail,
Hur will hur ferry quite away
   from off that nappy ale:
It makes hur foes, with hur red nose,
   hur seldom can agree;
But my Ale was tunn'd when I was young,
   and a little above my knee.

The Spaniard stout will have a bout,
   'cause he hath store of gold;
Till at the last he is laid fast,
   my Ale doth him so hold;
His Ponyard strong is laid along,
   yet he is good company;
For my Ale etc.

There's never a tradesman in England
   that can my Ale deny;
The Weaver, Taylor, and Glover,
   delights it for to buy:
Small money they do take away,
   if that they drink with me;
For my Ale etc.

There is Smug the honest Blacksmith,
   he seldom can pass by;

Because a spark lies in his throat,
    which makes him very dry;
But my old Ale tells him his tale,
    so finely we agree;
For my Ale etc.

The Brewer, Baker, and Butcher,
    as well as all the rest,
Both night and day will watch where they
    may finde Ale of the best:
And the gentle craft will come full oft
    to drink a cup with me;
For my Ale etc.

So to conclude, good-fellows all,
    I bid you all adieu;
If that you love a cup of ale,
    take rather old th⟨a⟩n new:
For if you come where I do dwell,
    and chance to drink with me,
My Ale was etc.

134

An Amorous Dialogue between John and his Mistress

Being a Compleat and True Relation of Some Merry
Passages Between the Mistris and Her Apprentice, Who
Pleased her so well, that she Rewarded him with Fifty
Broadpieces for his Pains.

> *Here by this Dialogue you may discern*
> *While old Cats nibble Cheese the young ones learn.*

Come, *John*, sit thee down I have somewhat to say,
In my mind I have kept it this many a day,

Your Master you know is a Fool and a Sot,
And minds nothing else but the Pipe and the Pot.
Till twelve or till one he will never come home,
And then he's so drunk that he lies like a Mome:
  Such usage as this would make any one mad,
  But a Woman will have it if 'tis to be had.

'Tis true forsooth mistris, the case is but hard,
That a woman should be of her pleasure debar'd:
But 'tis the sad fate of a thousand beside,
Or else the whole City is fouly beli'd:
There is not a man among twenty that thrives,
Not ten in fifteen that lie with their Wives:
  Yet still you had better be merry than sad,
  And take it wherever it is to be had.

But *John*, 'tis a difficult matter to find,
A man that is trusty and constantly kind:
An Inns-of-Court Gallant he cringes and bows,
He's presently known by his Oaths and his Vows,
And though both his cloaths and his speeches be gay,
Yet he loves you but only a night and away:
  Such usage as this would make any one mad,
  Yet a woman will have it, if 'tis to be had.

What think you of one that belongs to the Court,
They say they are youthful, and given to sport:
He'l present you with bracelets, and jewels, & Rings,
With stones that are precious, & twenty fine things;
Or if you are not for the Court nor the Town,
What think you forsooth of a man with a Gown?
  You must have a gallant, a good or a bad,
  And take it where ever it is to be had.

THE SECOND PART

No, John I confess that not any of these,
Had ever the power my fancy to please;
I like no such blades for a trick that I know,
For as soon as they've trod they are given to crow;
Plain dealing is best, and I like a man well,
That when he has kiss'd will be hang'd ere he'l tell:
  My meaning is honest, and thou art the Lad,
  Then give it and take it where 'tis to be had.

Alas! my dear mistris, it never can be,
That you can affect such a fellow as me;
Yet heaven forbid, since I am but your man,
I should ever refuse to do all I can;
But then if my master should know what we've done,
We both shou'd be blown up as sure as a Gun:
  For after our joys, he would make us sad,
  For taking it where it ought not to be had.

But how shou'd he know it thou scrupulous Elf,
Do'st think I'me so silly to tell him myself?
If we are but so wise our own counsel to keep,
We may laugh and lye down while the sot is asleep:
Some hundreds I know in the city that use
To give to their men what their masters refuse:
  The man is the master, the Prentice the Dad,
  For women must take it where 'tis to be had.

Some Prentices use it, forsooth, I allow,
But I am a Novice and cannot tell how:
However, I hope that I shall not be blam'd,
For to tell you the truth I am somewhat asham'd;
I know how to carry your Bible to Church,
But to play with my mistris I'me left in the lurch:
  Yet if you can show me the way good or bad,
  I'le promise you all that there is to be had.

376

You quickly may learn it, my *Johnny*, for . . . Thus,
Before you proceed you begin with a buss;
And then you must clasp me about with your arm;
Nay, fear me not *Johnny* I'le do thee no harm;
Now I sigh, now I tremble, now backwards I lye,
And now dear *Johnny,* ah now I must dye:
  Oh! who can resist such a mettlesome lad,
  And refuse such a pleasure when 'tis to be had.

Alas, pritty mistry the pleasure is such,
We never can give one another too much:
If this be the business the way is so plain,
I think I can easily find it again:
'Twas thus we began; and . . . Thus we lye down,
And thus . . . Oh thus! that we fell in a swoun:
  Such sport to refuse who was ever so mad,
  I'le take it where ever it is to be had.

Now, *Johnny* you talk like an ignorant mome,
You can have such pleasures no where but at home,
Here's fifty broad pieces for what you have done,
But see that you never a gadding do run:
For no new imployment then trouble your brains,
For here when you work you'l be paid for your pains:
  But shou'd you deceive me no woman so sad,
  To lose all the pleasure that once she has had.

A mistris so noble I never will leave,
'Twere a sin and a shame such a friend to deceive;
For my Master's shop no more will I care,
'Tis pleasanter handling my mistrisses ware:
A fig for Indentures, for now I am made
Free of a Gentiler and pleasanter trade:
  I know when I'me well, I was never so mad,
  To forsake a good thing when 'tis to be had.

135

The Ranting Wanton's Resolution; 1672

*Wherein you will find that her only Treasure
Consisteth in being a Lady of Pleasure.*

Oh! fye upon Care,
   Why should we despair?
Give me the Lad that will frollick,
   There is no disease,
   But Musick will please,
If it were the stone or the cholick
   The Lad that drinks Wine,
   Shall only be mine,
He that calls for a Cup of Canary,
   That will tipple and sing,
   Kiss, caper, and spring.
And calls for his Mab, and his Mary.

Such Sinners as these
   My pallat will please,
For this is a Lad that will knock it,
   Provided he be
   Not Niggard to me,
But carry good gilt in his pocket;
   I care not from whence
   He gets his expence,
Nor how he comes by his treasure,
   So I have the sweets
   When he and I meets,
For I am a Lady of Pleasure.

I love a young Heir,
   Whose fortune is fair,
And frollick in *Fishstreet*-dinners;

Who boldly doth call,
  And in private payes all,
These Boyes are the noble beginners;
  For what the old Father
  In long time did gather,
He toaps it away without measure,
  Hee'l lye in my lap,
  Like a Bird in a trap,
And call me his Lady of pleasure.

He wears gallant Cloaths,
  And studies new Oaths,
And gets pretty words from the players,
  He swaggers and Roars,
He calls the next Oars.   [*Oars* = *boat*
And cryes, Here's a peece for your fairs.
  Thus we in delight
  From morning till night,
Do study to cast away treasure,
  At night in my arms
  I secure him from harms,
For I am a Lady of pleasure.

THE SECOND PART

When this Gallant's broke,
  I've another be-spoke,
And he hath my protestation,
  I call him my Love
  My Jewel, my Dove,
And swear by my reputation,
  That I never did know
  What Love was till now,
Though I have had men beyond measure.
  With such tricks as these
  All Coxcombs I please,
  For I am a Lady of pleasure.

When they're in the Jayle,
  They wretchedly rail
And at me they cast all their curses,
  Let them laugh that win,
  I care not a pin,
When I have confounded their purses:
  While they have disgraces,
  I know not their faces,
When Warriers of *Wood-street* make seizure,
  But when they'r whole men
  I'le know them agen,
For I am a Lady of pleasure.

  I live by the quick,
  And not by the sick,
Or such whose estate lye a bleeding,
  My wa⟨i⟩st must be bound,
  By men that are sound;
For I am a Lass of high feeding;
  If once they get poor,
  No Money, no Whore,
And yet they shall wait on my leisure,
  I only fulfill
  My fancy and will,
Which shews me a Lady of pleasure.

  I laugh when they tell
  Me stories of Hell,
I think there is no such Cavern,
  If Heaven there be
  (As some will tell me)
I am sure it must be in the Tavern:
  Where there is no wine,
  There's nothing divine;
Wee'l think of a grave at more leisure,

Boy, fill th'other glass,
For I am a Lass
That will be a Lady of pleasure.

In freedom and joyes
I'le spend all my dayes,
For there is no greater blessing,
Than musick and meat,
Good wine and the feat,
And nothing to pay for the dressing.
Let Sisters precise
Go turn up their eyes,
And speak words by line and by leisure,
If death comes at last
And takes me in haste
Then there lies a Lady of pleasure.

136

A Satyre entituled the Witch

supposed to bee made against the Lady Francis Countes
of Somersett

Shee with whom troopes of Bustuary slaves,
(Like Legion) sojourned still amongst the Graves;
And there laid plots which made the silver Moone
To fall in Labour many times too soone:
Canidia now drawes on.

[Bustuary = funereal

Shee that in every vice did so excell
That Shee could read new principles to Hell;
And shew the Fiends recorded in her looks,
Such deeds, as were not in their blackest books:
Canidia now drawes on.

Shee that by spels could make a frozen stone
Melt and dissolve with soft affection;
And in an instant strike the Factours dead
That should pay duties to the Marriage bed:
    Canidia now drawes on.

Shee that consisted all of borrowed grace,
Could paint her heart as smoothly as her face,
And when her breath gave wings to silken words,
Poisons in thoughts conceive and murthering swords:
    Canidia now drawes on.

Shee that could reeke within the sheets of lust,
And there bee searcht, yet passe without mistrust;
Shee that could surfle upp the waies of sinne,
And make streight Posternes where wide gates had bin:
    Canidia now drawes on.

[*surfle* = *sew (embroidery)*]

Shee that could cheate the matrimoniall bed,
With a false-stampt adulterate maidenhead;
And make the Husband thinke those kisses chast,
Which were stale Panders to his Spouses wast.
    Canidia now drawes on.

[*adulterate* = *spurious, and adulterous*]

Whose brest was that Aceldama of blood,
Whose vertue still became the Cankers food;
Whose closett might a Golgotta bee stil'd,
Or else a charnell where dead bones are pil'd:
    Canidia now drawes on.

[*Aceldama* = *Judas' field*]

Whose waxen pictures made by Incantation,
Whose philters, potions for Loves propagation;
Count *Circe* but a novice in the trade,
And scorne all druggs that *Colchos* ever made:
    Canidia now drawes on.

Oh let no Bells bee ever heard to ring,
Let not a Chime the nightly houres sing;
Let not the Lyrique Larke salute the day,
Nor *Philomele* tune the sad dark away:
    Canidia still drawes on.

Let croaking Ravens, and death-boding Owles,
Let groning Mandrakes, and the ghastly howles
Of men unburied, bee the fatall knell
To ring *Canidia* downe from Earth to Hell:
    Canidia still drawes on.

Let Wolves and Tygers howle, let Serpents cry,
Let Basilisks bedew their poisoning eie;
Let Plutos dogg stretch high his barking note,
And chant her dirges with his triple throate:
    Canidia still drawes on.

Under his burthen let great *Atlas* quake,
Let the fixt Earth's unmoved center shake;
And the faire Heavens wrapp't as it were with wonder
That Devills dy, speake out their loudest thunder:
    Canidia still drawes on.

No longer shall the pretty Marigolds
Ly sepulchred at night in their owne folds;
The Rose should flourish, and throughout the yeare
No leaf nor plant once blasted would appeare:
    Were once *Canidia* gone.

The Starres would seeme as glorious as the Moone,
And Shee like Phœbus in his brightest noone;
Mists, clouds and vapours, all would passe away,
And the whole yeare bee as Halcyons day:
    Oh were *Canidia* gone.

137

Much has been said . . .

Much has been said of strumpets of yore
Of Lais whole volumes, of Messaline more,
But I sing of a lewder than e'er lived before
   Which nobody can deny.

From her mother at first she drew the infection,
And as soon as she spoke, she made use of injection,
And now she's grown up to a girl of perfection,
   Which nobody can deny.

If you told her of hell she would say 'twas a jest,
And swear of all gods, that Priapus was best,
For her soul was a whore when she suck't at ye breast,
   Which her nurses can't deny.

She once was call'd virgin, but 'twas but a shamm,
Her maidenhead never was gotten by man,
She frigg'd it away in the womb of her damm,
   Which the midwife couldn't deny.

At length Mr Foppling made her his bride,
But found (to bring down his ambition and pride)
Her fortune but narrow, and her c—t very wide,
   Which he himself can't deny.

In vain he long strove to satiate her lust,
Which still grew more vig'rous at every thrust,
No wonder the puny chitt came by the worst,
   Which nobody can deny.

And now she is free to swive where she pleases,
And where'er she swives, to scatter diseases,
And a shanker's a damn'd loving thing where it seizes,
   Which nobody can deny.

There's Haughton, and Elland, and Arran the sott,
(Shee deserves to be pox'd that would f—k with a Scott)
All charged the lewd harlott, and all went to pott,
   Which nobody can deny.

For that she has bubo'd and ruin'd as many
As Hinton, or Willis, Moll Howard or any,
And, like to those punks, will f—k for a penny,
   Is what nobody can deny.

To scower the town is her darling delight,
In breaking of windows, to scratch and to fight,
And to lay with her own brawny footmen at night,
   Which she herself can't deny.

Who, though they eternally pizzle her britch,
Can't allay the wild rage of her lech'rous itch,
Which proves our good lady a monstrous bitch,
   Which they themselves can't deny.

But now if there's any, or Christian or Jew,
That say I've bely'd her, I advise 'em to goe
And ask the fair creature herself if it's true,
   Which I'm certain shee won't deny.

138

The Roaring Lad and the Ranting Lass

OR

A Merry Couple Madly Met

In which you may see, in every degree,
How merry they be, when every side agree.

THOMAS

I met with a Jovial Girl,
That would have me handle her Stuff,
She told me 'twould pleasure an Earl,
For she had a delicate Muff:
She said we must go to the Tavern,
For she could drink nothing but Wine:
   But a pox of her Trade,
   Let her go for a Jade
She shall finger no money of mine

BETTY

I met with a Ranting Rogue,
That fain would be fingering my stuff,
And thus he began to collogue,
Good Madam pray lend me your Muff.
He said if I'd go to the Tavern,
He'd give me a glass of good Wine;
   But a pox on the Rogue,
   I scorn to cologue,
For he shall have nothing of mine

THOMAS

I pray Madam coy, entertain me,
For I am a Swaggering Boy;
I wonder that you will so disdain me.

386

BET. In troth sir, I nere was coy
Then let's to the Tavern and bouse it,
And taste of the fruit of the Wine,
   For I am a Lad,
   That will ever be mad
And Girl, all that I have shall be thine

[*Wine =
vine* (?)

BETTY

I love a kind cup of good Nectar,
Because it will mount in my blood,
But I fear me sir, you are a Hector,
And then you will do me no good.
Your tongues are so tipt with expressions
Of Dove, Duck, Dearest and Honey;
   But when you come near,
   To barter for Ware,
You fail both in measure and money

THOMAS

Sweet Madam you much are mistaken
For I am no Hector-like flash:
But you'll find when we come to reckon,
That I want neither Measure nor Cash;
I am a Casheer to a Merchant,
But Cupid hath made me a Lover;
   Therefore in my Pleasure,
   I'le give London Measure,
And that is a Handful over

BETTY

I see what your loving intent is,
And I no longer will be coy,
I fancy a Citizen's Prentice,
For he is my bonny fine Boy,
He toils not in getting of money,

And therefore in spending is free,
  He'l pay, and he'l call,
  And cry, Have at all;
Oh! that is a Lad for me

THOMAS

So loving a Lad I have brought thee
And therefore be merry and wise,
For Cupid hath courted and caught me,
With the Beames of thy black Eyes;
The Maiden-head Tavern lies open.
Ile slip in a liquor my head in't:
  With Claret and Sack
  We'l strengthen the back;
Come Boy show a Room with a Bed in't.

BETTY

A Maiden-head is a temptation
Provided your Claret be terse sir,
But the Bush is the best provocation,
If you can but handle your Piercer,
Which is the best Art of a Vinter,
Before he poluted his Wine:
  When the Red and the White
  both spring with delight,
Oh! that, 'tis a pregnant sign.

THOMAS

Then up the Bed-room we'l clamber,
The Drawer will be our conceler:
Fornication may be in the Chamber,
When Adultery is in the Cellar.
BET. Then drink a full bowl of Canary
Come kindle thy courage with wine,
  And what thou dost sip
  With a touch of my Lip
by a new Distillation is mine.

[*Adultery =
adulteration*

388

CONCLUSION

Come Boy then and fill us more Liquor,
The best that your Cellar affords
And bid the Drawer come quicker,
Unless he will taste of our Swords?
Here's a health to the utter confusion
Of damnable Usuring Elves
   That Cousen by stealth
   But a pox o'their Wealth
Come Boys a good health to our selves.

139

'The Maids of Honour'

(c. 1690)

The Maids of Honour are growne Wild
   And weary of colde Chastitie
Because their Temple is defild
   But that ne're troubles mee Boy.

Villers foretold that long agoe
   When shee flewe into Germany
Where now she sings hy-nonny-no
   But that ne're troubles mee Boy.

Seymer shee loves a Lord that's *Rich*
   Because shee would a *Lady* bee
But if her face can him bewitch
   t'shall never trouble mee Boy.

Arden is faire but very Nice
   No Chapman can for her agree
Shee stands too much upon her Price
   But that ne're troubles mee Boy.

Howard they say she cannot Loue
   Yet married would as others bee
It is a signe shee'le wanton prove
   But that ne're troubles mee Boy.

Hold up thy head my brave Queene Cis
   And lett them see thou are gentiv
When all are freed thou ranst not misse
   But that ne're troubles mee Boy

[*gentiv =*
gentil(?)]

Christien shee does Poute and Puffe
   Because of her Virginity
But shee'le gett one to starch her Ruffe
   That never troubles mee Boy.

140

The Town-Rakes

BY P. A. MOTTEUX (?)

What Life can compare with the jolly Town-Rakes,
When in his full swing of all Pleasure he takes?
At Noon he gets up for a wet and to Dine,
And Wings the swift Hours with Mirth, Musick and Wine,
Then jogs to the Play-house and chats with the Masques,
And thence to the Rose where he takes his three Flasks,
There great as a Caesar he revels when drunk,
And scours all he meets as he reels, as he reels to his Punk,
And finds the dear Girl in his Arms when he wakes,
What Life can compare to the jolly Town-Rakes, the jolly
   Town-Rakes.

He like the Great Turk has his favourite She,
But the Town's his Seraglio, and still he lives free;

Sometimes she's a Lady, but as he must range,
Black Betty or Oyster Moll serve for a Change:
As he varies his sports his whole Life is a Feast,
He thinks him that is soberest is most like a Beast:
All Houses of Pleasure, breaks Windows and Doors,   [*All* =
Kicks Bullies and Cullies, then lies with their Whores: *Att*(?)
Rare work for the Surgeon and Midwife he makes,
What Life can Compare with the jolly Town-Rakes.

Thus in Covent-Garden he makes his Campaigns,
And no Coffee-House haunts but to settle his Brains;
He laughs at dry Mortals, and never does think,
Unless 'tis to get the best Wenches and Drink:
He dwells in a Tavern and lives ev'rywhere,
And improving his Hour, lives an age in a Year:
For as Life is uncertain, he loves to make haste,
And thus he lives longest because he lives fast;
Then leaps in the Dark, and his Exit he makes,
What Death can compare with the jolly Town-Rakes.

141

The Epicure

Sung by one in the habit of a Town Gallant.

BY THOMAS JORDAN

Let us drink and be merry, dance, Joke and Rejoice,
With *Claret* and *Sherry, Theorbo* and *Voice*,   [*Theorbo* = *a*
The changeable World to our Joy is unjust,   *large kind of*
All *Treasure* uncertain, then down with your dust.   *lute*
  In Frollicks dispose your pounds, shillings, and pence,
  For we shall be nothing a hundred year hence.

Wee'l kiss and be free with *Nan*, *Betty* and *Philly*,
Have *Oysters* and *Lobsters*, and *Maids* by the *Belly*;
Fish-dinners will make a *Lass* spring like a *flea*,
Dame Venus (Love's Godess) was born of the *sea*.
With her and with Bacchus wee'll tickle the sence,
For we shall be past it a hundred year hence.

Your most beautiful *Bit*, that hath all Eyes upon her,
That her *Honesty* sells for a hogo of *Honour*;
Whose Lightness and Brightness, doth shine in such
      splendor,
That None but the *Stars* are thought fit to attend her.
Though now she be pleasant and sweet to the sence,
Will be damnable mouldy a hundred year hence.

[hogo = 'haut
   gout' : a
relish ; also a
'high stench'

Then why should we turmoil in cares and in Fears,
Turn all our Tranquillity to Sighs and Tears?
Let's eat, drink and play till Works do corrupt us,
'Tis certain that *post mortem nulla voluptas.*
Let's deal with our Damsels, that we may from thence,
Have broods to succeed us a hundred years hence.

The *Usurer* that in the *hundred* takes *Twenty*,
Who *wants* in his *Wealth*, and doth pine in his *Plenty*;
Lays up for a season which he shall ne'r see,
The Year of One thousand eight hundred and three.
His Wit and *his* Wealth, *his* Law, Learning and
      sence,
Shall be turn'd into nothing a hundred year hence.

Your *Chancery Lawyer* who by *Conscience* thrives,
In spinning of *Suits to the length of three* Lives;
Such *Suits* which the Clients do wear in *slavery*,
While the *Pleader* makes Conscience a *Cloak* for his
      knavery,
May boast of his subtlety i' th' Present tense,
But non est inventus, *a hundred year hence.*

Your most *Christian Monsieur* who rants it in Riot,
Not suffering his poor Christian Neighbours live quiet,
Whose numberless *Legions* that to him *belongs*,
Consists of more *Nations* than *Babel* has *Tongues*.
   Though num'rous as Dust in despight of defence,
   Shall all lie in ashes a hundred year hence.

[*Christian
Monsieur
=Louis XIV*

We mind not the Counsels of such Bloody Elves,
Let us set foot to foot, and be true to our selves:
Our Honesty from our Good-Fellowship springs,
We aim at no selfish preposterous things.
   Wee'l seek no preferment by subtle pretence,
   Since all shall be nothing a hundred year hence.

142

Molly Mog

OR

The Fair Maid of the Inn

BY JOHN GAY

Says my Uncle, I pray you discover
   What hath been the Cause of your Woes,
Why you pine, and you whine, like a Lover?
   I have seen *Molly Mog* of the *Rose*.

O Nephew! your Grief is but Folly,
   In Town you may find better Prog;
Half a crown there will get you a *Molly*,
   A *Molly* much better than *Mog*.

I know that by Wits 'tis recited,
   That Women at best are a Clog;
But I am not so easily frighted,
   From loving of sweet *Molly Mog*.

The School-Boy's desire is a Play-Day,
　　The School-Master's joy is to flog;
The Milk-Maid's delight is on *May-Day*,
　　But mine is on sweet *Molly Mog*.

Will-a-wisp leads the Trav'ler a gadding
　　Thro' Ditch, and thro' Quagmire and Bog;
But no light can set me a madding,
　　Like the Eyes of my sweet *Molly Mog*.

For Guineas in other Men's Breeches
　　Your Gamesters will palm and will cog;
But I envy them none of their Riches,
　　So I may win sweet *Molly Mog*.

The Heart, when half-wounded, is changing,
　　It here and there leaps like a Frog;
But my Heart can never be ranging,
　　'Tis so fix'd upon sweet *Molly Mog*.

Who follows all Ladies of Pleasure,
　　In Pleasure is thought but a Hog:
All the Sex cannot give so good measure
　　Of Joys, as my sweet *Molly Mog*.

I feel I'm in Love to Distraction,
　　My Senses all lost in a Fog;
And nothing can give Satisfaction
　　But thinking of sweet *Molly Mog*.

A Letter when I am inditing,
　　Comes *Cupid* and gives me a Jog,
And I fill all the Paper with writing
　　Of nothing but sweet *Molly Mog*.

If I would not give up the three *Graces*
   I wish I were hang'd like a Dog,
And at Court all the Drawing-Room Faces,
   For a Glance of my sweet *Molly Mog*.

Those Faces want Nature and Spirit,
   And seem as cut out of a Log;
Juno, Venus, and *Pallas's* Merit
   Unite in my sweet *Molly Mog*.

Those who toast all the Family Royal,
   In Bumpers of *Hogan* and *Nog*,
Have Hearts not more true or more loyal
   Than mine to my sweet *Molly Mog*.

Were *Virgil* alive with his *Phillis*,
   And writing another Eclogue;
Both his *Phillis* and *fair Amaryllis*
   He'd give up for sweet *Molly Mog*.

When she smiles on each Guest, like her **Liquor,**
   Then Jealousy sets me agog.
To be sure she's a Bit for the *Vicar*
   And so I shall lose *Molly Mog*.

143

Ballad

BY JOHN GAY

Of all the Girls that e'er were seen
   There's none so fine as *Nelly*,
For charming Face, and Shape, and Mien,
   And what's not fit to tell ye:

Oh! the turn'd Neck, and smooth white Skin
   of lovely dearest *Nelly*!
For many a Swain it well had been,
   Had she ne'er pass'd by *Calai*.

For when as *Nelly* came to *France*,
   (invited by her cosins,)
Across the *Tuilleries* each glance
   Kill'd *Frenchmen* by whole dozens;
The king, as he at dinner sat,
   Did beckon to his *Hussar*,
And bid him bring his Tabby Cat
   For charming *Nell* to buss her.

The Ladies were with Rage provok'd,
   To see her so respected:
The men look'd arch, as *Nelly* stroked,
   And Puss her tail Erected.
But not a man did look imploy,
   Except on pretty *Nelly*,
Then said the duke *de Villeroy*,
   Ah! qu'elle est bien jolie!

But who's that grave Philosopher,
   That carefully looks a' ter?
By his Concern it should appear
   The Fair One is his Daughter.
Ma foy! (quoth then a courtier sly,)
   He on his Child does leer too;
I wish he has no Mind to try
   What some Papas will here do.

The Courtiers all, with one Accord
   Broke out in *Nelly's* praises,
Admired her *Rose* and *Lys sans farde*
   (Which are your *Termes Françoises*)

396

Then might you see a painted Ring
    Of Dames that stood by Nelly:
She, like the Pride of all the Spring,
    And they like *Fleurs du Palais*.

In *Marli's* gardens and *St. Clou*
    I saw this charming *Nelly*,
Where shameless Nymphs, expos'd to view
    Stand naked in each *Allee*:
But Venus had a Brazen Face,
    Both at *Versailles* and *Meudon*,
Or else she had resign'd her Place,
    And left the Stone she stood on.

Were *Nelly's* Figure mounted there,
    'Twould put down all th' *Italian*:
Lord! how those Foreigners would stare!
    But I should turn *Pygmalion*:
For, spite of Lips, and Eyes, and Mien,
    Me, nothing can delight so,
As does that Part that lies between
    Her Left Toe, and her Right Toe.

144

Wil the Merry Weaver, and Charity the
Chamber-Maid

OR

A Brisk Encounter between a Youngman
and his Love

Her straying eyes, such Beauties did discover,   [*Her : His*(?)]
As made him caper to approach his Lover;
And she a longing Maid as other be,
Desired for to learn her A.B.C.
He put the Fescue in her Lilly-white hand
And taught her how the same to understand.

I am a Weaver by my Trade
And I fell in love with a Servant Maid
And if I can but her favour win,
Then I will weave, and she shall spin.

At first I was a bashful fool,
And not well vers'd in Cupids School,
But as I bolder grew indeed
To tell you plain I did thus proceed.

I went to my loves Chamber door,
Where I had been many a night before;
But upon the Bed whereas she lay,
What I did there I dare not say.

I went to my love late in the night
And by the Stars that did shine so bright.
Where such a light sprung from her clothes,
As if the morning star had rose.

I folded down her Milk-White sheet,
To view her body so fair and clear,
Where down below I did espy,
Two Pillars of White Ivory.

Beneath those Pillars a fountain laid,
Which my poor wandering eyes betray'd,
But of all Fountains that e're was found,
I could have wish't my self there drown'd.

In a sweet slumber whilst she lay,
I had no power for to go away;
For the more I view'd her, the more I might
Her beauty dazled so my sight.

At length she did awake from sleep,
And fetched many a sigh most deep,
Oh shall I dye a Maid quoth she,
Will no young-man come pitty me.

This Damozel she was wondrous fair
And her age it was not above fifteen;
And oftentimes complained she,
That she could not learn her A.B.C.

I would some scholler would me show
The Letters of my criss-cross-row;
That my words in order might placed be,
And I might learn my A.B.C.

I wonder young-men are such fools,
To keep so long from Venus Schools,
If they did not know so much as me,   [*did not:*
They would ne'er forget their A.B.C.   *did(?)*]

I hearing of her thus complain,
Quoth I fair Maid from tears refrain
You need not troubled thus to be,
For learning of your A.B.C.

If you will be (kind sir, she said)
So courteous to a simple Maid,
Most thankful I shall ever be
For learning me my A.B.C.

With that I did my self prepare,
And near I drew to this Maiden fair,
There is some hopes I find, quoth she,
That I shall learn my A.B.C.

I gave her a Fescue in her hand,
And bid her use it at her command;
She said you best know where it should be,
Come put it to my A.B.C.

I found her very ripe of wit,
And for a scholar wondrous fit,
She us'd her art as well as me,
And all to learn her A.B.C.

When I had taught her Lesson plain,
She would repeat it o're again;
Quoth she, this Lesson pleases me,
I like to read my A.B.C.

And now if any Maidens have
A mind to learn this Lesson brave
Though I'm a Weaver of low degree,
Ile teach them to read their A.B.C.

145

As Oyster Nan Stood By Her Tub

As Oyster Nan stood by her Tub,
    To shew her vicious Inclination;
She gave her noblest Parts a Scrub,
    And sigh'd for want of Copulation:
A Vinter of no little Fame,
    Who excellent Red and White can sell ye,
Beheld the little dirty Dame,
    As she stood scratching of her Belly.

Come in, says he, you silly Slut,
　'Tis now a rare convenient Minute;
I'll lay the Itching of your Scut,
　Except some greedy Devil be in it:
With that the Flat-capt Fusby smil'd,   [*Fusby*=
　And would have blush'd, but that she cou'd not;   '*Fusby*'
Alass! says she, we're soon beguil'd,   *squat* (?)
　By Men to do those things we shou'd not.

From Door they went behind the Bar,
　As it's by common Fame reported;
And there upon a Turkey Chair,
　Unseen the loving couple sported:
But being call'd by Company,
　As he was taking pains to please her;
I'm coming, coming Sir, says he,
　My Dear, and so am I, says she, Sir.

Her Mole-hill Belly swell'd about,
　Into a Mountain quickly after;
And when the pretty Mouse crept out,
　The creature caus'd a mighty Laughter:
And now she has learnt the pleasing Game,
　Altho' much Pain and Shame it cost her;
She daily ventures at the same,
　And shuts and opens like an Oyster.

146

Sally in our Alley

BY HENRY CAREY

Of all the girls that are so smart
　There's none like pretty Sally;

She is the darling of my heart,
  And she lives in our alley.
There's ne'er a lady in the land
  That's half so sweet as Sally;
She is the darling of my heart,
  And she lives in our alley.

Her father he makes cabbage-nets,
  And thro' the streets does cry 'em;
Her mother she sells laces long
  To such as please to buy 'em;
But sure such folks could ne'er beget
  So sweet a girl as Sally;
She is the darling of my heart,
  And she lives in our alley.

When she is by I leave my work,
  I love her so sincerely;
My master comes like any Turk
  And bangs me most severely;
But let him bang his bellyfull,
  I'll bear it all for Sally;
She is the darling of my heart,
  And she lives in our alley.

Of all the days that's in the week
  I dearly love but one day,
And that's the day that comes betwix
  A Saturday and Monday,
For then I'm dressed all in my best
  To walk abroad with Sally;
She is the darling of my heart,
  And she lives in our alley.

My master carries me to church,
  And often am I blam'd

Because I leave him in the lurch
   As soon as text is nam'd;
I leave the church in sermon time
   And slink away to Sally;
She is the darling of my heart,
   And she lives in our alley.

When Christmas comes about again,
   O, then I shall have money;
I'll hoard it up, and box and all,
   I'll give it to my honey;
And would it were ten thousand pounds,
   I'd give it all to Sally;
She is the darling of my heart,
   And she lives in our alley.

My master and the neighbours all
   Make game of me and Sally,
And, but for her, I'd better be
   A slave and row a galley;
But when my seven long years are out,
   O, then I'll marry Sally;
O, then we'll wed, and then we'll bed,
   But not in our alley.

147

The Widow that Keeps the Cock Inn

A traveller for many long years I have been,
   But I never went over to France –
Most cities and all market towns I've been in,
   From Berwick on Tweed to Penzance,

Many hotels and taverns I've been in my time,
    And many fair landladys seen –
But of all the fair charmers who other outshine
    Give me the sweet widow –
      The dear little widow,
I mean the sweet widow that keeps the Cock Inn.

Her lips are as roses as e'en is her wine,
    And like all her liquors, she's neat,
She's full of good spirits, that's really devine
    And while serving her bitters, looks sweet,
Excuse these outpourings, they spring from the heart,
    You may laugh – so shall I, if I win,
One smile of consent, how 'twould lessen the smart,
    From the active young widow,
      The spruce little widow.
The little widow that keeps the Cock Inn.

There's Bet at the 'Blossom' and Poll of the 'Crown',
    Fat Dolly who owns the 'Red Heart'.
There's Kate of the 'Garter and Star', of renown
    And Peggy who keeps the 'Skylark'.
Spruce Fan of the 'Eagle' and Nan of the 'Bell'
    Pretty Jane of the 'Man drest ⟨?in Green⟩'
But of all the fair creatures ⟨?that⟩ others excel.
    Give me the sweet widow,
      The nice little widow.
My neat.pretty widow who keeps the Cock Inn.

<!-- marginal note: [Broadside torn -->

There's Nance at 'the Old Woman clothed in Gray'
    I look black upon her I vow,
Even Letty who graces 'the Old Load of Hay',
    I don't care a straw for her now,
There's another decanter'd just now in my heart
    I for none of the rest care a pin.

Oh, that Cupid the rogue, would but let fly his dart,
 At the plump little widow,
 The gay little widow,
The spirited widow that keeps the Cock Inn.

When last in her little bar parlour I sat
 I joked her about her lone state,
A brood of young chicken's dear widow mind that,
 Would be better around you prate,
Says she, pray don't reckon 'fore they are hatch'd,
 says I, where's the harm or the sin?
You can manage a second, we're very well match'd
 You dear little widow,
 You charming young widow,
You're a nice little widow to keep the Cock Inn.

Then here's to the dear little charmer I prize,
 In a bumper now filled to the brim,
For who could resist such a pair of black eyes,
 As in rich liquid moisture they swim,
Away, then away, with my bachelor's vow
 My hand then is hers, with the ring,
For if she be willing to take me in tow,
 I'll marry the widow,
 The dear little widow,
I'll marry the widow, and keep the Cock Inn.

148

Black Thing

Ye nymphs and ye swains that trip over the plains
Come listen a while to my innocent tale,
And hear ⟨me with⟩ pity while I do sing,
Its no less than the loss of my little black thing.

[Broadsheet:
my wife

405

As I sat at cards with a friend t'other day
To pass some dull hours and drive care away
Young Colin as brisk as a bird in the spring,
He wanted to play with my little black thing.

On me his sly looks were constantly bent
To gaze on my beauty it was his intent,
His looks towards me he did frequently fling,
While he gently handled my little black thing.

I dreamt of no hurt but thought him quite blunt,
And gave him the pleasure to play with my c—
Then got up his p— quite stiff for a fling,
And ran it slap into my little black thing.

Ten thousand soft whispers he forced in my ear,
I bid him begon but ⟨he⟩ still would not hear,
I had no power left from him to spring,
He got so fast hold of my little black thing.

I squeaked and I squealled and bid him let go,
He smiled in my face and a⟨n⟩swered me no,
A crown in my lap he did instantly fling,
To let him enjoy my little black thing.

Then a full p— he put in my hand
I wanted no coaxing to make it stand,
⟨I⟩ measured it round with a nine inch string
And found it just fit for my little black thing

Then I got on the ground and lay on my back
He drew his p— and b— my c— in a crack
My legs round his body I fixed as a spring,
And draged out the brains with my little black
        thing.

[Broadsheet
    A

149

Johnny Raw and Polly Clark

One night quite bang up to the mark,
                    Ri tol de lol.
A drunken swell met Polly Clark,
                    Ri tol de lol.
And said, dear Poll if you'll be mine,
A swigging gin we'll spend our time,
Agreed, said she, that's bang up prime,
                    Ri tol de lol.
He married her – sad tale to tell,
                    Ri tol de lol,
She got no max so blow'd up well,   [*max = gin*
                    Ri tol di lol,
At length she vow'd she'd serve him out,
Bung up his eyes and crack his snout
And send the duds all up the spout.   [*duds = clothes;*
                    Ri tol de lol,   *up the spout =*
Thus she would bore him with her jaw,   *in pawn*
                    Ri tol de lol.
And call him spooney Johnny Raw   [*spooney =*
                    Ri tol de lol,   *foolish*
Then claps her fins and bully him,   [*claps =*
And wild passion at him grin,   *clasp (?)*
She'd bawl you dog where is my gin,
                    Ri tol de lol.
One time while thinking of his state
                    Ri tol de lol.
He cried, you Poll, I'll break your pate,
                    Ri tol di lol.
For every thing that I have got,
You've hauled off to the pop shop
And there bang up they're like to stop,
                    Ri tol de lol.

With that she gave him such a twister
                Ri tol de lol
And tipt him such a precious fister
                Ri tol de lol.
That laid him sprawling in the grate
There now said she you hold your prate,

[claret = nose-blood

For your claret flows at a prime rate,
                Ri tol de lol.
That night while snoring in his bed,
                Ri tol de lol,
He dreamt his wife had from him fled
                Ri tol de lol,
Then full of joy, he woke 'tis true
And found his rib had proved untrue,
And bolted with the Lord knows who.
                Ri tol de lol
I'm glad the vixen's gone said he,
                Ri tol de lol,
For long I've liv'd in misery
                Ri tol de lol

*[brush'd = run away
[mug myself = 'make myself cosy'

But now she's brush'd I'll spend my
    time,
And mug myself with gin and wine,
So now once more I'm bang up prime,
                Ri tol de lol.

150

The Trumpeter

A forward young woman, Miss Chaos,
  Whose bosom had oftentimes thought of love,
One night in the pit of a playhouse,
  Had her heart suddenly brought to love,

She sat near the orchestra music,
    Whence Cupid a crotchet shot bump at her,
She was charmed and immediately grew sick,
    For she fell in love with the trumpeter.

She gazed on him while he was blowing,
    His mouth seemed all musical knowledge,
His nose was as sharp and as knowing,
    As a student of Brazen nose college,
She saw his left eye look over to her,
    In fact it looked constantly plump at her
And it seemed like an amorous overture,
    Play'd on the heart by the trumpeter.

She thought he was charmed with her graces
    With his she was now deeply smitten,
And she manag'd with one to change places,
    To get nearer where he was sitting,
She at him then nodded and smiled,
    And she thought his left eye seemed to comfort her,
But alas! he remained unbeguiled,
    For blind of that eye was the trumpeter.

She thought with her flasket of brandy,
    She could bring him to smile and ⟨prattle too⟩   [MS.:
She shew'd it – he took it quite handy,   'to prattle'
    And drank 'til he emptied the bottle too
As he drank, 'side the stage her eye caught
    A one-armed wench shaking her stump at her,
She wondered but little she thought
    This was the wife of the trumpeter.

She still squeezed his hand and kept making,
    Dumb motions of love to the trumpeter,
When his wife in a deuce of a taking,
    Spank from the stage made a jump at her,

She soon black'd the eyes of Miss Chaos,
    With her stump she made many a thump at her,
And in spite of the roar of the playhouse,
    She turn'd round and thump'd the poor trumpeter.

Now this one-arm'd wife had with surprise
    Struck doubly dump her poor dumb creature,
And Miss with her blue and black eyes,
    Sat as mute and as mum as the trumpeter,
But she thought best to scamper away,
    For the wife said she would pelt and thump at her
But whenever she goes to the play,
    She never sits near to the trumpeter.

[dump = dumb (?)]

151

The Naughty Lord & The Gay Young Lady Damages, £10,000

There is a pretty piece of work,
    It is up in high life,
Upon my word an amorous lord,
    Seduced another man's wife;
She was a lady of title,
    She was charming, young, and fair,
With her daddy and her mammy once
    She lived in Belgrave Square.

The trial now is over,
    And his lordship, with a frown,
For kissing Lady Nelly
    Has to pay ten thousand pounds.

Lord G— was a naughty lord,
　　Oh! how could he engage,
To seduce young Lady Ellen, –
　　He is sixty years of age.
The verdict of the jury
　　Made his lordship quake and jump,
Ten thousand pounds he has to pay,
　　For playing tiddly bump.

Lady Nelly left her husband,
　　And would with his lordship be,
She would trim his lordship's whiskers
　　As she sat upon his knee.
Some said oh, lack-a-daisy,
　　She was in a comical way!
His lordship was bald-pated,
　　And his hair and whiskers grey.

My lord was very fond of lamb, –
　　The cook said so at least, –
And neighbours you must understand
　　He liked the belly piece.
His lordship loved the lady,
　　And the lady she loved he,
His lordship played by music,
　　The tune called fiddle-de-dee.

His lordship when he heard the news,
　　Caused his eyes to flash like fire then
He looked around, ten thousand pounds
　　His lordship holloaed 'wire-em'.
He sold his hat, he pawned his coat,
　　To pay the browns, we find,
And then he run round Hyde Park sqre,
　　With his shirt hanging out behind.

Sweet Ellen was a daughter
　Of my Lord and Lady C—
And once lived in a mansion,
　Yes she lived in Belgrave Square,
Sweet Ellen had an husband,
　An honest upright man,
And his lordship went a trespassing
　Upon her husband's land.

My lord was fond of sporting,
　And hunting of the hare,
He has to pay ten thousand pounds,
　The damage to repair;
His lordship played the fiddle,
　Down in Scotia's land, 'tis said,
And his lordship must have fiddled well
　Both in and out of bed.

Now all young lords take warning,
　When a hunting you do go,
In the evening or the morning
　Pray beware of 'Tally-ho!'
If you are caught a trespassing
　On other people's ground,
Perhaps you'll be like old Lord G—
　Made to pay ten thousand pounds.

The lady's injured husband,
　Has nobly gained the day,
And beat old Mr December,
　Who seduced young Lady May.

152

Verses on Daniel Good

(Who was executed this morning May, '42, for the Murder of Jane Jones)

(1842)

Of all the wild deeds upon murder's black list,
Sure none is so barbarous and cruel as this,
Which in these few lines unto you I'll unfold,
The recital's enough to turn your blood cold.

In the great town of London near Manchester square,
Jane Jones kept a mangle in South street we hear,
A gentleman's coachman oft visiting came,
A cold-blooded monster, Dan Good was his name.

As a single man under her he made love,
And in course of time she pregnant did prove,
Then with false pretences he took her from home,
To murder his victim and the babe in her womb.

[*under* = *unto*(?)

To his master's stables in Putney Park Lane,
They went, but she never returned again,
Prepare for your end then the monster did cry,
You⟨r⟩ time it is come for this night you must die.

Then with a sharp hatchet her head did cleave,
She begged for mercy but none he would give,
Have mercy dear Daniel my wretched life spare,
For the sake of your own child which you know I bear.

No mercy, he cried, then repeated the blow,
Alive from this stable you never shall go,

Neither you nor your brat shall e'er trouble me more,
Then lifeless his victim he struck to the floor.

And when she was dead this sad deed to hide,
The limbs from her body he straight did divide,
Her bowels ript open and dripping with gore,
The child from the womb this black monster he tore.

He made a large fire in the harness room,
Her head, arms, and legs in the fire did consume,
But e'er his intentions were fulfilled quite,
This dark deed by Providence was brought to light.

To a pawn-shop the coachman he did go one day,
A boy said some trowsers he did take away,
A policeman followed unto Putney Lane,
The coachman and trouwsers to bring back again.

When in searching the stable the body he spied,
Without head, legs, or arms, and ript open beside,
Then a cry of murder he quickly did raise,
And the coachman was taken within a few days.

And when he was tried, most shocking to state,
The evidence proved what I now relate,
That Daniel Good murdered his victim Jones,
Then cut up and burnt her flesh and bones.

He soon was found guilty and sentenced to die,
The death of a murderer on the gallows high,
The blood of the murder'd must not cry vain,
An we hope that his like we shall ne'er see again.

THREE

VOCATIONAL

153

The Merry Bagpipes

The Pleasant Pastime Betwixt a Jolly Shepherd and a Country
Damsel, On a Mid-summers-day in the Morning

A Shepherd set him under a Thorn,
   he pull'd out his Pipe and began for to play,
It was on a *Mid-summers-day* in the morn
   for honour of that Holy-day:
A Ditty he did Chant along,
   goes to the Tune of *Cater-Bordee*
And this was the burthen of his Song,
   if thou wilt Pipe Lad, I'll dance to thee,
     To thee, to thee, derry, derry, to thee &c,

And whilst this Harmony he did make,
   a Country Damsel from the Town,
A Basket on her Arm she had,
   a gathering Rushes on the Down;
Her Bongrace of wended Straw;
   from the Sun's hot Beams her Face is free,
And thus she began when she him saw,
   if thou wilt Pipe &c.

[*Bongrace* =
*A broad-
brimmed hat*

Then he pull'd out his Pipe, and began to sound,
   whilst tempting on her Back she lay,
But when his quivering note she found,
   how sweetly then this Lass could play:
She stop'd all jumps, and she reveal'd,
   she kept all time with harmony,
And looking on him, sighing said,
   if thou wilt Pipe &c.

She never so much blusht at all,
   the Musick was so charming sweet,
But e'er anon to him she'd call,
   and bid him be active, turn and meet;
As thou art a bonny Shepherd's Swain,
   I am a Lass am come to Wooe thee
To play me another double Strain,
   and doubt not but I will dance to thee &c.

[*silly = simple*

Altho' I am but a silly Maid,
   who ne'er was brought up at Dancing-School,
But yet to the Jig that thou hast plaid,
   you find that I can keep time and Rule;
Now see that you keep your stops aright,
   for Shepherd I am resolv'd to view thee,
And play me the Damsel's chief Delight,
   then never doubt but I'll Dance to thee &c.

The Shepherd again did Tune his Pipe,
   and plaid her a Lesson loud and shrill,
The Damsel his Face did often wipe,
   with many a Thank for his good will;
And said, I was ne'er so pleas'd before,
   and this is the first time that I knew thee,
Come play me this very Jigg once more,
   and never doubt but I'll Dance to thee &c.

The Shepherd, he said, as I am a Man,
   I have kept Playing from Morning till Noon,
Thou know'st I can do no more than I can;
   my Pipe is clearly out of Tune;
To ruine a Shepherd I'll not seek,
   said she, for why should I undo thee,
I can come again to the Down next Week,
   and thou shalt Pipe, and I'll Dance to thee,
     To thee, to thee, derry, derry, to thee, &c.

154

Gee Ho, Dobin

As I was driving my Waggon one Day,
I met a young Damsel tight, buxom and gay;
I kindly accosted her with a low Bow,
And I felt my whole Body I cannot tell how;
   Ge ho Dobin, hi ho Dobin, Ge ho Dobin, Ge ho, Ge ho.

I long'd to be at her and gave her a kiss,
She thought me but civil, nor took it amiss;
I knew no recalling the minutes were past,
I began to make hay while the sunshine did last;
   Ge ho Dobin, &c,

I've six score of sheep, and each Ram has his Ewe,
And my cows when they lack to the Parsons Bull go;
We're made for each other, so prithee comply;
She blush'd, her eyes twinkled, She could not tell why;
   Ah poor Jenny, fearful Jenny, ah poor Jenny, hi ho.

I kiss'd her again, she reply'd with Disdain,
No kisses I want, prithee take them again,
Then whisper'd me softly the Weather was hot,
And her Mind ran on something, She cou'd not tell what;
   Ah poor Jenny, Coaxing Jenny, ah poor Jenny, hi ho.

Then down in my Waggon this Damsel I laid,
But still I kept driving, for driving's my Trade;
I rumpl'd her Feathers, and tickl'd her scutt,
And play'd the round Rubbers at two handed Put;
   Well put Roger, well put Jenny, well put Roger, hi ho.

Her Breasts were as soft and as white as New Cream,
And her motion kept Time with the Bells of my Team;
When her Bubbies went up, her plump Buttocks went
   down,
And the Wheels seem'd to stand, and the Waggon go
   round;
   Ah brave Roger, drive on Roger, ah brave Roger, hi ho.

Then too, and again to our Pastime we went,
And my Cards I plày'd fairly to Jenny's Content;
I work'd at her Pump till the Sucker grew dry,
And then I left pumping, a good Reason why;
   Ah poor Roger, broken back Roger, ah poor Roger, hi
      ho.

I thought e'er we parted to had t'other Blow,
When slap went the Waggon Wheel into a Slough;
Which shatter'd her Premises out of Repair,
Then Roger's Pump handle ran the Devil knows where;
   Ah poor Roger, flimsy Roger, ah poor Roger, hi ho.

155

The Jovial Tinker

OR

The Willing Couple

A Tinker by a maid put to his dumps
Til he was fain to turn her up for trumps
She fretted his hammers went so slow
They always hit to high or else to loe
At first he was unapt and therefore told
Her Kettles crackt & so it will not hold
At last with double fee she brought him on
And then he prov'd himself a mettle'd man.

418

There was a Tinker liv'd of late
   as I to you will show;
And how he us'd a maiden kind
   you presently shall know,
He'd undertake to cure a crack
   i'th Kettle at a blow:
Although his hammers they did beat
to high, to low, to high, to low, to low.

And as this Tinker walkt the streets
   for work as he did cry;
A handsome proper maid did meet,
   and call him by and by:
Tinker said the maid draw neer to me,
   my kettle I will show;
Although thy hammers they do beat
   &c.

She took the Tinker by the hand,
   and led him in at door;
fair maid said he your Kettles crackt
   'twas mended once before:
With that she call'd the Tinker rogue
   fair maid why sayst thou so
Because thy hammers they do beat
   &c

And as the Tinker sate at work,
   this maid began to chide;
Because he did not clench the nail
   upon the other side.
Thou dost not work, ⟨not⟩ workmanlike   [Broadsheet:
fair maid why sayest thou so   *'and'*
Because thy hammers they do beat
   &c

The Tinker then took up his pack
  and fain would go his way;
The fair maid she perceiving that,
  desired him to stay;
I'le give thee meat, I'le give thee drink
  I'le pay thee e're thou go;
Although thy hammers they do beat
  &c

Cause she was neat he did retreat,
  and come e're she could send,
Fair maid said he I needs must see
  what hole you have to mend:
She took the Tinker by the hand,
  Into a Room they go,
But still she cry'd his hammers beat
  &c

The Tinkers job did hold him back
  till it was almost dark.
It seem'd her Kettle was so black,
  he could not hit the mark:
Which made the maiden for to cry,
  Strike home before you go
For yet the hammers they do beat &c

The Tinker see his work in vain
  the cause he plainly told,
there hath so many nails been drove
  that mine will not take hold,
It hath been peec't so many times
  'twill not endure a blow,
No wonder if my hammers beat &c

The maid thereat was sore perplex⟨t⟩
    and troubled at this ill:
Said she it hath endur'd some knocks
    and more it may do still;
I'me sure good liquor it would hold,
    if it were fill'd I know:
The reason is your hammers beat &c

She bid the Tinker mend his work   [=mend
    and she would mend his wage;   improve,
He us'd his hammers like a Turk   better
    and did himself engage
And at the last when all was past
    the Tinker pleas'd her so
She said his hammers did not beat &c

The Tinker he for double fee
    did please with much a do,
But yet e're forty weeks were gone
    her kettle fell in two:
he⟨d⟩ knockt her till she Big'd again
    as boys they us'd to do
I hope she will not now complain
to high, to low, to high, to low, to low.

156

Room for a Jovial Tinker: Old Brass to Mend

Here is a Tinker full of mettle,
The which can mend pot, pan, or Kettle;
For stopping of holes is his delight,
His work goes forward day and night.
If there be any women brave
Whose Coldrons need of mending have,
Send for this Tinker nere deny him,
He'l do your work well if you try him.
A proof of him I'le forthwith show,
'Cause you his workmanship may know.

It was a Lady of the North she lov'd a Gentleman,
And knew not well what course to take, to use him now and
  than.
Wherefore she writ a Letter, and seal'd it with her hand,
And bid him be a Tinker, to mend both pot and pan,
With a hey ho, hey, derry derry down; with hey trey,
    down down, derry.

And when the merry Gentleman the Letter he did read,
He got a budget on his back, and Apron with all speed,
His pretty shears and pincers, so well they did agree,
With a long pike staff upon his back, came tripping o're
  the Lee.
With a hey ho, hey, derry derry down; with hey trey,
    down down, derry.

When he came to the Ladye's house, he knocked at the
  gate,
Then answered this Lady gay, Who knocketh there so
  late?
'Tis I, Madam, the Tinker said, I work for gold and fee:
If you have any broken pots or pans, come bring them all
  to me.
With a hey ho, hey, derry derry down; with hey trey,
    down down, derry.

I am the bravest Tinker that lives beneath the Sun,
If you have any work to do, you shall have it well done;
I have brasse within my budget, and punching under my
  Apron,
I'm come unto your Ladyship, and means to mend your
  Coldron.
With a hey ho, hey, derry derry down; with hey trey,
    down down, derry.

I prethee, said the Lady gay, bring now thy budget in
I have store of work for thee to do, if thou wilt once begin.
Now when the Tinker he came in, that did the budget bear,
God blesse, quoth he, your Ladyship! God save you Madam
    fair.
With hey ho, hey, derry derry down; with hey trey,
    down down, derry.

But when the Lady knew his face, she then began to wink,
Hast, lusty Butler! then quoth she, to fetch the man some
    drink.
Give him such meat as we do eat, and drink as we do use,
It is not for a Tinker's Trad good liquor to refuse.
With hey ho, hey, derry derry down; with hey trey
    down down, derry.

But when that he had eat and drunk, the truth of all is so,
The Lady took him by the sleeve, her work to him to show,
Let up thy Tools, Tinker, quoth she, and see there be
    none lost,
And mend my Kettle handsomely, what ere it doth me cost.
With hey ho, hey, derry derry down; with hey treys,
    down, down, derry.

Your work, Madam, shall be well done, if you will pay me
    for't;
For every nayl that I do drive, you shall give me a mark.
If I do not drive the nayl to th'head, I'le have nothing for
    my pain,
And what I do receive of you shall be return'd again.
With hey ho, hey, derry derry down; with hey trey,
    down down, derry.

At last being come into the Room, where he the work
    should do,
The Lady lay down on the bed, so did the Tinker too:

Although the Tinker knockt amain, the Lady was not
    offended,
But before that she rose from the bed, her Coldron was
    well mended.
With hey ho, hey, derry derry down; with hey trey,
      down down, derry.

But when his work was at an end, which he did in the
    dark,
She put her hand into her purse and gave him twenty mark,
Heres mony for thy work, said she, and I thank thee for
    thy pain,
And when my Coldron mending lacks I'le send for thee
    again.
With hey, ho, hey, derry derry down; with hey trey,
      down down, derry.

The Tinker he was well content for that which he had
    done,
So took his budget on his back, and quickly he was gone.
Then the Lady to her husband went, O my dear Lord,
    quoth she,
I have set the bravest Tinker at work that ever you did see.
With hey ho, hey, derry derry down; with hey trey,
      down down, derry.

No fault at all this Tinker hath, but he takes dear for his
    work,
That little time that he wrought here it cost me twenty
    mark.
If you had been so wise, quoth he, for to have held your
    own,
Before you set him to this work the price you might have
    known.
With hey ho, hey, derry derry down; with hey trey,
      down down, derry.

Pray hold your peace, my Lord, quoth she, and think it not
　　too dear.
If you cou'd doo't so well 'twould save you forty pound a
　　year.
With that the Lord most lovingly, to make all things
　　amends,
He kindly kist his Lady gay, and so they both were friends.
　　With hey ho, hey, derry derry down; with hey trey,
　　　　down down, derry.

You merry Tinkers, every one, that hear this new-made
　　Sonnet,
When as you do a Lady's work be sure you think upon it;
Drive home your nayls to the very head, and do your work
　　profoundly,
And then no doubt your Mistresses will pay you for it
　　soundly.
　　With hey ho, hey, derry derry down; with hey trey,
　　　　down down, derry.

157

The Tinker

There was a Lady in this Land,
　　That lov'd a Gentleman,
And could not have him secretly
　　As she would now and then,
Till she divis'd to dress him like
　　A Tinker in Vocation:
And thus, disguis'd, she bid him say,
　　He came to clout her Cauldron.　　　　　　　　[*clout = mend*

425

His face full fair she smother's black
   That he might not be known
A leather Jerkin on his back,
   His breeches rent and torn;
With speed he passed to the place,
   To knock he did not spare:
Who's that, quoth the lady ⟨'s Porter⟩ then,
   That raps so rashly there.

I am a Tinker, then quoth he,
   That worketh for my Fee,
If you have Vessels for to mend,
   Then bring them unto me:
For I have brass within my bag,
   And target in my Apron,
And with my skill I can well clout,
   And mend a broken Cauldron.

The Porter went into the house
   Where Servants us'd to dine,
Telling his Lady, at the Gate
   There staid a Tinker fine:
Quoth he, much Brass he wears about
   And Target in his Apron,
Saying that he hath perfect skill
   To mend your broken Cauldron.

Quoth she, of him we have great need,
   Go Porter, let him in,
If he be cunning in his Craft
   He shall much money win:
But wisely wist she who he was,
   Though nothing she did say,
For in that sort she pointed him
   To come that very day.

When he before the Lady came,
   Disguised stood he there,
He blinked blithly, and did say,
   God save you Mistris fair;
Thou'rt welcome, Tinker, unto me,
   Thou seem'st a man of skill,
All broken Vessels for to mend,
   Though they be ne'er so ill;
I am the best men of my Trade,
   Quoth he, in all this Town
For any Kettle, Pot, or Pan,
   Or clouting of a Cauldron.

Quoth she, our Cauldron hath most need
   At it we will begin,
For it will hold you half an hour
   To trim it out and in:
But give me first a glass of drink,
   The best that we do use,
For why ⟨,⟩ it is a Tinkers guise
   No good drink to refuse.

Then to the Brew-house hyed they fast
   This broken piece to mend,
He said he would no company,
   His Craft should not be kend,
But only to your self, he said,
   That must pay me my Fee:
I am no common Tinker,
   But work most curiously.

And I also have made a Vow
   I'll keep it if I may,
There shall no mankind see my work,
   That I may stop or stay:
Then barred he the Brew-house door,

The place was very dark,
He cast his Budget from his back,
   And frankly fell to work.

And whilst he play'd and made her sport
   Their craft the more to hide,
She with his hammer stroke full hard
   Against the Cauldron side:
Which made them all to think and say,
   The Tinker wrought apace,
And so be sure he did indeed,
   But in another place.

Quoth he, fair Lady, unto her,
   My business I have ended,
Go quickly now and tell your Lord
   The Cauldron I have mended:
As for the price that I refer
   Whatsoever he do say,
Then come again with diligence,
   I would I were away.

The Lady went unto her Lord
   Where he walkt up and down,
Sir, I have with the Tinker been,
   The best in all the Town:
His work he doth exceeding well,
   Though he be wondrous dear,
He asks no less than half a mark
   For that he hath done here.

Quoth he, that Target is full dear,
   I swear by God's good Mother:
Quoth she, my Lord, I do protest,
   'Tis worth five hundred other;

He strook it in the special place,
   Where greatest need was found,
Spending his brass and target both,
   To make it safe and sound.

Before all Tinkers in the Land,
   That travels up and down,
Ere they should earn a Groat of mine,
   This man should earn a crown:
Or were you of his Craft so good,
   And none but I it kend,
Then would it save me many a Mark,
   Which I am fain to spend.

The Lady to her Coffer went,
   And took a hundred Mark,
And gave the Tinker for his pains,
   That did so well his work;
Tinker, said she, take here thy fee,
   Sith here you'll not remain,
But I must have my Cauldron now
   Once scoured o'er again.

Then to the former work they went
   No man could them deny;
The Lady said, good Tinker call
   The next time thou com'st by;
For why ⟨,⟩ thou dost thy work so well,
   And with so good invention,
If still thou hold thy hand alike,
   Take here a yearly Pension.

And ev'ry quarter of the year
   Our Cauldron thou shalt view;
Nay, by my faith, her Lord gan say,
   I'd rather buy a new;

Then did the Tinker take his leave
    Both of the Lord and Lady,
And said, such work as I can do,
    To you I will be ready.
From all such Tinkers of the Trade
    God keep my Wife, I pray,
That comes to clout her Cauldron so,
    I'll swing him if I may.

158

'Missy sick'

Missy sick of she did not know what
And perhaps of too much health Sir
Complaind of this & complaind of that
But going one night by stealth Sir
To the Vice-Chamberlain
She told all her pain
Who slyly look'd upon her
And said he'd a pill
Woud cure every ill
Belong'd to a maid of honour

Oh Lord she cryd pray give it me quick
Not knowing what twas he meant Sir
Just now I've a fit just now I am sick
So she took it & in it went Sir
But she made a strange Rout
To have it got out
As soon as twas in let me tell ye
She cryd I'm undone
As sure as a Gun
Twill make such work in my belly

Away says the vice with your simple fears
Already the worst is over
Quoth she if it comes to my sister maids ears
The whole court will say you're my lover
To the Queen twill be told
And Grantham will scold
But when we are out of sight Sir
I'm resolved to endure
What you say is my cure
You shall give it me every night Sir.

159

The Hunt

Some in the Town go betimes to the Downs,
   To pursue the fearful Hare;
Some in the Dark love to hunt in a Park,
   For to chace all the Deer that are there:
Some love to see the Faulcon to flee,
   With a joyful rise against the Air;
But all my delight is a Cunny in the Night,
   When she turns up her silver Hair.

[*cunny* = *rabbit*
(*equivocal*)

When she is beset, with a Bow, Gun, or Net,
   And finding no shelter for to cover her;
She falls down flat, or in a Tuft does squat,
   'Till she lets the Hunter get over her:
With her breast she does butt, and she bubs up her Scut,
   When the Bullets fly close by her Ear;
She strives not to escape, but she mumps like an Ape,
   And she turns up her silver Hair.

The Ferret he goes in, through flaggs thick and thin,
   Whilst Mettle pursueth his Chace;
The Cunny she shows play, and in the best of her way,
   Like a Cat she does spit in his Face;
Tho' she lies in the Dust, she fears not his Nest,
   With her full bound up Sir, career;
With the strength that she shows, she gapes at the Nose,
   And she turns up her silver Hair.

The sport is so good, that in Town or in Wood,
   In a Hedge, or a Ditch you may do it;
In Kitchen or in Hall, in a Barn or in a Stall,
   Or wherever you please you may go to it:
So pleasing it is that you can hardly miss,
   Of so rich Game in all our Shire;
For they love so to play, that by Night or by Day,
   They will turn up their Silver Hair.

160

The Merchant and the Fidler's Wife

It was a Rich Merchant Man,
   That had both Ship and all;
And he would cross the salt Seas,
   Tho' his cunning it was but small.

The Fidler and his Wife,
   They being nigh at hand;
Would needs go sail along with him,
   From Dover unto Scotland.

The Fidler's Wife look'd brisk,
   Which made the Merchant smile;
He made no doubt to bring it about,
   The Fidler to beguile.

Is this thy Wife the Merchant said,
　　She looks like an honest Spouse;
Ay that she is, the Fidler said,
　　That ever trod on Shoes.

Thy Confidence is very great,
　　The Merchant then did say;
If thou a Wager darest to bet,
　　I'll tell thee what I will lay.

I'll lay my Ship against thy Fiddle,
　　And all my Venture too;
So Peggy may gang along with me,
　　My Cabin for to View.

If she continues one Hour with me,
　　Thy true and constant Wife;
Then shalt thou have my Ship and be,
　　A Merchant all thy Life.

The Fidler was content,
　　He Danc'd and Leap'd for joy;
And twang'd his Fiddle in merriment,
　　For Peggy he thought was Coy.

Then Peggy she went along,
　　His Cabin for to View;
And after her the Merchant-Man,
　　Did follow, we found it true.

When they were once together,
　　The Fidler was afraid;
For he crep'd near in pitious fear,
　　And thus to Peggy he said.

Hold out, sweet Peggy hold out,
    For the space of two half Hours;
If thou hold out, I make no doubt,
    But the Ship and Goods are ours.

In troth, sweet Robin, I cannot,
    He hath got me about the Middle;
He's lusty and strong, and hath laid me along,
    O Robin thou'st lost thy Fiddle.

If I have lost my Fiddle,
    Then am I a Man undone;
My Fiddle whereon I so often play'd,
    Away I needs must run.

O stay the Merchant said,
    And thou shalt keep thy place;
And thou shalt have thy Fiddle again,
    But Peggy shall carry the Case.

Poor Robin hearing that,
    He look'd with a Merry-chear;
His wife she was pleas'd, and the Merchant was eas'd,
    And jolly and brisk they were.

The Fidler he was mad,
    But valu'd it not a Fig;
Then Peggy unto her Husband said,
    Kind Robin play us a Jigg.

Then he took up his Fiddle,
    And merrily he did play;
The Scottish Jigg and the Horn-pipe,
    And eke the Irish Hey.

It was but in vain to grieve,
    The Deed it was done and past;
Poor Robin was born to carry the Horn,
    For Peggy could not be Chast.

Then Fiddlers all beware,
    Your Wives are kind you see;
And he that's made for the Fidling Trade,
    Must never a Merchant be.

For Peggy she knew right well,
    Although she was but a Woman;
That Gamesters Drink, and Fidlers Wives,
    They are ever Free and Common.

161

My Thing is My Own

I a tender young Maid have been courted by many,
Of all sorts and Trades as ever was any:
A spruce Haberdasher first spake me fair,
But I would have nothing to do with Small ware.
    My Thing is my own, and I'll keep it so still,
    Yet other young Lasses may do what they will.

A sweet scented Courtier did give me a Kiss,
And promis'd me Mountains if I would be his,
But I'll not believe him, for it is too true,
Some Courtiers do promise much more than they do.
    My thing is my own, and I'll keep it so still,
    Yet other young Lasses may do what they will.

A fine Man of Law did come out of the Strand,
To plead his own Cause with his Fee in his Hand;
He made a brave Motion but that would not do,

For I did dismiss him, and Nonsuit him too.
　My thing is my own, and I'll keep it so still,
　Yet other young Lasses may do what they will.

Next came a young Fellow, a notable Spark,
(With Green Bag and Inkhorn, a Justices Clark)
He pull'd out his Warrant to make all appear,
But I sent him away with a Flea in his Ear.
　My thing is my own, and I'll keep it so still,
　Yet other young Lasses may do what they will.

A Master of Musick came with an intent,
To give me a Lesson on my Instrument,
I thank'd him for nothing, but bid him be gone,
For my little Fiddle should not be plaid on.
　My thing is my own, and I'll keep it so still,
　Yet other young Lasses may do what they will.

An Usurer came with abundance of Cash,
But I had no mind to come under his Lash,
He profer'd me Jewels, and great store of Gold,
But I would not Mortgage my little Free-hold.
　My thing is my own, and I'll keep it so still,
　Yet other young Lasses may do what they will.

A blunt Lieutenant surpriz'd my Placket,
And fiercely began to rifle and sack it,
I mustered my Spirits up and became bold,
And forc'd my Lieutenant to quit his strong hold.
　My thing is my own, and I'll keep it so still,
　Yet other young Lasses may do what they will.

[stitch =
dividing balk
of land

A Crafty young Bumpkin that was very rich,
And us'd with his Bargains to go thro' stitch,
Did tender a Sum, but it would not avail,
That I should admit him my Tenant in tayl.

436

My Thing is my own, and I'll keep it so still,
Yet other young Lasses may do what they will.

A fine dapper Taylor, with a Yard in his Hand,
Did profer his Service to be at Command,
He talk'd of a slit I had above Knee,
But I'll have no Taylors to stitch it for me.
  My Thing is my own, and I'll keep it so still,
  Yet other young Lasses may do what they will.

A Gentleman that did talk much of his Grounds,
His Horses, his Setting-Dogs, and his Grey-hounds,
Put in for a Course, and us'd all his Art,
But he mist of the Sport, for Puss would not start,
  My Thing is my own, and I'll keep it so still,
  Yet other young Lasses may do what they will.

A pretty young Squire new come to the Town,
To empty his Pockets, and so to go down,
Did profer a kindness, but I would have none,
The same that he us'd to his Mother's Maid Joan.
  My Thing is my own, and I'll keep it so still,
  Yet other young Lasses may do what they will.

Now here I could reckon a hundred and more,
Besides all the Gamesters recited before,
That made their addresses in hopes of a snap
But as young as I was I understood Trap.
  My thing is my own, and I'll keep it so still,
  Until I be Marryed, say Men what they will.

162

The Jolly Trades-Men

Sometimes I am a Tapster new,
And skilful in my Trade Sir,
I fill my Pots most duly,
Without deceit or froth Sir:
A Spicket of two Handfuls long,
I use to Occupy Sir:
And when I set a Butt abroach,
Then shall I no beer run by Sir.

Sometimes I am a Butcher,
And then I feel fat Ware Sir;
And if the Flank be fleshed well,
I take no farther care Sir;
But in I thrust my Slaughtering-Knife,
Up to the Haft with speed Sir;
For all that ever I can do,
I cannot make it bleed Sir.

Sometimes I am a Baker,
And Bake both white and brown Sir;
I have as fine a Wrigling-Pole,
As any is in all this Town Sir:
But if my Oven be over-hot,
I dare not thrust it in Sir;
For burning of my Wrigling-Pole,
My Skill's not worth a Pin Sir.

Sometimes I am a Glover,
And can do passing well Sir;
In dressing of a Doe-skin,
I know I do excel Sir:

[Spicket=spigot

*[Occupy =to
follow one's
trade, and
(cant term) to
fornicate.*

438

But if by chance a Flaw I find,
In dressing of the Leather;
I straightway whip my Needle out,
And tack 'em close together.

Sometimes I am a Cook,
And in Fleet-Street I do dwell Sir:
At the sign of the Sugar-loaf,
As it is known full well Sir:
And if a dainty Lass comes by,
And wants a dainty bit Sir;
I take four Quarters in my Arms,
And put them on my Spit Sir.

In Weavering and in Fulling,
I have such passing Skill Sir;
And underneath my Weaving-Beam,
There stands a Fulling Mill Sir:
To have good Wives displeasure,
I would be very loath Sir;
The Water runs so near my Hand,
It over-thicks my Cloath Sir.

Sometimes I am a Shoe-maker,
And work with silly Bones Sir;
To make my Leather soft and moist,
I use a pair of Stones Sir:
My Lasts for and my lasting Sticks,
Are fit for every size Sir;
I know the length of Lasses feet,
By handling of their Thighs Sir.

The Tanner's Trade I practice,
Sometimes amongst the rest Sir;
Yet I could never get a Hair,
Of any Hide I dress'd Sir;

For I have been tanning of a Hide,
This long seven Years and more Sir;
And yet it is as hairy still,
As ever it was before Sir.

Sometimes I am a Taylor,
And work with Thread that's strong Sir;
I have a fine great Needle,
About two handfuls long Sir;
The finest Sempster in this Town,
That works by line or leisure;
May use my Needle at a pinch,
And do themselves great Pleasure.

163

A Ballad of All the Trades

Oh the Miller, the dusty, musty Miller,
  The Miller, that beareth on his Back;
He never goes to Measure Meal,
  But his Maid, but his Maid, but his Maid holds
  ope the sack.

O the Baker, the bonny, bonny Baker,
  The Baker that is so full of Sin;
He never heats his Oven hot,
  But he thrusts, but he thrusts, but he thrusts
  his Maiden in.

O the Brewer, the lusty, lusty Brewer,
  The Brewer that Brews Ale and Beer;
He never heats his Liquor hot,
  But he takes, but he takes, but he takes his
  Maid by the Geer.

O the Butcher, the bloody, bloody Butcher,
   The Butcher that sells both Beef and Bone;
He never grinds his Slaught'ring Knife,
   But his Maid, but his Maid, but his Maid must
     turn his Stone.

O the Weaver, the wicked, wicked Weaver,
   That followeth a weary Trade;
He never shoots his Shuttle right,
   But he shoots, but he shoots, but he shoots
     first at his Maid.

O the barber, the neat and nimble Barber,
   Whose Trade is ne'er the worse;
He never goes to Wash and Shave,
   But he trims, but he trims, but he trims his
     Maiden first.

O the Taylor, the fine and frisking Taylor,
   The Taylor that gives no good regard;
He never goes to measure Lace,
   But his Maid, but his Maid, but his Maid holds
     out his Yard.

O the Blacksmith, the lusty, lusty Blacksmith,
   The best of all good Fellows;
He never heats his Iron hot,
   But his Maid, but his Maid, but his Maid must
     blow the Bellows.

O the Tanner, the Merry, Merry Tanner,
   The Tanner that draws good Hides into Leather;
He never strips himself to work,
   But his Maid, but his Maid, but his Maid and
     he's together.

O the Tinker, the sturdy, sturdy Tinker,
　　The Tinker that deals all in Mettle;
He never clencheth home a Nail,
　　　But his Trull, but his Trull, but his Trull
　　　　holds up the Kettle.

164

The Wanton Trick

If anyone long for a Musical Song,
　　Altho' that his Hearing be thick,
The sound that it bears will ravish his Ears,
　　Whoop, 'tis but a Wanton Trick.

A pleasant young Maid on an Instrument play'd,
　　That knew neither Note, nor Prick;
She had a good Will to live by her Skill,
　　Whoop, 'tis but a Wanton Trick.

[*Prick* =note of music

A Youth in that Art well seen in his Part,
　　They call'd him Darbyshire Dick,
Came to her a Suiter, and wou'd be her Tutor,
　　Whoop, 'tis but a Wanton Trick.

To run with his Bow he was not slow,
　　His Fingers were nimble and quick,
When he play'd on his *Bass*, he ravish'd the Lass,
　　Whoop, 'tis but a Wanton Trick.

He Woo'd her and Taught her, until he had brought her
　　To hold out a Crotchet and Prick,
And by his direction, she came to Perfection,
　　Whoop, 'tis but a Wanton Trick.

With Playing and Wooing he still would be doing,
   And call'd her his pretty sweet Chick:
His reasonable Motion brought her to Devotion,
   Whoop, 'tis but a Wanton Trick.

He pleas'd her so well, that backwards she fell,
   And swoon'd, as tho' she were sick;
So sweet was his Note, that up went her Coat,
   Whoop, 'tis but a Wanton Trick.

The string of his *Viol* she put to the Trial,
   Till she had the full length of the Stick;
He⟨r⟩ white Belly'd *Lute* she set to his *Flute*,
   Whoop, 'tis but a Wanton Trick.

Thus she with her *Lute*, and he with his *Flute*,
   Held every Crotchet and Prick;
She learned at leisure, yet paid for the Pleasure,
   Whoop, 'tis but a Wanton Trick.

His *Viol-string* burst, her Tuten she Curst,
   However she play'd with the Stick,
From *October* to *June* she was quite out of Tune,
   Whoop, 'tis but a Wanton Trick.

[*Tuten* =
tutor (?)]

With sheming her Hand to make the Pin stand,
   The Musick within her grew Thick,
Of his *Vial* and *Lute* appeared some Fruit,
   Whoop, 'tis but a Wanton Trick.

And then she repented that e'er she consented,
   To have either Note or Prick;
For Learning so well made her Belly to swell,
   Whoop, 'tis but a Wanton Trick.

443

All Maids that make trial of a *Lute* or a *Viol*,
  Take heed how you handle the Stick:
If you like not this Order, come try my *Recorder*,
  Whoop, 'tis but a Wanton Trick.

And if this Ditty forsooth doth not fit ye,
  I know not what Musick to Prick,
There's never a Strain but in time will be twain,
  Whoop, 'tis but a Wanton Trick.

165

The Maids Conjuring Book

A Young Man lately in our Town,
  He went to Bed one Night;
He had no sooner lay'd him down,
  But was troubled with a Sprite:
So vigorously the Spirit stood,
  Let him do what he can,
Sure then he said it must be lay'd,
  By Woman not by Man.

A Handsome Maid did undertake,
  And into Bed she leap'd;
And to allay the Spirits Power,
  Full close to him she crep'd:
She having such a Guardian care,
  Her Office to discharge;
She open'd wide her Conjuring Book,
  And lay'd the Leaves at large.

Her office she did well perform,
    Within a little space;
Then up she rose, and down he lay,
    And durst not show his Face;
She took her leave, and away she went,
    When she had done the Deed;
Saying, if't chance to come agin,
    Then send for me with speed.

166

'A Soldier and a Sailor'

BY WILLIAM CONGREVE

(1695)

A Soldier and a Sailor, a Tinker and a Taylor,
    Had once a doubtful Strife, Sir,
    To make a Maid a Wife, Sir,
Whose Name was Buxome Joan,
Whose Name was Buxome Joan:
For now the time was ended
    When she no more intended
    To lick her lips at Man, Sir,
And gnaw the Sheets in vain, Sir,
And lie a Nights alone,
And lie a Nights alone.

The Soldier swore like Thunder,
He lov'd her more than Plunder;
    And show'd her many a Scar, Sir,
    Which he had brought from far, Sir
With fighting for her sake:
The Taylor thought to please her,

With offering her his Measure;
    The Tinker too with Mettle,
    Said he wou'd mend her Kettle,
And stop up ev'ry Leak.

But while these three were prating,
The Sailor slily waiting;
    Thought if it came about, Sir,
    That they shou'd all fall out, Sir,
He then might play his part;
And just e'en as he meant, Sir,
To Loggerheads they went, Sir,
    And then he let fly at her,
    A Shot 'twixt Wind and Water,
Which won this fair Maids Heart.

167

The Cooper o' Dundee

Ye coopers and hoopers, attend to my ditty,
    I sing o' a cooper wha dwelt in Dundee;
This young man he was baith am'rous and witty,
    He pleas'd the fair maids wi' the blink of his e'e.

He wisna a cooper, a common tub-hooper,
    The maist o' his trade lay in pleasin' the fair;
He hoopt them, he coopt them, he bor'd them, he
    plug'd them,
    An' a' sent for Sandie when out o' repair.

For a twelvemonth or sae this youth was respected,
    And he was as busy as weel he could be,
But bis'ness increas'd so, that some were neglected,
    Which ruin'd trade in the toun o' Dundee.

A baillie's fair daughter had wanted a coopin',
   An' Sandie was sent for, as oft time was he,
He yerkt her sae hard, that she sprung an end-hoopin',
   Which banish'd poor Sandie frae bonnie Dundee.

168

She's Hoy'd Me Out o' Lauderdale

There liv'd a lady in Lauderdale,
   She lo'ed a fiddler fine;
She lo'ed him in her chamber,
   She held him in her mind;

She made his bed at her bed-stock,
   She said he was her brither;
But she's hoy'd him out o' Lauderdale,
   His fiddle and a' thegither.

First when I cam to Lauderdale,
   I had a fiddle gude,
My sounding-pin stood the aik   [*aik = oak*
   That grows in Lauder-wood;
But now my sounding-pin's gaen down,
   And tint the foot for-ever;   [*tint = ruined,*
She's hoy'd me out o' Lauderdale,   *lost*
   My fiddle and a' thegither.

First when I came to Lauderdale,
   Your Ladyship can declare,
I play'd a bow, a noble bow,
   As e'er was strung wi' hair:
But, dow'na do's come o'er me now,
   And your Ladyship winna consider;
She's hoy'd me out o' Lauderdale,
   My fiddle and a' thegither.

The Ploughman

The ploughman he's a bonnie lad,
　His mind is ever true, jo;
His garters knit below the knee,
　His bonnet it is blue, jo.
　　Sing up, wi't a', the ploughman lad,
　　And hey the merry ploughman;
　　O' a' the trades that I do ken,
　　Commend me to the ploughman.

As walkin' forth upon a day,
　I met a jolly ploughman;
I tauld him I had lands to plough,
　If he wad but prove true, man.
　　Sing up wi't a', &c

He says, My dear, tak ye nae fear
　I'll fit ye til a hair, jo;
I'll cleave it up, and hit it down,
　And water-furrow't fair, jo.
　　Sing up wi't a', &c

I hae three ousen in my plough,
　Three better ne'er plough'd ground, jo,
The foremost ox is lang and sma',
　The twa are plump and round, jo.
　　Sing up wi't a', &c

Then he wi' speed did yoke his plough,
　Which by a gaud was driven, jo!
But when he wan between the stilts,
　I thought I was in heaven, jo!
　　Sing up wi't a' &c

But the foremost ox fell in the fur,
   The tither twa did founder;
The ploughman lad he breathless grew,
   In faith it was nae wonder.
     Sing up wi't a', &c

But a fykie risk, below a hill,
   The plough she took a stane, jo,
Which gart the fire flee frae the sock,
   The ploughman gied a grane, jo.
     Sing up wi't a', &c

I hae plough'd east, I hae plough'd west,
   In weather foul and fair, jo;
But the sairest ploughing e'er I plough'd,
   Was ploughing amang hair, jo.
     Sing up wi't a', the ploughman lad,
      And hey the merry ploughman;
     O' a' the trades that I do ken,
      Commend me to the ploughman.

170

As I Came O'er Cairney Mount

As I came o'er the Cairney Mount
   And down the blooming heather
The Highland laddie drew his dirk
   And sheath'd it in my wanton leather.

O my bonnie, bonnie Highland lad,
   My handsome, charming Highland laddie;
When I am sick and like to die,
   He'll row me in his Highland plaidie.

With me he play'd his warlike pranks,
    And on me boldly did adventure,
He did attack me on both flanks,
    And pushed me fiercely in the centre.

O, My bonnie &c

A furious battle then began,
    Wi' equal courage and desire,
Altho' he stuck me three to one,
    I stood my ground and receiv'd his fire.

O, my bonnie &c

But our ammunition being spent,
    And we quite out o'breath an' sweating,
We did agree with ae consent,
    To fight it out at the next meeting.

O, my bonnie &c

171

The Mower

It was one summer's morning on the fourteenth day of
    May,
I met a fair maid, she ask'd my trade, I made her this
    reply,
For by my occupation I ramble up and down,
With my taring scythe in order to mow the meadows
    down.

She said, my handsome young man, if a mower that
    you be,
I'll find you some new employment if you will go with
    me,
For I have a little meadow long kept for you in store,
It was on the dew, I tell you true, it ne'er was cut before.

He said, my pretty fair maid, if it is as you say,
I'll do my best endeavours in cutting of your hay,
For in your lovely countenance I never saw a frown,
So my lovely lass, I'll cut your grass, that's ne'er been
    trampled down.

With courage bold undaunted she took him to the
    ground,
With his taring scythe in hand to mow the meadow
    down;
He mowed from nine till breakfast time, so far beyond
    his skill,
He was forced to yield and quit the field, for the grass
    was growing still.

She says, my handsome young man, you did promise me
    and say
You'd do your best endeavours in cutting of the hay,
For in my little meadow, you'll ne'er find hills nor rocks,
So I pray young man don't leave me, till you see my hay
    in cocks.

He said, my pretty fair maid, I can no longer stay,
But I'll go to Newry, in cutting of the hay,
But if I find the grass is cut in the country where I go,
It's then perhaps I may return, your meadow for to mow.

Now her hay being in order, and harvest being all o'er,
This young man's gone and left her sad case for to deplore,

451

But where he's gone I do not know, so far beyond my
    skill,
I was forced to yield and quit the field, for grass is
    growing still.

172

The Little Farm

OR

The Weary Ploughman

You husbandmen and ploughmen, of every degree,
I pray you give attention and listen unto me,
I hope it will offend not ⟨not⟩ meaning any harm
But concerning of a bonny lass who kept a little farm.

CHORUS
    I was both weak and weary by daylight in the morn,
    I thought it young and growing but to stubble it
        was worn.

I stept up to this blooming lass thinking to get employ,
She said young man be civil and do not me annoy,
My farm though in the lowlands was never overflown,
I've made a resolution to keep ⟨it⟩ as my own.

I said my charming fairmaid I am a husbandman,
And have had great experience in cultivating land,
There's nothing comes amiss to me in the farming line I
    vow,
You'll find me likewise useful in working at your plough.

She said no longer time delay your mind shall be at ease,
My farm-house lies in the valley between two poplar trees,

Surrounded too with rushes I've long kept in store,
There is a tree you'll see growing each side of the door.

I said with your permission I there will enter in,
Command me at your leisure my labour to begin,
You'll find me use⟨d⟩ to ploughing likewise my seed to
    sow
If we agree you soon will see it for to thrive and grow.

With courage in good order she said come try your skill,
The plow is near the furrough at the bottom of the hill,
Above the hill two milking-⟨pails⟩ resemble cocks   [Broadsheet:
    of hay   '*maids*'
If you feel weak no further seek a pillow for to seek   [*seek* = '*stay*',
                                                      '*lay*' (?)]

At length with toil being weary, I laid my head between
Those milking-pails that were so white although the
    grass was green.
The land being in bad order it made me sweat and groan,
I was forc'd to yield and quit the field for it was overflown.

She said when you have rested your strength for to regain,
If its your intention commence ploughing again,
No said I excuse me and do not on me frown
Although I'm young and in my prime my courage is
    pull'd down.

173

The Jolly Driver

  I am a jolly young fellow,
    My fortune I wish to advance,
  I first took up to London,
    And I next took a tour to France,

I understand all kinds of servitude,
   And every fashion so tight,
If you hire me as your coachman,
   I am a safe driver by night.

CHORUS

So my darling I'll go along with you,
   Stick to you while I have life,
I would rather ten times be your coachman,
   Than tie⟨d⟩ to a drunken old wife.

Up came a lady of fashion,
   And thus unto me did say,
If I hire you as my coachman,
   You must drive me by night and by day,
Ten guineas a month I will give you
   Besides a bottle of wine,
If you keep me in plenty of drink,
   I will drive you in a new fashion style.

She brought me into the kitchen,
   Where she gave me liquors so quick,
She told me drink that in a hurry,
   She wish'd to see my driving whip;
O when that she seen it
   She eyed it with a smile,
Saying, I know by the length of your lash,
   You can drive in a new fashion style.

She bid me get into her chaise box,
   And drive both mild and discreet,
And handle my whip with much judgment,
   And drive her quite through the street,
Three curls I gave to my cracker,
   And then I was up to her rigg,
And the very first turn the wheel got,
   I broke the main-spring of her gig.

[rigg = ridge(?)

454

She brought me into the cellar,
    And gave me a bottle of wine,
She told me drink that in a hurry,
    As I had to drive her three miles;
She being a nice little young thing,
    And just in the height of her bloom,
And I being a dashing young fellow,
    I drove her nine times round the room.

My mistress being tired and weary,
    In order to take a rest,
She call'd for her waiting-maid, Sally,
    The maid that she loved the best,
Saying, Sally, we've got a good coachman,
    That understands driving in style,
And while my gig wheel is repairing,
    I'll let him drive you for a mile.

So now to conclude and finish,
    Driving I mean to give o'er,
Carriages, cars, gigs, and coaches,
    I ne'er will drive any more;
When the Ladies of honour all heard it.
    The truth they did declare,
They ne'er could meet with a coachman,
    That understood driving so fair.

174

Six Jolly Wee Miners

Six jolly wee miners, an' miner lads are we.
We've travelled broad Scotland for many a long day.
We've travelled east, we've travelled west, the country
    round an' round,
For to find out the treasures that do lie below the ground.

You should see my miner lad as he walks down the street,
All dressed in his best, lookin gentle and sae neat.
His teeth are white as ivory, his eyes are black as sloes.
You can easy tell a miner lad everywhere he goes.

Some hae got money, an' some hae none at a',
And them that hae money, the bottle they will draw.
We'll fill our glasses to the tip, the toast goes round and
  round,
My health to every wee collier lad that works below
  the ground.

[grovet =
cravat (?)
[doggie = stylish

I'll knit my love a grovet, as doggie as it can be,
The colours that I'll put in it will fairly tak his e'e.
His chums will a' come up to him, and say: Where'd
  ye get that?
Oh, I got it frae ma wee doggie moll, an' whit dae ye
  think o' that?

I'll build my love a castle, a castle of renown,
Neither kings, dukes nor earls will pull my castle down.
The king loves the queen an' the emperor does the same,
I love my wee miner lad an' wha can me blame?

175

Mutton and Leather

A Coblerone I'm told,
    A wicked and rakish young fellow,
He was such a chap for the girls;
    And now and then used to get mellow.
His wife was as fat as a but,
    He could hardly put both ends together,
But he hammered away for his life,
    With his bristles, and lapstone and leather.

456

VOCATIONAL

A butcher's shop in the same street,
  Was kept by a widow of forty,
She was handsome, and sold such fine meat,
  And never done anything naughty
The Cobbler, and her I'm told,
  They were very friendly together,
For a chop or a steak off her rump,
  He'd make up the difference in leather.

And all the young fellows declared,
  They never did taste such a treat,
Her buttock was tender as lamb,
  Her rump was the sweetest of meat,
The Ladies they envied her much,
  At her custom they felt quite concerned,
Said her meat must be tainted and queer,
  And some of it terribly turned.

The cobler's wife jealous grew,
  And said that she knew it for certain,
That the widow disposed of her meat,
  Often behind the bed curtain,
She swore she would catch him the rogue,
  And if she should catch them together,
Of her mutton she would make a hash,
  And damage the cobbler's leather.

She watched him, and saw the old widow,
  The hair on her head hissed and frizzles,
With the cobbler's stone in her lap,
  Along with his awl and his bristles,
And he with her buttock and rump,
  Was tearing away like a glutton,
And scattered about to be seen.
  Were the widow's fat plump legs of mutton.

She caught hold of a large bullock's tail,
   With fury her passion did deepen,
It was awful nobby and thick,
   By law, 'twas an unlawful weapon,
She swung it about in her fright,
   And smash went the rump of the widow,
She battered her chops too in style,
   And gave her no time to consider.

The widow she called out police,
   Of peelers there soon was a muster,
The cobbler began to show fight,
   And show'd them a bit he could bluster,
Keep your hands off of my wife,
   She's vexed so dont agrevate her,
But bob pulled his long thing from behind,
   And gave him a smash on his tater.

When before the old beak they were brought,
   Mrs. Cobbler says he you're a vixen,
For using that stunning long tail,
   I shall give two months snug at brixton,
And you Mr. Cobbler too,
   Lone women they shall not be put on,
You've damaged the widow's best rump,
   And played some queer tricks with her mutton.

You rakes take warning and try,
   At home to put both ends together,
For it is owned by the wisest of men
   On earth there is nothing like leather.
Don't go smelling about after meat,
   When strange it's not worth a button,
Remember the widow's fat rump,
   And see how I'm served thro' her mutton.

The Cunning Cobbler Done Over

A story, a story to you I will tell,
Concerning of a butcher in London did dwell,
The butcher was possessed of a beautiful wife,
And a cobbler he loved her as dear as his life.
        To my fal riddle I do riddle lal di ra.

Now the butcher went to market to purchase an ox,
And then the little cobbler as sly as any fox,
He put on his Sunday clothing a courting he did go,
It was to the jolly butcher's wife, because he loved her so.

The cobbler then stept into the butcher's shop,
The butcher's wife knew what he meant and bid him for
    to stop,
For the cobbler said my dearling have you got a job for
    me
The butcher's wife so cunning said, I'll go up and see.

She went up to the bed-room and gave the snob a call,   [snob =
Saying I have found an easy job if you have brought   journeyman
    your awl,   cobbler
And if you do it workman-like some cash to you I'll pay
I thank you said the cobbler and began to stitch away.

But as the cobbler was at work a tap came at the door,
The cobbler crawled beneath the bed and laid upon the
    floor,
Lay still says the butcher's wife what will my husband
    say
Then she let the policeman in along with her to play.

The cobbler he lay shivering and frightened to move,
The butcher's wife she said my dear, my darling and
　my love,
But the cobbler thought within himself O how he'd treat
　his wife,
I really think the bed will fall I do upon my life.

Now the butcher came from market and it put them in
　a fright,
The policeman scrambled down the stairs and soon was
　out of sight,
The butcher's wife so nimbly did lock the bedroom door
And in her fright she quite forgot the cobbler on the
　floor.

The butcher then found out when he lay down in bed,
O something here is very hard the butcher smiled and
　said,
His wife said, it is my rolling pin, the butcher could
　but laugh,
Saying how came you to roll your dough with a
　policeman's staff?

The butcher threw the trunnel underneath the bed,
And there he broke the c . . . . . r-pot and cracked the
　cobbler's head;
The cobbler bawled out 'murder', said the butcher,
　who are you?
Why, I am the little cobbler that mends your ladies shoes.

O if you are the cobbler, said the butcher come with me
I'll pay you well for mending shoes before I'm done
　with thee,
He locked him in the bullock's pen, the bull began to
　roar,
And the butcher laughed to see the bull roll him o'er and
　o'er!

Then early next morning when the people was about,
The butcher rubbed his face with blood and turned the
   cobbler out,
He pinn'd a paper on his back and on it was the news
The cobbler in the bed-room goes to mend the ladies
   shoes.

The people seemed all frightened as home the cobbler ran
His coat and breeches were so torn, he nearly showed
   his bum;
His wife was frightened as in he ran, and knocked her
   on the floor,
He said you brute, I'll never go out mending any more.

177

The Beverley Maid and the Tinker

In Beverley town a maid did dwell,
A buxton lass I knew her well,   *[buxton =*
Her age it was near twenty-two,   *buxom(?)*
And for a man she had in view.

This maid being generous, kind, and free,
And willing to travel the country,
She went to live with a gentleman,
A tinker came to soldier her pan.   *[soldier =*
                              solder(?)

The gentleman being from home one day,
The tinker with her did kiss and play,
He slyly got her behind the door,
And gave her kisses o'er and o'er.

461

When all was o'er and at an end
She slipt him 20 guineas in hand,
Saying when will you come this way again,
For I've another kettle to mend.

In travelling hard and being dry,
He call'd to an ale house close hard by,
Saying landlord bring me a pot of ale,
For twenty guineas I've earn'd to day.

The landlord says well done my cock,
Your rivets you have boldly knock'd,
My liquor is good, your money is fine,
And you shall stay with me to dine.

If all is true as I've been told,
The tinker spent all his gold,
The tinker may do as he's done before,
Kiss the girl behind the door.

FOUR

CLERICAL

178

As I Lay Musing

As I lay musing all alone
fa : la
A pretty Jest I thought uppon
fa la
Lisening a while and I will you tell
off a fryer yt lovd a bonny lass well   [*yt =that*
fa la fa la

The fryer came to ye maidens bed
and said he must have her maiden head
but shee deny'd at his desire
and tould him that shee did fear hell fire.

Tush quoth the fryer thou need not doubt
if thou wert in hell I could sing thee out
Nay then quoth ye maid you shall have yr request,
the fryer was as glad as a fox in his nest.

But one thing of you I must require
before you have yt as you desire
before yt you doe the thing
An Angell of money you must bring.

Tush quoth ye fryer wee twoe shall agree
Noe money shall part my love and me
before yt I will see the lacke   [*the =thee*
Ile pawne my gray gown of my backe

[whyle = wile

This maid she bethoughte her off a whyle
how she might the fryer beguile,
when he was gon the truth to tell
she hangs a cloth before the well.

The fryer he came as his convenant was
with money unto the bonny lass
good morrow faire maid, good morrow quoth she
here is they money I promised thee

Shee thankt him well and tooke the money
Now let us goe to it quoth he sweet honey
Nay stay quoth shee some respite make
my ffather is coming & he will us take.

[Ah las =
    alas (?)

[yn = then

Ah las quoth the fryer where shall I run
to hide me until that he be gone
Behind yon cloth yn run quoth shee
& there my ffather he cannot you see

Behind the Cloth the fryer he crept
& into the well he suddainly lept
Alas quoth fryer I am in the well
its noe matter quoth shee if thou wert in hell

Thou saydest thou couldest sing me out of hell
I prithee now sing they selfe out of the well
The fryer he sung with a pitty full sound
O help me out or I shall be drownd

Then for sweet st francis sake
& his disciples pitty take
Quoth she st fra.⟨ncis⟩ never taught
Scholars to tempt young maids to naught

The fryer he did intreat her still
Yt shee would help him out of the well
She heard him make such pitty full mone
She helpt him out & she bid him be gone

Quoth he let me have my money again
wch thoust of me before hannd taine
Now stay quoth shee there is noe such matter
Ile make you pay for fouling my water

[*thoust = thou
hadst*

The fryer went all along the street
dropping like a new washt sheepe
both old and young commended the mayd
that shee such a pretty prank had playd.

179

A Lovely Lass to a Friar Came

BY JOHN WILMOT, EARL OF ROCHESTER (?)

A lovely Lass to a Friar came
To confess in the morning early:
In what, My Dear, are you to blame?
Come, tell to me sincerely;
I have done, Sr, what I dare not name,
With a Lad that loves me dearly.

The greatest fault in myself I know
Is what I now discover;
You for that fault to Rome must go,
And Discipline must suffer:
Lack a day, Sr, if it must be so,
Pray with me send my Lover.

Oh! no, no, no, My Dear, you do dream,
We'll have no double dealing.
But if you'll with me repeat the same
I'll pardon your past failing:
I must own, Sr, but I blush indeed with Shame,
Your Pennance is prevailing.

180

Off a Puritane

It was a puritanicall ladd
    that was called Mathyas,
& he wold goe to Amsterdam
    to speake with Ananyas.
he had not gone past halfe a mile,
    but he mett his holy sister;
he layd his bible under her breeche,
    & merylye hee kist her.

'Alas! what wold they wicked say?'
    quoth shee, 'if they had seen itt!
my Buttocckes thé lye to lowe: I wisht
    appocrypha were in itt!'
'but peace, Sweet hart, or ere wee part, –
    I speake itt out of pure devotion, –
by yee & nay Ile not away
    till thou feele my spiritts motion'.

Thé huft & puft with many heaves,
    till that thé both were tyred,
'alas!' quoth shee, 'youle spoyle the leaves;
    my peticoates all Myred!
if wee professors shold bee knowne
    to the English congregation
eyther att Leyden or Amsterdam,
    itt wold disgrace our nation;

'But since itt is, that part wee must,
    tho I am much unwilling,
good brother, lets have the tother thrust,
    & take thee this fine shilling
to beare thy charges as thou goes,
    & passage ore the ocean'.
then downe shee Layd, & since tis sayd,
    shee quencht his spirits motion.

181

The Quaker's Song

Amongst the pure ones all,
    Which Conscience doth profess;
And yet that sort of Conscience,
    Doth practice nothing less:
I mean the Sect of those Elect,
    That loath to live by Merit;
That leads their lives with other Mens Wives,
    According unto the Spirit.

One met with a Holy Sister of ours,
    A Saint who dearly lov'd him:
And fain he would have kiss'd her,
    Because the Spirit mov'd him:
    But she deny'd and he reply'd,
    You're damn'd unless you do it;
Therefore consent, do not repent,
    For the Spirit doth move me to it.

She not willing to offend, poor Soul,
    Yielded unto his Motion;
And what these two did intend,
    Was out of pure Devotion:

To lye with a Friend and a Brother,
 She thought she shou'd die no Sinner,
But e'er five Months were past,
 The Spirit was quick within her.

But what will the Wicked say,
 When they shall hear of this Rumour,
They'd laugh at us every Day,
 And Scoff us in every Corner:
Let 'em do so still if that they will,
 We mean not to follow their Fashion,
They're none of our Sect, nor of our Elect,
 Nor none of our Congregation.

But when the time was come,
 That she was to be laid;
It was no very great Crime,
 Committed by her they said:
'Cause they did know, and she did show,
 'Twas done by a Friend and a Brother,
But a very great Sin they said it had been,
 If it had been done by another.

182

The Four-Legg'd Elder

OR

A Horrible Relation of a Dog
and an Elder's Maid

BY SIR JOHN BIRKENHEAD

All Christians and Lay-Elders too,
 For Shame amend your Lives;

I'll tell you a Dog-trick now,
   Which much concerns your Wives:
An Elder's Maid near Temple-Bar,
   (Ah, what a Quean was she?)
Did take an ugly Mastiff Cur,
   Where Christians use to be.
     Help House of Commons, House of Peers,
       Oh now or never help!
     Th' Assembly having sat Four Years
       Has now brought forth a Whelp.

One Evening late she stept aside,
   Pretending to fetch Eggs;
And there she made her self a Bride,
   To one that had four Legs:
Her master heard a Rumblement,
   And wonder<'d> she did tarry;
Not dreaming (without his consent)
   His Dog would ever Marry.
     Help House of Commons, House of Peers &c.

Her Master peep'd, but was afraid,
   And hastily did run,
To fetch a Staff to help his Maid,
   Not knowing what was done:
He took his Ruling Elders Cane,
   And cry'd out help, help, here:
For Swash our Mastiff, and poor Jane,
   Are now fight Dog, fight Bear.
     Help House of Commons &c

But when he came he was full sorry,
   For he perceiv'd their Strife;
That according to the Directory,
   They Two were Dog and Wife:

Ah! (then said he) thou cruel Quean,
   Why hast thou me beguil'd?
I wonder Swash was grown so lean,
   Poor Dog! he's almost spoil'd.
     Help House of Commons &c

I thought thou hadst no Carnal Sense,
   But what's in our Lasses:
And could have quench'd thy 'Cupiscence,
   According to the Classes:
But all the Parish sees it plain,
   Since thou art in this pickle;
Thou art an Independent Quean,
   And lov'st a Conventicle.
     Help House of Commons &c

Alas! now each Malignant Rogue,
   Will all the World perswade;
That she that's Spouse unto a Dog,
   May be an Elder's Maid:
They'll jeer us if abroad we stir,
   Good Master Elder stay;
Sir, of what Classis is your Cur?
   And then what can we say?
     Help House of Commons &c

[*Classis* = a
presbytery;
pl. '*classes*':
v. *above*

They'll many graceless Ballads sing,
   of a Presbyterian;
That a Lay Elder is a thing
   Made up half Dog, half Man:
Out, out, said he, (and smote her down)
   Was Mankind grown so scant?
There's scarce another Dog i' th'Town,
   Had took the Covenant.
     Help House of Commons &c

Then Swash began to look full grim,
   And Jane did thus reply;
Sir, you thought nought too good for him,
   You fed your Dog too high:
'Tis true he took me in the lurch,
   And leap'd into my Arm;
But (as I hope to go to Church)
   I did your Dog no harm.
     Help House of Commons &c

Then she was brought to Newgate Jail,
   And there was naked stripp'd;
They whipp'd her till the Cords did fail,
   As Dogs us'd to be whipp'd:
Poor City Maids shed many a Tear,
   When she was lash'd and bang'd;
And had she been a Cavalier,
   Surely she had been hang'd.
     Help House of Commons &c

Hers was but Fornication found,
   For which she felt the lash:
But his was Bugg'ry presum'd,
   Therefore they hanged Swash:
What will become of Bishops then,
   Or Independency?
For now we find both Dogs and Men
   Stand for Presbytry.
     Help House of Commons &c

She might have took a Sow-gelder,
   With Synod-men good store,
But she would have a Lay-Elder,
   with Two Legs and Two more:
Go tell th'Assembly of Divines,
   Tell Adoniram blue;

Tell Burgess, Marshall, Case and Vines,
   Tell Now-and-Anon too.
      Help House of Commons &c

Some say she was a Scottish Girl,
   Or else (at least) a Witch;
But she was born in Colchester,
   Was ever such a Bitch:
Take heed all Christian Virgins now,
   The Dog-Star now prevails;
Ladies beware your Monkeys too,
   For Monkeys have long Tails.
      Help House of Commons &c

Bless King and Queen, and send us Peace,
   As we had Seven Years since:
For we remember Dog-days,
   While we enjoy'd our Prince:
Bless sweet Prince Charles, Two Dukes, Three Girls,
   Lord save his Majesty;
Grant that his Commons, Bishops, Earls,
   May lead such lives as he.
      Help House of Commons, House of Peers,
         Oh now or never help!
      Th'Assembly having sat Four Years,
         Has now brought forth a Whelp.

183

The Four-Legg'd Quaker

All that have two or but one ear,
   (I dare not tell ye half)
You of an *Essex* Colt shall hear
   Will shame the very *Calf.*

In *Horsley* Fields near *Colchester*
  A Quaker would turn Trooper;
He caught a Foal and mounted her
  (O base!) below the Crupper.
    Help, Lords and Commons, once more help,
      O send us Knives and Daggers!
    For if the Quakers be not Gelt
      Your Troopes will have the Staggers.

Ralph Green (it was this Varlet's name)
  Of *Colchester* you'll swear,
From thence the *Four-legg'd Elder* came,
  was ever such a Pair!
But though 'twas foul 'tween *Swash* and *Jane*,
  yet this is ten times worse,
For then a Dog did play the Man,
  but Man now play'd the Horse.
    Help, Lords and Commons &c

The owner of the Colt was nigh,
  (observing their Embrace)
And drawing nearer did espye
  The Quaker's sorrell Face:
My Foal is ravish'd (then he cryes,
  and fiercely at him ran),
Thou Rogue, I'll have thee halter'd twice,
  as Horse and eke as Man!
    Help, Lords and Commons &c

O Friend (said *Green*, with sighs and groans)
  let this thy wrath appease!
(And gave him eight new half-Crowns
  to make him hold his peace)
The Man reply'd, though I for this
  conceal thy Hugger Mugger,

Do'st think it lawfull for a Piece
    a silly Foal to Bugger?
       Help, Lords and Commons &c

The Master saw his Colt defil'd
    which vex'd his soul with doubt;
For if his Filly prov'd with Child
    he knew all would come out:
Then he afresh began to rave,
    (for all his Money taking)
Neighbours, said he, I took this Knave,
    i'th very act of *Quaking*.
       Help, Lords and Commons &c

Then to the Pinfold (Gaol I mean)
    they dragg'd him by the Mane,
They call'd him Beast, they call'd her Quean,
    as if she had been *Jane*
O stone him (all the women cry'd),
    nay Geld him (which is worse),
Who scorn'd us all and took a Bride
    that's Daughter to a Horse!
       Help, Lords and Commons &c

The Colt was silent all this while,
    and therefore 'twas no Rape,
The virgin Foal he did beguile,
    and so intends to scape:
For though he got her in a Ditch
    where she could not revolt,
Yet he had no *Scott'sh Spurr* nor Switch
    to ride the willing Colt.
       Help, Lords and Commons &c

O *Essex, Essex, England*'s pride,
  go burn this long-tail'd Quean,
For though the *Thames* runs by thy side,
  it cannot wash the clean!   *[the = thee*
'Tis not thy Bleating Sonn's complaints,
  hold forth such wanton courses,
Thy Oysters hint the very Saints
  to horn the very Horses.
    Help, Lords and Commons &c

Though they salute not in the Street
  (because they are our Masters)
'Tis now reveal'd why Quakers meet
  in Meadows, woods, and Pastures.
But Hors-men Mare-men, all and some
  who Man and Beast perplex,
Not only from East-Horsley come,
  but from *West-Middle-Sex*.
    Help, Lords and Commons &c

This was not GREEN the *Feltmaker*,
  nor willow GREEN the *Baker*,
Nor GEORGE the Sea-GREEN *Mariner*,
  but RALPH the Grass-GREEN *Quaker*.
Had GREEN the Sow-gelder but known,
  and done his office duly,
Though RALPH was GREEN when he came on,
  he had come off most blewly.
    Help, Lords and Commons &c

Alass you by Man's flesh came
  The *Foul* disease to *Naples*,
And now we fear the very same
  is brake into our Stables;
For death has stolen so many Steeds
  from Prince and Peer and Carrier,

That this new Murrain rather needs
   a FARRAR[1] than a Farrier.
      Help, Lords and Commons &c

Nay if this GREEN within the Walls
   of Colchester left forces,
Those Cavaliers were Caniballs,
   eating his humane Horses!
But some make man their *second course,*
   (in cool blood will not spare)
Who butcher Men and favour Horse
   will couple with a Mare.
      Help, Lords and Commons, &c

This Centaur, unquoth *Other* thing,
   will make a dreadful Breach:
Yet though an Ass[2] may Speak or Sing
   o let not Horses Preach!
But Bridle such wild Colts who can
   when they'll obey no Summons,
For things begot 'tween Mare and Man
   are neither Lords nor Commons.
      Help, Lords and Commons &c

O *Elders, Independents* too
   though all your Powers combin'd,
Quakers will grow too strong for you
   now Horse and Man are joyn'd:
While Cavaliers, poor foolish Rogues,
   know only Maids Affairs,
She-Presbyters can deal with Dogs,
   and Quaking Men with Mares.
      Help, Lords and Commons &c

   1. Physician to the Earl of Pembroke who is no Quaker nor
Quacker. [Note in original broadside.]
   2. A new sect of young men and women who pray, eat and sing
ex tempore. [Note in original broadside.]

Now as when *Milan* Town was rear'd,
   a Monstrous Sow untam'd,
With black half Hair half Wool appear'd,
   'twas *Mediolanum* nam'd:
Colchester must have recourse
   to some such four legg'd Sister,
For sure as *Horsley* comes from Horse
   from Colt 'twas call'd Colchester.
    Help, Lords and Commons, once more help,
      O send us Knives and Daggers!
     For if the Quakers be not Gelt
      Your Troopes will have the Staggers.

184

The Lusty Fryer of Flanders

How in a Nunnery at the City of Gaunt this Fryer got Thirty
Nuns with Child in three Weeks time, and afterwards made
his escape.

Not long ago from hence I went,
   to travel into Flanders
To learn the Art of War, was sent
   under those great Commanders;
At Gaunt I saw a pleasant fun,
   As you shall hear hereafter,
Betwixt a fryar and a Nun,
   may well deserve your laughter.

The Fryar like a Jolly Dad,
   a propagating Father,
Hid not the Talent which he had,
   but chose to use it rather:
The Nun was pretty, young, and fair,
   as if design'd for pleasure,
And pity 'twas that she should swear
   to keep her Virgin Treasure.

Unto this lusty Fryar she went,
   and there her sins confessed,
Which they unto her heart's content,
   forgave and her released;
But this he said, before you rise,
   for all your sad offences,
By good St. Francis, i'le Chastise
   with Rods your Preter Tenses.

Her hinder Quarters up she turns
   and there she lay most fairly,
The Fryar now in Lust he burns,
   and flaug'd her off most rarely:
Her prayers and tears at last prevail
   upon the cruel fryar,
That he'd no more correct her tail,
   nor would he now deny her.

*[flaug'd =
flogged*

Thou pretty Nymph arise he said,
   and let me now imbrace thee,
Bestow on me your Maiden-head,
   fear not that i'le disgrace thee;
What tho' my Robe be black my dear,
   my skins as white as may be,
And I have that has pleas'd i'le swear
   oh many a gallant Lady.

The Charming Nun then blushing said,
   oh tempt me not to evil,
Have I not sworn to live a Maid,
   and to renounce the Devil,
But should I now commit this Crime,
   and break my vow by sporting,
My belly will grow big in time,
   and then you'll leave your Courting.

478

The Sin, my Dear, is Venial
   and to indulge is easie,
Sin on and i'le forgive you all,
   my Love, if you'll but please me
But since you fear to breed young bones,
   i'le tell you to their Glory,
The Lady Abess and her Nuns
   have done the like before you.

[*Presumably
once '*ye*'—v.
*also the rhyme
to* '*Ven-i-al*'
above

This Nun she grew big at last,
   and dayly it increases,
And e'er ten months were fully past,
   the Nuns fell all a pieces;
The crafty fryer away he went
   that he should 'scape 'twas pity,
and he left behind a Regiment
   of bastards to the City.

Thus he this Creature did beguile,
   but tell me wasn't he dirty.
Twenty nine Nuns he'd got with Child,
   and this made up the thirty;
He had a faculty to Cure
   each longing expectation.
So this religious rascal sure
   is able to Stock a nation.

185

The Penurious Quaker

OR

The High Priz'd Harlot

Quaker. My Friend thy Beauty seemeth good
    We Righteous have our failings;
  I'm Flesh and Blood, methinks I cou'd,
    Wert thou but free from Ailings.

Harlot. Believe me Sir I'm newly broach'd,
    And never have been in yet;
  I vow and swear I ne'er was touch'd,
    By Man 'till this day sennight.

Quaker. Then prithee Friend, now prithee do,
    Nay, let us not defer it;
  And I'll be kind to thee when thou
    Hast laid the Evil Spirit.

Harlot. I vow I won't, indeed I shan't,
    Unless I've Money first, Sir;
  For if I ever trust a Saint,
    I wish I may be curst, Sir.

Quaker. I cannot like the Wicked say,
    I Love thee and Adore thee,
  And therefore thou wilt make me pay,
    So here is Six pence for thee.

Harlot. Confound you for a stingy *Whig,*
    Do ye think I live by Stealing;
  Farewel you Puritannick Prig,
    I scorn to take your Shilling.

[*Prig* =
precisian

186

The Presbyterian Wedding

A certain Presbyterian Pair
   Were wedded t'other day;
And when in Bed the Lambs were laid,
   Their Pastor came to pray.

But first he bade each Guest depart,
   Nor sacred Rites prophane;
For carnal Eyes such Mysteries
   can never entertain.

Then with a puritannick Air,
   Unto the Lord he pray'd,
That he would please to grant Encrease
   To that same man and maid:

And that the Husbandman might dress
   Full well the Vine his Wife;
And like a Vine she still might twine
   About him all her Life.

Sack posset then he gave them both,
   And said with lifted Eyes,
Blest of the Lord! with one Accord
   Begin your Enterprize.

The Bridgroom then drew near his Spouse,
   T'apply Prolifick Balm;
And while they strove in mutual Love,
   The Parson sung a Psalm.

187

The Crafty Miss of London

OR

The Fryar well Fitted

A Fryar was walking in *Exeter-street*
Drest up in his Garb like a Gentleman neat,
He there with a wanton young Lady did meet,
And freely did offer and earnestly proffer, to give her
   a bottle of Wine.

Love, let us not stand to Discourse in the Cold
My amorous Jewel I prithee behold
Then straight he pull'd out a whole handful of Gold,
And said, my dear Honey, here's plenty of Money I'll
   give thee a Guinny or two.

The glittering Guinnies soon dazel'd her eyes
That privately straight she began to devise
By what means she might get this rich Golden prize,
Two is but a trifle, his pockets I'll rifle
[MS.: '*now*']   I ⟨hope⟩ to have all now or none

She seemingly Bashful, disputing did stand,
And said, I dare not to the Tavern with Man;
But this was to bring him more eagerly on,
So that the Old Fryar, did burn with desire, and she
   to his humour did yield

Away to the Tavern they went in all haste,
A glass of Canary resolving to taste,
And there the Old Fryar he freely Embrac'd
This Lady of pleasure, she aim'd at his Treasure,
   which constantly run in her mind.

The Drawer supply'd them with Liquor good store,
And when all was out, still they call'd for more,
Her amorous Charms he did dearly adore,
And as they sat drinking, she paid it with thinking
   how she might his Guinnies obtain.

The Fryar to Court her he thus did begin,
Sweet Madam step out of these Robes you are in,
That I may behold thy white delicate Skin,
The which will inflame me, sweet creature don't blame me,
   I'll give you three Guinnies the more.

This Lady of Pleasure she thus did reply,
That Civil Request, Sir, I will not deny,
If that you'll strip naked now as well as I,
To which he consented, both being contented,
   they scamper'd a while round the Room.

While naked they danc'd at this frolicsome rate,
His Wigg did flye off, and she see his bald Pate,
I have an Old Fryar, thought she, for my Mate,
I'faith I will fit him, if that I can get him
   to change his Apparel with me.

Then straight with a Smile to the Fryar she goes,
And said, worthy Sir, here's one thing I propose,
Let us in this Frolick now change our Cloaths,
He grants her desire, they change their Attire,
   she like a Town-Bully appear'd.

The Fryar immediately sets himself down,
He puts on her Smicket, her Top-Knot and Gown,
And look'd like a Hag-ridden Bawd of the Town,
In Ribbons and Laces, but she had her Paces,
   and fitted the Fryar at last.

[*Smicket* =
smock

His Cloaths with his Watch and his Guinnies, she got,
Then made an excuse to go down to the Vault,
Yet ne'er came again, but left him all the Shot
To pay without Money, his Amorous Honey
   did leave the Old Rogue in the Lurch.

He found she had left him the Dog for to hold,
Then calling the Drawer his Grief to unfold,
He had not a penny of Silver nor Gold,
Then counting his Losses, his Beads and his Crosses
   he near was so Riffl'd before.

The Drawer he told him the Shot must be pay'd,
The Fryar stood quaking, but little he said;
They stripp'd off the Gown in which he was array'd,
His Ribbons and Laces, he made sower faces
   to see his most desperate Doom.

They found that he was of Jesuit breed,
And one that had been a great Rascal indeed;
Now therefore they sent him to *Newgate* with speed;
A woful disaster, he says Pater-Noster,
   but has neither Money nor Cloaths.

188

The Patriarch

BY ROBERT BURNS

As honest Jacob on a night,
   Wi' his beloved beauty,
Was duly laid on wedlock's bed,
   And noddin' at his duty,

'How lang,' she says, 'ye fumbling wretch,
　　Will ye be fucking at it?
My eldest wean might die of age,
　　Before that ye could get it.

'Ye pegh, and grane, and goazle there,　　[*pegh = puff*
　　And mak an unco splutter,　　　　　　[*goazle = look dazedly*
And I maun lie and thole you here　　　　[*thole = endure*
　　And fient a hair the better'　　　　　[*fient = the devil*

Then he, in wrath, put up his graith,　　[*graith = tool,
　　'The deevil's in the hizzie!　　　　　　*implement*
I maw you as I maw the lave,　　　　　　[*maw = mow*
　　And night and day I'm busy.　　　　　[*lave =
　　　　　　　　　　　　　　　　　　　　　remainder

'I've bairned the servant gypsies baith,
　　Forbye your titty Leah;
Ye barren jad, ye put me mad,
　　What mair can I do wi' you?

'There's ne'er a maw I've gi'en the lave,
　　But ye hae got a dizzen;
And damn'd a ane ye'se get again,
　　Although your cunt should gizzen'　　　[*gizzen = dry up*

Then Rachel, calm as ony lamb,
　　She claps him on the waulies,　　　　[*from 'wawlie'
Quo' she, 'Ne'er fash a woman's clash,　　*= choice*
　　In trowth ye maw me braulies.　　　　*braulies =
　　　　　　　　　　　　　　　　　　　　splendidly

'My dear, 'tis true, for mony a maw
　　I'm your ungratefu' debtor
But ance again, I dinna ken
　　We'll aiblins happen better'　　　　　[*aiblins =
　　　　　　　　　　　　　　　　　　　　perhaps

Then, honest man! wi' little wark
    He sune forgot his ire;
The patriarch he coost the sark
    And up and till't like fire!!!

[*till't* = *to it*

189

Godly Girzie

BY ROBERT BURNS

The night it was a holy night,
    The day had been a holy day;
Kilmarnock gleam'd wi' candle light,
    As Girzie hameward took her way.
A man o' sin, ill may he thrive!
    And never holy meeting see!
With godly Girzie met belyve,
    Amang the Craigie hills sae hie.

[*stark* = *bold; violent*
[*chap* = *haggle*

The chiel' was wight, the chiel' was stark
    He wad na wait to chap nor ca'
And she was faint wi' holy wark,
    She had na pith to say him na.
But ay she glowr'd up to the moon,
    And ay she sigh'd most piouslie,
'I trust my heart's in heaven aboon,
    'Whare'er your sinfu' pintle be.'

190

For A' That an' A' That

BY ROBERT BURNS (?)

The bonniest lass that ye meet neist,
  Gie her a kiss an' a' that,
In spite o' ilka parish priest,
  Repentin' stool, an' a' that.
    For a' that an' a' that
      Their mim-mou'd sangs an' a' that,
    In time and place convenient,
      They'll do't themselves for a' that.

*[mim-mou'd =
prim-lipped,
mealy-mouthed*

Your patriarchs in days o' yore,
  Had their handmaids an' a' that;
O' bastard gets, some had a score,
  An' some had mair than a' that.
    For a' that an' a' that,
      Your Langsyne saunts, an' a' that,
    Were fonder o' a bonny lass
      Than you or I, for a' that.

*[Langsyne
saunts =
bygone saints*

King Davie, when he waxed auld,
  An's bluid ran thin an' a' that,
An faund his c-s were growin' cauld,
  Could not refrain for a' that.
    For a' that an' for a' that
      To keep him warm an' a' that,
    The daughters o' Jerusalem
      Were waled for him, an' a' that.

[waled = chosen

Wha wouldna pity thae sweet dames
  He fumbled at, an' a' that,
An' raised their bluid up into flames,

He couldna drown for a' that.
  For a' that an' a' that,
    He wanted pith an' a' that;
  For, as to what we shall not name
    What could he do but claw that.

191

The Frolicsome Parson Outwitted

Come all you hearty roving blades, and listen to my song,
A verse or two I will unfold, and will not keep you long,
It is of a frolicsome parson, as you shall quickly hear,
That dwelt in the town of Ledbury, in the county of
  Herefordshire.

The parson being a rakish blade, and fond of sporting
  games,
He fell in love with the pretty cook, as I have heard the
  same;
The parlour-maid found out the same, and in the fruit
  room looked,
And there she saw the parson sporting with the cook.

It was in nine months after she brought him forth a child,
Within the rectory it was born, it drove him nearly wild;
It proved to be a male child, at least they tell us so,
Then this damsel from the rectory was quickly forced to go.

Then the secret to unfold, it was her full intent,
During the time of service into the church she went,
Holding the child up in her arms, and on the parson gazed,
Saying, lovely babe, that is your dad, which filled him
  with amaze.

The congregation they all stared, the parson seemed
  confused,
And many a lad and lass no doubt, within them felt
  amused;
Such a scene as this was never known within the church
  before,
Let us hope that it will be the last, and the like shall be
  no more.

'Twas then a court was called in town, for to invest the
  case.
There the parson, cook, and parlour-maid they met face
  to face,
And many more in court appeared, to hear the sport and
  fun,
This damsel swore the parson was the father of her son.

Your reverence; you are found to blame the Justices
  declared,
Although some honest country lad (*sic*) you thought for
  to ensnare;
So with all your doctrine and your skill unto him they
  did say,
A half-a-crown each week to the child you've got to pay.

His reverence felt dissatisfied with such a glorious treat,
To a higher court he did proceed, and there was quickly
  beat,
So this damsel she's victorious, the truth I now declare,
And his reverence is suspended for the period of five
  years.

Come all you blooming servant maids a warning take
  by this,
When in service with the parsons don't be treated to a
  kiss;

Or it may cause much jealousy, as you may all well
    know,
Then you from service must be gone your sorrows for
    to rue.

Now to conclude and make an end and finish up my
    song,
All you young men that's deep in love, be sure don't
    stay too long;
Join hand in hand in wedlock's band without the least
    delay
Before the fairest of all girls is by parsons led astray.

192

The Parson Grocer

'Thou shalt not covet thy neighbour's wife'

Come my friends and listen unto me,
    A story I'll relate
Of a wicked minister
    And his unhappy fate:

Down in Bethnal Green he preach'd
    Among the rich and poor,
And oft did speak of sinners
    And wicked deed deplore.
        O wicked man,
        The truth we must relate.
    Your deeds so dark, we bid you mark
        The terrors of your fate.

CLERICAL

This man among his people
   Was so very *modest*,
You'd scarcely think that he did
   Anything not honest,
And yet, behind their faces,
   A devil in human form,
And often spent his evenings
   Amid a brothel's storm.

Among the things that this man did, –
   He took a neighbour's wife,
From her family and home,
   To live with him in strife.
Friends with indignation fill'd
   Soon found the monster out,
Th'people heard the sad disgrace,
   And sent him right about.

From Ebenezer Chapel,
   And Hampden Chapel kick'd,
To Old Kent Road and Walworth,
   And Kennington he sneak'd,
In these and other places,
   He'd nightly play his tricks.
But from each in turn, afraid,
   He soon pack'd up his sticks.

Now to seek a close retreat,
   To Gravel Lane he's fled,
Instead of preaching sermons,
   Sells grocery instead.
He who acts the traitors part –
   Who steals another's wife,
Must be a wretch – a villain,
   For any mischief rife.

FIVE

MARITAL

193

Keep a Good Tongue in your Head
for

Here's a good woman in every respect,
But only her tongue breeds all the defect.

BY MARTIN PARKER

I marry'd a wife of late –
  the more's my unhappy fate!
I tooke her for love,
As fancy did me move,
  and not for her worldly state.
For qualities rare
Few with her compare;
  let me doe her no wrong:
I must confesse
Her chief amisse
Is onely this,
As some wives is,
  she cannot rule her tongue.

She hath as sweet a face
  as any in seven miles space,
Her eyes christalline
Like diamonds do shine,
  she looks with a modest grace:
Her hair is like flax,
Her lips are red wax,
  that seale the bond so strong
Twixt her and I,

That till I die
Ile justifie
Her constancy,
   but she cannot hold her tong

Her cheeks are red as the rose
   (which June for her glory shows);
Her teeth on a row
Stand like a wall of snow
Between her round chin and her nose.
Her shoulders are decent,
Her armes white and pleasant,
   her fingers are smal and long;
No fault I finde,
But, in my minde,
Most womenkind
Must come behind:
   O that she could rule her tong!

[decent =
   shapely

[smal = slender

Her breasts like pyreene hills,
   which nature yearely fils
With liquor that by ods
Doth passe the drink o' th' gods,
   all Nectar it far excels.
With this she doth feed
The twigs that proceed
   from our affections strong;
Shee's fruitful as
The springing grasse,
No time's let passe,
And yet, alas!
   she cannot rule her tongue.

Her body, which I have oft
   embraced, so smooth and soft!
Is slender and white,

Proportioned aright,
  'tis straight as any shaft.
Her leg is compleat,
Her foot's fine and neat,
  'tis neither too short nor too long;
In every part
Dame Nature's art
Gives her the start:
With all my heart
  I wish she could rule her tong!

[*compleat =
perfect*

194

The Wooing Maid

OR

*A faire maid neglected,
Forlorne and rejected,
That would be respected:
Which to have effected,
This general summon
She sendeth in common;
Come tinker, come broomman:
She will refuse no man.*

BY MARTIN PARKER

I am a faire Maide, if my glasse doe not flatter,
Yet, by the effects, I can find no such matter;
For every one else can have Suters great plenty;
Most marry at fourteene, but I am past twenty.
*Come gentle, come simple, come foolish, come witty,
Oh! if you lack a maid, take me for pitty.*

I see by experience – which makes me to wonder –
That many have sweethearts at fifteene and under,
And if they passe sixteen, they think their time wasted;
O what shall become of me? I am out-casted;
Come gentle &c

I use all the motives my sex will permit me,
To put men in mind, that they may not forget me:
Nay, sometimes I set my commission o' th' tenters,[1]
Yet let me doe what I will, never a man venters.
Come gentle &c

When I goe to weddings, or such merry meetings,
I see other maids how they toy with their sweetings,
But I sit alone, like an abject forsaken;
Woe's me! for a husband what course shall be taken?
Come gentle &c

When others to dancing are courteously chosen,
I am the last taken among the halfe dozen,
And yet among twenty not one can excell me;
What shall I do in this case, some good man tell me.
Come gentle &c

THE SECOND PART

'Tis said that one wedding produceth another –
This I have heard told by my father and mother –
Before one shall scape me, Ile goe without bidding;
O that I could find out some fortunate wedding!
Come gentle, come simple, come foolish, come witty,
Oh! if you lack a maid, take me for pitty.

Sure I am unfortunate, of all my kindred,
Else could not my happiness be so long hindred:
My mother at eighteene had two sons and a daughter,
And I'm one and twenty, not worth looking after.
Come gentle &c

1. Frame for stretching cloth. Hence 'in a state of strain' (Cp. mod. 'on tenterhooks').

My sister, that's nothing so handsome as I am,
Had sixe or seven suters and she did deny them;
Yet she before sixteene was luckily marry'd:
O Fates! why are things so unequally carr'd?
Come gentle &c

My kinswoman Sisly, in all parts mis-shapen,
Yet she on a husband by fortune did happen
Before she was nineteene years old (at the furthest)
Among all my Linage am I the unworthiest.
Come gentle &c

There are almost forty, both poorer and yonger,
Within few yeares marry'd, yet I must stay longer,
Within four miles compasse – O is't not a wonder?
Scant none above twenty, some sixteene, some under.
Come gentle &c

I hold my selfe equall with most in the parish
For feature, for parts, and what chiefly doth cherish
The fire of affection, which is store of money;
And yet there is no man will set love upon me.
Come gentle &c

Who ever he be that will ease my affliction,
And cast upon me an auspicious affection,
Shall find me tractable still to content him,
That he of his bargaine shall never repent him.
Come gentle &c

Ile neither be given to scold nor be jealous,
He nere shall want money to drink with good fellows:
While he spends abroad, I at home will be saving,
Now judge, am not I a lasse well worth the having?
Come gentle &c

Let none be offended, nor say I'm uncivill,
For I needs must have one, be he good or evill:
Nay, rather then faile, Ile have a Tinker or Broomman,
A Pedler, an Inkman, a Matman, or some man.
Come gentle, come simple, come foolish, come witty,
O let me not die a maid, take me for pitty.

195

The Merry Cuckold

Who frolickly taking what chance doth befall
Is very well pleased with Wife, hornes and all.

You married men, whom Fate hath assign'd,
To marry with them that are too much kind,
Learn, as I do, to beare with your wives;
All you that doe so, shall live merry lives.

I have a Wife, so wanton and so free,
That she, as her life, loves one besides me.
What if she doe, I care not a pin;
Abroad I will goe, when my rivall comes in.

I can be merry and drinke away care
With Claret and Sherry and delicate fare.
My Wife has a Trade that will maintain me:
What though it be said that a Cuckold I be!

While she at home is taking her pleasure,
Abroad I do rome, consuming her treasure:
Of all that she gets, I share a good share;
She payes all my debts, then for what should I care?

She keepes me brave and gallant in cloathing:
All things I have, I do want for nothing.
Therefore I connive and winke at her faults,
And daily I strive against jealous assaults.

While for small gaines my neighbours worke hard,
I live (by her meanes), and never regard
The troubles and cares that belong to this life;
I spend what few dares: gramercy, good Wife!

Should I be jealous, as other men are,
My breath, like to bellowes, the fire of care
Would blow and augment; therefore I thinke it best
To be well content, though I were Vulcans crest.   [*were = wear*

Many a time upbraided I am;
Some say I must dine at the Bull or the Ramme:
Those that do jeere cannot do as I may,
In Wine, Ale, and Beere spend a noble a day.

THE SECOND PART

I by experience, rightly do know
That no strife or variances (causes of woe,)
Can make a wife so bent⟨,⟩ to live chast.
Thou in stead of strife, let patience be plac't.   [*Thou;
Then*(?)

If a man had all Argus his eyes,
A wife that is bad will something devise
To gull him to's face: then what boores mistrust,   [*boores =
The hornes to disgrace, though weare it I must!   behoves*

Ile be content with this my hard chance,
And in merryment my head Ile advance,
Wishing I were but as rich as some men,
Whose wives chast appeare, yet they'l kisse now and then.

One trying to me a great comfort is: [*trying =
Still quiet is she, though I do amisse.   thing*(?)
She dares do no other, because she knows well,
That gently I smoother what most men would tell.

If I should rave, her minde would not alter;
Her swing she will have, though't be in a halter:
Then sith that I get good gaines by her vice,
[*let* = *hinder* I will not her let, but take share of the price.

Why should I vexe and pine in dispaire?
I know that her sexe are all brittle ware;
[*canstant* = And he that gets one who canstant abides,
constant Obtaines that which none, or but few, have besides.

Yet will I not accuse my wife,
For nothing is got by railing, but strife.
I act my own sence, intending no wrong:
No Cuckold nor Queane will care for this song.

[*Wife* But a merry Wife, that's honest⟨,⟩ I know it,
that's ... (?) As deare as her life, will sure love the Poet;
And he thats no Cuckold, in Countrey or City,
However lucke hold, will buy this our Ditty.

196

The Scolding Wives Vindication

OR

An Answer to the Cuckold's Complaint

Wherein she shows what just Reasons she had to exercise
Severity over her insufficient Husband.

I have been abus'd of late
by some of the Poets Crew
Who says, I broke my Husbands Pate,
but this I did never do.

500

'Tis true I his Ears did cuff,
  and gave him a kick or two;
For this I had just Cause enough,
  because he would nothing do.

He's lain like a Log of Wood,
  in bed, for a year or two,
And won't afford me any good,
  he nothing at all would do.

I am in my blooming Prime,
  dear Neighbours I tell you true,
I am loth be to loose my Teeming Time,
  yet nothing at all he'll do.

He says that I keep a friend,
  but what if I did keep two,
There's no one can me discommend
  for nothing at all he'll do.

I make it full well appear,
  to be both just and true,
I kept my Maiden-head two year,
  for nothing at all he'd do.

Sometimes he'd give me a Kiss,
  and I would return him two,
But when he comes to farther Bliss
  he nothing at all would do.

I am a young Buxome Dame
  and fain would my Joys renew,
But my poor Cuckold is to blame
  he nothing at all would do.

Sure never was wife so fool'd
   as I, for a year or two;
I did for him what e'er I could
   yet nothing at all would do.

I feasted him e'ery day,
   with Lamb-stones, and Cock-broths too,
Yet all this Cost was thrown away,
   he nothing at all would do.

I fed him with Jelly of Chicks,
   and curious Egg-Caudles too,
I'se good feed him with Faggot-sticks
   for nothing at all would do.

He lyes like a lump of Clay,
   such Husbands there is but few,
'Twould make a Woman run astray,
   When nothing at all would do.

Now let him take his ease,
   and sleep while the sky looks blue,
I have a friend my mind to please
   since nothing at all would do.

Long, long, have I liv'd at strife,
   I kick'd, and I cuff'd him too,
He's like to live no better life,
   since nothing at all he'll do.

I solemnly do declare,
   believe me this is true,
He shall dig Gravel next Horn-Fair
   and that he is like to do.

197

The Lamentation of Chloris

for the Unkindness of her Shepherd, shewing

How she by her Strephon was strangely beguil'd,
And is almost Distracted for want of a child:
But if any brisk Lad will come her to Imbrace,
She's free, can they find a convenient place.

My Shepherd's unkind; alas, what shall I do?
Who shall I direct my sad Speeches unto?
Whilst in secret I mourn for the loss of my dear,
Down from my poor eyes drops many a Tear.

He takes much delight with his flocks for to keep,
And minds not poor *Cloris*, who for him doth Weep:
But in vain I lament, for I plainly do see
It is all one to him what becometh of me.

In the morning he's gone before I'm awake,
Then I miss my dear Shepherd, my heart it doth ake:
The Sighs and the Groans by my self I do fetch
Would move him to pitty a sorrowful wretch.

THE SECOND PART

At night he doth think for to make me amends,
And with his fair looks for to make us good friends;
But, alas! he's so weary, he cannot be kind:
And this adds great sorrow to my pensive mind.

But I have no hopes that I e're shall injoy
As the fruits of my labour a Girl or a Boy;
Which so much I desire, but I fear all in vain;
For my *Strephon's* unkind, which doth make me complain.

But if thus he continues, I'le tell you my mind,
I'le find out some friend who knows how to be kind:
For I'm sure flesh and blood long cannot endure
The pain that I feel, without looking for cure.

When I walk in the fields, not thinking of harms,
And meet but a woman with a Babe in her arms,
It tormenteth me more than my tongue can relate
Which makes me deplore my too rigid fate.

Well, *Strephon*, thy fore-head I will certainly graft
With a large pair of Horns, yet do't with such Craft,
Thou shalt ne'er be the wiser; and when this is done,
I fear not to bring thee a Daughter or Son.

And for my so doing can any me blame,
If they do but consider, what a scurrilous Name
Poor women receive that no Children do bear;
Though the fault be their husbands, such dry souls they are?

Besides, I am young, and my nature requires
A lusty young Ladd for to please my desires:
Yet I have as little of Lover's content
As ever had woman, which makes me lament.

Then pitty poor *Cloris*, all you that injoy
The content of your hearts, and do frequently toy
With your Lovers in private, and use *Venus'* Game,
For you cannot deny but my shepherd's to blame.

198

The New Married Couple

OR

A Friendly Debate between the Country Farmer and his Buxome Wife

Dear *Gill* I ne'er thought till last night
   that Cupid had yielded such sweet delight
But when thy soft arms with mine were twin'd
   the Joy the Oak, did not closer bind: [*Joy* = *Ivy* (?)
Thou gav'st me sweet kisses that might invite,
   in old Shepheards a new delight:
Young *Colin* did ne'r with Mirtilla so bright
   enjoy such a sweet, such a pleasing night.

My *Neede* (quoth she) since I love thee here
   I will be a Port for to please my Dear:
And in the soft Circuit of thy Pale
   feed either upon the high hill or the Dale;
Graze on my soft *Lypis,* if those hills be dry
   Stray down where fountains lye:
The Doe thy fair breeder, will always be nigh,
   to please her young Wanton with Art and Eye.

Thou shalt be a banquet to my Taste,
   on which, I will always delight to feast;
As sweet as young *Colley* the Farmer⟨'s⟩ Cow
   as sweet as the hay in his Barn I vow:
As sweet as young Roses that all admire
   as may Blossoms upon the Briar:
As sweet as blind midnight with Maidens desire
   as sweet as Sack-Posset by Sea-Coal fire.

Uds boars (quoth stout *Nedde*) I'le forsake my dumps
    and briskly bestir my old hobnail stumps
The Lasses shall foot it, the Lads shall sing
    and Ecchoes all round with our Joys shall ring:
Doll shall leave Dairy and Dames Brown-Cow
    and brisk *Roger* his Cart and Plough,
To meet us young *Nancy* amd *William* come now
    we shall have rare Daunces and Jigs enow.

Rough Batchellors may live merry lives
    yet we will not change that have Buxom wives;
Upon the soft Pillow of their Breast
    we Love-sick lie warm in *Cupids* Nest.
[*need*=*heed*(?)]   What though there be Cuckolds we need not
    Our Wives always will take such care
Although the Brows bud the Horns shant appear
    to make us look noble and like the Dear.

If *Gill* should within the Curtains chide
    my Antlers and head in the sheets il'e hide
And when my Good Houswifes-Pot boyles ore
    to cool her hot Broth i'le attempt no more
It is I confess the depth of skill
    to lead women by their own Will
But while her tongue gallops my Tongue shall be still,
    and thus I'le endeavour to please *Gill*, *Gill*.

Dear *Neddy* (quoth *Gill*) name not things so soon
    with us 'tis but yet our Honey-moon
Come let us to please each other strive
    and gather like Bees within our Hive.
Thou must not be like a dull Idle drone,
    nor mind Horns for Thou shalt have none:
But follow thy Plough by *Dobbin* and *Roan*
    and I to my milking will go with *Joan*.

Dear *Gill* there are many old Complaints
  all Wives that look fair dont prove all Saints
For many mens wives are like the moon
  that alters each morning, each night and noon
Yet for my own part, I will never fear,
  but try always to please my Dear
If I can, my Wife will hold almost a year,
  this Riddle me Riddle nine months will clear.

199

A Ballade upon a Wedding

BY SIR JOHN SUCKLING

I tell thee *Dick* where I have been,
Where I the rarest things have seen;
  Oh things without compare!
Such sights cannot be found
In any place on English ground
  Be it at Wake, or Fair.

At *Charing-Crosse*, hard by the way
Where we (thou know'st) do sell our Hay,
  There is a house with stairs;
And there did I see comming down
Such folk as are not in our Town,
  Vorty at least, in Pairs.

Amongst the rest, one Pest'lent fine,
(His beard no bigger though then thine)
  Walkt on before the rest:
Our Landlord looks like nothing to him:
The King (God blesse him) 'twould undo him
  Should he go still so drest.

[*Course-a-Park*
=*A country
game in which a
girl called out a
boy to chase her*

At Course-a-Park, without all doubt,
He should have first been taken out
   By all the maids i'th Town:
Though lusty *Roger* there had been,
Or little *George* upon the Green,
   Or *Vincent* of the Crown.

But wot you what? the youth was going
To make an end of all his woing;
   The Parson for him staid:
Yet by his leave (for all his haste)
He did not so much wish all past
   (Perchance) as did the maid.

The maid (and thereby hangs a tale)
For such a maid no Whitson-ale
   Could ever yet produce:
No Grape that's kindly ripe, could be
So round, so plump, so soft as she,
   Nor half so full of Juyce.

Her finger was so small, the Ring
Would not stay on which they did bring,
   It was too wide a Peck:
And to say truth (for out it must)
It lookt like the great Collar (just)
   About our young Colt's neck.

Her feet beneath her Petticoat,
Like little mice stole in and out,
   As if they fear'd the light:
But oh! she dances such a way!
No sun upon an Easter day
   Is half so fine a sight.

He would have kist her once or twice,
But she would not, she was so nice,
　　she would not do't in sight,
And then she lookt as who should say
I will do what I list today;
　　And you shall do't at night.

Her Cheeks so rare a white was on,
No Dazy makes comparison,
　　(Who sees them is undone)
For streaks of red were mingled there,
Such as are on a Katherine Pear,
　　(The side that's next the Sun.)

Her lips were red, and one was thin,
Compar'd to that was next her Chin;
　　(Some Bee had stung it newly.)
But (*Dick*) her eyes so guard her face;
I durst no more upon them gaze
　　Then on the sun in *July*.

Her mouth so small when she does speak,
Thou'dst swear her teeth her words did break
　　That they might passage get,
But she so handled still the matter,
They came as good as ours, or better,
　　And are not spent a whit.

If wishing should be any sin,
The Parson himself had guilty bin;
　　(she lookt that day so purely,)
And did the Youth so oft the feat
At night, as some did in conceit,
　　It would have spoil'd him, surely.

Just in the nick the Cook knockt thrice,
And all the waiters in a trice
   His summons did obey,
Each serving man with dish in hand,
Marcht boldly up, like our Train Band,
   Presented, and away.

When all the meat was on the Table,
   What man of knife, or teeth, was able
   To stay to be intreated?
And this the very reason was,
Before the Parson could say Grace
   The Company was seated.

The bus'nesse of the Kitchin's great,
For it is fit that men should eat;
   Nor was it there deni'd,
Passion oh me! how I run on!
There's that that would be thought upon,
   (I trow) besides the Bride.

Now hatts fly off, and youths carouse;
Healths first go round, and then the house,
   The Brides came thick and thick:
And when 'twas nam'd another health,
Perhaps he made it hers by stealth,
   (And who could help it? *Dick*)

O' th' sodain up they rise and dance;
Then sit again and sigh, and glance:
   Then dance again and kisse:
Thus sev'ral waies the time did passe,
Till ev'ry Woman wisht her place,
   And ev'ry Man wisht his.

By this time all were stoln aside
To cousel and undresse the Bride;
  But that he must not know:
But yet 'twas thought he ghest her mind
And did not mean to stay behind
  Above an hour or so.

When in he came (*Dick*) there she lay
Like new-faln snow melting away,
  ('Twas time I trow to part)
Kisses were now the onely stay,
Which soon she gave, as who would say,
  Good Boy! with all my heart.

But just as leav'ns would have to crosse it,
In came the Bridemaids with the Posset:
  The Bridegroom eat in spight;
For had he left the Women to't
It would have cost two hours to do't,
  Which were too much that night.

At length the candles out and out,
All that they had not done, they do't;
  What that is, who can tell?
But I beleeve it was no more
Then thou and I have done before
  With *Bridget*, and with *Nell*.

200

To Friend and Foe

To Friend and to Foe, to all that I know
  That to marriage Estate do prepare,
Remember your days in several ways
  Are troubled with sorrow and care:

For he that doth look in the Mans book
    And read but his Items all over,
Shall find them to come at length to a sum
    Which shall empty Purse, Pocket and Coffer.

In the pastimes of love, when their labours do prove,
    And the fruit beginneth to kick,
For this and for that, and I know not for what,
    The Woman must have, or be sick;
There's *Item* set down for a loos-bodyed Gown,
    In her longings you must not deceive her;
For a Bodkin, a Ring, or the other fine thing,
    For a Whisk, a Scarf, or a Beaver.

Deliver'd and well, who is't cannot tell
    Thus while the child lyes at Nipple,
There's *Item* for Wine, and Gossips so fine,
    And Sugar to sweeten their Tipple;
There's *Item*, I hope, for Water and Sope,
    There's *Item* for Fire and Candle,
For better or worse, there's *Item* for Nurse
    The Baby to dress and to dandle.

When swadled in lap, there's *Item* for pap,
    And *Item* for Pot, Pan and Ladle;
A Coral with bells which custom compels,
    And *Item* ten groats for a Cradle;
With twenty odd knacks which the little one lacks,
    And thus doth thy pleasure bewray thee:
But this is the sport in Country and Court,
    Then let not these pastimes betray thee.

201

The Old Man and Young Wife

There was an Old-man and a jolly Old-man
  Come love me whereas I lay,
And he would marry a fair young Wife
  The clean contrary way.

He Woo'd her to wed, to wed,
  Come love me whereas I lay,
And after she kick't him out of the bed
  The clean contrary way.

Then for her dinner she looked due,
  Come love whereas I lay,
Or she would make her Husband rue
  The clean contrary way.

She proved a gallant Houswife soon,
  Come love me whereas I lay,
She was up every morning by noon
  The clean contrary way.

She made him go wash and wring,
  Come love me whereas I lay,
And every day to Dance and Sing
  The clean contrary way.

She made him do a worse thing than this,
  Come love me whereas I lay,
To Father a Child was none of his
  The clean contrary way.

R

202

A Westminster Wedding
OR
Like unto Like, quoth the Devil to the Collier

Heres two in marriage joyn'd you see
Better one house than two should troubled be
For I may boldly speak without erring
There's neither Barrel of them better Herring
Then buy this Bull if you e're bought any
For I dare say 'tis richly worth a penny

There liv'd of late in Luteners Lane
A painted whore and a rogue in grain
Tom come tickle me, Tom come tickle ⟨me⟩
     Tom come tickle me once again

They often meeting at Venus play
Agreed to be married without delay
Tom come etc.

This girl was the finest of all the flock
With her Taffety gown, and her Holland smock
Tom come etc.

Her hair it was powder'd, her locks was curl'd
In Rings like a Lady for all the world
Tom come etc.

And she of a bargain was very well sped
To take a rude Royster unto her bed
Tom come etc.

One that was thrice of Newgate made free
And hardly escaped the three-leg'd tree
Tom come etc.

A hopeful couple in mischief deep
A thousand times better to hang than to keep
Tom come etc.

But hap at a venture it must be so
To bind up the bargain they needs must go
Tom come etc.

The wedding appointed and day being set
Mark what a company there was met
Tom come etc.

First came Dorothy with her mate
B⟨onny⟩ Bridget and boney Kate   [Print worn
Tom come etc.

Jumping Joan that can play in the dark
Sue and Sarah from Whetstones Park
Tom come etc.

Mat so merry came with a good will
Peg and Prudence from Saffron-hill
Tom come etc.

Smiling Cisscily worthy regard
Frank and Mary from Dog and Bitch Yard,
Tom come etc.

Beck and Maudlin as it was meet
Hasted hither from Turnbull Street
Tom come etc.

Quoth Gillian ile go though it cost me a fall
And call all my Sisters at Hutton-Wall,
Tom come etc.

As far as from Ratcliff thither they came
From Wells-close and from Rosemary-Lane
Tom come etc.

But she of all others that bore the bell
Came as they told me from Clerkenwell
Tom come etc.

Thus tag, rag, and sorrel came flocking amain
I think at a Wedding was ne're such a train
Tom come etc.

For Luteners Lane, it was never so grac't
With so many Girls of the game at a feast
Tom come etc.

Nor never at Westminster went such a pair
A couple so exactly matcht to a hair
Tom come etc.

They had not been married above one hour
But there was, thou rogue and thou art a whore
Tom come etc.

I wish the Apprentices had been there
That time to frighten them from their cheer
Tom come etc.

But now I must leave them to shake up their bedding
And there is an end to a Westminster wedding
Tom come etc.

203

To Chuse a Friend, but never Marry

BY JOHN WILMOT, EARL OF ROCHESTER (?)

To all young Men that love to Wooe,
To Kiss and Dance, and Tumble too;
Draw near and Counsel take of me,
Your faithful Pilot I will be:
Kiss who you please, Joan, Kate, or Mary,
But still this counsel with you carry,
                    Never marry.

Court not a Country Lady, she
Knows not how to value thee;
She hath no am'rous Passion, but
What Tray, or Quando has for Slut:
To Lick, to Whine, to Frisk, or Cover,
She'll suffer thee, or any other,
                    Thus to Love her.

Her Daughter she's now come to Town,
In a rich Linsey Woolsey Gown;
About her neck a valued Prize,
A Necklace made of Whitings Eyes:
With List for Garters 'bove her Knee
And Breath that smells of Firmity,
                    's not for thee.

[List = a strip of cloth

[Firmity = frumenty: milk pudding of wheat

Of Widows Witchcrafts have a care,
For if they catch you in their Snare;
You must as daily Labourers do,
Be still a shoving with your Plow:
If any rest you do require,
They then deceive you of your Hire,
                    And retire.

The Maiden Ladies of the Town,
Are scarcely worth your throwing down;
For when you have possession got,
Of Venus Mark, or Hony-pot:
There's such a stir with, marry me,
That one would half forswear to see
                    Any she.

If that thy Fancy do desire,
A glorious outside, rich Attire;
Come to the Court, and there you'll find,
Enough of such to Please your Mind:
But if you get too near their Lap,
You're sure to meet with the Mishap,
                    Call'd a Clap.

[*fucus* =
cosmetic cream

With greasy painted Faces drest,
With butter'd Hair, and fucus'd Breast;
Tongues with Dissimulation tipt,
Lips which a million have them sipp'd:
There's nothing got by such as these,
But Achs in Shoulders, Pains in Knees
                    For your Fees.

In fine if thou delight'st to be,
Concern'd in Woman's Company:
Make it the Studies of thy Life,
To find a Rich, young, handsome Wife:
That can with much discretion be
Dear to her husband, kind to thee,
                    Secretly.

In such a Mistress, there's the Bliss,
Ten Thousand joys wrapt in a Kiss;
And in th'Embraces of her Wast,
A Million more of Pleasures taste:

Who e'er would marry that could be
Blest with such Opportunity,
        Never me.

204

The Wife-Hater

He that intends to take a Wife,
I'll tell him what kind of Life,
  He must be sure to lead;
If she's a young and tender Heart,
Not documented in Love's Art,
  Much Teaching she will need.

For where there is no Path, one may
Be tir'd before he find the way;
  Nay, when he's at his Treasure:
The Gap perhaps will prove so strait,
That he for Entrance long may wait,
  And make a toil of's Pleasure.

Or if one old and past her doing,
He will the Chambermaid be wooing,
  To buy her Ware the cheaper;
But if he chuse one most formose,
Ripe for't, she'll prove libidinous,
  Argus himself shan't keep her.

[*formose =
beautiful*

For when these Things are neatly drest,
They'll entertain each wanton Guest,
  Nor for your Honour care;
If any give their Pride a Fall,
They've learn'd a Trick to bear withal,
  So you their Charges bear.

Or if you chance to play your Game,
With a dull, fat, gross, and heavy Dame,
   Your Riches to increase,
Alas, she will but jeer you for't,
Bid you to find out better Sport,
   Lie with a Pot of Grease.

If meager — be thy delight,
She'll conquer in veneral Fight,
   And waste thee to the Bones;
Such kind of Girls, like to your Mill,
The more you give, the more crave they will,
   Or else they'll grind the Stones.

[to = too

If black, 'tis Odds, she's dev'lish proud;
If short, Zantippe like to loud,
   If long, she'll lazy be:
Foolish (the Proverb says) if fair;
If wise and comely, Danger's there,
   Lest she do Cuckold thee.

If she bring store of Money, such
Are like to domineer too much,
   Prove Mrs. no good Wife:
And when they cannot keep you under,
They'll fill the House with scolding Thunder,
   What's worse than such a Life.

But if their Dowry only be
Beauty, farewel Felicity,
   Thy Fortune's cast away;
Thou must be sure to satisfy her,
In Belly, and in Back desire,
   To labour Night and Day.

And rather than her Pride give o'er,
She'll turn perhaps an honour'd Whore,
   And thou'lt Acteon'd be;
Whilst like Acteon, thou may'st weep,
To think thou forced art to keep,
   All such as devour thee.

If being Noble thou dost wed,
A servile Creature basely bred,
   Thy Family it defaces;
If being mean, one nobly born,
She'll swear to exalt a Court-like Horn,
   Thy low Descent it graces.

If one Tongue be too much for any,
Then he who takes a Wife with many,
   Knows not what may betide him;
She whom he did for Learning Honour,
To scold by Book will take upon her,
   Rhetorically chide him.

If both her Parents living are,
To please them you must take great care,
   Or spoil your future Fortune;
But if departed they're this Life,
You must be Parent to your Wife,
   And Father all be certain.

If bravely Drest, fair Fac'd and Witty,
She'll oft be gadding to the City,
   Nor can you say nay;
She'll tell you (if you her deny)
Since Women have Terms, she knows not why,
   But still to keep them may.

If thou make choice of Country Ware,
Of being Cuckold there's less fear,
   But stupid Honesty
May teach her how to Sleep all Night,
And take a great deal more Delight,
   To Milk the Cows than thee.

Concoction makes their Blood agree,
Too near, where's Consanguinity,
   Then let no Kin be chosen;
He loseth one part of his Treasure,
Who thus confineth all his Pleasure,
   To th'Arms of a first Couzen.

He'll never have her at Command,
Who takes a Wife at Second hand,
   Than chuse no Widow'd Mother;
The First Cut of that Bit you love,
If others had, why mayn't you prove,
   But Taster to another.

Besides if She bring Children many,
'Tis like by thee she'll not have any,
   But prove a Barren Doe;
Or if by them She ne'er had one,
By thee 'tis likely she'll have none,
   Whilst thou for weak Back go.

For there where other Gardeners have been Sowing
Their Seed, but never could find it growing,
   You must expect so too;
And where the Terra Incognita
So's Plow'd, you must it Fallow lay,
   And still for weak Back go.

Then trust not a Maiden Face,
Nor confidence in Widows place,
　　Those weaker Vessels may
Spring Leak, or Split against a Rock,
And when your Fame's wrapt in a Smock,
　　'Tis easily cast away.

Yet be she Fair, Foul, Short, or Tall,
You for a time may Love them all,
　　Call them your Soul, your Life;
As one by one, them undermine,　　　　　　　　*[As = And (?)]*
As Courtezan, or Concubine,
　　But never as a Married Wife.

He who considers this, may end the strife.
　Confess no trouble like unto a Wife.

205

Sally Sweetbread

BY HENRY CAREY

Now the good man's away from home
　　I could cast away care,
And with some brisk fellow
　　Steal out to the fair;
But some are too bashful,
　　And some are too bold,
And woman's intentions
　　Are not to be told.

But could I once meet
　　With a spark to my mind,
One fit to be trusted,

I then might prove kind;
With him I'd steal out,
And I'd range the fair round,
Both eating and drinking
The best could be found.

Oh! there I shall see
The fine gentleman rakes,
And hear the sweet cry
Of beer, ale, wine and cakes;
While I in blue apron
And clean linen gown
Allure all the sparks
From the flirts of the town.

Fairground
proprietors
and
entertainers

There's Fielding and Oates
There's Hippesley and Hall,
There's Pinchbeck and Fawkes,
There's the devil and all.
I'll have the best place
And I'll see ev'ry sight,
And revel in pleasure
From morning to night.

Then home get secure
E'er my husband comes back;
And cry most demurely,
What d'ye buy, what d'ye lack;
Thus courted and treated,
Gallanted and kiss'd
Can deary be cheated
When nothing is miss'd.

206

Mog the Brunette

Young Jockey he courted sweet Mog the Brunette,
Who had lips like carnations, and eyes black as jet
He coax'd, and he weedl'd, and talk'd with his eyes,
And look'd, as all lovers do, wonderful wise:
Then he swore like a lord how her charms he ador'd,
That she'd soon put an end to his suff'rings implor'd,
For a heart unaware thus his trammels he set,
And soon made a conquest of Mog the Brunette.

They pannell'd their dobbins, and rode to the fair,
Still kissing and fondling until they came there,
They call'd at the church and in wedlock were join'd
And Jockey was happy, for Moggy was kind:
'Twas now honeymoon, time expired too soon,
They revell'd in pleasure night, morning and noon.
He call'd her his charmer, his joy, and his pet,
And the lasses all envy sweet Mog the Brunette.

Then home they return'd, but return'd most unkind
For Jockey rode on and left Moggy behind;
Surpriz'd at this treatment she call'd to her mate,
Why, Jockey, you're alter'd most strangely of late:
Come on, fool, he cri'd, thou now art my bride,
And when folks are married they set fooling aside;
Hard names and foul words were the best she could get,
Strange usage this, sure, for sweet Mog the Brunette.

He took home poor Moggy new conduct to learn,
She brush'd up the house while he thatch'd the old barn,
They laid in a stock for the cares that ensue,
And now live as man and wife usually do:

As their humours excite they kiss and they fight.
'Twixt kindness and feuds pass the morn, noon, and night.
To his sorrow he finds with his match he has met,
And wishes the devil had Mog the Brunette.

207

My Wife's a Wanton Wee Thing

My wife's a wanton wee thing,
My wife's a wanton wee thing,
My wife's a wanton wee thing,
   She winna be guided by me.

She play'd the loon ere she was married,
She play'd the loon ere she was married,
She play'd the loon ere she was married,
   She'll do it again ere she die.

She sell'd her gown and she drank it,
She sell'd her gown and she drank it,
She row'd hersel' in a blanket,
   She winna be guided by me.

She did it altho' I forbad her,
She did it altho' I forbad her,
I took a rung and I claw'd her,
   An' a braw guid bairn was she.

208

Duncan Gray

BY ROBERT BURNS

Can ye play me Duncan Gray,
  Ha, ha, the girdin' o't
O'er the hills and far away',
  Ha, ha, ha, the girdin' o't.
Duncan came our Meg to woo,
Meg was nice and wadna do,
But like an ether puff'd and blew
  At offer o' the girdin' o't.

Duncan, he cam' here agin,
  Ha, ha, the girdin' o't.
A' was out an' Meg her lane
  Ha, ha, ha, the girdin' o't.
He kiss'd her butt, he kiss'd her ben,
He bang'd a thing against her wame;
But troth, I now forget its name,
  But, I trow, she gat the girdin' o't.

She took him to the cellar then,
  Ha, ha, the girdin' o't,
To see gif he could do't again,
  Ha, ha, the girdin' o't.
He kiss'd her ance, he kiss'd her thrice,
Till deil a mair the thing wad rise,
  To gie her land the girdin' o't.

But Duncan took her to his wife,
  Ha, ha, the girdin' o't.
To be the comfort o' his life,
  Ha, ha, the girdin' o't.

[*girdin'* =
striking,
energetic
working

[*ether* = *adder*

[*her lane* = *alone*

[*but and ben* = *in the kitchen and parlour*

[*wame* = *belly*

An' now she scauls baith night and day,
Except when Duncan's at the play;
An that's as seldom as he may,
    He's weary o' the girdin' o't.

209

John Anderson, My Jo

BY ROBERT BURNS (?)

John Anderson, my jo, John
    I wonder what ye mean
To lie sae lang i' the mornin'
    And sit sae late at e'en?
Ye'll blear a' your een, John,
    And why do ye so?
Come sooner to your bed at e'en,
    John Anderson, my jo.

John Anderson, my jo, John,
    When first that ye began,
Ye had as good a tail-tree
    As ony ither man;
But now it's waxen wan, John,
    And wrinkles to and fro,
And aft requires my helping hand,
    John Anderson, my jo.

When we were young and yauld, John
    We've lain out-owre the dyke,
And O! it was a fine thing
    To see your hurdies fyke; –
To see your hurdies fyke, John,
    And strike the rising blow;

'Twas then I lik'd your chanter-pipe,
   John Anderson, my jo.

John Anderson, my jo, John,
   You're welcome when you please;
It's either in the warm bed,
   Or else aboon the claes.
Do ye your part aboon, John,
   And trust to me below;
I've twa gae-ups for your gae-down,
   John Anderson, my jo.

When ye come on before, John
   See that ye do your best;
When I begin to haud ye,
   See that ye grip me fast;
See that ye grip me fast, John,
   Until that I cry 'Oh!'
Your back shall crack, or I do that,
   John Anderson, my jo.

I'm backet like a salmon,
I'm breastit like a swan
My wyme is like a down-cod,
   My waist ye weel may span;
My skin fra tap to tae, John,
Is like the new fa'n snaw
   And it's a' for your conveniency,
   John Anderson, my jo.

210

The Sandgate Girl's Lamentation

I was a young maid truly,
And lived in Sandgate Street.
I thought to marry a good man
To keep me warm at neet.

He's an ugly body, a bubbly body
An ill-fared, hideous loon;
And I have married a keelman,
And my good days are done.

*[keelman = a
dealer in keel
or ruddle*

I thought to marry a parson
To hear me say my prayers;
But I have married a keelman
And he kicks me down the stairs.

I thought to marry a dyer
To die my apron blue;
But I have married a keelman
And he makes me sorely rue.

I thought to marry a joiner
To make me chair and stool;
But I have married a keelman,
And he's a perfect fool.

I thought to marry a sailor
To bring me sugar and tea;
But I have married a keelman
And that he lets me see.

He's an ugly body, a bubbly body,
An ill-fared, hideous loon;
And I have married a keelman,
And my good days are done.

211

The Silly Old Man

Come listen awhile, and I'll sing you a song,
I am a young damsel just turn'd twenty-one;
I married a miser for gold it is true,
And the age of his years were seventy-two.

CHORUS

Will you live for ever you silly old man,
I wish that your days they were all at an end;
To please a young woman is more than you can,
It's not in your power, you silly old man.

For every night when I go to bed,
He lays by my side like one that is dead;
Such spitting and coughing it makes me run wild,
Tho' I'm never disturb'd by the noise of my child.
   Will you live for ever &c

Was there ever a woman so sorely oppress'd,
For every morning I've got him for to dress;
And like a young child I have got him for to nusse,
For he's got ne'er a tooth to mumble a crust.
   Will you live for ever &c

When I go to bed to him he makes me run wild,
For he's got no more use in his limbs than a child,
He feels all as cold, as a piece of lead
That I have a great mind to get out of bed
   Will you live for ever &c

There's a buxom young fellow that lives in this town
That pleases me well, so we'll cut out the clown;
I'il make him wear horns as long as a stag,
So we'll cuckold the miser and seize his gold bag
   Will you live for ever &c

When I go to bed to him I do not lay nigh,
He grunts and he groans like a pig in a sty;
I'm sure a young woman would soon wish him dead
He's as bald as a coot and no teeth in his head.

Will you live for ever you silly old man?
I wish that your days they were all at an end;
I'll spend all your gold with some lusty young man
So go to your grave, you silly old man.

212

Good & Bad Wives

A BATCHELOR leads an easy life
   Few folks that are wed live better,
A man may live well with a very good wife,
   But the puzzle is how to get her.

There are pretty good wives and pretty bad wives,
   And wives neither one thing nor t'other
And as for wives who scold all their lives
   I'd soon wed Adam's grandmother.

Then ladies and gents if to marriage inclin'd
   May deceit nor ill humour ne'er trap ye, ·
May those that are single get wive⟨s⟩ to their mind
   And those who are married live happy

Some chuse their ladies for ease and for grace,
   Or pretty turn'd foot as they're walking
Some chuse for figure and some for face
   But very few chuse them for talking

Now as for the wife I could follow through life,
   Tis she who can speak sincerely,
   Who not over nice can give good advice
   And love a good husband dearly:

So ladies and gent⟨s⟩ when to wedlock inclin'd,
   May deceit nor ill humour e'er trap ye
May those who e'er single find wives to their mind   [*e'er* = *are* (?)
   And may those who are married live happy.

213

Prince of Wales' Marriage

Everybody stop and listen to my ditty,
And let the news spread from town to city,
The Prince of Wales has long enough tarried,
And now we know he has got married.

  For he went to sleep all night
    And part of the next day,
    The Prince of Wales must tell some tales,
    With his doo dah, doo dah, day.

His pastime for a week there's no disputing,
For the first three days he went out shooting,
He's like his father I don't deceive her,
And she like Vick is a good feeder.

The next two days, so it is said, sir,
He began to dig out the parsley bed, sir,
Like his dad he does understand,
And knows how to cultivate a bit.

The first day over he laid in clover,
And just alike he felt all over;
At fox-hunting he's clever and all races,
Yet she might throw him out of the traces.

He must not go larking along with the gals,
Keep out of the Haymarket and Pall Mall;
And to no married woman must he speak,
She'll stand no nonsense or half-crowns a-week.

In November next she must not fail
But have a little Prince of Wales,
Young Albert he must not be beat,
But contrive to make both ends meet.

When his wife is in a funny way,
Then he must not go astray;
Of all those things he must take warning,
Nor go out with the girls and stop till morning.

The last Prince of Wales was a good'un to go,
He would ride with the girls in Rotten Row,
He use⟨d⟩ to flare-up, he was no joker,
He was as fat as a Yarmouth bloater.

He must look to his stock and cultivation,
He must be a father to the nation;
He must begin to reap and sow,
Be a rum'un to look at, but a good'un to go.

He wants six maids as light as fairies,
To milk the cows and look to the dairy,
To his wife the household affairs confiding,
While the Prince of Wales goes out riding.

Long life to the Prince and his fair lady,
May she have health and bouncing babies,
May the Prince be King, we want no other,
And take the steps of his father and mother.

214

Johnny Sands

A man whose name was Johnny Sands
   Had married Betty Haigh,
And tho' she brought him gold and lands,
   She proved a terrible plague.
For, oh, she was a scolding wife,
   Full of caprice and whim,
He said that he was tired of life,
   And she was tired of him
   And she was tired of him.

Says he, then I will drown myself –
   The river runs below
Says she, pray do you silly elf,
   I wished it long ago

Says he, upon the brink I'll stand,
   Do you run down the hill
And push me in with all your might.
   Says she, my love, I will
   Says she, my love, I will.

For fear that I should courage lack
   And try to save my life,
Pray tie my hands behind my back.
   I will, replied his wife.
She tied them fast as you may think,
   And when securely done,
Now stand, she says, upon the brink,
   And I'll prepare to run,
   And I'll prepare to run.

All down the hill his loving bride,
   Now ran with all her force
To push him in – he stepped aside
   And she fell in of course
Now splashing, dashing, like a fish,
   Oh, save me, Johnny Sands,
I can't my dear, tho' much I wish,
   For you have tied my hands
   For you have tied my hands.

215

The Female Husband, who had been Married to another Female for Twenty-one Years

What wonders now I have to pen, sir,
Women turning into men, sir,
For twenty-one long years, or more, sir,
She wore the breeches we are told, sir,

A smart and active handsome groom, sir,
She then got married very soon, sir,
A shipwright's trade she after took, sir,
And of his wife, he made a fool sir.

  Sing hey! sing O! 'twas my downfall sir,
  To marry a man with nothing at all, sir.

Well Mother Sprightly, what do you think of this Female Husband; it appears to me a strange piece of business. Why, Mother Chatter, I do not believe half what is said about it – Pho, pho, do you think I would have been in bed with my husband twenty-one minutes without knowing what he was made of, much more twenty-one years, for I should never have patience to wait so long. My old man cuddles me as close as wax these cold winter nights, and if he was to turn his back to me I would stick a needle into it.

  If the wife asked for a favour,
  Then she flew into a fever,
  Gave to her a precious thump, sir,
  Which after left a largeish lump, sir,
  Then her limbs so straight and tall, sir,
  She turn'd her face against the wall, sir,
  And oft have quarrel'd and much strife, sir,
  Because he would not cuddle the wife, sir.

Why I must say, Mother Chatter, if he had been my husband, I think after hard work all day he must have slept sound, and I would have seen what he was before I rose in the morning, or I'd know the reason why.

  Was woman ever so perplex'd, sir,
  And through life so grievously vex'd, sir,
  And disappointments oft did meet, sir,
  And instead of a kiss, I oft got beat, sir,

Sometimes cuff'd and sometimes scouted,
Because I asked what woman wanted,
And if ever that I marry again, sir,
I'll surely marry a perfect man, sir.

Mother Chatter, – Man, indeed! yes, I hope she will take
care next time she marries, and not be duped in that way
again; and as she was such a bad judge I would advise her
to taste and try first next time.

Mother Sprightly, – I have no doubt but she'll examine
the beard and whiskers of the next man she marries, and
not take a beardless thing at his own word.

With this pretty handsome groom, sir,
She went and spent the honey-moon, sir,
The very first night my love should cuddle,
Up in the clothes he close did huddle;
And with his face against the wall, sir,
He never spoke a word at all, sir,
A maid to bed I then did go, sir,
And a maiden am now, heigho! heigho! sir.

Well, Mother Frisky, how is your old man? Why he is
quite hearty, and every inch a man, none of your sham
husbands; give me the real man or none at all. Well, I am
of your way of thinking, and I hope the next husband she
has she will have thumping children.

Pretty maidens list I pray, sir,
Unto what I now do say, sir,
Taste and try before you buy, sir,
Or you'll get bit as well as I, sir;
See he's perfect in all parts, sir,
Before you join your hand and heart, sir,
You then with all your strength may try, sir,
To be fruitful, increase, and multiply, sir.

216

The Old Marquis and his Blooming Wife

Oh, here's a jolly lark,
   Some strife perhaps there may be,
A Marquis had a wife,
   Oh, such a blooming lady;
She married him they say,
   For title, and remember,
'Twas lovely Miss May,
   And old Mister December.

Old Fidgets lost his wife,
   And sorely now does grumble
When he goes to bed at night,
   He's nobody to fumble.

The old man is seventy eight,
   As sprightly as a donkey,
Such a noble friend is he
   To the Italians and the monkeys.
The lady he did wed,
   He married her one Monday,
Blooming, young, and fair,
   Only seventeen come Sunday.

He cuddled her so sweet,
   The damsel he did flatter,
Singing I for Bobbing Joan,
   And she for stoney batter;
An angel from above,
   The poor old man did think her,
But oh dear, she ran away
   One morning with a tinker.

The old Marquis lost his wife,
   And he was in a sad mess,
Miss was a lady gay,
   An Irish Marchioness;
Lovely seventeen,
   He could not discard her –
Wedded she thought she'd been
   Unto her great grandfather.

Five hundred bright pounds,
   The damages, that got he,
Against the naughty man
   Who robbed him of his lady.
The lawyers they did chaff,
   What fun in court, oh law there
They caught her snug in bed,
   In Sheffield town, in Yorkshire.

This blooming damsel fair,
   Has such a lovely pimple,
Such pretty chesnut hair
   And nigh her mouth a dimple;
A bustle made of gold,
   And I can now remember,
A crinoline to hold
   Poor old Mister December.

Old men, take my advice,
   Or taken in you may be,
If you should wed a nice,
   Sweet frolicsome young lady;
A gay, young Mister June,
   Perhaps they may connive at,
To play to her a tune,
   Just now and then in private.

The poor old man is mad,
    Though he has lots of riches,
He wants another wife,
    Or a larger pair of breeches;
Though past three score and ten,
    If one should meet his fancy,
He says he'll marry again, –
    Oh! don't I love my Nancy.

When he married his sweet wife
    He didn't care for nothing,
He used to lace her stays,
    And then tie up her stockings
He kissed her lovely lips,
    What a darling he did think her,
But she soon gave him the slip,
    And bolted with the tinker.

A single man again,
    His lordship now will be, sirs,
Just threescore and eighteen,
    But another wife wants he, sirs,
To cuddle him at night,
    And his old knees be warming,
What a lark if his next wife
    Should cut away in the morning.
She got old Fidgets off,
    Made cock sure all right,
And with the Yorkshire blade
    She danced a jig at night.

217

Washing Day

The sky with clouds was overcast
    The rain began to fall
My wife she beat the children
    And rais'd a pretty squall
She bade me with a frowning look
    To get out of the way
The deil a bit of comfort is there
    On a washing day
For its thump thump scold scold
    Thump thump away
The deil a bit of comfort is there.

My Kate she is a bonny wife,
    There's no more free from evil,
Except upon a washing day.
    And then she is a devil
The very kittens on the hearth,
    They dare not even play
Away they jump with many a thump
    Upon a washing day
        For its thump, thump etc.

A friend of mine once ask'd me
    How long's poor Jenny's dead,
Lamenting the good creature
    And sorry I was wed
To such a scolding vixen
    Whilst he had been at sea
The truth it was he chanc'd to come
    Upon a washing day
        For its thump, thump etc.

I ask'd him to stay and dine
  'Come come' said I
I'll no denial take – you shall
  Though Kate is in the suds;
But what he had to dine upon
  in faith I shall not say
But I'll wager he'll not come again
  Upon a washing day
    For its thump, thump etc.

On that sad morning when I rise
  I make a fervent prayer
Unto the gods that it may be
  Throughout the day quite fair
That not a gown or handkerchief
  May in the ditch be laid
For should it happen so egad
I should catch a broken head
    For its thump, thump etc.

SIX

WISE AND FOOLISH VIRGINS

218

The New Balow

OR

A Wenche's Lementation for the loss of her Sweetheart, he having left her with a Babe to play her, being the fruits of her folly.

Balow, my Babe, weep not for me:
Whose greatest grief's for wronging thee
But pity her deserving smart,
Who can but blame her own kind heart,
For trusting to a flattering friend;
The fairest tongue, the falsest mind.
   Balow, my babe &c

Balow, my Babe, ly still and sleep,
It grieves me sore to hear thee weep:
If thou be still I will be glad,
Thy weeping makes thy mother sad;
Balow, my boy, thy mother's joy,
Thy father wrought me great annoy.
   Balow, balow &c

First when he came to court my love,
With sugred words he did me move:
His flattering and fained chear
To me that time did not appear.
But now, I see that cruel he
Cares neither for my babe nor me.
   Balow, balow, &c

I cannot choose but love him still,
Altho' that he hath done me ill,
For he hath stolen away my heart,
And from him it cannot depart:
In weal or wo, where ere he go,
I'le love him though he be my foe.
    Balow, balow, &c

But peace my comfort, curse not him.
Who now in seas of grief doth swim,
Perhaps of death: for who can tell
Whether the Judge of heaven or hell,
By some predestined death,
Revenging me hath stopt his breath,
    Balow, balow &c

If I were near those fatal bounds,
Where he ly groaning in his wounds,
Repeating as he pants for breath,
Her name that wounds more deep than death,
O then what woman's heart so strong
Would not forget the greatest wrong?
    Balow, balow &c

If linen lack, for my love's sake,
Whom I once loved, then would I take
My smock even from my body meet,
And wrap him in that winding sheet;
Ay me how happy had I bin,
If he had nere been wrapt therein.
    Balow, balow, &c

Balow, my babe, spare thou thy tears,
Until thou come to wit and years;
Thy griefs are gathering to a sum,
Heaven grant thee patience till they come,

A mother's fault, a father's shame,
A hapless state, a bastard's name.
 Balow, balow, &c

Be still, my babe, and sleep awhile,
And when thou wakes then sweetly smile!
But smile not as thy father did
To cusen maids: O heaven forbid
And yet into thy face I see
Thy father dear, which tempted me.
 Balow, balow, &c

O! if I were a maid again,
All young men's flatteries I'd refrain:
Because unto my grief I find
That they are faithless and unkind;
Their tempting terms hath bred my harm,
Bear witness babe lyes in my arm.
 Balow, balow, &c

Balow, my babe, spare yet thy tears,
Until thou come to wit and years;
Perhaps yet thou may come to be
A courteour by disdaining me:
Poor me, poor me, alas, poor me,
My own two eyes have blinded me.
 Balow, balow, &c

On Love and fortune I complain,
On them, and on my self also:
But most of all my own two eyes
The chiefest workers of my wo;
For they have caused so my smart,
That I must die without a heart.
 Balow, balow, &c

Balow, my babe, thy father's dead –
To me the Prodigal hath plaid:
Of heaven and earth regardless, he
Prefer'd the wars to me and thee,
I doubt that now his cursing mind
Make him eat acorns with the swine.
 Balow, balow, &c

Farewel, farewel, most faithless youth
That ever kist a woman's mouth,
Let never a woman after me
Submit unto the curtesie;
For if she do, O cruel thou,
Would wrong them: O who can tell how?
 Balow, balow, &c

219

The Maid's Complaint for want of a Dil doul

> *This Girl long time had in a sickness been,*
> *Which many maids do call the sickness green:*
> *I wish she may some comfort find, poor Soul,*
> *And have her belly fill'd with a* Dil *doul.*

Young men give ear to me a while,
 if you to merriment are inclin'd,
And i'le tell you a story shall make you to smile,
 of late done by a woman kind:
And as she went musing all alone,
 I heard her to sigh, to sob and make moan,
For a dill doul, dil doul, dil doul doul
(*quoth she*) *I'm undone if I ha'nt a dil doul.*

548

For I am a Maid and a very good Maid,
   and sixteen years of age am I,
And fain would I part with my Maiden-head,
   if any good fellow would with me lye:
But none to me ever yet proffer'd such love,
   as to lye by my side and give me a shove
With his dil doul, dill doul, dil doul,
   O happy were I &c

At night when I go to bed,
   thinking for to take my rest,
Strange fancies comes in my head,
   I pray for that which I love best:
For it is a comfort and pleasure doth bring
   to women that hath such a pritty fine thing,
Call'd a dill doul, dill doul, dill doul doul,
   then happy were I &c

Last week I walked in the *Strand,*
   I met with my Sister, a handsome Lass,
I kindly took her by the hand,
   this question of her I did ask;
Whether she kept still a Maiden alone,
   or whether her maiden-head was fled or gone,
For a dill doul, dill doul, dill doul doul,
   O happy were &c

THE SECOND PART

Kind sister, quoth she, to tell you the truth,
   it has gone this twelve months day;
I freely gave it to a handsome youth,
   that us'd to sport and play:
To grieve for the loss of it I never shall,
   if I had ten thousand I would give um all
For a dill doul, dill doul, dil doul doul,
   O my &c

She making this answer, I bid her adieu,
   and told her I could no longer stay,
I let go her hand, and I straight left the *Strand*,
   and to *Covent-Garden* I hasted away:
Where lively young gallants do use to resort,
   to pick up young lasses & shew um fine sport
With a dil doul, dil doul, dil doul doul,
   yet none &c

I would i'de a sweet heart, as some Maids have,
   that little know how to pleasure a man,
I'de keep him frolicksome, gallant and brave,
   and make as much on him as anyone can:
Before any good thing he should lack,
   i'de sell all my Coats & Smock from my back
For his dil doul, dil doul, dill doul doul,
   and all my &c

Besides, young men, I have store of money,
   good red gold and Silver bright,
And he shall be master of every peny,
   that marries with me and yields me delight.
For why, t'other night I heard my dame *Nancy*
   declare how her master did tickle her fancy,
With his dill doul, dill doul, dill doul doul,
   then what e're it cost me i'le have a dil doul.

Then come to me my bonny Lad,
   while I am in the prime, I pray,
And take a good bargin while it is to be had,
   and do not linger your time away.
'Tis money, you see, makes many a man rich:
   then come along rub on the place that doth itch
For a dill doul, dil doul, dil doul doul,
   take all my money, give me a dill doul.

220

The Thankful Country Lass

OR

The Jolly Batchelor Kindly Entertained

I met with a Country Lass,
　　and thus I began to wooe,
'Shall I lay thee upon the Grass?'
　'*I, marry, and thank you too!*'

'And shall I embrace thee then,
　　as Lovers are wont to do?'
Her Answer was to me agen,
　'*I, marry, ⟨and thank you too⟩.*'

'Wilt thou give me leave', I said,
'to dally a while with you,
And make a Mother of a Maid?'
　'*I, marry, ⟨and thank you too⟩.*'

'In case I am loath to live,
　　as marry'd men often do;
Yet wilt thou take what I can give?'
　'*I, marry, ⟨and thank you too⟩.*'

'My dear, to enjoy the bliss,
　　I crave but this boon of you,
To give me leave to court and kiss.'
　'*I, marry, ⟨and thank you too⟩.*'

'Give me thy Virginity,
　　and thou shalt have mine in lieu:
You may have what you please of me'.
　'*I, marry, ⟨and thank you too⟩.*'

'But what if thy Belly swell;
   my dearest, now tell me true.
Wilt thou be free to take it well?'
   '*I, marry, ⟨and thank you too⟩.*'

'I'll get thee a Champion Boy,
   and will thy pleasures renew,
If I thy charms may but enjoy.'
   '*I, marry, ⟨and thank you too⟩.*'

'My Jewel and heart's delight,
   if that thy Lodging I knew,
I'll come and lye with thee all night.'
   '*I, marry, ⟨and thank you too⟩.*'

'I live in the Town of *Lynn*,   (*She replies*)
   next door to the *Anchor* blew;
Come night or day, I'll let you in,
   I, marry, ⟨and thank you too⟩.'

'I never intend to wed,
   for fear my heart should rue;
Yet shall I have thy Maiden-head?'
   '*I, marry, ⟨and thank you too⟩.*'

She made not the least demur,
   While he did kiss and wooe,
But took what e'er he proffer'd her,
   '*I, marry, and thank you too!*'

221

The Lass of Lynn's New Joy, for finding a Father for her Child

Come listen, and hear me tell
    the end of a Tale so true,
The Lass that made her Belly Swell,
    with *Marry and thank ye too*.

With many hard Sobs and Throws,
    and Sorrow enough (I wot)
She had wept Tears, the whole Town knows,
    could fill a whole Chamber-pot.

For Pleasure with Pain she pays,
    her Belly and Shame to hide
So hard all day she Lac'd her Stayes,
    as pinch'd both her Back and Side.

Oh! were not my Belly full,
    a Husband I'de have to Night;
There's *George* the *Tapster* at the *Bull*,
    I'm sure I'm his whole Delight.

This day on his Knees he Swore
    he Lov'd me above his Life,
Were not my Pipkin Crackt before,
    I vow I would be his Wife.

Her Mother that heard her, spoke,
    O take him at's word, said she,
A Husband, Child's, the only Cloak
    to cover a Great Belly.

Her Mother she show'd the way,
   and straight without more ado,
She took him to the Church next day,
   and *Marry'd and thank'd him too.*

But Oh! when he came to Bed,
   the saddest News now to tell ye;
On a soft place his hand he laid,
   and found she'd a Rising Belly.

At which he began to Roar,
   Your Fancy it has been Itching;
By th'Meat in your Pot, I find, you Whore,
   you've had a Cook in your Kitchin.

O fie, my dear Love, said she,
   what puts you into this Dump?
For what tho' Round my Belly be,
   it is only Fat and Plump.

Good Flesh it is all, ye Chit,
   besides, the plain truth to tell,
I've eat so much, the Sack-Posset
   has made my poor Belly Swell.

Nay, then I've wrong'd thee, he crys,
   I beg thy sweet pardon for't;
I'll get thee a Son before we rise,
   and so he fell to the Sport.

No, the Boy it was got before,
   the Midwife soon wisht him Joy:
But, Oh! e're full five Months were o're,
   she brought him a lusty Boy.

My Wife brought to Bed, says *George*,
    I hope she has but Miscarry'd;
A Boy! says he, how can that be,
    when we are but five Months Marry'd.

Five Months! has the man lost his Wits?
    crys Midwife, what does the Fool say?
Five months by Days, and five by Nights,
    sh'has gone her full time to a day.

The Child's all your own, by my truth,
    the pritty Eyes do but see,
Had it been spit out of your Mouth,
    more like you it could not be.

Nay then, my kind Gossips all,
    says *George*, let us Merry make;
I'll Tap a Barrel of stout Ale,
    and send for a Groaning-Cake.

The Gossips they Laugh'd and Smil'd,
    and Mirth it went round all through;
She'd found a Father for her Child,
    Hye, Marry and thank him too.

222

The Unfortunate Miller

OR

The Country Lasses witty Invention
Shewing

How he would have Layn with A Maid in his own house; As also the manner of the Cheat put upon him. By which meanes his man *Lawrence* grafted a large pair of *horns* upon his Masters Head.

here = hear] All you that desire to here of a jest,
Come listen a while and it shall be exprest;
It is of a Miller that liv'd very near,
The like of this ditty you never did here,
A handsome young Damsel she came to his Mill,
To have her Corn Ground with a Ready good Will,
' see' in
original As soon as he saw her fair beauty so bright,
He caused this young Damosel to tarry all night.

Said he, my dear Jewel, it will be ne'r Morn,
Before my Man Lawrence can grind my Dears Corn,
And therefore if thou wilt be ruled by me,
At home in my Parlour thy Lodging shall be,
For I am inflam'd with thy Amorous Charms,
And therefore this Night thou shalt sleep in my arms,
I swear it, and therefore it needs must be so,
It is but in vain for to answer me no.

At this the young Damsel she blushing did stand,
But strait ways the Master took her by the hand,
And leading her home to young *Gillian* his wife,
Said he, my sweet honey, the joy of my Life,
Be kind to this Maid, for her Father I know,
And let her lye here in the Parlour below,
Stout Lawrence my servant, and I, we shall stay
All night in the Mill till the dawning of Day.

To what he desir'd she straitways agreed,
And then to the Mill he did hasten with speed,
He ready was then to leap out of his skin,
To think of the Bed which he meant to Lye in;
Now when he was gone, the Maid told his intent,
To *Gillian*, and they a new Project invent,
By which they well fitted this Crafty young blade;
The Miller by Lawrence a Cuckold was made.

The Maid and his Wife they chang'd Bed for that night,
So that when the Miller came for his delight,
Straight way to the Parlour Bed he did Repair,
Instead of the Damsel wife *Gillian* was there,
Which he did Imagin had been the young Lass,
When after some hours in pleasure they past,
He ris, and return'd to the Mill, like one wild,
For fear he had Got the young Damsel with child.

Then to his man Lawrence the miller did say,
I have a young damsel both bony and Gay,   [*bony = bonny*]
Her Eyes are like diamonds, her cheeks sweet & fair,
They may with the Rose and the Lilly Compare,
Her lips they are like the rich coral for Red,
This Lass is at home in my Parlour a Bed,
And if you go home you may freely enjoy,
With her the sweet pleasure, for she is not Coy.

His masters kind Proffer he did not refuse,
But was brisk and Airy, and pleased with the News,
But said, to your self much beholding I am,
And for a Requital i'le give you my Ram;
This done lusty Lawrence away home he goes,
And stript of his Coat, Breeches, likewise shooes and hose,
And went into Bed to *Gillian* his dame,
Yet Lawrence for this was not worthy of blame.

He little Imagen'd his Dame was in bed,
And therefore his heart was the freeer from dread,
The minutes in Pastime and pleasure they spent,
Unknown to them both she injoy'd true content,
Now after a while he his dame had Imbrac'd,
He Rose and Return'd to the mill in all hast,
Telling his master of all the delight,
Which he had injoy'd with that damsel this Night.

Next morning the maid to the mill did Repair,
The miller and Lawrence his servant was there,
His master then whisper'd this word in her Ear,
How like you to lye with a miller, my dear?
At this the young damsel then laughing out Right;
And said I chang'd Beds with young *Gillian* last Night;
If you injoy'd any it was your sweet wife,
For my part I ne'r lay with man in my Life.

At this he began for to Rave, stamp and stare,
Both scratching his Elbows and Hauling his hair,
And like one distracted about he did Run,
And oftentimes Crying, ha! what have I done,
Was ever poor miller so finely betray'd,
By Lawrence my man, I am a Cuckold made,
The damsel she laught, and was pleas'd in her mind,
And said he was very well serv'd in his kind.

223

Amintas and Claudia

OR

The Merry Shepherdess

Calm was the Evening and clear was the Sky
    when the new budding flowers do spring,
When all alone went *Amintas* and I
    to hear the sweet nightingales sing.
I sate and he laid him down by me,
    and scarcely his breath he could draw,
      But when with a fear,
      He begun to draw near,
He was dasht with a ha, ha, ha, ha, ha, ha, ha,
  ha, ha, ha, ha, ha, ha.

He blusht to himself and lay still for a while
    and his modesty curb'd his desire,
But strait I convinc'd all his fears with a smile
    and added new flames to his fire:
Ah, *Silvia*, said he, thou art cruel,
    to keep thy poor lover in awe,
      And once more he prest
      His hands to my brest,
But was dasht with a &c.

I know 'twas his passion which caused all his fear,
    and therefore I pittied his case,
I whispered him softly, there was nobody near,
    and I laid my cheek close to his face:
But as he grew bolder and bolder,
    a Shepherd came by us and saw,
      And just as our bliss
      Began with a kiss,
He burst out, &c.

Come my own dear, lets retire a while,
    and hasten us down to the Grove,
      Where in some shade
      That nature hath made,
We'l make a rehearsal of love,
And when with love tales we are tired,
    and occasion does bid us withdraw,
      We then from our feat,
      Will make a retreat,
And laugh out, &c.

I having consented, away we did go,
    and found out the thick of the Wood;
      But when we came there,
      I began for to fear,
His meaning portended no good:

My beauty likewise he would oftentimes praise,
  for the rarest that ever he saw,
    And there he would skip,
    From my hand to my lip,
But was dasht with a ha, ha, ha, ha, ha, ha, ha,
  ha, ha, ha, ha, ha, ha.

Sometimes he wou'd sigh, and sometimes he wou'd weep,
  and pray me to pitty his case;
    But I found out by that
    What he would be at,
His meaning I read in his face:
I bid him desist and give over his suit,
  For I told him my Will was a law,
    And if he were pleas'd
    To have his pain eas'd,
He must laugh, &c.

You know, said *Amintas*, how long I have lov'd,
  and ever restrain⟨'d⟩ my desire,
    And now with your scorn,
    Which cannot be born⟨e⟩,
You seek to extinguish my fire.
My vertue will justifie all that I do,
  to keep you at distance and awe:
    And your loose desire
    Will sooner expire,
Then mirth, &c.

He sat like a Mute, and was still for a while,
  consulting what answer to make,
    When all in hast
    He imbraced my Wast,
And no more denyals would take.
He vow'd, though my heart it were frozen,
  his indeavour he'd use, it to thaw;

If the heat of your blood
Could do any good,
Which made &c.

I found that his passion began to Rebel,
   and Reason no more could prevail,
      Thought I to myself,
      I am now on a shelf,
And know not which way for to fall;
But if by my Policy I can get off,
   and my honor preserve without flaw,
      Ile ingage me no more,
      On such dangerous shore,
But at home, &c.

I used some perswasions that Evening was nigh,
   for the Sun it began to decline,
      And fearing some Swain,
      Of the neighboring plain,
Might come for to water his Kine;
I pray'd him return and walk softly along,
   when 'twere dark i'd submit to his law,
      Where in my own Bower,
      For the space of an hour
He should kiss, &c.

His thoughts being transported with joy, he conceiv'd,
   ne're feared, but my promise i'd keep,
      But instead of a Wench,
      He found such a Drench,
As charm'd all his senses a sleep:
The vertue whereof through his vitals disperst
   and his faculties purer did draw;
      and when I had done,
      Away I did run,
And laught out with a ha, ha, ha, ha, ha, ha, ha,
   ha, ha, ha, ha, ha, ha.

224

The Country Girl's Policy

OR

The Cockney Outwitted

All you that are to mirth inclin'd, come tarry here a little while:
Pray read it once, and I do not fear, but soon it will make you
to smile.
The Londoners call us 'country Fools,' and laugh at us every day;
But I'll let them see, before I have done, we know as good things as
they.

A jolly young girl in *Hertfordshire*, who lately had learned
to Dance;
In less than the Space of one whole Year she light of a
Child by chance.
Being very poor this cunning whore, upon a Certain
Day,
Resolved was she the City to see, so to *London* she took
her way.

With an old straw Hat, and her tail pinn'd up, and with
Dirt instead of Fringe,
Not long ago, this cunning slut did come to the *Royal*
Exchange;
With the Child in a Basket under her arm, close covered,
as it is said,
With a clean white cloth, and at each end hung out a
Goose's head.

She saw two Stock-jobbers standing by, she then unto
one did say,
Gaffer, what stately Church is this? come tell me now I
pray!

The other to her smiling said, How like a Fool you talk!
This is no church, it is the '*Change*, where all the
    Merchants walk.

Is this the '*Change*, good Sir? she said, a glorious place it
    be;
A finer place, in all my life, I never before did see:
I'll warrant you there's fine Chambers in't, as you and I
    do live!
Now if you'll let me go and see, a Penny to you I will
    give.

The one said, Your basket I will hold, and tarry here
    below,
Whilst my Consort goes up with you, the Chambers for
    to show.
She answered, I am afraid, that when I do come down,
You will be gone, and I would not lose my basket for a
    crown.

I am not such a Man, ⟨he⟩ cry'd, and that I'd have you
    know;
She gave it him, and with her guide she up the stairs did
    go;
She view'd the pictures very fine, and did them much
    admire;
He soon dropp'd her, she downstairs run, and after him
    did enquire.

She straight runs up to a Merchant, Good honest man,
    said she,
Did you not see a thick tall man that had two Geese of
    me?
Alas! said he, poor country girl, our Cocknies are too
    quick;
Go home and tell your Country Girls of this fine *London*
    trick.

She stamp'd and cry'd, Thus to be bit, would make a
    body swear.
I'll never come to the *Royal Exchange* any more to sell
    my ware;
For by a couple of cheating knaves, alas! I am undone.
She gave a stamp, and laugh'd aloud, and then away she
    run.

But now we will to the Jobbers turn, who thought they
    had got a Prize;
They stept into an Ale-house, and sent for both their
    wives.
They told them the story, with hearts both merry and
    light,
Said they, We'll have a Frolic on't, and roast them both
    at night.

The women cry'd, No, one at a time, the further they
    will go;
the other we'll have at another house, and order the
    matter so.
Thus they began to jangle, and got on either Side;
But all the while the Basket stood, without ever a Knot
    unty'd.

Then opening of the Basket, as I the Truth unfold,
There did they find a curious Boy, just about five Weeks
    old.
The women flew into a damnable rage; O how they did
    scold and curse!
Instead of a Cook, ye rogues, said they, you must run
    and call a Nurse.

The one said, This is your bastard, sirrah, you have had
    by some common whore.
If these be your Geese, ye Rogues! she said, I never shall
    love Geese more.

The one she kick'd the drink all down, the other whipp'd
    up the Glass,
And after she had drunk the Beer, she threw it and cut
    his face.

There was helter-skelter, the Devil to pay, oh how the
    Pots did fly!
Just as they were in the midst of the Fray, the child began
    to cry:
There were clouts and blankets all beshit, such sights are
    seldom seen;
I hope it will learn them both more wit, how they
    meddle with Geese again.

They put it out for three shillings a week, which is
    Eighteen-pence a piece,
Which they pay every Saturday Night, in remembrance
    of the Geese.
Come, here's a health to the Country Lass, I think she
    was not to blame;
If she has but Wit to take care of her T—, she may pass
    for a Maid again.

225

There was a Knight and he was Young

There was a Knight and he was Young,
    A riding along the way, Sir;
And there he met a Lady fair,
    Among the Cocks of Hay, Sir:
Quoth he, shall you and I Lady,
    Among the Grass lye down a;
And I will have a special Care,
    Of rumpling of your Gown a.

If you will go along with me,
    Unto my Father's Hall, Sir;
You shall enjoy my Maiden-head,
    And my Estate and all, Sir:
So he mounted her on a milk-white Steed,
    Himself upon another;
And then they rid upon the Road,
    Like Sister and like Brother.

And when she came to her Father's House,
    Which was moated round about, Sir;
She stepped streight within the Gate,
    And shut this Young Knight out, Sir,
Here is a Purse of Gold, she said,
    Take it for your Pains, Sir;
And I will send my Father's Man,
    To go home with you again, Sir.

And if you meet a Lady fair,
    As you go thro' the next Town, Sir;
You must not fear the Dew of the Grass,
    Nor the rumpling of her Gown, Sir:
And if you meet a Lady Gay,
    As you go by the Hill, Sir;
If you will not when you may,
    You shall not when you will, Sir.

There is a Dew upon the Grass,[1]
[Your=My(?)]   Will spoil your Damask Gown a;
[Your=My(?)] Which has cost your Father dear,
    Many a Shilling and a Crown a:
There is a Wind blows from the *West*
    Soon will dry the Ground a;
And I will have a special Care,
[My=Your(?)]   Of the rumpling of my Gown a.

        [1]Presumably the second stanza, misplaced.

226

The Lass of Islington

There was a Lass of *Islington*,
  As I have heard many tell;
And she would to Fair *London* go,
  Fine Apples and Pears to sell:
And as along the Streets she flung,
  With her basket on her Arm:
Her Pears to sell, you may know right well,
  This fair Maid meant no harm.

But as she tript along the Street,
  Her pleasant Fruit to sell;
A Vintner did with her meet,
  Who lik'd this Maid full well:
Quoth he, fair Maid, what have you there?
  In basket decked brave;
Fine Pears, quoth she, and if it please ye,
  A taste Sir you shall have.

The Vintner he took a Taste,
  And lik'd it well, for why;
This Maid he thought of all the rest,
  Most pleasing to his Eye:
Quoth he, fair Maid I have a Suit,
  That you to me must grant;   [*that*=*then* (?)
Which if I find you be so kind,
  Nothing that you shall want.

Thy Beauty doth so please my Eye,
  And dazles so my sight;
That now of all my Liberty,
  I am deprived quite:

Then prithee now consent to me,
   And do not put me by;
It is but one small courtesie,
   All Night with you to lie.

Sir, if you lie with me one Night,
   As you propound to me;
I do expect that you should prove,
   Both courteous, kind, and free:
And for to tell you all in short,
   It will cost you Five Pound,
A Match, a Match, the Vintner said,
   And so let this go round.

When he had lain with her all Night,
   Her Money she did crave,
O stay, quoth he, the other Night,
   And thy Money thou shalt have:
I cannot stay, nor I will not stay,
   I needs must now be gone,
Why then thou may'st thy Money go look,
   For Money I'll pay thee none.

This Maid she made no more ado,
   But to a Justice went;
And unto him she made her moan,
   Who did her Case lament:
She said she had a Cellar Let out,
   To a Vintner in the Town;
And how that he did then agree
   Five Pound to pay her down.

But now quoth she, the Case is thus,
   No Rent that he will pay;
Therefore your Worship I beseech,
   To send for him this Day:

Then strait the Justice for him sent,
   And asked the Reason why;
That he would pay this Maid no Rent?
   To which he did Reply.

Although I hired a Cellar of her,
   And the Possession was mine
I ne'er put any thing into it,
   But one poor Pipe of Wine:
Therefore my Bargain it was hard,
   As you may plainly see;
I from my Freedom was Debarr'd,
   Then good Sir favour me.

This Fair Maid being ripe of Wit,
   She strait reply'd again;
There were two Butts more at the Door,
   Why did you not roul them in?
You had your Freedom and your Will,
   As is to you well known;
Therefore I do desire still,
   For to receive my own.

The Justice hearing of their Case,
   Did then give Order strait;
That he the Money should pay down,
   She should no longer wait:
Withal he told the Vintner plain
   If he a Tennant be;
He must expect to pay the same,
   For he could not sit Rent-free.

But when the Money she had got,
   She put it in her Purse:
And clapt her Hand on the Cellar Door,
   And said it was never the worse:

Which caused the People all to Laugh,
    To see this Vintner Fine:
Out-witted by a Country Girl,
    About his Pipe of Wine.

227

'As I sat at my Spinning-Wheel'

As I sat at my Spinning-Wheel,
A bonny Lad there passed by,
I kenn'd him round, and I lik'd him weel,
Geud Feth he had a bonny Eye:
    My Heart new panting, 'gan to feel,
    But still I turn'd my Spinning-Wheel.

Most gracefully he did appear,
As he my Presence did draw near,
And round about my slender Waste
He clasp'd his Arms, and me embrac'd:
    To kiss my Hand he down did kneel,
    As I sat at my Spinning-Wheel.

[small = slender

My Milk white Hand he did extol,
And prais'd my Fingers long and small,
And said, there was no Lady fair,
That ever could with me compare:
    Those pleasing Words my Heart did feel,
    But still I turn'd my Spinning-Wheel.

Altho' I seemingly did chide,
Yet he would never be deny'd,
But did declare his Love the more,
Until my Heart was Wounded sore;
    That I my Love cou'd scarce conceal,
    But yet I turn'd my Spinning-Wheel.

As for my Yarn, my Rock and Reel,
And after that my Spinning-Wheel,
He bid me leave them all with Speed
And gang with him to yonder Mead:
  My panting Heart strange Flames did feel,
  Yet still I turn'd my Spinning-Wheel.

He stopp'd and gaz'd, and blithly said,
Now speed the Wheel, my bonny Maid,
But if thou'st to the Hay-Cock go,
I'll learn thee better Work I trow,
  Geud Feth, I lik'd him passing weel,
  But still I turn'd my Spinning-Wheel.

He lowly veil'd his Bonnet oft,
And sweetly kist my Lips so soft;
Yet still between each Honey Kiss,
He urg'd me on to farther Bliss:
  'Till I resistless Fire did feel,
  Then let alone my Spinning-Wheel.

Among the pleasant Cocks of Hay,
Then with my bonny Lad I lay,
What Damsel ever could deny,
A Youth with such a Charming Eye?
  The pleasure I cannot reveal,
  It far surpast the Spinning-Wheel.

228

The Fair Maid of the West

Who sold her Maidenhead for a High-crown'd Hat

I pray attend unto this Jest,
A youthful maiden in the West,
She was gay and handsome too,
As I in truth may tell to you.

And therefore now I pray attend,
Unto these lines which I have penn'd
And if you do not say the same,
I think you will be much to blame.

Upon a day it happen'd so,
That she would to market go,
Taking her money great and small,
To buy a high-crown'd hat withal.

As soon as e'er she did come there,
Unto a shop she did repair;
Where soon a young batchelor,
Did fix his wanton eyes on her.

Kind Sir, said she, a hat I'd have,
And pray let me have what I crave,
One that is fine and light to wear,
He straight did fit her to a hair.

What is the price? she then reply'd,
Seven shillings I have deny'd;
I will fit you well he said
Because you are a hansome Maid.

I'll let you have it for a crown,
If that you'll let me lay you down
Upon my soft and downy bed,
There to enjoy your Maidenhead.

She seem'd to blush and stand awhile,
At length she answer'd with a smile,
What Maidenhead and money too,
No, kind sir, that will not do.

He strait did whisper in her ear,
I will befriend thee now my dear,
Let me enjoy my heart's delight,
And you shall have the Hat outright.

This maid she did no longer stand,
But struck the bargain out of hand:
And having given the Youth content,
She took her Hat and away she went.

Now as she past along the way,
She to herself these words did say,
With a fine hat I now am sped,
And all for a silly Maidenhead.

Then coming to her mother strait,
This hopeful bargain to relate,
O Mother! o mother! as sure as I'm true,
I have a Hat and money too.

Why Hussey her Mother then reply'd
How was the haberdasher paid?
He had my Maidenhead said she,
Which was a great plague unto me.

The good old wife flew in a rage,
And nothing could her wrath assuage,
Thrusting her daughter out of doors,
And said, she'd never own her more

If this same Hat she did not take,
And to the Town again make haste,
And give it him with whom she had lain
And bring her Maidenhead back again.

With sighs and tears she did lament,
As to the market town she went,
To tell the shopkeeper therefore,
He must her Maidenhead restore.

For why, my mother won't agree
That I should part with it, said she.
Why then, come in, I will freely part
With it to thee with all my heart.

As soon as she did it receive,
Poor heart she did no longer grieve,
But made a curtsey to the ground,
Because she had this kindness found.

Then home again this lass did hie,
And told her mother presently,
An honest man he seem'd to be,
For he restor'd it willingly.

Well daughter had it not been so,
It might have been your overthrow;
But since he did it you restore,
See that you play the fool no more.

229

Roger and Dolly

BY HENRY CAREY

Young Roger came tapping at Dolly's window,
    Tumpaty, tumpaty, tump.
He begg'd for admittance, she answer'd him, No!
    Glumpaty, glumpaty, glump.
My Dolly, my dear, your true love is here,
    Dumpaty, dumpaty, dump.
No, Roger, no, as you came you may go,
    Clumpaty, clumpaty, clump.

Oh! what is the reason, dear Dolly, he cried,
    Pumpaty, pumpaty, pump.
That thus I'm cast off and unkindly deny'd,
    Frumpaty, frumpaty, frump.
Some rival more dear I guess has been here,
    Crumpaty, crumpaty, crump.
Suppose there's been two; pray, sir, what's that to you?
    Numpaty, numpaty, nump.

O, then with a sigh a sad farewell he took,
    Lumpaty, lumpaty, lump.
And all in despair he leapt into the brook,
    Flumpaty, flumpaty, flump.
His courage it cool'd, he found himself fool'd,
    Trumpaty, trumpaty, trump.
He swam to the shore and saw Dolly no more,
    Rumpaty, rumpaty, rump.

And then she recall'd and recall'd him again,
    Humpaty, humpaty, hump.

But he like a madman ran over the plain,
    Stumpaty, stumpaty, stump.
Determin'd to find a damsel more kind,
    Plumpaty, plumpaty, plump.
While Dolly's afraid she shall die an old maid,
    Mumpaty, mumpaty, mump.

230

Three Maids a-Milking would Go

Three maids a milking would go,
Three maids a milking would go,
The wind it blew high, the wind it blew low,
Which toss'd their milk pails to and fro.

They met with a man by the way,
And one of them to him did say,
Saying, kind sir, have you got any skill,
For to catch us a small bird or two.

O yes, I have a very great skill,
O yes, I have a very great skill.
If you would go with me to yonder shady tree,
I will catch you a bird to your will.

To yon shady green grove they went
To yon shady green grove they went
And he caught her a bird upon her own ground,
As soon as he knew her intent.

Then he set her against a green tree,
Then he set her against a green tree,
And he beat the bush and the bird flew in,
A little above my love's knee.

[two = tway(?)]

Then her sparklin' eyes turn'd round
As if she had been in a sound.
Saying I caught a bird upon my will,
Picking upon its own ground.

[sound =
swound (?)

This pretty fair maid she fell sick,
This pretty fair maid she fell sick,
The bird it stop'd up, and the apron tuck'd in,
Until it was forty weeks old.

Pretty maidens be ruled by me,
Pretty maidens be ruled by me.
Never catch a small bird upon the green ground,
But catch them upon the green tree.

So here's a health to the bird in the bush,
Likewise to the linnet and t⟨h⟩rush,
For birds of a feather will all flock together,
Let their parents say little or much.

231

The Foggy Dew

When I was a batchelor early and young,
    I followed the weaving trade,
And all the harm ever I done,
    Was courting a servant maid.
I courted her the summer season,
    And part of the winter too,
And many a night I rolled her in my arms,
    All over the Foggy dew.

One night as I lay on my bed,
    As I laid fast asleep,

There came a pretty fair maid,
   And most bitterly did weep.
She wept she mourned she tore her hair,
   Crying, alas what shall I do,
This night I'm resolved to come to bed with you
   For fear of the Foggy dew.

It was in the first part of the night,
   We both did sport and play,
And in the latter part of the night,
   She slept in my arms till day.
When broad day-light did appear,
   She cried I am undone,
Hold your tongue you foolish girl,
   The Foggy dew is ⟨gone⟩.

[Broadside:
   '*done*'

Suppose that we should have a child,
   It would cause us to smile,
Suppose that we should have another
   It would make us laugh awhile.
Suppose that we should have another,
   And another one too,
would make you leave off your foolish tricks
   And think no more of the Foggy dew.

I love this young girl dearly,
   I loved her as my life,
took this girl and married her,
   And made her my lawful wife.
never told her of her faults,
   Nor never intend to do,
But every time she winks or smiles,
   Sh⟨e⟩ th⟨i⟩nks of the Foggy ⟨dew⟩.

Tragic Verses

Come all fair maids both far and near and listen unto me,
While unto you I do relate a dreadful Tragedy,
A deed of blood I will unfold which lately came to light,
When 'tis made known, you'll surely own you never
   heard the like.

'Tis of an honest farmer's child, a damsel fair and young,
Who was in tender years beguil'd all by a flattering
   tongue,
The finest lady in the land could not with her compare,
Her dimpled cheeks and rosy looks how charming sweet
   they were.

Crowds of admirers flocking came, to gain fair Susan's
   love;
But none her favour could obtain, nor her affections
   move,
Till by mischance a youth she met, as fate would have it
   so,
Who caught her heart in Cupid's net and prov'd her
   overthrow.

A naval Captain of renown, beguil'd her tender youth,
Deceit and lies he did disguise with air of seeming truth,
He prais'd her looks, her shape, her air, vow'd she should
   be his wife,
And thus did vilely her ensnare – then took her precious
   life.

When he had thus her ruin prov'd by many a solemn vow,
The very maid he vow'd to love was hateful in his view.

With bitter tears she did implore that he'd his vows
fulfil;
But all in vain – she charm'd no more now he had had
his will.

She wrote a letter which she thought would grieve his
heart full sore,
And tenderly she him besought, to mind the vows he
swore,
T'was you that did my heart trepan, which now in tears
I rue –
Slighted many an honest man all for the love of you.

I wish that my young babe was born and on the nurse's
knee,
And I myself was dead and gone and the grass grown
over me.
When he this letter through had read, which expos'd his
villainy,
A deadly thought came in his head her butcher for to be

With seeming kindness in his face which made poor
Susan gay,
He did appoint a lonely place to meet with her next day
The hour arriv'd, she hasten'd there to the appointment
true,
Where the deceitful murderer the lovely damsel slew.

When she beheld his deadly knife she rais'd her lovely
face,
Crying, Oh! spare, Oh! spare my life and leave me to
disgrace,
Have pity on your unborn babe tho' you have none for
me;
Alas! a dark untimely grave, my bridal bed will be.

Her lovely face, her beauteous eyes, for mercy plead in
    vain,
Of no avail were tears or cries unmov'd he did remain,
He rais'd his arm, – a deadly plunge, and down she
    weltering lay,
And while her heart's-blood stain'd the ground, with
    dying breath did say.

'Monster, the fearful crime you've done heaven's Lord
    will bring to light,
No human eye is looking on – none sees the cruel sight.
Yet righteous King of heaven and earth my blood doth
    cry to thee,
To visit my untimely death that all mankind may see.'

Now when this deed of blood was done he dug a hole
    so deep,
And thrust her murdered body in, then homeward did
    retreat,
But vengeance did his crime requite for to his great
    dismay,
The horrid murder came to light all in a wond'rous way.

He did confess – they dug the ground while hundreds
    came to view,
And here the murder'd corpse they found, of her who
    lov'd so true,
In irons now in Prison strong lamenting he does lie;
And, by the laws condemn'd ere long, most justly he
    will die.

233

Leicester Chambermaid

It's of a brisk young butcher, as I have heard 'em say
He started out of London town upon a certain day,
Says he, a frolic I will have, my fortune for to try,
I will go into Leicestershire some cattle for to buy.

When he arrived at Leicester town he went into an inn,
He called for an ostler, and boldly walked in,
He called for liquors of the best, he being a roving blade
And quickly fixed his eyes upon the chambermaid.

The day it being over, the night it being come,
The butcher came to the inn, his business being done,
He called for his supper, reck'ning being left unpaid,
Says he, this night I'll put a trick upon the chambermaid.

She then took a candle to light him up to bed,
And when they came into the room, these words to her
   he said
One sovereign I will give to you all to enjoy your charms
This fair maid did sleep all night within the butcher's
   arms.

He rose up in the morning and prepared to go away,
The Landlord said, your reckoning, sir, you have forgot
   to pay,
O, no, the Butcher did reply, pray do not think it strange,
I gave a sovereign to your maid, but did not get the
   change.

He straightway called the chambermaid and charged her
   with the same,

The sovereign she did lay down, fearing to get the blame,
The butcher he went home, well pleased with what was
    past,
For soon this pretty chambermaid grew thick about the
    waist.

Twas in a twelvemonth after, he came to town again.
And then as he had done before, he stopped at the inn,
Twas then the buxom chambermaid she chanc'd him to
    see,
She brought the babe just three months old, and placed it
    on his knee.

The butcher sat like one amazed, and at the child did
    stare,
But when the joke he did find out, how he did stamp
    and swear,
She said, kind sir, it is your own, so do not think it
    strange,
One sovereign you gave to me, and I have brought the
    change.

The company they laugh'd amain; the joke went freely
    round,
And the tidings of the same was spread through
    Leicester town,
The butcher was to a justice brought, who happened to
    live near,
One hundred pounds he did lay down, before he could
    get clear.

So all you brisk and lively blades, I pray be ruled by me,
Look well into your bargains, before you money pay,
Or soon, perhaps, your folly, will give you cause to
    range,

For if you sport with pretty maids you are sure to have
your change.

234

The Very Pretty Maid of this Town, and the Amorous 'Squire not One Hundred Miles from the Place

A pretty maid both kind and fair,
    Dwells in this very town,
Her pleasant smiles and easy air,
    Engages fop and clown.

Being accosted t'other day,
    By a clumsy 'squire,
Who ask'd her if she knew the way
    To quench a raging fire.

Water, Sir, reply'd the maid,
    Will quench it in a trice,
O no, said he, you little jade,
    I've try'd that once or twice.

Then Sir, said she, 'tis past my skill,
    To tell you what will do;
I'm sure, said he, you know what will;
    There's nothing can but you.

Alas-a-day, what do you mean,
    Reply'd the pretty fair;
I'd have you try it once again,
    You never should despair.

Despair I cannot, cry'd the 'squire,
　　While you are in my sight,
'Tis you must quench the burning fire,
　　You set it first alight.

Then strait he clas'p [*sic*] her round the waist,
　　And forc'd from her a kiss;
Ho! ho! said she, is that your tale,
　　Then pray you, Sir, take this.

And with a pail, placed at the door,
　　She sluic'd the amorous 'squire;
You're welcome, Sir, to this and more,
　　To quench your raging fire.

235

Pretty Maids Beware!!!

A Love Letter from Sarah to Charles

The following epistle was written by a girl at Deal to her
sweetheart, a sailor on board a man of war in the Downs.
The lieutenant of the ship found it on board, twisted up
with tobacco in it, by which it seems our seafaring spark
had as little regard for his mistress, after enjoyment, as if
he had been of a more illustrious rank.

Lovin Der Charls,

This mi kind love to yow is to tell yow, after all owr
sport and fon, I am lik to pay fort, for I am with child; and
wors of al, my sister Nan knos it, and cals me hore and
bech, and is redy to ter my sol owt, and curs Jack Peny lies
with her evry tim he cums ashor; and the saci dog wold
have lade with me to, but I wold not let him, for I wil be

always honest to yow; therfor der Charls com ashor, and let us be mared to safe my vartu: and if yow have no munni, I will paun my new stais and sel mi new smoks yow gave me, and that will pay the parsen and find us a diner; and pray der lovin Charls cum ashor, and der Charls dont be frad for wont of a ring, for I have stole mi sister Nans, and the nasty tod shall never have it no mor; for she tels abot that I am goin to have a bastard, and God bles yowr lovin sol cum sune, for I longs to be mared accordin to yowr promis, and I will be yowr der vartus wife til deth,

SARAH JOHNSON

Feb. 19th.

PS. – Pray dont let yowr mesmat Jack se this, if yow do hel tel owr Nan, and shel ter mi hart owt then, for shes a devil at me now.

A POETICAL VERSION OF THE FOREGOING

Dear object of my love, whose manly charms
With bliss extatic fill'd my circling arms;
That bliss is past, and nought for me remains
But dire reproach, and sharp unpitied pains:
For (Death to me, and food to others pride)
My sister has my growing shame descry'd,
Ev'n she assails me with opprobious name,
When the prude's conscious she deserves the same
Her loose associates, sated, from her flies,
And vainly to seduce my virtue tries:
True, as a wife, I only want the name;
O! haste and wed me, and preserve my fame.
Unlike most modern matches ours shall be, ⎫
From settlement, the lawyers fetters free; ⎬
I'll quit my All, and be content with thee. ⎭
Then haste away, and strike detraction dead;
The nuptial feast awaits you, and the bed;
Nor fear the hand that will endure for life,
With me, your loving and your faithful wife.

POSTSCRIPT

These earnest dictates of my anxious heart
I beg you will not to your friend impart;
For oft beneath fair friendship's specious show,
The traitor lurks, the undermining foe.

R.A.

APPENDIX: CONTEMPORARY DESCENDANTS OF THE STREET BALLAD

(A) PRINTED EXAMPLES

(B) ORAL EXAMPLES CURRENT IN THE FORCES

A

I

Blackpool Breezes

She was a sweet country lassie,
    But to Blackpool she went on the spree,
With a beautiful face and a chassis
    As shapely as any could be.
But oh! for the pitfalls of Blackpool,
    She fell into one after dark,
At the point of a gun, all her virtue had gone,
    When they found her in Stanley Park.

  Refrain (with feeling)
    And the Tower looks down with a terrible frown,
    On the time and the money ill-spent,
    Oh maidens beware! please do have a care,
    Try and come back as glad as you went.

She was a siren named Flossy,
    A sort of platinum blonde,
But a trifle too forward and bossy,
    That's the reason why she's gone beyond.
While going the rounds up in Blackpool
    On the Pleasure Beach she'd have a go,
'Til a big Yankee guy, with a caste in his eye,
    With one wave of his hand laid her low.

2

What he Took

He took her fancy when he came
    He took her hand, he took a kiss:
He took no notice of the shame

That glowed her happy cheek at this:
He took to coming afternoons:
   He took an oath he'd ne'er deceive:
He took her father's silver spoons,
   And after that he took his leave.

B

FORCES' BALLADS

SOCIAL AND POLITICAL

3

H—y P—tt

H—y P—tt was a Bolshie, and one of Lenin's lads,
Till he was foully murdered by reactionary cads,
   By reactionary cads? Sir, reactionary cads,
   Till he was foully murdered by reactionary cads.

Up spoke the soul of H—y, 'In death I will not lie,
I'll go and do some party work in the Kingdom up on
   high.'

He stood before the portal, all trembling at the knees,
'A message here for Comrade God, from H—y P—tt
   please.'

Said God, 'Who is this person, all humble and contrite?
A friend of Neville Chamberlain's? Oh that will be all
   right.'

They put him in the choir, put a harp into his hand,
He taught the Internationale to the Hallelujah band.

They put him in the choir, but the hymns he did not like,
He organized the angels and he brought them out on
   strike.

They brought him up on trial before the Holy Ghost
For spreading disaffection amongst the Heavenly Host.

The verdict it is 'Guilty', and H—y he said 'Swell'.
He tucked his nightie round his knees and floated down
   to Hell.

Now seven long years have passed away, and H—y's
   doing well,
He's just been made first People's Commissar of Soviet
   Hell.

The moral of this story, is very plain to tell:
If you want to be a Communist you'll have to go to
   Hell.

4

They're Shifting Father's Grave

They're shifting father's grave to build a sewer
They're shifting it regardless of expense
They're shifting his remains to make way for ten-inch
   drains
To suit some local high-class residents.

Now what's the use of having a religion
If when you die your bones can't rest in peace.
Because some high-born twit wants a pipeline for his
   sh—t
They will not let poor father rest in peace.

But father in his life was ne'er a quitter
I don't suppose he'll be a quitter now.
He'll dress up in a sheet and he'll haunt that sh—t house
    seat
And never let those bastards sh—t nohow.

Now won't there be an age of constipation
And won't those bastards howl, and rant, and rave
But they'll have got what they deserve, 'cause they had
    the bleeding nerve
To desecrate a British workman's grave.

5

Ops in a Wimpey[1]

Now the first silly bastard he got in an aeroplane,
He thought he could fly over Germany,
And the crew all sang as they pranged upon the boundary,
'Who'll come on ops in a Wimpey with me?'

CHORUS

Ops in a Wimpey, ops in a Wimpey
Who'll come on ops in a Wimpey with me?
And the crew all sang as they pranged upon the boundary,
'Who'll come on ops in a Wimpey with me?'

Now the second silly bastard he got in an aeroplane,
He set course o'er the cold North Sea.
And the crew all sang as they swam back to the coast
    again,
'Who'll come on ops in a Wimpey with me?'
    Chorus

   1. Vickers-Armstrong Wellington Bomber.

Now the third silly bastard he got over Hanover
Up came the flak like a Christmas tree,
And the crew all sang as the navigator sh—t himself,
'Who'll come on ops in a Wimpey with me?'
   Chorus

Now the fourth silly bastard he got over Magdeburg,
Up came the fighters, one, two, three.
And the rear-gunner sighed as he reached for his
   parachute,
'Who'll come on ops in a Wimpey with me?'
   Chorus

AMATORY

6

The Keyhole in the Door

The party finished early, 'twas on the stroke of nine;
By a strange coincidence, her room was next to mine;
And having had a good time and desirous of some more,
I took up my position by the keyhole in the door.
   O the keyhole, keyhole, the keyhole in the door –
   I took up my position by the keyhole in the door.

She was standing by the fireplace her figure for to warm
With only a pair of Frenchies to cover up her form:
Oh how I wished that she would drop them to the floor.
By God I saw her do it through the keyhole in the door.
   O the keyhole &c.

My fingers they rapped lightly on the panel of the door
And after many a pleading I crossed the threshold floor
And so that others should not see what I had seen before

I stuffed that pair of Frenchies through the keyhole in
   the door.
    O the keyhole &c.

That night I slept in glory and many a place beside
And on her lily-white breasts had many a glorious ride,
But when I woke next morning my p—k was red and sore;
It felt as if I'd stuffed it through the keyhole in the door.
    O the keyhole &c.

7

The Highland Tinker

(A modern oral version of earlier ballads, the punning
'vocational' point having, however, been lost. See Introduction, p. 49.)

The Lady of the Manor was dressing for the ball
When she saw a highland tinker p—g up against a wall
   With his dirty great kidney-wiper and b—s the size of
     three
   And half a yard of parkin hanging down below his
     knee.

The lady wrote a letter, and in it she did say
She rather would be f—d by the tinker than her husband
    any day,
   With his &c.

The tinker got the letter, and when it he did read
His p—k began to fester and his b—s begin to bleed
   With his &c.

The Tinker mounts his charger, and into town he rides
With his p—k flung over his shoulder and his b—ks by
   his side
  With his &c.

He f—d her in the pantry, he f—d her in the hall
God save us, said the butler, *he has come to f—k us all*.
  With his &c.

8

My Husband

(Cp. ballads in the 'Vocational' section, Part II)

My husband's a jockey, a jockey, a jockey,
A bloody fine jockey is he.
All day he rides horses, rides horses, rides horses,
At night he comes home and rides me.

My husband's a stoker, &c.
A bloody fine stoker is he.
All day he pokes fire, &c.
At night he comes home and pokes me.

My husband's a pork-butcher, &c.
A bloody fine pork-butcher is he.
All day he stuffs sausages, &c.
At night he comes home and stuffs me.

My husband's a sergeant, &c.
A bloody fine sergeant is he.
All day he f—ks men about, &c.
At night he comes home and f—ks me.

9

The Monk of Great Renown
(Cp. the anti-friar ballads in the 'Clerical' section, Part. II.)

There was an old monk of great renown
There was an old monk of great renown
There was an old monk of great renown
Who f—d all the women of London town.
The old s—d, the dirty old s—d
The b—r deserves to die.
Glory, glory Allelujah

The other monks cried out in shame
The other monks &c.
The other monks &c.
But he turned them over and did them again.
      The old &c.

The other monks to stop his frolics
The other monks &c.
The other monks &c.
They took a great knife and cut off his b—ks.
      The old &c.

And now deprived of all desire
And now &c.
And now &c.
He sings soprano in the choir.
      The old &c.

BIBLIOGRAPHY AND
ABBREVIATIONS

(Abbreviations used in the notes are printed
before the work to which they refer.)

N.B. Only short titles are given.

Amanda – *The Amanda Group of Bagford Poems*, ed. J. W.
Ebsworth for the Ballad Society, 1880.

Ashmole – Ashmole MSS. Bodl.

Ashton M.S.B. – *Modern Street Ballads*, ed. John Ashton
(Chatto and Windus), London, 1888.

Ballad Society – *The Roxburghe Ballads reprinted by The Ballad
Society* (London), 1869–80 (8 vols.), ed. Wm. Chappell and
J. W. Ebsworth.

Bagford – *The Bagford Ballads*, *c.* 1600–1715 (Original Broadsides, 2 vols., B.M.).

Bell, Robert – *Ancient Poems, Ballads and Songs of the Peasantry
of England*, ed. R. Bell, London, 1856.

B.M. – British Museum.

Bodl. – Bodleian Library.

Carey – *The Poems of Henry Carey*, ed. F. T. Wood (The
Scholartis Press), London, 1930.

C.A.Y.B.M. – *Come all Ye Bold Miners: Ballads and Songs of
the Coalfields*, ed. A. L. Lloyd (Lawrence and Wishart),
London, 1952.

Chappell, W. – *A Collection of Natural Airs* (1838); *Popular
Music of the Olden Time* (1859, revised edition, 1893).

Choyce Drollery – *Choyce Drollery: Songs & Sonnets*, ed.
J. W. Ebsworth (R. Roberts), Boston, Lincs., 1886.

C.N.I.P. – *A Collection of the Newest and Most Ingenious Poems,
Songs, Catches &c against Popery, Relating to the Times*,
London, 1689.

C.S.L. – *The Curiosities of Street Literature Comprising Cocks or
Catchpennies, a large and curious assortment of street drolleries,
squibs, Histories, comic tales in verse and prose* [ed. Charles
Hindley] (Reeves and Turner), London, 1871 (limited
edition).

Douce – The Douce Collection of Original Broadsides, Bodl.

D'Urfey, Thomas – *Wit and Mirth or Pills to Purge Melancholy*

(1719–20, 6 vols. Reprinted 1870 and 1960) [see also under P.P.M. below].

Farmer – *Merry Songs and Ballads*, ed. J. S. Farmer, 1897, 5 vols. (Privately printed).

Firth Bodl. – The Firth Collection of original broadsides, Bodl.

Firth N.S.B. – *Naval Songs and Ballads,* selected and edited by C. H. Firth. Printed for the Navy Records Society (No. XXXIII), London, 1908.

Firth, Sir Charles – 'Ballads and Broadsides', by C. H. Firth, in *Shakespeare's England* (Oxford University Press), Oxford, 1916, Vol. II, pp. 511–38.

Fragmenta Aurea – *Fragmenta Aurea. A Collection of all the Incomparable Peeces written by Sir John Suckling*, London, 1646.

Henderson, H. – *Ballads of World War II*, ed. H. Henderson, 1947.

Hindley, Charles – *History of the Catnach Press*, London, 1886 [see also under C.S.L. above].

H.P.D. – *A Handfull of pleasant delites*, London, 1584 (ed. H. E. Rollins, Cambridge, U.S.A., 1924).

Hughes, Thomas – *The Scouring of the White Horse*, Cambridge, 1859.

Jordan, T. O. L. – *The Triumphs of London* by Thomas Jordan, 1675.

Legman, G. – *The Horn Book*, New York, 1964.

Luttrell – Luttrell Collection of Original Broadsides, B.M.

Marvell, Andrew: *The Poems and Letters of Andrew Marvell*, ed. H. Margoliouth (Oxford, at the Clarendon Press), 1927 (2 vols.).

Mayhew – *London Labour and the London Poor*, compiled by Henry Mayhew (Griffin, Bohn and Co.), London, 1862 (3 vols.).

Merry Drollery – *Merry Drollery Collected by W.N., C.B., & J.G.,* London, 1661.

Merry Muses – *The Merry Muses of Caledonia* (*c.* 1800; Crochallan Edition, collected by Robert Burns).

Miscellanies in Verse – *Miscellanies in Verse*, Printed for Benjamin Motte, London, 1727. (By Pope, Swift and others.)

Musical Miscellany – *The Musical Miscellany Being a Collection of Choice Songs*, London, 1729 (5 vols.).

Nottingham 118/B2 – Nottingham University Library Collection of Original Broadsides (mainly nineteenth century): loose broadsides unnumbered in File r/PR 118/B2.

Nottingham 89375 – same collection. Original broadsides (mainly nineteenth century) collected in album 89375 and numbered in two parts.

P.B. – *The Pepys Ballads*, ed. H. E. Rollins (Harvard University Press), 1930 (7 vols.).

Percy Folio – *Percy Folio MS. c. 1620–1650* privately printed and ed., F. J. Furnivall, 1868.

Pinto, V. de S. – 'The Street Ballad and English Poetry', *Politics and Letters* Nos. 2 and 3, Winter-Spring 1947. 'Broadsheets' article in *Chambers's Encyclopaedia*, new edition, 1950.

P.M.L.A.A.–*Publications of the Modern Language Association of America*.

P.O.A.S. – *Poems on Affairs of State From the Time of Oliver Cromwell, to the Abdication of K. James the Second*, London, 1697.

Portland – The Duke of Portland's MSS., Nottingham University Library.

P.P. – *A Pedlar's Pack of Ballads and Songs*, ed. W. H. Logan (W. Paterson), Edinburgh, 1869.

P.P.M. – *Pills to Purge Melancholy*, i.e. '*Songs Compleat, Pleasant and Divertive,* Written by Mr D'Urfey', London, 1719–20 (5 vols.) [an expanded and rearranged edition of *Wit and Mirth or Pills to Purge Melancholy* (1699–1714)].

Rawlinson – Rawlinson Collection of original broadsides (Quarto), Bodl.

Reeves, James – *The Idiom of the People*, London, ed. J. Reeves, 1958; *The Everlasting Circle*, ed. J. Reeves, London, 1960.

Rochester, John Wilmot, Earl of – *Poems by John Wilmot, Earl of Rochester*, ed. V. de S. Pinto (Routledge), London, revised edition, 1964.

Rollins, Hyder E.–'The Black Letter Broadside', by Hyder E. Rollins, *Publications of the Modern Language Association of America*, XXXIV, 2, 1919.

Rollins O.E.B. – *Old English Ballads 1553–1625*, ed. Hyder E. Rollins (Cambridge University Press), 1920.

Rollins P.G. – *A Pepysian Garland*, ed. Hyder E. Rollins (Cambridge University Press), 1922.

Rollins P.O.A. – *The Pack of Autolycus*, ed. Hyder E. Rollins (Harvard University Press), 1927.

Roxburghe – *The Roxburghe Ballads* (Original Broadsides in 4 parts), *c.* 1540–1790, B.M.

S.A. – Society of Antiquaries (Collection of Original Broadsides in the Society's Library, Burlington House, London).

S.C.N.I.P. – *A Second Collection of the Newest and Most Ingenious Poems, Satyrs, Songs &c against Popery*, London, 1689.

Sedley, Sir Charles – *The Poetical and Dramatic Works of Sir Charles Sedley*, ed. V. de S. Pinto (Constable), London, 1928 (2 vols.).

Shirburn – *The Shirburn Ballads,* ed. A. Clark (Oxford University Press), 1907.

Songs Comic and Satirical – *Songs Comic and Satirical,* by G. A. Stevens, Oxford, 1782.

Swift's Poems, ed. Williams – *The Poems of Jonathan Swift*, ed. Harold Williams (Oxford at the Clarendon Press), 1927 (3 vols.).

Taverham – Taverham MS. (*c.* 1600–40), Nottingham University Library.

V.S.B. – *Victorian Street Ballads*, ed. W. Henderson (Country Life Ltd), London, 1937.

W.C.N.P. – *The Works of the Most Celebrated Minor Poets Volume the First*, printed for H. Cogan, London, 1749.

Westminster Drolleries – *Westminster Drolleries,* ed. J. W. Ebsworth, 1875 (2 vols.).

Wit and Mirth – *Wit and Mirth*, ed. H[enry] P[layford], London, 1682.

Wood – Wood Collection of Broadsides, *c.* 1600–95, Bodl.

WORK IN PROGRESS

Simpson, Claude, Jr, of Stanford University, is compiling a very ambitious book of the tunes of the broadside ballads – i.e. those demonstrably associated with the ballads at the time of printing. It is to be called *The British Broadside Ballad and its Music* and will be published by Rutgers University Press (New Brunswick, New Jersey) in the autumn of 1965.

Sedley, Stephen, of Birmingham University, is compiling a critical anthology of street ballads, folk songs and folkstyle songs; many are in the nature of modern extensions of *The Common Muse* idiom. They will be accompanied by a commentary and supported by sets of tapes, to be deposited in appropriate archives. It is to be published by Chatto & Windus.

SELECT DISCOGRAPHY

An asterisk indicates singers who have their material purely from oral tradition (always allowing for broadsides intervening at some point in the past).

All records listed are LPs except where indicated.

1. Records containing versions of songs included in *The Common Muse*

THE MERRY MUSES OF CALEDONIA : Ewan MacColl (Folk Lyric DLP 2).

WHEN DALLIANCE WAS IN FLOWER, vols. I–III: Ed McCurdy (Elektra EKL 110, 140 and 160; vols. I–II issued in Britain on Transatlantic TRA 115 and 119).

SONGS OF DALLIANCE: Ed McCurdy (Elektra EKL 170).
Note: The 'Dalliance' albums are drawn principally from *Wit and Mirth*, *Pills to Purge Melancholy* and the *Drolleries* (see Bibliography and Notes), but a good deal of the material has been reworked.

THE IRON MUSE : edited by A. L. Lloyd (Topic 12 T 86): *The Durham Lock-Out* (Bob Davenport), *The Recruited Collier* [or *Jimmy's Enlisted*] (Ann Briggs).

CHORUS FROM THE GALLOWS : Ewan MacColl (Topic 12 T 16): *Van Dieman's Land.*

STEVE BENBOW SINGS : Steve Benbow (Folklore F-LEUT 6): *Van Dieman's Land, ·There was a Knight and he was Young* (sub nom. *The Baffled Knight*).

ADMIRAL BENBOW : Steve Benbow (HMV CLP 1603): *The Death of Admiral Benbow.*

THE FOLK SONGS OF BRITAIN,* vols. I–V: edited by Alan Lomax and Peter Kennedy (Caedmon Records, New York): vol. II – *The London Prentice* (sub nom. *Blow the candle out*) (Jimmy Gilhaney, Belfast), *The Foggy Dew* (Phil Hammond, Norfolk), *Room for a Jovial Tinker* (sub nom. *The Jolly Tinker*) (Thomas Moran, Co. Leitrim), *The Cunning Cobbler Done Over* (George Spicer, Sussex); vol. V – *There was a Knight and he was Young* (sub nom. *The Baffled Knight*) (Emily Bishop, Herefordshire), *The Jolly Beggar* (Jeannie Robertson, Aberdeenshire).

FOLKSONG TODAY*: edited by Peter Kennedy (HMV DLP 1143): *The Foggy Dew* (Harry Cox, Norfolk).

SONGS OF LOVE, LUST AND LOOSE LIVING: Isla Cameron and Tony Britton (Transatlantic TRA 105): *The London Prentice* (sub nom. *Blow the candles out*), *John Anderson, My Jo*.

ALL FOR ME GROG: A. L. Lloyd (Topic EP TOP 66): *The Foggy Dew, The Leicester Chambermaid* (sub nom. *The Butcher and the Chambermaid*).

STEAM WHISTLE BALLADS: Ewan MacColl (Topic 12 T 104): *The Coal-Owner and the Pitman's Wife*.

CEILIDH AT THE CROWN: The Ian Campbell Folk Group et al. (Topic EP TOP 76): *The Jolly Beggar*.

THE BEST OF A. L. LLOYD (Prestige International INT 13066): *The Mower*.

BRITISH BROADSIDE BALLADS: Paul Clayton (Folkways FW 8708): *Three Maids a-Milking would Go*.

THE ROVING JOURNEYMEN: Tom, Chris and Ben Willet (Topic 12 T 84): *The Maid of Tottenham* (sub nom. *As I was going to Salisbury*); this record also contains a version of *A Blacksmith Courted Me,* the folksong from which Vaughan Williams derived his famous melody (*Monksgate*) for Bunyan's *Pilgrim Song*.

HEROES IN LOVE: Shirley Collins (Topic EP TOP 95). Contains another variant of *A Blacksmith Courted Me* with a tune closer to *Monksgate*.

MCCAFFERTY: Dominic Behan (Collector EP JEL 2): *Van Diemen's Land*.

STEVE BENBOW'S FOLK FOUR (Collector EP JEB 2): *The Coal-Owner and the Pitman's Wife*.

STORMY WEATHER BOYS: Bob Roberts (Collector EP JEB 6): *The Foggy Dew*.

THE FOGGY DEW: Shirley Collins (Collector EP JEB 3).

2. Records containing songs akin to those in *The Common Muse*.

A. Traditional

BAWDY BRITISH BALLADS: Big Theo Johnson (Surprise Records ILP 1011)

BROADSIDE BALLADS, vols. I and II: Ewan MacColl (Folkways FW 3043 and 3044).

PEELERS AND PRISONERS: Dominic Behan (Topic EP TOP 85).

EASTER WEEK AND AFTER: Dominic Behan (Topic 12 T 44).

STREETS OF SONG: Dominic Behan and Ewan MacColl (Topic 12 T 41).

WOR GEORDIE: Bob Davenport (Topic EP TOP 83).

THE UNFORTUNATE RAKE (Folkways FS 3805): 21 variants of one street ballad archetype.

SCOTTISH POPULAR SONGS: Ewan MacColl and Peggy Seeger (Folkways FW 8757).

THE COLLIER'S RANT: Johnny Handle and Louis Killen (Topic EP TOP 74).

SONGS FOR SWINGING LANDLORDS TO: Stan Kelly (Topic EP TOP 60); includes some newly composed songs.

THE BUTCHER BOY AND OTHER BALLADS: Enoch Kent (Topic EP TOP 81).

A HUNDRED YEARS AGO: A. L. Lloyd and Ewan MacColl (Top EP TOPIC 99)

BOLD SPORTSMEN ALL: A. L. Lloyd and Ewan MacColl (Topic 10 T 36); includes one newly composed song.

GAMBLERS AND SPORTING BLADES: A. L. Lloyd and Ewan MacColl (Topic EP TOP 71).

BARRACK-ROOM BALLADS: Ewan MacColl (Topic 10 T 26): World War II and later songs.

GLASGOW STREET SONGS: Robin Hall and Jimmy MacGregor: vols. 1–3 (Collector EPs JES 2, JES 5, JES 9).

SONGS OF THE STREETS: Dominic Behan (Collector EP JEL 3).

B. Recently written

REVIVAL IN BRITAIN: Matt M'Ginn, Stan Kelly, Johnny Handle, Alan Rogerson, Enoch Kent, Charles Parker (Folkways FW 8728).

STOTTIN DOON THE WAAL: Johnny Handle (Topic EP TOP 78).

SONGS FOR CITY SQUARES: Leon Rosselson (Topic EP TOP 77).

THE NEW BRITON GAZETTE, vols. I and II: Ewan MacColl and Peggy Seeger (Folkways FW 8732 and 8734).

NOTES AND REFERENCES

PART I

1. *A Ballade of the Scottyshe Kynge*. B.M.C.39.e.1. See Introduction, p. 32. This ballad by John Skelton, probably the oldest English printed street ballad in existence, is printed in black letter without title or pagination on four quarto leaves with a rude woodcut illustration. The unique copy in the British Museum was discovered in 1878 inside the cover of a French romance printed in 1513. It must have been written and printed hastily very soon after the battle of Flodden Field (9 September 1513) as it appears from the text that Skelton was still unaware of the fact that James IV was killed in the battle and believed he had been taken prisoner. See the excellent facsimile edition with introduction by John Ashton (London, 1882).

2. *Fragment of an Anti-Papist Ballad*. B.M. Cup.651. e.2. This fragment of a broadside ballad in black letter was probably printed in 1548. Attention was first drawn to it by Hyder E. Rollins in the Introduction to O.E.B. The ballad refers to the Popish rebellion in Devon and Cornwall in 1548 following the attempt of Edward VI's ministers to introduce Protestant services in village churches. The person called 'bodye' in l. 2 is a certain William Body who was killed in the rebellion.

3. *A New Ballade of the Marigolde*. S.A. Broadsides Henry VIII–Elizabeth, No. 36, reprinted in the *Harleian Miscellany*, X.253, and in Rollins O.E.B. William Forrest, the author of this ballad, was one of the chaplains to Mary I. See Introduction, p. 34.

4. *A Songe betwene the Quenes majestie and Englande*. S.A. Broadsides Henry VIII–Elizabeth, No. 47. A shortened and modernized version of this fine ballad is printed by Miss M. C. Bradbrook in *The Queen's Garland* (Royal Society of Literature, 1952).

5. *Upon Sir Francis Drake's return*. Ashmole, 36, 37. According to Norman Ault (*Elizabethan Lyrics*, p. 104) this poem was written about 1584. It obviously refers to Drake's return from his voyage round the world in 1581 and the

Queen's visit to him on his ship *The Golden Hind* at Deptford when she knighted him. The last stanza refers to the loss of Sir Humphrey Gilbert on his return from Newfoundland in 1584. The text in the present collection is taken from a manuscript in the Bodleian, but the poem is undoubtedly a street ballad. Ebsworth, in *The Roxburghe Ballads* (Ballad Society, 1887), VI, 377, quotes what appears to be a broadside version, but gives no reference. According to Ebsworth the three Sir Francises of the first line of the poem are Sir Francis Drake, Sir Francis Walsingham and Sir Francis Vere, all knighted on this occasion by Elizabeth I.

6. *Lord Willoughby*. Roxburghe, II, 93. The 'brave lord Willoughby' of this ballad is Peregrine Bertie, Lord Willoughby de Eresby (1555–1601) one of the chief commanders of the English forces in the Low Countries in Elizabeth's reign, where he served with Leicester, Sidney and Norris. According to the article on Bertie by Sir Sidney Lee in the D.N.B., this ballad 'relates one of Willoughby's exploits in Flanders with no very strict adherence to historical fact'. It may be dated about 1586, when Willoughby and Norris were serving together.

7. *A Joyfull New Ballad*. *The Works of Thomas Deloney*, ed. F. O. Mann, pp. 468–73. Entered in *Stationer's Register* 10 August 1588. This ballad refers to the taking of the galleon of Pedro de Valdes by Drake off the Devonshire coast on 21 July 1588 and of De Monçadas's galleon off Calais on 29 July.

8. *The Winning of Cales*. *The Garland of Good Will*, by Thomas Deloney, Part III. '*Cales*' is the Elizabethan form of 'Cadiz'. This ballad refers to the capture and sack of Cadiz by the expedition under the command of the Earl of Essex, 20 June to 5 July 1596.

9. *A Famous Sea-Fight*. Manchester Free Reference Library, II.36. A unique, but mutilated copy of the original broadside of this ballad, which refers to a naval battle between Spanish and Dutch ships in the Channel in September 1639. Another ballad on the same subject, called *A New Spanish Tragedy*, is printed in Rollins O.E.B. from Wood 401 (137).

10. *The Famous Fight at Malago*. Roxburghe, II, 146. Firth N.S.B., p. 47. This fight took place in July 1656.

11. *The Lancashire Puritane*. Taverham, pp. 77–8.

12. *An Essay on The Fleet riding in the Downes*. Luttrell, III, 91. This fine ballad in the unusual form of the heroic couplet refers to the Third Dutch War of 1672, when Charles II joined with Louis XIV to attack Holland.

13. *On the Lord Mayor and Court of Aldermen, etc.* P.O.A.S., 1697. First printed in the Second Collection of Poems on Affairs of State, 1689, and then in P.O.A.S., 1697, where it is first ascribed to Marvell. Another version is printed by Margoliouth in his *Poems and Letters* of Andrew Marvell, I, 181, 182. This ballad refers to the presentation of the freedom of the City of London to Charles II in December 1674, when he was made an honorary member of the Grocers' Company.

14. *The History of Insipids. A Second Collection of the Newest and most Ingenious Poems, Satyrs, Songs &c. Against Popery and Tyranny, Relating to the Times*. London, 1689. 4to. pp. 9, 10; (B.M. 1077, L.32). Printed with full notes and bibliographical detail in V. de S. Pinto's edition of Rochester, London, 1953, 1964.

15. *A Ballad upon the Popish Plot*. Luttrell, III, 143. Ascribed in the printed broadside to 'A lady of Quality', but according to a MS. note in the B.M. copy in a seventeenth-century hand it is by 'John Gadbury ye Astrologer'. John Gadbury (1672–1704) was a well-known figure in Restoration London and was consulted by many eminent people. The ballad refers to the Popish Plot agitation of 1678–79. The 'Politick Statesman' of Stanza II is Shaftesbury and his 'Instrument' (Stanza III) is Titus Oates.

16. *England's Darling*. Roxburghe, II, 140. A Whig ballad written probably in the Autumn of 1679 when Monmouth, the bastard son of Charles II and darling of the Whigs, had been exiled to Holland.

17. *England's Triumph or The Subjects' Joy*. Dated by Ebsworth 1679. Though this and the following ballad were printed later than No. 22, they have been inserted before it, as they are typical Cavalier ballads probably written a good deal earlier.

18. *The Courtier's Health*. Roxburghe, II, 89. Dated by Ebsworth 1681.

19. *A Carrouse to the Emperor*. Roxburghe, II, 58 2. This ballad refers to the raising of the Siege of Vienna in September 1683. The 'much wrong'd Duke Lorrain' is Charles Leopold, Duke of Lorraine, who had been deprived of his dominions by Louis XIV and commanded the Emperor's troops against the Turks in 1683. 'Starenberg' is either Count Starhemberg, who commanded the Vienna garrison, or his nephew, who played a prominent part in the defence of the city. The 'Royal Pole' is John Sobieski (John III), King of Poland, who, with the Duke of Lorraine, commanded the relieving armies.

20. *The Dutchess of Monmouth's Lamentation*. Ballad Society, 1885, V, 3, 640. This ballad is a monologue placed in the mouth of Anne, the beautiful and popular wife of the worthless Monmouth. It was probably written in 1684, when Monmouth had fled to Holland after the failure of the plot to assassinate Charles II and the Duke of York in which he had been implicated.

21 *A New Song*. C.N.I.P., 1689. This is the famous Lillibulero, the song of the Revolution, said to have been written by the Earl of Wharton, who boasted that with it he had 'sung a King out of three kingdoms'. 'In this little poem an Irishman congratulates a fellow Irishman, in a barbarous jargon, on the approaching triumph of Popery and the Milesian Race' (Macaulay, *History of England*, ed. Firth, III, 1072). The tune (far superior to the words) is printed with the ballad in a broadside reproduced in Firth's edition of Macaulay's History, III, 1075.

22. *A New Song of an Orange*. S.C.N.I.P., 1689. A ballad of the Revolution. The 'Orange' is, of course, William of Orange, afterwards William III.

23. *The Lord Chancellours Villanies Discovered*. S.C.N.I.P., 1689. 'The Lord Chancellour' is the hated Judge Jeffreys, who was arrested in disguise in Wapping in 1688 and died shortly afterwards in the Tower.

24. *Sir T. J.'s Speech to his Wife and Children*. S.C.N.I.P., 1689. This ballad also certainly refers to Judge Jeffreys, whose Christian name was really George. The author of the ballad seems to have thought that his initial was T.

25. *The Death of Admiral Benbow*. B.M. 11621, i. II. (14). A

broadside printed by Fowler of Salisbury about 1785. There are several versions of this famous and excellent naval ballad which refers to the death of Admiral John Benbow, who died of wounds in 1702 at Port Royal after a heroic struggle with a French fleet off Santa Marta. He had to give up the pursuit of the French fleet because his captains (Kirby and Wade) disagreed with his plan of battle. See the note by Sir C. H. Firth in N.S.B., pp. 348, 349.

26. *Jack Frenchman's Lamentation*. B.M. 12350.m. 18/3. Broadside printed by Morphew probably in 1708, reprinted by H. Williams in his edition of Swift's Poems, I, 1079. The ballad, which has been attributed to Swift, Congreve and Prior, refers to the battle of Oudenarde, 11 July 1708. Two other broadside versions in the B.M. (1876.f. I/40 and C.40 m. 10/103) have a clumsy additional stanza between stanzas 6 and 7 (here printed in square brackets), which Williams considers to be probably an interpolation.

27. *A New Song Entitled the Warming Pan*. Roxburghe, III, ii, 724. Refers to the birth of a son (the Old Pretender) to James II and Mary of Modena on 10 June 1688. According to Whig legend this child was really a foundling introduced into the Palace in a warming-pan.

28. *Victory*. Ashton M.S.B., p. 223.

29. *A New Song Composed on the Death of Lord Nelson*. Firth N.S.B., p. 302. This was a very popular ballad and several different versions of it exist in broadsides printed in the first half of the nineteenth century. Thomas Hughes in *The Scouring of The White Horse* describes it as being sung in a Berkshire public house about 1859. See Firth's note in N.S.B., p. 360.

30. *The Battle of Navarino*. Ashton M.S.B., p. 223. This and the following ballad refer to the battle of Navarino, when Admiral Codrington, in command of a combined British, French and Russian fleet, annihilated the Turkish fleet in Navarino Bay in October 1827 and thus secured the independence of Greece.

31. *The Glorious Victory of Navarino!* Nottingham, 89375, I, 27.

32. *A New Hunting Song*. Ashton M.S.B., p. 340.

33. *Queen Victoria.* Ashton M.S.B., p. 273.

34. *A New Song on the Birth of the Prince of Wales.* C.S.L., p. 65. Refers to the birth of Albert Edward, Prince of Wales, afterwards Edward VII.

35. *The Slave Chase.* Nottingham, 1181/B2, Firth N.S.B., p. 335. This fine ballad is probably mid-Victorian. It refers to one of the numerous occasions when British warships in this period stopped slave ships on the high seas and freed their human cargoes.

36. *Elegy on Albert Edward the Peacemaker.* B.M. 1896.b.15. A number of street ballads were written on the occasion of the death of Edward VII and were hawked in the streets of London at his funeral. This seems to have been the last occasion when a public event evoked a considerable body of English popular poetry. This specimen has been chosen from several preserved in an album in the British Museum. It seems to be one of the least sophisticated in the collection and to represent the same sort of popular feeling that found expression in the ballads on the accession of Mary I (No. 3) and Elizabeth I (No. 4). It is printed in crimson letters on one side of a single sheet with a silver border, and in this form it is a piece of early twentieth century popular art comparable with the decorations of contemporary public houses, where it was probably sold and read.

37. *London Lickpenny.* B.M. Harl. 542 ff. 102-104. This famous poem is, perhaps, the oldest extant English street ballad. It was probably written in the last quarter of the fifteenth century, and it survives in two manuscripts in the Harleian collection, which give slightly differing texts. The more authentic of the two is that which is reproduced in the present collection; it is in the hand of John Stowe (1525–1605), the sixteenth century antiquary, who had obviously copied it from an older MS. The other is a transcript in an unknown hand also of the sixteenth century headed 'London-lyck-penny a Ballade compyled by Dan John Lydgate Monke of Bery and now newly oversene & amended'. This is obviously a text which has been altered and modernized, as, indeed, the title implies. The ascription to Lydgate is now generally agreed by all competent authorities to be false.

Both MSS. were printed by E. P. Hammond in *Anglia*, XX, 1898, and a kind of composite text by E. Holthausen in *Anglia*, XLIII, 1919.

38. *The Map of Mock-Begger Hall*. Roxburghe, I, 252–253.

39. *The Poore Man Payes for All*. Roxburghe, I, 326–327.

40. *The Downright Country-Man or The Faithful Dairy Maid*. Ballad Society, vol. VII, 1891, pt 2, p. 276.

41. *The Old and the New Courtier. Le Prince d'Amour*, 1660. Reprinted Ballad Society, 1889, VI, 4, 756. This famous ballad must have been written in the reign of James I, though the earliest known printed edition is that of 1660.

42. *All things be Dear but Poor Mens Labour*. Wood, E.25.119.

43. *An Excellent New Song Upon His Grace Our good Lord Archbishop of Dublin*. Swift's Poems, ed. Williams, I, 341. First appeared as an anonymous broadside in 1724. The Archbishop is William King, Archbishop of Dublin (1650–1729). The references in ll. 12 and 35 are to the debased coinage supplied to the Irish Government by William Wood, the contractor, who was denounced by Swift in *The Drapier's Letters* (1724).

44. *An Excellent New Song on a Seditious Pamphlet*. Swift's Poems, ed. Williams, I, 236, first printed in Faulkner's edition of Swift's Works (1735). This ballad was part of Swift's campaign in favour of the use of Irish manufactures. The 'seditious pamphlet' is Swift's *Proposal for the Universal Use of Irish Manufacture*, which appeared in April or May 1720. The printer of the pamphlet was prosecuted, but the jury found a verdict of 'not guilty'.

45. *The Red Wig*. Nottingham, 89375, II, 28.

46. *Good English Hospitality. Poetry and Prose of William Blake*, ed. G. Keynes (Nonesuch Press, 1927), p. 882. In this fragment from his comic fantasy, *An Island in the Moon* (written about 1787), Blake has caught the style and the idiom of the street ballad of the eighteenth century perfectly.

47. *My Master and I*. V.S.B., p. 123.

48. *An Ode to the Framers of the Frame Bill. Byron's Works, Poetry*, ed. E. H. Coleridge (John Murray), VII, 13, 14. This vigorous poem in true street-ballad style was published by

Byron in the *Morning Chronicle* on 2 March 1812. It refers to the Luddites, or Nottinghamshire weavers, whose miseries drove them to revolt in the winter of 1812. Byron, in an impassioned speech in the House of Lords on 27 February, had defended the Luddites and condemned the Government's repressive policy. The persons mentioned in ll. 1–3 were all members of the Government responsible for this policy.

49, 50. *The Framework-knitters Lamentation* and *The Framework-knitters Petition*. From original broadsides ,communicated to the editors by Mr M. J. Graham of the Notts Free Press, Sutton-in-Ashfield. These broadsides are owned by Mr W. E. Cowpe, Newlands Farm, Forest Road, Nr Mansfield, Notts. Like Byron's poem they refer to the distress among the Nottinghamshire frameworkers at the time of the Luddite disturbances in 1812.

51. *The Times have Altered*. P.P., p. 435. An early nineteenth-century ballad. Cf. Cobbett's remarks on old and new types of farmer in *Rural Rides*, 20 October 1825.

52. *The Fine Old English Gentleman, New Version. The Poems and Verse of Charles Dickens*, ed. F. G. Kitton, 1903, pp. 59–63.

53. *The Bishop's See*. V.S.B., p. 120.

54. *The Coal-Owner and the Pitman's Wife*. C.A.Y.B.M., p. 93. A. L. Lloyd, in his note on this poem, states that the text was communicated to him by J. S. Bell of Whiston, Lancs., and that the ballad, according to Mr Bell, refers to the Durham strike of 1844.

55. *The Song of the Lower Classes*. Ashton M.S.B., p. 338. Ernest Jones (1819–69), the author of this famous ballad, was one of the principal leaders of the Chartist movement of the eighteen-forties. He published several volumes of prose and verse. See article in D.N.B. by Lord Sumner of Ibstone.

56. *The Durham Lock-Out*. C.A.Y.B.M., p. 101. Refers to great lock-out of Durham Colliers which began on 18 March 1892.

57. *Turners Dish of Lentten Stuffe or a Galymaufery*. Rollins P.G., p. 31. Pepys, I. 206. According to Rollins, this ballad was originally printed in 1612. A Second Part (inferior to the first) is also printed by Rollins and contains some comments on contemporary actors. Like a number of the seventeenth-

century balladists, Turner makes effective use of the old London street cries.

58. *The Journey into France*. Taverham, ff. 156ᴿ–158ᵛ. A version of this poem called *Cantilena Politico-Jucunda* is printed by Hamilton Thompson in his edition of *The Works of Sir John Suckling* (Routledge, 1910), p. 71. He states in his note that his version comes from Harl. MS. 367, where no author's name is given, but that there is an endorsement on it by Sir H. Ellis attributing it to Suckling. He points out that 'Suckling's authorship is by no means certain'. Actually it is very unlikely: the ballad seems to have been written about 1623, when Suckling was only fourteen.

59. *The Innocent Country-Maid's Delight*. Roxburghe, II, 230.

60. *The Man in the Moon Drinks Clarret*. Roxburghe, I, 298.

61. *The Old Man's Wish*. Roxburghe, II, 386. This famous ballad is by Walter Pope (d. 1714), a distinguished mathematician and astronomer, who became a Fellow of Wadham College, Oxford, in 1651, and Professor of Astronomy at Gresham's College, London, in 1660.

62. *Advice to the Ladies of London*. Roxburghe, II, 5.

63. *The Beau's Receipt for a Lady's Dress*. Roxburghe, III, ii, 463. From the style of dress described in this and the following ballad they would seem to belong to the first quarter of the eighteenth century. I am unable to identify 'monsieur Pantin' in the last line of No. 64.

64. *The Lady's Receipt for a Beau's Dress*. Roxburghe, III, ii, 465.

65. *London is a Fine Town*. P.P., p. 315. First printed apparently in *A New Academy of Compliments*, 1789. Probably mid eighteenth century. 'Farinelli' in l. 16 was the stage name of the Italian singer, Carlo Broschi (1705–82).

66. *A New Song called The Curling of the Hair*. Roxburghe, III, 776.

67. *The Dandy O*. Nottingham, 89375, I, II. Early nineteenth century. According to the O.E.D. the word 'dandy' was in use in London for 'an exquisite or swell' about 1813–19.

68. *The Maunding Souldier*. Roxburghe, I, 474, 475.

69. *The Souldiers Farewel.* Rollins P.G., pp. 173–5, Pepys IV, 42.

70. *Saylors for my Money.* Ballad Society, VI, 4, 797. Perhaps the masterpiece of the famous ballad poet Martin Parker (d. *c.*1656). It was imitated but not excelled by Thomas Campbell (1777–1844) in his well-known poem *Ye Mariners of England.*

71. *The Jovial Marriner.* Ballad Society, VI, 2, 369. Reprinted by Firth in N.S.B., pp. 42–4. Ebsworth attributes this ballad to John Playford and dates it 1670–84.

72. *Song Written at Sea. The Works of the Most Celebrated Minor Poets,* 1749, pp. 128–30. This famous poem by one of the chief Restoration Court Wits is a true street ballad written to the tune of an older ballad called 'Shackerley Hay'. It was published anonymously as a broadside and entered in the Stationers' Register on 30 December 1664 as *The Noble Seaman's Complaint to the Ladies at land.* Unfortunately no copy of this broadside is known to survive. The price was 6d. and Pepys bought a copy of it on 2 January 1664–5. (See Pepys's Diary, ed. Wheatley, IV, 301.)

73. *A Ballad* (1715). From the Farce *The What d'ye Call It* (see Introduction p. 15 and p. 44).

74. *Captain Death.* P.P., pp. 31, 32. There are other versions of this poem in Ritson's *Select Collection of English Songs,* Vol. 2. Early Naval Ballads, ed. Halliwell (Percy Society), and Firth N.S.B., pp. 205, 206. The ballad deals with the fate of an English privateer called *The Terrible* of 26 guns and 200 men under the command of Captain Death, which captured a French ship called *Le Grand Alexandre* on 23 March 1757. A few days later, when sailing to England with the prize, Captain Death's ship was attacked by a much larger French privateer, which retook the prize. The two ships then bore down on *The Terrible.* There was a furious engagement in which Captain Death, most of his officers and nearly all his crew were killed before their ship was captured in a shattered state by the French.

75. *My Bonny Black Bess.* Ashton M.S.B., p. 366. Refers to the famous highwayman Dick Turpin hanged at York in 1739.

76. *A Shining Night or Dick Daring, the Poacher*. Nottingham, 89375, I, 66. The refrain of this ballad is taken from the famous Lincolnshire Poacher's Song, a text of which will be found in the *Oxford Book of Light Verse*, ed. W. H. Auden, p. 373. It has not been reprinted in this collection as it is so well known.

77. *Van Dieman's Land*. Nottingham, 89375, I, 76.

78. *Lancashire Lads*. Nottingham, 89375, I, 38.

79. *Jimmy's Enlisted*. C.A.Y.B.M., p. 42.

80. *The Soldier's Farewell to Manchester*. Nottingham, 89375, I, 68.

81. *A Description of a Strange Fish*. Rollins P.G., p. 438, Wood 401 (127).

82. *A Ballad of the Strange and Wonderful Storm of Hail*, etc. Rollins P.O.A., pp. 207–9, Pepys II, 137.

83. *Man's Amazement*. Rollins P.O.A., pp. 216, 218, Pepys, II, 175. Printed for I. Deacon. Undated, but according to Rollins printed in 1684. The story of T. Cox is told in a prose pamphlet of that date quoted in full by Rollins.

84. *A Lementable New Ballad upon the Earle of Essex Death*. Shirburn, LXXIX. Refers to the execution of Robert Devereux, Earl of Essex, on 25 February 1601. It is not known to whom 'Sauit' in line 9 refers. It may be a misprint for 'Saint'.

85. *Sir Walter Rauleigh his Lamentation*. Rollins P.G., p. 89. Original broadside in Pepys Collection, I. iii.

86. *A Ballad to the Tune of Bateman*. *The Poetical and Dramatic Words of Sir Charles Sedley*, edited by V. de S. Pinto (Constable, 1927), I, 33, 34. This ballad by Sir Charles Sedley, the well-known Restoration courtier poet, refers to the killing of a barrister called Hoyle by a young man called George Pitts near Temple Bar on the night of 27 May 1692.

87. *Clever Tom Clinch going to be hanged*. *Swift's Poems*, ed. Williams, II, 399. First published in Faulkner's edition of Swift's Works, 1735. Though no broadside version is known, this is a true sheet ballad in the manner of those commonly hawked at executions in the eighteenth century. 'Wild' mentioned in l. 17 is Jonathan Wild, the notorious organizer of thieves and thief-taker who was executed in 1705 and

whose career inspired Gay's *Beggar's Opera* and Fielding's *History of Jonathan Wild*.

88. *Confession and Execution of William Corder*. C.S.L., p. 189. This broadside deals with the murder of Maria Marten by William Corder near Ipswich in 1827. It formed the basis of the well-known popular contemporary melodrama.

89. *A Ballad from the Seven Dials Press*. C.S.L., p. 160.

90. *Farewell to the World of Richard Bishop*. C.S.L., p. 220. Printed by H. Disley of 67 High Street, St Giles. This ballad must belong to the eighteen-sixties, when Disley seems to have been in business.

91. *To Pass the Place where Pleasure is*. Rollins O.E.B., pp. 213–15, from B.M. Add. MS. 15, 5225 ff. 17ᵛ–18. This ballad was entered for publication in *The Stationer's Register* in 1561–2. (See Arber's *Transcript*, I, 179, 265.)

92. *A Song made by F. B. P.* Rollins O.E.B., pp. 164–9 (from B.M. Add. MS. 15, 225 ff. 36ᵛ–37ᵛ). There are several versions of this fine Catholic ballad including a black-letter broadside in the Bodleian Library (Rawl 566, f. 167). 'F. B. P.' was almost certainly a priest. It has been suggested that the initials are a mistake for J. B. P., standing for John Brerely Priest.

93. *Here followeth the Songe of the Death of Mr Thewlis*. Rollins O.E.B., pp. 88–100 (from B.M. Add. MS. 15, 225 ff. 22ᵛ–25). This remarkable ballad is one of two printed by Rollins, op. cit., dealing with the execution of John Thewlis of Upholland, a seminary priest at Lancaster, on 18 March 1616.

94. *The Pilgrim Song. The Pilgrim's Progress from This World to that Which is to come The Second Party by John Bunyan*, London, 1684. This famous lyric sung by Mr Valiant-for-Truth in *The Pilgrim's Progress*, Part II, is perhaps the finest example of the use of the street-ballad style and metre for religious poetry. Bunyan tells us in *A Few Sighs from Hell, or The Groans of a Damned Soul* that ballads, newsbooks and romances were his favourite reading before his conversion.

PART II

95. *The Jolly Beggar.* Farmer, II, 5. (See Introduction, p. 45, for Byron's debt to this poem.) Attributed to James V of Scotland.

96. *The Complaint of a Lover Forsaken of his Love.* Roxburghe, I, 54, 55. (This is Desdemona's Willow Song, see Introduction, p. 21.)

97. *On Dulcina.* Westminster Drolleries, ii, 59. Attributed to Sir Walter Ralegh. The evidence for this ascription, and details of variants, is to be found in *Westminster Drolleries*, App. li.

98. *A New Courtly Sonnet of the Lady Greensleeves.* H.P.D., 1584.

99. *Phillida Flouts Me.* Roxburghe, III, 142. (See Introduction p. 23.)

100. *The Happy Husbandman.* Roxburghe, II, 205. (See Introduction p. 24.)

101. *Flora's Lamentable Passion.* Roxburghe, IV, 15.

102. *The Wandering Maiden.* Bagford, II, 165.

103. *The Shepheard and the Milkmaid.* Amanda, p. 538.

104. *The Coy Shepherdess.* Roxburghe, ii. 85.

105. *There was a Brisk Girle.* Portland. A longer, but not superior, version is to be found in the Roxburghe Ballads, II, 77.

106. *The Merry Hay-Makers.* Douce, II, 154.

107. *A Pleasant New Court Song.* Roxburghe, II, 22.

108. *The Wooing Rogue.* Westminster Drolleries, I, 16. (See Introduction, p. 22.)

109. *Young Coridon and Phillis.* P.P.M., III, 205.

110. *The Maid of Tottenham.* Choyce Drollery, p. 45.

111. *The Mourning Conquest.* Douce, II, 155b.

112. *The Sound Country Lass.* P.P.M., II, 211. To 'double Chops' is presumably to use 'plumpers' to fill out the cheeks.

113. *A Ballad of the Courtier and the Country Clown.* P.P.M., II, 99.

114. *The Green-Gown.* P.P.M., II, 26. This poem is an answer to *The Feast of the Gods*, a popular 'Drolleries' song.

115. *A Shepherd kept Sheep on a Hill so High.* P.P.M., III, 107.

116. *Have-at a Venture.* Roxburghe, II, 207.

117. *A Ballad of Andrew and Maudlin.* P.P.M., II, 65. (See Introduction, p. 23.)

118. *A Pastoral.* Songs Comic and Satyrical, p. 46. (See Introduction, p. 23.) Probably intended as a parody of Shenstone's *Pastoral Ballad.*

119. *Green Grow the Rashes.* Merry Muses (not numbered). Folk poems collected, edited, and sometimes written or rewritten by Burns.

120. *Gie the Lass her Fairin'.* Merry Muses.

121. *Sweet Robinette.* Nottingham, 89375, II, 32.

122. *Blue Ey'd Mary.* Nottingham 118/B2.

123. *The Frolicksome Farmer.* Nottingham 118/B2.

124. *Squire and Milkmaid.* Nottingham 118/B2.

125. *Don't Be Foolish Pray.* Nottingham, 89375, I, 17.

126. *The Lovely Village Fair.* Nottingham, 89375, I, 48.

127. *Shocking Rape and Murder of Two Lovers.* C.S.L., p. 'd'.

128. *Fain would I have a prettie thing.* H.P.D.

129. *A Pleasant New Ballad of Two Lovers.* Roxburghe, I, 316. The first line is probably an allusion to Wyatt, *My Lute Awake.*

130. *Come Turn to Mee.* Roxburghe, III, 140.

131. *The London Prentice.* P.P.M., VI, 342.

132. *The Suburbs is a Fine Place.* P.P.M., III, 99. A middle-class attack on the area outside the puritan City Council's control.

133. *The Merry Hoastess.* Roxburghe, I, 536–7.

134. *An Amorous Dialogue between John and his Mistress.* Roxburghe, II, 12.

135. *The Ranting Wanton's Resolution.* Roxburghe, III, 252–3.

136. *A Satyre entituled the Witch.* Taverham, p. 67.

137. *Much has been said.* Farmer, p. 21, c. 1600; supposed to refer to Lady Southesk.

138. *The Roaring Lad and the Ranting Lass.* Rawlinson 566.87.

139. *The Maids of Honour*. Portland.

140. *The Town-Rakes*. Farmer, IV, 107. Attributed to Peter Anthony Motteux (1660–1718).

141. *The Epicure*. Jordan, T.O.L. This seems to be the original version of this fine poem. It first appears in Jordan's *The Triumphs of London* (1675). There is a more extended broadside version in Bagford III, 53 and another in Bodl. quarto Rawl. 566 printed by N. Ault in his *Seventeenth Century Lyrics*, 387. (See introduction, p. 30.)

142. *Molly Mog*. Miscellanies in Verse, pp. 202–6. Printed for Benjamin Motte. Written by John Gay, probably with some assistance from Pope and Swift. Variant versions to be found in other collections and on broadsheets. Full details are to be found in *The Poetical Works of John Gay*, ed. G. C. Faber (O.U.P.), pp. 188–9.

143. *Ballad*. Miscellanies in Verse, pp. 168–71. Ascribed both to Arbuthnot and Gay. (See *The Poetical Works of John Gay*, ed. G. C. Faber (O.U.P.), pp. xxiv, 642.)

144. *Wil the Merry Weaver, and Charity the Chamber-Maid*. Rawlinson 566.50.

145. *As Oyster Nan Stood By Her Tub*. P.P.M., V, 107.

146. *Sally in our Alley*. Firth Bodl., 626.141. See also Carey, p. 151.

147. *The Widow that Keeps the Cock Inn*. Nottingham 118/B2.

148. *Black Thing*. Firth Bodl. B.34.31.

149. *Johnny Raw and Polly Clark*. Nottingham, 89375, I, 35.

150. *The Trumpeter*. Nottingham, I, 76.

151. *The Naughty Lord & The Gay Young Lady*. C.S.L., p. 134.

152. *Verses on Daniel Good*, C.S.L., p. 195.

153. *The Merry Bagpipes*. Roxburghe, II, 363.

154. *Gee Ho, Dobin*. Farmer, II, 202.

155. *The Jovial Tinker*. Wood, E. 25.45.

156. *Room for a Jovial Tinker*. Roxburghe, III, 230. (See Introduction, p. 49.)

157. *The Tinker*. Merry Drollery, p. 134.

158. '*Missy Sick*'. Portland.

159. *The Hunt*. P.P.M., VI, 127.

160. *The Merchant and the Fidler's Wife*. P.P.M., III, 153.

161. *My Thing is My Own*. P.P.M., II, 234.

162. *The Jolly Trades-Men*. P.P.M., VI, 91.

163. *A Ballad of All the Trades*. P.P.M., II, 61.

164. *The Wanton Trick*. P.P.M., II, 94.

165. *The Maids Conjuring Book*. P.P.M., VI, 180.

166. *A Soldier and a Sailor*. P.P.M., I, 227. By Congreve, *Love for Love*, 3, iv.

167. *The Cooper o' Dundee*. Merry Muses. (See note to 119.)

168. *She's Hoy'd Me Out o' Lauderdale*. Merry Muses. (See note to 119.)

169. *The Ploughman*. Merry Muses. (See note to 119.)

170. *As I Came O'er Cairney Mount*. (See note to 119.)

171. *The Mower*. Nottingham 118/B2.

172. *The Little Farm*. Firth Bodl. B34.236.

173. *The Jolly Driver*. Nottingham 118/B2. This poem is still current orally among Kent gypsies.

174. *Six Jolly Wee Miners*. C.A.Y.B.M., p. 47.

175. *Mutton and Leather*. Nottingham 118/B2.

176. *The Cunning Cobbler Done Over*. Nottingham 118/B2.

177. *The Beverley Maid and the Tinker*. Firth Bodl., 626.

178. *As I Lay Musing*. Portland. (See Introduction, p. 18, note 1.)

179. *A Lovely Lass to a Friar Came*. Portland. Ascribed to John Wilmot, Earl of Rochester.

180. *Off a Puritane*. Percy Folio, p. 182.

181. *The Quaker's Song*. P.P.M., III, 185.

182. *The Four Legg'd Elder*. Bagford, III, 57.

183. *The Four Legg'd Quaker*. Wit and Mirth, p. 81.

184. *The Lusty Fryer of Flanders*. Douce, II, 143.

185. *The Penurious Quaker*. P.P.M., VI, 294.

186. *The Presbyterian Wedding*. Musical Miscellany, V, 602.

187. *The Crafty Miss of London*. Douce, I, 39.

188. *The Patriarch*. Merry Muses. (See note to 119.)

189. *Godly Girzie*. Merry Muses. (See note to 119.)

190. *For A' That an' A' That*. Merry Muses. This is not in the original Crochallan edition, but in a very early one. Probably written by Burns.

191. *The Frolicsome Parson Outwitted*. C.S.L., p. 156.

192. *The Parson Grocer.* Firth Bodl., 634.223.

193. *Keep a Good Tongue in your Head.* Roxburghe, I, 512–13.

194. *The Wooing Maid.* Roxburghe, I, 452–3.

195. *The Merry Cuckold.* Roxburghe, I, 256–7.

196. *The Scolding Wives Vindication.* Douce, II, 1906.

197. *The Lamentation of Chloris.* Roxburghe, II, 277.

198. *The New Married Couple.* Douce, II, 165b.

199. *A Ballade upon a Wedding.* Fragmenta Aurea, p. 37.

200. *To Friend and Foe.* Wit and Mirth, p. 104.

201. *The Old Man and Young Wife.* Wit and Mirth, p. 17.

202. *A Westminster Wedding.* Wood, E25.94.

203. *To Chuse a Friend, but Never Marry.* P.P.M., III, 342.

204. *The Wife-Hater.* P.P.M., I, 120.

205. *Sally Sweetbread.* Carey, p. 125.

206. *Mog the Brunette.* Firth Bodl., b.33.46.

207. *My Wife's a Wanton Wee Thing.* Merry Muses. (See note to 119.)

208. *Duncan Gray.* Merry Muses. (See note to 119.)

209. *John Anderson, My Jo.* Merry Muses. (See note to 119.)

210. *The Sandgate Girl's Lamentation.* C.A.Y.B.M., p. 41.

211. *The Silly Old Man.* Nottingham, 89375, Pt I, p. 66.

212. *Good & Bad Wives.* Nottingham, 89375, Pt I, p. 28.

213. *Prince of Wales' Marriage.* C.S.L., p. 68.

214. *Johnny Sands.* Firth, b.26.220.

215. *The Female Husband.* C.S.L., p. 119.

216. *The Old Marquis and his Blooming Wife.* C.S.L., p. 131.

217. *Washing Day.* Douce, IV, 51.

218. *The New Balow.* Roxburghe, II, 573.

219. *The Maid's Complaint.* Bagford, II, 163.

220. *The Thankful Country Lass.* Amanda, p. 542.

221. *The Lass of Lynn's New Joy.* Bagford, II, 141.

222. *The Unfortunate Miller.* Bagford, II, 155.

223. *Amintas and Claudia.* Bagford, II, 147. The first three stanzas are taken from a song in *An Evening's Love or The Mock-Astrologer*, by John Dryden (1671), IV, i.

224. *The Country Girl's Policy.* Roxburghe, III, 300.

225. *There was a Knight and he was Young.* P.P.M., III, 192.

226. *The Lass of Islington.* P.P.M., III, 118.

227. *As I sat at my Spinning-Wheel*. P.P.M., III, 88.

228. *The Fair Maid of the West*. Douce, III, 28.

229. *Roger and Dolly*. Carey, p. 205.

230. *Three Maids a-Milking Would Go*. Nottingham, 118/B2.

231. *The Foggy Dew*. Nottingham, 89375, Pt I, p. 23. Cf. the present-day students' song, derived via Benjamin Britten and Peter Pears from Carl Sandburg's version:

Now I am a bachelor, I live by myself, and I work at
　the weaving trade.
And the only thing that I ever did wrong
　Was to woo a fair young maid.
I wooed her in the summertime, and in the winter too,
And the only thing I ever did wrong
Was to save her from the foggy, foggy dew.

One night she came tiptoeing to my bedside as I lay there
　fast asleep.
She laid her pretty head upon my bed and she began to
　weep.
She sighed, she cried, she damned near died: she said
　'What shall I do?'
So I took her into bed and I covered up her head
Just to save her from the foggy, foggy dew.

Now I am a bachelor and so are my sons and we work
　at the weaving trade
And ev'ry single time that I look into their eyes
They remind me of that fair young maid.
They remind me of the wintertime and of the summer
　too,
And of the many many times that I took her into bed,
Just to save her from the foggy, foggy dew.

232. *Tragic Verses*. C.S.L., p. 11.

233. *Leicester Chambermaid*. Nottingham 118/B2.

234. *The Very Pretty Maid of this Town*. C.S.L., p. 35.

235. *Pretty Maids Beware !!!* C.S.L., p. 34.

APPENDIX

1. *Blackpool Breezes.* Billy's Weekly Liar, 19, 1952.
2. *What he Took.* 'England's Glory' 391/1 (matchbox 1953).
3. *H—y P—tt.* Oral.
4. *They're Shifting Father's Grave.* Oral.
5. *Ops in a Wimpey.* Oral.
6. *The Keyhole in the Door.* Oral.
7. *The Highland Tinker.* Oral. (See Introduction, p. 49.)
8. *My Husband.* Oral.
9. *The Monk of Great Renown.* Oral.

INDEX OF TITLES AND FIRST LINES

Note: Where the title is repeated in the first line,
only a title entry has been made

INDEX OF AUTHORS